Black Sails
White Rabbits;

ISBN: 151880988X
ISBN 13: 9781518809880

CANCER WAS THE EASY PART

BLACK
SAILS

KEVIN A. HALL

"Kevin's memoir is a GIFT, an insider's view of life with bipolar illness. Stunning & swift-moving, written in a vulnerable spirit, the book is a funny, bumpy ride, laced with passion, perspective, and poetry."
    -Rev. Mary Johnstone

"An exceptionally clear depiction of the lifelong struggle to cope with bipolar disorder. Kevin's compelling prose captures mania when words flow too fast, moods change too erratically, and actions occur without a filter, as well as severe bouts of depression and the tremendous toll the illness can have on family and friends. Yet, there is a hopefulness for living well with bipolar disorder that threads throughout the book, and will pull in readers."
    - Jeffrey Hunt, MD, professor,
    Department of Psychiatry and Human Behavior,
    Alpert Medical School at Brown University

"Coming from a family with multi-generational bipolar in our DNA, I found this a riveting memoir. I could not put this book down. It promises to be an eye opener for any families and friends living with the disorder."
    - Peter Johnstone, Founder, Gunboat

"I am still mesmerized by the journey Kevin took me on. *Black Sails White Rabbits* is a poignant, brutally honest and insightful ride on the rollercoaster that is the bipolar experience of a highly intelligent and skilled young man trying to find success in the normal world against tremendous abnormal obstacles. I was blown away by Kevin's ability to take a medium that is very two dimensional (words on a page) and create a three-dimensional experience (with emotion, humor and depth) that allowed me to experience what I can't see and what I don't know anything about."
    - Dave Perry, author of *Winning in One-designs*

"This is simply the best book about competitive sailing I have ever read."
    - Nathaniel Philbrick, author of *In the Heart of the Sea* and *Why Read Moby-Dick*

Dedicated to
King Lewis and Queen Alice P L
King James and Queen Anna L P
King Time and Queen Amanda J H
and Me.

⤴ ⤴ ⤴

Who are *you*?

-The Caterpillar

Alice's Adventures in Wonderland

What ails thee?

-Percival

Arthurian legend

Why are there so many songs about Rainbows /
and what's on the other side?

-Kermit the Frog

The Rainbow Connection

T HE SCENE WAS GOING BEAUTIFULLY. The "homeless people" in line with me for bread and hot stew couldn't have been better cast and costumed. Nice touch by the Director to have some of them smell the part, too. Made it real easy to stay in character. I sat down at an empty table with my brown plastic tray, its patterns worn smooth by years of use. Nodded my head very briefly in gratitude, and dug in. A volunteer sat down across from me and smiled gently.

"Is this your first time with us at Pine Street Inn Shelter? I'm Brett. We're glad you're here," he said.

I took another gulp of stew, tore off a big hunk of bread, pretended to be too hungry to answer. Furtive glance up and slightly to the left, then face back down to within inches of my bowl. It had been at least two or three, well, *hours* since I ate some spicy wings, a cheeseburger, fries, onion rings, a vanilla milkshake, a coke, and a piece of mudpie. My credit card worked just fine at the upscale Boston sports grill. The only problem was, I didn't feel like I belonged there anymore.

I was going to struggle to keep the stew down and hit my lines if I ate any more.

"Wow you must be hungry," he said.

I grunted and flashed my eyes at him. '*Ya think?*

"That's a really cool scarf. You warm enough? I can probably find you an old sweater or something," he said.

"Thanks," I said, putting my spoon down and almost looking him in the eye.

I slowly remove my scarf. A bell chimes. Everyone looks up for a split second. I begin a scarf performance-art improv.

"Check it out! It doesn't just represent linear time, like when I stretch it out flat like this—"

Brett, meet Mr. Hyde. Dr. Jekyll had to leave. Summoned by bell. Last minute change to the script. Just hang with me, your cues will be obvious.

Timing my hand movements with my words and with standing up in a smooth ballet of poise and presence, "—it can also represent some sort of Samsara, like this," I say, my eyes wider than Brad Pitt's in *12 Monkeys* as I fold one end of the scarf back to the other, hold the ends together with one hand, and gracefully lift the scarf into a circle.

I have Brett's attention, although there are supposed to be four or five extras converging on the table around us by now. They're all late.

"But that's not really how the Universe works, not space, not time…" *Don't rush this…where the hell is the rest of the audience? Well, you can't hang on this beat any longer.*

"The way it works, the way *we* work, the way it was and ever will be, has no inside/outside…" I slide one end of the scarf slowly away from the other "No above/below…" pull the two ends apart and taut so there is an obvious top and bottom "No left and right…" hold it vertically "Or us and them…" diagonally now "Time, space, you, I, the past, the future, the sun and moon, kings and queens and dog and bitch, hills and valleys and God and snitch…" I am now twisting the right side over half a turn, and have laid the middle of the scarf on the table as I bring my two hands together, the scarf making a sideways eight: an infinity. I put my hands together with the twist, and remember to project to the galleries, deep from the diaphragm, "We…are all…One!"

I bow. Quickly bring Dr. Jekyll back on stage to mumble, "Er, that's a Möbius strip, just for the record. For the archives. In case the camera didn't catch the twist. It will mean more to the geeks. Peace."

I sit back down and drop my pie hole into my stew and keep my head down, counting silently, as long as I can until I must rise for a breath. I get to twenty-three-mississippi and sit up, stew dripping from my nose.

Brett can't help the laugh, but his eyes are wide with the concern of somebody sitting across from a proper madman.

"Let's play a game," I say to him, wiping the dark gloppity-glop off my nose and chin onto the sleeve of my faded jean jacket.

"Uh, sure." He looks around for support, quickly cocks his head toward me and raises his eyebrows. If there had been a little red button under the edge of the table, he would have pushed it a while ago.

"It's called pick the real me. Ready?" I say.

"Not quite ready. Almost though. Maybe just tell me your name first?" Brett says.

"We'll get to that. Now…" I pull my leather wallet out. Slam it down on the table, flick it open. Thumb the cards snick, snick—plastic sliding past plastic and leather to get free. I fan the laminated rectangles out in front of Brett. IDs, credit cards, backup credit cards, ATM cards, licenses for cars, for airplanes, membership cards for more than one yacht club. I tell him to pick one. He looks at it, shows it to me.

Kevin Hall, Brown University.

"So you're Kevin?" Brett says.

"Nope, try another one," I say.

"Visa, name on card Kevin Hall. Same name."

"Not me. Try this one." I push one up a little, like you do

to help your adorable niece pick the right card playing Go Fish.

"Kevin Hall, member 1989 US Sailing Team," Brett says. "Still not you?"

"None of them are me—" I throw everything but my bouncer-fooling fake ID at him. "This is me! *This* one! It's the only fake one! I'm a fraud! This is my proof." And I flick it at him sideways, just missing Brett's eye. It flutters to the floor. He bends down to pick it up.

"OK, uh…Anson. Do you want me to call you Anson?" Brett says.

"No, not an-son, not a-son, not in-the-sun, not over done. Call me Shaun. No Shem. Sorry, nevermind. Call me whatever you want. Just make it stop. Please, make it stop." I slam my forehead onto the table and burst into tears, real tears. Anguished, imploring, running-river tears.

Then I hop up, smile, bow quickly to Brett, to the left, to the right, grab my scarf, and run out of the shelter into the cold December night.

CHAPTER 2

BOSTON '89 WAS MY FIRST experience with the imagined Director. I was twenty years old. My reality, viewed from the outside, had a population of exactly one. Inside my head, the whole world was in on it. They knew I was The One.

Twenty-four years later, I hadn't been hospitalized for fourteen years when I lost track of consensus reality during a family reunion. My kin managed to lure me out of Legoland and into an afternoon intervention. The cheap Days Inn bedspread scratching the back of my legs was the only thing I was sure was real. Actors pretending to be my wife, sister, and parents said things scripted to provoke me. Mean things. Sad things. Impossible things. They were not my family. My family, was *They*.

∞

A year after Legoland, I flew from New Zealand to see Dad in LA for Thanksgiving. I asked if he wanted to talk about raising a son with mental illness. I asked what that day at Legoland was like for him. He didn't sugarcoat:

"I felt disrespected. I couldn't believe I had to waste a thousand dollars and a week of my life to be a part of that."

I didn't go on to ask about how he felt about the family line ending with me, as a result of my two separate bouts with cancer. I didn't need to hear that my ancestors feel disrespected too.

If you had asked me whether I believed in myself when I was nineteen, I would have told you I didn't understand the question. I would have told you I knew my place in the world. That I was exactly where I belonged. I might have told you that I was the best sailor in the world.

I started sailing when I was five years old. By the time I was twelve, I had read every book about sailboat racing in print, along with *The Agony and the Ecstasy* about Michelangelo, some Michener, and all of my parents' Time Life Series books about artists. I read a few Time Life books about World War II for good measure. It was all about Winslow Homer, Leonardo da Vinci, and P-51 Mustangs for me.

I was lovingly provided the support and resources necessary to excel at anything. I chose sailing. Mom drove me up and down California to compete on the weekends. I won my first world championship at age sixteen.

I got to do a lot of flying with Dad, earning my pilot's license soon after becoming a sailing world champion. I was chosen for early admission to the Ivy League. I finished high school, left my pretty and popular girlfriend back in California, and headed east. Long blond hair. Confidence to spare. If the world wasn't my oyster, it's because I was on top of it.

Then, junior year at Brown, my mind betrayed me. Senior year my body did too. Then my mind, then again my mind. Then my body, then again body. Then mind, mind, mind…like that. For ten years straight.

I was one of the last people to have the words manic-depressive written on my chart. And, among the first wave to be relabeled with bipolar disorder. As if euphemizing the name made it better. The mood swings got larger, more frequent, and far more dangerous well after the name for my natural disposition was castrated.

There are two ways to look at what happened to me in the fall of 1989. The safe, sanctioned explanation is to simply say my body attacked my brain, like this:

I got a fever of 104° F. My skin erupted in a violent rash all over my back, legs, and face. My brain swelled and pressed against the inside of my skull. My neurons short circuited. My brain caught fire. I went mad. It wasn't MY fault, it was my body's.

The damage done by those tempestuous weeks of fever and rash left my brain vulnerable. My previously dormant biological psychiatric illness never slept again. I was born manic-depressive. It was only a matter of time. My fate was always to make a scene. The diagnosis was simply the last one on stage.

It's a forgiving perspective, which explains everything. This is helpful.

How I am is not me. It's my Illness. It has a name, symptoms, and cure.

The other way to look at my challenges used to be unthinkable to me. Now, I see it as part of a wider perspective on a very complicated picture.

I had two academic passions. Mathematics, and French literature. I know, a bit schizo right? Backing up, I had only applied to two colleges. Brown University, and the United States Naval Academy. Not exactly sister schools. I was accepted for admission by both. Navy was an efficient path to having the Government pay for my fuel to fly jets. The easiest way to boil down the decision is to say that I didn't want to be told when to brush my teeth or cut my hair.

I really liked math. But I was used to being the best thinker in math class. Not anymore. Not at Brown. As the leaves turned to reds and golds the fall semester of my junior year, I enrolled in two upper-level math classes. Differential Geometry and Topology conspired to shunt me away from my handful of exceptionally bright classmates into the dunce's corner of Euclid fans.

I adored French literature. When I opened a French book, I fell ass over teakettle into imaginary worlds two steps removed from waking, Anglophone life. Seventeenth century, nineteenth, twentieth…didn't matter. A dreamer is freer in a second language. (Samuel Beckett, though Irish, wrote much of his best stuff in French.)

A description of my two majors as "bipolar" isn't silly. Math: practical, precise, proven to be helpful in a world of men and money. French Lit: navel-gazing, or escapist. Or else super-serious Absurdism.

Not long before I was to graduate from Brown, I got ambushed picking up a girlfriend in New York City for one of our early dates. The whole clan was there in her parents' Upper East-Side apartment to size up the new tribeless boyfriend. Some had driven in from halfway out on Long Island. As I stepped through the front door, my date's aunt fired point-blank: "What are you gonna *do* with a degree in math and French literatchuh?"

So here's the second, more complicated way to look at my meltdown: I was disintegrating, right down to my core. I wanted to continue to pursue math, I loved it. But it was becoming clear that I sucked. I also wanted to pursue French Lit, I loved it, but Aunt Mary-Bette was right to ask. What, exactly, *would* I do with a degree in French literature?

I used to cling to the absolution that came with putting all my struggles down to bad luck, to a body playing mean tricks on me, and to a trendy diagnosis. However, I now believe that my mind—or perhaps my Soul—made sure I didn't miss the invitation to see that I might be barking in the middle of a forest of hollow trees.

Joseph Campbell talks about the seat of the soul being that

place where the outer world and one's inner world meet. My outer and inner worlds were colliding head-on when I dragged myself to the infirmary with a violent rash. I had midterms the following week, and I was going to fail.

Instead of stepping down, resting, and reflecting, I did the opposite. The second I got off the IV drip, I doubled down on the stress, tripled up on the caffeine, and went for broke on the determination. Then, I cracked.

Did my stress divert all remaining powers from my sanity force field? Did madness pass into me from a fraternity party sneeze, or maybe the morning dew? Once inside my body, did the insurgents give me a fever, swell my brain, and cause me to lose track of what was real and what wasn't? Maybe. That's the chicken theory.

The egg theory is messy. It's jagged. It has taken me twenty five years to swallow: the arrow points the other direction.

I was in trouble. I was smacked from peacock to feather-duster when I realized that in the world of math I was barely a guppy in an ocean of white whales. There was no map for passing through magic French doors which led to a roof over my head and food on the table. At least, not a table set with the silver and privilege to which I had become accustomed.

In a world where "what do you do?" and "who are you?" seem to be interchangeable to potential future in-laws, I couldn't answer either question. I went insane fighting to keep the ideas of who I was and what I did separate. My mind was well on its way to splitting—which would have shown up soon enough—when my body flinched first with a fever and a rash. A few short weeks later, I played the madman and the fool, got arrested, then locked up to sit still and drool.

The Western, medical model had the cause outside the patient. So, give him pills, restore the neuro-electrico-biochemical balance, and get him back in the game. Job done. Case closed.

As soon as I stopped drooling, moved out of the locked

ward, and caught my breath, I ran right back out on the field. Like nothing with spiritual or self-identity implications had happened. I didn't slow down. Not in class, not in training, not on the racecourse.

Well, my body tried its hand again at getting my Soul's attention. This time, instead of crazy, it was cancer.

Losing one nut is, in a relative sense, not a big deal. That's not how it felt at the time, and I don't mean to be glib. But with a remaining testicle, the system still works. It's actually easier to answer the question, "How's it hangin' ?" And hearing about how something must have "really taken balls" doesn't clang the same way it clangs once you have none.

So to review:

Junior year: Crazy.

Senior year: Cancer.

Fast forward through the next ten years: Following year—crazy again. Next year—huge operation to remove the lymph nodes from my sternum to my groin and clean out the metastasized cancer. But the nodes were all negative, benign. Nothing there. Major medical mystery! Not exactly the way I wanted to be unique, fascinating, and deserving of great attention. The mystery solved itself a few weeks later when my remaining testicle hemorrhaged, announcing I was to become a crazy castrato at twenty-three.

Over the next seven years, I rode along for seven more acute manic episodes. That makes it sound tidy. It was not tidy.

Police arrests, gurney restraints, nightmares while strapped to a plastic bed wet with my own urine, locked wards, Group therapy, Day/Night Room, and the eventually earned euphoria of the five minutes of freedom for a cigarette during "*smoke* break!". I only smoked with my peeps in the nuthouse, but there were times that cigarette was all I lived for.

Ensuing depressions. Some suicidal.

Once the chronic bipolar disorder diagnosis won out over encephalitis, Lyme disease, or any other temporary physiological or neurological causes, father came to believe that all of my psychiatric challenges were avoidable. This has been hard on our relationship recently. To Dad, the times of uncertainty have always been a simple case of medication regimen noncompliance.

He was always there for me. He has always loved me. He has always wanted me to be healthy, happy, and prosperous. But his model of me proposes that manic episodes betray a simple lack of willpower. Essentially, the choice to fuck it all up.

He's entitled to boil my life down to whether or not I took the purple pill. As an emergency room doctor I'm sure it seems that cut and dry. Symptom/cure. Gushing blood/tourniquet. Broken leg/cast. Just take your medicine, and if you haven't, don't call me.

But right there, hidden in the evasive name of the condition, is the truth. There are two sides to the story. Maybe stopping the medicine is an attempt to cure something deeper, and far more painful or scary than losing jobs, friends, or even sanity.

I have lots to show for the times I did exactly what the world asked of me. I took my MEDS. I drank the protein shakes, lifted the weights, incurred the debts, kept the jobs, paid off the credit cards, jumped through the hoops, and sailed around and around the buoys. I got the leather jacket—the one with the Olympic rings on the back. I'm an Olympian. "Never Former, Never Past" it says on my keychain. I've won races as the navigator in the America's Cup finals. And I have a marvelous, loving family.

But when my friend died in a tragedy of splintering black

carbon fiber and foaming salt spray two years ago and I helped pull his dead body out of the water, there it was again. Life is unbelievably fragile. I only have one chance—this life—to find out who I really am.

Maybe there are clues in my past. In the place my outer world and my inner worlds first collided head-on. Maybe my soul knew itself already then, and my head has been getting in the way ever since.

My French honors thesis won an award, which came with a very practical $200 prize. American dollars. The ultimate vote of confidence.

"Les lettres d'amour de Marguerite Duras et Ludwig van Beethoven" - *The Love Letters of Duras and Beethoven* proposed that Beethoven's famous "Immortal Beloved" letter was never sent to a particular woman, because it was written to Love itself. The letter was a breakwater against his desperate isolation, and an optimistic transmission to a future self. The mystery surrounding her identity is the wrong question.

Beethoven's famous letter begins *"My angel, my all, my very self."* I believe those words could be taken at face value. My thesis ends *"L'imortelle bien aimée, c'est donc l'amour."* *The Immortal Beloved, therefore, is Love.*

So there you are. Twenty-two years old, three-time All-American sailor. Now, do you sign up for the immediate status and paycheck of turning pro, or do you walk the other way and hope the news that his son is going to be an Artist garners Dad's support? Yeah, right.

* If you choose to be an artist, close the book.

* If you choose to be a pro sailor, turn the page.

I don't actively begrudge my professional-athlete self. Competitive sailing, the quest to become an Olympian, the striving with a team to win the America's Cup, were quintessentially purposeful. They gave direction and meaning to a man who desperately needed those things to define himself and even to survive.

My midlife unraveling two years ago at Legoland comes down to a simple series of questions: Is *Who I am* the same as *What I do*? Is *What I do* the same as *My job*? And finally, *If I hang up my jersey, if I dare to try my hand at something else, will I survive?*

Searching for answers to those questions has been every bit as challenging and terrifying as a narrow escape from a lethal crash, as living with bipolar disorder, even as scary as facing cancer a second time.

I used to quip that the book I wanted to write some day should be called *Cancer Was the Easy Part*. Meaning, living with bipolar is much harder. What's been really hard, is only now appreciating just how much all of the desperate strivings for external validations which I have leaned on all my life occluded my soul from its call.

David Foster Wallace was a much better writer than I am competitive sailor. His last day on earth was September 12th, 2008. He was forty-six years old when he hung himself from his patio rafter. In his garage nearby, he left the lights shining on a two page note and the unfinished novel *The Pale King*.

I am forty-five years old, I was born September 11th, and I believe in ghosts. There are days when I'd find peace sooner if I followed him into that garage, wrote the note, and ended the drama. If you harbor the capacity for infinite sadness, once the dangling carrot of Achievement reveals itself to be a spiritual mirage….

Look, I'll stop name dropping soon. Promise. Mostly, it's that

I'm insecure, and like Alanis Morissette says, "If I am cultured my words would somehow garner respect...(and still it would not come)."

I'm not asking you to accept my life. I'm begging myself to. If there is such thing as a vocation, if there is such thing as an Authentic Self, the fatal crash was my wake-up call to search for it more courageously.

CHAPTER 3

⌒

B ACK IN BOSTON, ANSON, KEVIN, Shaun and Shem, Jekyll, Hyde, me, myself, and I…we all spent the rest of that chilly night in 1989 walking around, talking to ourselves. Looking for the original hen, the one that pecks for the letter with the tea stain in James Joyce's *Finnegans Wake*.

I can't wait to review the recordings, that last bit was absolutely hilarious…proving by algebra that Hamlet's grandson is Shakespeare's grandfather—ha!….

It was a serious mistake to run out of the shelter without my wallet or any of its contents. Damn. Walking all night to stay warm meant I really was hungry now that the sun was coming up. I retraced Paul Revere's ride before noon, ending up in Beacon Hill.

A hill that's also a beacon? Perfect. I want to go to that!

"May I help you?" was the most common way the antique-shop owners tried to communicate that their patience would very soon turn inside out, and that my freeloading on their central heating was of distinctly finite duration. Also, that I was unlikely to find much of interest in their shops. I only struck out once in four or five visits, when I was asked to leave immediately. The conversations usually went about like this:

"Seventeenth century. Flemish, right?" I said, running my

hand along the telescope with reverence.

"Ah, yes. Yes precisely. Monsieur is a collector?"

How do they all know how to raise their eyebrow so far? Another shop: "Do you have the dining room table that pairs with this credenza?"

Again, the eyebrow. I'm Eddie Murphy in *Trading Places*, well after he moves off the streets and into the brownstone with the infamous jacuzzi and has decided to wear the Harvard tie. Or maybe I'm Dan Akroyd, having been ejected from my home with the butler and my snug life with Penelope. I spend quite a long time standing very still, silently wondering whether I can be both, before I am finally asked to leave.

It won't be long until I'm behind bars, having to explain why the phone in my limo is busted. And it won't be the last time I feel that someone out there, that *They*, have hijacked my life. I sure hope it's for a good cause because I'm on fire here.

CHAPTER 4

I STILL WISH I COULD APOLOGIZE to the woman in the park. I dropped out of my tree, right in front of her. It would have been startling and then, seeing the look in my eyes, frightening. I could tell right away I had scared her. I took a half-step back, and used a very soft voice.

"Ophelia? Oh, Ophelia, it is such a relief to find you! I've been to hell and back and—"

She doesn't recognize me.

I take a full step back. She is trembling. She hasn't recovered from the adrenaline of nearly being flattened by a human bomb. She is standing in front of a docile—though not diminutive—young man in a jean jacket and a scarf, who is calling her Ophelia.

"I'm sorry, but my name is Joelle," she says.

"Right. Sorry. I knew that. I mean I knew that it wasn't Ophelia. I was just practicing. Tell her I'm ready to do the scene, OK? And can she please hurry; I'm freezing my nuts off up *theyah.*" I point to the tree.

The woman moves to step past me. I turn sideways and step back. *Sorry, I'm so sorry.* The voice is very faint, and very, very meek, but it's there. Is that little voice me? If it is, then who just jumped out of the tree?

I climb back up to my perch.

18

The cops stopped by next. They talked me down from the tree, asked if I would be able to remain calm and just walk with them to their car. It was warm, 'ya know, and they could maybe help me find my friend Ophelia and sort this all out.

It would be a couple months before I realized that it was, in fact, possible for the cops to know who I was looking for without having cameras and microphones throughout the park, or a director feeding them info and lines. After my near miss with Joelle, my mind very quickly discarded the information that I had spoken Ophelia's name to her.

That information did not support my own completely coherent but very bizarre reality.

CHAPTER 5

IN 1989, THE DSM-III—the third iteration of the *Diagnostic and Statistical Manual of Mental Disorders*—still called it bizarre, that special reality. Delusions of grandeur, of persecution, this, that, the other, but ultimately, bizarre. There was no such thing as "Truman Show Delusion" back then. Put more accurately, there was no explicit name for the experiences I was having in Boston. It would be another eight and a half years before Jim Carey played Truman Burbank in a movie that I still enjoy very much, but which also still gives me the shivers. That movie made me feel a lot less alone about the times in my life I thought I was so "special." Sure, it was just a movie. A brilliant, entertaining caricature of itself. A Hollywood movie which deftly satirized Entertainment.

Years later, as I studied the evolving versions of *The Truman Show* script (originally set in New York), I had the feeling that someone, somewhere, knew exactly where I was coming from. About ten years after the movie was in theaters, Doctor Joel Gold noticed that a string of his many psychiatric patients told him the same story: they were all being watched, filmed, and broadcast to the world. Dr. Gold named it "Truman Show Delusion".

I had it before it was cool. I had it before *The Truman Show*.

Recently, the tag *bizarre* has been removed from the description of my psychiatric diagnosis. No longer bizarre. Something about catching up with the times, and/or removing cultural bias. Before, my delusional scenario was utterly impossible. It was impossible to be under constant video and audio surveillance in the nineteenth century, for example. Now it is—however unlikely that one is singled out from the entire world's population—plausible. Don't believe me? Tell it to the NSA. Copy in MI-6, OK?

When I'm on my medication, the little voice that wanted to apologize to the woman in the park becomes the big voice. Mr. Real World. He gets real busy recognizing clear boundaries between citizens, clear lines between right and wrong, clear discourses of should and maybe-shouldn't, of relative moralism and moral relativism.

The big man. Large and in charge. The guy who secures the mortgage to buy the house, or gets the paperwork notarized for the newest arrow in the quiver of Homunculus Number One, safely hidden behind a new pair of sunglasses on the head of its treadmill-capitalist, dancing monkey body. Underneath those sunglasses, there's a splinter in my mind. "Born, pay taxes, die," can't be the whole story. It just can't.

Occasionally, when the stars align and the air in my area code is electrified, music brings me to my knees, waves of conversation in a bar or on the street cascade over me like a waterfall, and the edges between colors grow sharper as the edges between me and the rest of the Universe blur.

Friends and family tell me that the crystal methamphetamine world vibrates with compulsion to chase a similar-sounding high. Feelings of omnipotence and invincibility. Of everything being in it's place, things lining up according to a personalized master plan. Exactly where we're meant to be, except more so. Sights and sounds, stars and the moon, soft touches and hard sex, all better, incredible but really happening. Perfect but forever.

Much of my struggle to stay on this planet is because I get those feelings. Except, I get them when I *don't* take my drugs.

CHAPTER 6

A FTER BEING TALKED OUT OF MY TREE, I don't remember exactly
how long I was with the police before I was moved by
ambulance to the next joint. I remember tiny bright flashlights
stabbing my eyes, questions about whether or not I was on angel
dust.

"Please count backwards by sevens, from ninety-three," said
the woman in the white coat.

"Sixteen," I said immediately.

"Excuse me?"

"Ninety-three minus seventy-seven is sixteen."

"I meant, say ninety-three, eighty-six, seventy-nine, like that.
If you are able," Dr. Desai suggested.

"You're kidding, right? What say you give me pen and paper
and I jot you down the proof to Fermat's Last Theorem?"

"It would be better if you just did the exercise," the doctor
said with some frustration.

"No. I already proved I could subtract efficiently. What else
you got on your checklist?"

I think we tried the date, the president, my family's names
and phone numbers, whether or not I had health insurance.

Vague memories of EEGs, EKGs, ink blots and short
storyboard illustration sequencing exercises. Of my mother

22

being there, somewhere there.

I do remember drawing the heart on the curved triangular mirror hiding the surveillance camera. I had (somehow) concealed a red crayon before being sent back into my padded observation cell. It took quite a few jumps to make the humps for the top of the heart, because I could only make marks when I was sure they were going to be right. I was still able to focus on my very short-term goals, because I hadn't been given downers for droolers yet. I had, however, been provided a room with a view (through a tiny, thick plexiglass window and a deadbolted door).

I completed the bottom half of the crayon heart, where the V comes together in a point, standing on my tippy toes.

But how did I get a red crayon? Unless…unless they wanted to me to have one, and put it somewhere I would find it. Which means they wanted me to draw something. A test. It's a test. They want to see what I draw. Should I have drawn a heart? No. Not a heart. I should have drawn just a circle. That would have been better. Now they'll think I'm trying to say more than I am. I'm just part of the circle. But that means love. And love means hearts. Even better if they're on a mirror. Even better if the mirror is curved. Even better if there's a camera behind the mirror. Hey, wouldn't it be cool if I could see myself looking into that mirror on a TV underneath it? Wait, would the TV be on the TV? Guess that depends if you mean "look directly at your face" by "see yourself," or you mean look at your face in the mirror. What's the difference? Well, one is direct, the other is a reflection. Direct? Are you kidding me? Direct if you call passing through a lens, some hocus pocus, some wires, and then being projected onto a 2D screen direct. Whatever. Shut Up. I was having fun. I just mean would I see more than one TV, looking at myself looking at myself in the mirror on a TV under the mirror? Oh! Hey! No, not just one TV. That would be a loop. There'd be lots of TVs. Lots and lots. Like in Mom and Dad's bathroom with the mirrored closets behind the mirror over the sinks. Lots of me's.

Mise en abîme. That's what it's called. In French, anyway. When they put my face on the cereal box, holding the box of cereal with my face on it... Recursive virus. Recursive violence. Regurgive file-this. Detergent smile-piss. Divergent trial-dys. Emergent Nile-sis. Niobe. Carnal bliss....

Things got harder, very quickly, after that.

CHAPTER 7

EVENTUALLY I STOPPED DROOLING. Step one with containment of escalating psychotic break tends to be something we all share. I call it the horse tranquilizer, and I always picture the old-school stainless steel syringes with a pair of rings for the index and middle fingers of Nurse Ratchet, thumb giving two quick taps to squirt ominously for the camera before the stab through the Sharpie's big X and into the heart. Or maybe the side of the neck; that one looks pretty good too.

I've had as many as five huge orderlies hold me down to get the junk into me, wait for it to take, and transfer me to the bed with the vertical-metal-bars headboard, the black rubber mattress, and the leather straps.

Waking up disoriented is a rite of passage. Whether from a big night out, physical exhaustion sleep, or emerging from a psychotic or drug high, it's kind of a cool feeling. The *me* which has been pulling the levers for as long as it can remember, is long gone. AWOL. No evidence of departure. No tell-tale white rose or note or empty valise. Just a strong odor of *absence*. Missing context, missing recent browse history, missing contacts, missing timeline, missing family, missing future, and, worst of all, missing hope. It's exhilarating, provided that it's fleeting. When the statute is up for briefness, but the feeling just sits there on your shoulder cackling like a wicked witch, it's terrifying.

I gaze slowly around the sterile room. I need to scratch my temple, it itches and the scratching should also help me think. I lift my arm all of an inch before the leather bind asserts its grip. I look down at the hand which is not obeying the very simple order to come scratch my face. Sure enough, there's a leather strap on it. *What the hell?*

The idea of things stretching out into a personal hell hasn't hit yet. Maybe I can scratch with the other hand. If I raise it quickly, maybe the restraint won't catch me. Jerk, snap. Ouch! Nope. My CPU is running in molasses time, but inside, I am panicking at the speed of light. I try to kick my legs. Similar feeling to both wrists. Ankles, meet fetters. Fetters, Kevin's ankles. Try to scream. Ever tried to scream while your head is submerged in tar?

Breathe faster, maybe that will help. The command comes from the panicking insides and the oozing CPU both. Okay, think. Think. Think. Wait, all I seem to be able to think is that I want to think. Nothing happens after that. Blinking cursor on a blank screen. Revved engine in neutral. Asshole strapped to black rubber by leather restraints. This sure seems to be my body. And I seem to be stuck in this body. Which means…I'm really here.

Right. *Here.* Good word. Helpful. Let's see. Now. Is this now? Am I awake? Oh, that's better. What a relief! I'm *dreaming.* Everything's going to be okay. I'll wake up soon. Cornflakes and Sunday papers, here I come. Hmm. Just need to find the first page…uh oh. Can't find the light cord. Can't find the words in the books. I'm still dreaming.

Those walls sure look real, I can't see past any of them, or over. And I've never felt straps cut into me in a dream, they're usually more, like, symbolic. Not good. This is not good. I am awake. How can I not know if I'm awake?

Why doesn't my brain work? Maybe it's not my brain? Wait that makes no sense at all. Whose would it be? ***HELP.***

F ADED SNAPSHOTS OF PEOPLE VISITING ME. Like the movies where a picture is flashed up with a slow heartbeat, *lub,* then the screen is black for the downbeat, *dub.* A friend from Tufts, *lub,* dark screen, *dub.* A woman I don't know brings me a book. She's someone's mom. She's says she's the mom of my little brother. But I only have a little sister. Oh, she means my fraternity little brother. She tells me I meant a lot to him this semester. That I helped him stay in school. *Wonder how I did that? Dub.*

There's a note, a short French letter from my thesis advisor. She has come to visit but I was asleep. She writes that sleep is beautiful and essential, that this is a time to be patient. *Try not to drool on the letter. You should save the letter.*

I need to get out of here. I have exams, and papers, and, and, and. I can't be here.

"I need you to calm down, Kevin," says the nurse as she walks in the room. Apparently I've been yelling out loud about getting out.

"I have to go, I have to get back to Providence. Right now!" I implore.

Lots of little pills, triangles and circles, white and pink and orange maybe. All there in the tiny ruffled white paper cup, like the ones you pump ketchup into at burger franchises. It's fun to just stare deeply into the little cup at the pills and see how agitated you can get the orderlies before finally tossing it all back like a shot of tequila. Big gulp of water—all at once is my style. In the movies they always show the hero pretending to take the MEDS but really hiding them under his tongue. I spat quite a few out, but I never got the hang of hiding them under my tongue. Plus, once the water hits them and they start to dissolve, some of them taste like death.

The girl with the impossibly long slender fingers who looks like she might wear a veil when she's out and about, takes her pills one by one. First she holds them up to the light as if trying to see the secret message inside. Places one pill gently on the tip of her outstretched tongue. Slowly retracts her tongue as she sets the pill cup down and picks up her water cup. Takes a sip, sets the water cup down, wipes her mouth with the back of her hand like she's just polished off an ice-cold Budweiser, which seems incongruous but gives her the chance to affect a shit-eating grin and survey her audience. She looks around to see who's watching (there are a few of us), then starts on the next one. She takes six or seven pills, each one done exactly the same way. She tells me later that if they're going to make her a robot with the meds, well then she might as well act like one, right?

We have a little private room, the doc and I. A couple of chairs sturdy enough to lean back. I like tipping back pretty far. I almost fall over backward a few times before the first question.

"Any drugs before you got on the bus?" asks the psychiatrist in the starched white coat with the name stitched in red cursive on the patch stitched on the coat.

To the coat was stitched a patch. On the patch was stitched a name. In the name was stitched a game. Into the game was pushed a pen. And in the pen was put a pig. The big fat hen and pretty pig made eggs of small and ham of big. The shrink's the hen so I'm the pig. Committed.

"What? Oh. No. No drugs," I say.

"Alcohol?"

"I'm in college. What do you think?"

"I think that means there's a good chance you also used drugs. It will help us a lot, it will help you, if we understand what happened leading up to your arrest and transfer here to HRI," says the doc.

"No drugs. No alcohol. Caffeine, maybe. Glorious caffeine."

"OK. Family history?"

"It's all in my file; it's all there. You're kind of pissing me off. Why don't you just check my dossier?"

"You don't have a file, Kevin. You've never been here before. We can't check something that doesn't exist."

"Of course I have a dossier. They can't plan all this without very detailed files…whatever. Why don't you ask my family if they have a history?"

"I have spoken to your mother. I'm asking you what you think."

"I think you should turn the cameras off and make them stop. Make them leave me alone. I didn't ask for this. I quit. I just quit."

"Quit what?"

"You know what. That's all for today, Doc," I say, dropping my chin to my chest. He tries a few more questions and finally gives up.

CHAPTER 9

M EDS ARE TRICKY BUSINESS. Our minds are all over the map
with their cryptic, combination-lock tumblers of serotonin
and dopamine, synapses and gotta-stay-clean. No such thing as
one size fits all in that terrain. The same handful of medications
might work great for one patient and cause drastic problems for
another. Not exactly Russian roulette, but certainly not a sniper
shot from close range with no wind.

What goes up must come down. A brain in warp drive and a
soul on fire qualify as up. Way up. Doesn't matter how you got
there, you're Icarus.

Maybe the desire to be free helps you find the willpower to
demonstrate that you choose to actively participate in Group,
and clean up after yourself at meals (extra credit and early parole
if you clean up after others), speak straight to the docs and be
polite to the orderlies when your meds come around the bend
again, share your toys and especially your cigarettes, those sorts
of things. Maybe it's just the sound, the buzz of the deadbolt
mechanism on the door to the lockdown ward, that you have to
get away from more than anything.

Something, an almost unconscious or primal or preternatural
need, gets you into position to sell them on your release. At this
point there are lots of words flying around about support nets

and backup plans and patience and, if they think they can get away with it, words like optimism and hope. If it's your first time, you probably think it's smooth sailing from here: sweet freedom. Your family might already be planning your reentry into normal life for you, back to college or your power job or your half-finished novel.

Words are all well and good: "It's a biological illness; it has to do with trauma from your childhood, or it has to do with continued feelings of insecurity and impotence, or maybe both. Lots of important people had your disorder. You know, like Herman Melville. Did you know that?"

Words or no words, when you get out—when you get to where you will eat and shit, shave and sleep without the assisted living which inpatient care provides—you still have to move eventually. You still have to will yourself out of bed sometime after the sun comes up and before it goes back down.

If you don't, you're a bigger failure than when you landed in the nuthouse in the first place.

So what about "everything happens for a reason"? It's not a good time, when you still don't feel much like getting out of bed, to go looking for reasons. It's really not. I needed one, though, and I needed it bad. No family history, not of alcoholism, not of suicides, not much of anything. Just law-abiding, hardworking Scottish, English, Irish, and French folks who crossed the pond and got on with it. Mom's side in French Quebec selling high-quality liquor, Dad's side in the Midwest, being Midwestern.

CHAPTER 10

D AD TOOK A LEAVE FROM his work at the volatile downtown
Los Angeles CIGNA Hospital Emergency Room. Car
crashes, drug deals gone bad, fevers and stubbed toes, broken
arms and broken noses. I'm sure it was much harder for him now
with only one patient in the whole building, but not the person
he knew or recognized as his son. Not at all. Just someone with a
plastic, emotionless face who looked a lot like him.

Dad took me to his house in Big Bear, California. When I
did manage to get out of bed, I'd listen to music, sort of. Try to
read, sort of. Try to talk about it all, not-even-sort-of because I
didn't have much language for whatever went down in Boston
and now its aftermath. Shovel snow after the storms, sort of.
Cook grilled cheese, successfully, and open chips successfully as
well, and eat and eat and eat and eat.

Eating was rewarding because I could do it successfully, as
in every bit as well as I ever had. Even if I didn't really taste
much I could still chew and swallow. Eating was also reassuring
because it was the only thing in the world I had control over
anymore. Sure, medication side effects contributed to the weight
gain (other possible side effects included weight loss, impotence,
priapism, agitation, sedation...), but the main reason I
gained at least ten pounds was that when my poor little brain

32

said, *Hey, I have an idea, I'm getting that hungry sensation which means I should go get food and then eat it,* my body could follow orders and things happened pretty much about the way I willed them to. Except when we ran out of sliced cheese, which usually happened just before also running out of butter and bread and chips. Once, we ran out the same day we bought it all.

Sometime around Christmas, I felt well enough to try to go skiing. I do not underestimate my good fortune to have left the Boston psych ward and landed in Dad's house, with Dad and his laser-retinal-surgeon-graduated-from-Harvard-at-nineteen second wife Meimei. She seemed to get me, in a way that helped.

What's better than living up in the mountains, with open skies and winter air? On the the windy days, friendly ghosts whispered their stories through the forest and across the back deck, to where I sat on the other side of the window. On the calm days, snow thumped to the ground beneath an overburdened branch.

Mozart and Bob Marley seemed to keep getting put on the stereo when I wasn't looking. Maybe it was in the medical literature somewhere, the suggestion to favor Mozart over late Beethoven, and reggae over death metal, for the listening enjoyment of recently derailed souls.

The skiing went just fine for my body. The only problem was how restless I felt. Sort of an existential claustrophobia, or even a real claustrophobia. Like I was held down in a tiny little box by some unseen hand, and I would never get out. Even out in the middle of the widest run on a completely cloudless day. The word Dad kept using is akathisia (say ack-ah-THEE-sia). It's a side effect of the strong downer, the Haldol, the one I still needed in addition to Lithium to make sure I didn't relapse into delusion.

It's one of those weird "I'm definitely not in Kansas anymore" sensations, that I felt far more acutely claustrophobic and restless outside, than inside. Doesn't make sense, but I was starting to apprehend the vague notion that not much made sense in my life anymore.

CHAPTER 11

A FEW WEEKS BEFORE JUMPING OUT of trees, I was noticeably agitated on campus. To the point where I responded to a "Roommate Wanted" ad placed by a biomed grad student. Tsen-tsen was very soft spoken, pretty and elegant in a super-smart-scientist way. I still can't quite comprehend how I gave off the right vibe for her to choose me to share the rent and all her great soups. I know I wasn't the only person interviewing for the second bedroom in her off-campus apartment. It's best to let her tell it from the words in her card:

> December 17, 1989
> Wish you a Merry Christmas and
> Enjoy every moment in 1990
> the beginning of Another
> New Decade—New Dream
>
> Hi, Kevin,
>
> Still remember the very first phone call about
> looking for the apartment. I tried so hard,—
> tried to turn you down because you are junior
> + undergrad...But you told me that you were

different and I was surprised by your clear
self-identity. Being touched by the Suffering you
was going through in the very last two nights, I
felt your difference—you have already been years
ahead of your age!

I felt sorry, guilty, at a moment. That I could
not help. But I realized later that you (and me)
indispensable to no one but yourself. We can
only become a real self-made after having been
through our lonely inward journey. Imagine one
day. We both were standing on the certain horizon
(from mentality point of view), smiling at the
trails behind us—and said Joseph Campbell, didn't
lose our mind. Precisely because we had been
through the same darkness and met under the
sun eventually.

Tsen-tsen

Looking all the way back, I stagger at the prescience and
self-knowledge suggested by the fact that I got an off-campus
room and a gentle, wise grad student roommate before I hopped
the bus to Boston. I knew I needed to reduce complications,
social stress, noise, and get away from the Friday and Saturday
nights in the fraternity I lived in with fellow sailors, soccer
players, and musicians. (There was a common denominator to
our open-minded cohort, but if you didn't know what it was
it was probably better that way for you and especially for the
image your parents had of you.) I was the token odd-duck,
almost-militant teetotaler.

I'm a huge, as in fanatic groupie huge, fan of Joseph Campbell
and his work. For starters, there's the credit George Lucas gives
him for seeding the genesis of Star Wars. Enough said. But also,
one of Campbell's posthumous compilations, and my favorite, is

called *Mythic Worlds, Modern Words: On the Art of James Joyce.* The first book Campbell published, fifty years earlier, is *A Skelton Key to Finnegans Wake,* which is James Joyce's last book. After a career of trailblazing in mythology and cultural anthropology— the soundbite of which says all you have to do is look at the stories we (humans) tell and have always told, to realize that we're all far more alike than we are different—Campbell came back to his first love, and he looked at Joyce through the lens of a lifetime of mythology scholarship.

Finding Tsen-tsen's card recently and then looking at my bookshelf of Joseph Campbell books gave me a spooky, wonderful, frightening feeling. The feeling that there are things we don't understand, that there is a world beneath the one we see, and it is teeming with magic. *Meant to be. Waiting to be discovered. Providence. Destined. Mysterious and Enchanted.*

There's no way I could have gone back to the dorms at Brown six weeks after being strapped down, if I hadn't met Tsen-tsen. If she hadn't believed in me, in a me that I didn't even know yet but whom she had already met, this might be a very different story.

Here's what I did. Dad and I talked to the dean. He gave the okeydokey to the plan to finish all my coursework from the fall and enroll in one French Lit grad seminar, on Autobiographical Fiction. It went without saying but was said anyway that I could and really should leave if the stress of reintegration or schoolwork threatened my mental health. I had already failed and face-planted once. There was no way I was going to ever again.

(That's what I thought at the time.)

I took *no distractions* to a new level, including things like speaking, laughing, crying, or basically doing anything besides eating, sleeping, or studying. Friends tried to stand by me, but it was hard to know what to do with a person who had so little to say and who seemed to want nothing more than to be left alone with his math proofs, and French books.

Goldfish didn't survive the neglect.

CHAPTER **12**

⤚⟿

THERE WERE FIVE OF US in the French graduate seminar on Autobiographical Fiction that spring. I presented on Roland Barthes. One of the candidates preparing to defend for his doctorate said my presentation was good. He added, "by any standards, not just for an undergrad." It meant a lot at the time, and still does, because my head, and my heart, and my soul were all in there somewhere. When I wasn't working on the French presentation, I was making up classwork from the fall.

The lithium did a great job of keeping me on the ground junior spring. Too good a job. I started on antidepressants some time around midsemester, and none too soon. My thoughts were getting pretty dark, my outlook wasn't very optimistic, but I gritted my teeth and pretended I didn't have feelings, just goals.

Without Olympic aspirations still clamoring and harking from the mountaintop of childhood dreams, I might have been sunk within weeks of my Roland Barthes talk. I mean, what *was* I going to do with a degree in math and French literature? What's the point if there's no such thing as color, or music, or fun, or variety, or even anger anymore? I'm not interested in life as an android, thanks.

Unfortunately, I sure as hell felt like one.

Fortunately, way back in fourth grade, at St. Paul's Episcopal

37

Day School, I had told Father Henry's obnoxious son, the one who was forever teasing me about being uncoordinated and the last to be picked, that he could tease me all he wanted. I said, "I am going to the Olympics, and you sure as heck never are, unless it's the meanie Olympics."

There's something etched deep and indelibly when you're teased in fourth grade about fundamental things like being a total loser because you can't throw or catch. My quickness with numbers and my mature vocabulary conferred zero points of respect or self-esteem in fourth grade. More like negative points.

Revenge of the Nerds was still five years from being born, and the concept of twenty year-olds taking over the world because they invented an app was not on anyone's radar. I'd like to find that mean kid, and I'd like to thank him, because he probably saved my life.

CHAPTER 13

~⟡~

H ERE'S THE LOGIC I WAS RAISED ON.

> Ultimate goal = retirement + gold watch =
> fulfillment and happiness.
> College + hard work = good first job.
> Good first job + lots more hard work = good
> retirement (including gold watch).

Nobody told me there was any luck involved. Nobody told me that "Why me?" was the wrong question when things went wonky, and a much better meditation, far more healthy and sustaining, is "Why not?" It doesn't have an answer either, but at least in the meantime you query the life stories of the rest of the world's population and then try to see just where you fit in—as opposed to standing off to the side of the middle school dance of life while a seagull poops on your head, and deciding then and there that he did it on purpose.

Late in my sophomore year at Brown, one of my former national youth coaches recruited me to pair up in a two-person Olympic boat called a 470. I was on the US Sailing Team now, immediately ranked second in the country as a result of my new partnership. I remember wearing my shiny new jacket to a homecoming football game at Brown, like advertising. Like a big sign that said with one of those neon arrows pointing down at me and flashing, "Look here at me! Now you have proof. I'm *Somebody*."

Fast-forward to spring of junior year, when I believed I had perhaps lost what the French call a "reason to be". Wait, there, in the closet, what's that? Hey! It's my US Sailing Team jacket! I remember now, I still have to prove to the fat kid that I really am going to the Olympics. And poof! Just like that, I had my *raison d'être*. Things to do. Places to go. Back to the gym. Out on the water. Off to Holland and eventually Barcelona for the Pre-Olympics. Check. Check. Check.

Here's what happened at the Pre-Olympics. We sucked. Real bad. We were way too big in the little underpowered 470, especially for the light airs of the Mediterranean in northeastern Spain. I wasn't super reliable as a teammate. (I might have decided that a good way to protect my "self" from a shocking result was to at least be able to say I "won the party." Barcelona is a great city to vie for that title. Believe me.)

The second to last day of racing we were in a tiny collision which in any other universe should have just meant a scratch. Somehow, in those waters, on that day, it meant our boat started leaking, but we didn't realize it until we tried to pull it out of the water. We just thought we were that bad, back in the cheap seats trying desperately not to be last. We cursed the wind gods, and finally started cursing each other. The leaky boat explained a lot, but the damage was done.

I had never quit anything before. Not ever. Not even my MEDS at this point. But the last day of the event, just after we pulled in the sails, with a huge statue of Christopher Columbus pointing westward and looking on, I jumped out of the boat and started swimming for shore. I kept swimming. I got out of the filthy water and tiptoed through the minefield of hypodermic needles and empty bottles of cava, to my clothes, to the hotel, and into town for a day of art museums and stare-down contests with living statues, followed by a big night of soul searching and admirable efforts to charm the local ladies with two years of college Spanish and quite a few French words to bridge the gaps. I think it eventually worked, I can't really say for sure.

Olympic dream: *over.* Good thing school is about to start again, because I never really believed in that whole Olympic thing that much. I just told myself I did.

I had taken junior year off of collegiate sailing to focus on studies and devote the remaining thirty minutes a day to my physical Olympic training, meaning dropping weight and upping the sets of twenty pull-ups, doing lots of sit-ups, and stretching. Sometimes I wonder if so much time away from the water contributed directly to my agitation and eventual first breakdown. Harry Hindsight isn't that helpful, not really. But still, maybe sailing was how I meditated, and meditation was how I kept it all together.

I'm pretty sure that I was a lot of fun for the first four or five months Meg and I dated. As I flew closer and closer to the sun, there was plenty of love in the air. When I crashed, I clung fiercely to her. She stood by the zombie that was me for longer than I deserved.

I now see where Meg was coming from when she dumped me. Antidepressants might have saved my life, but they weren't an instant, magic bullet for something as carefree as a college romance should be. I was on boyfriend probation already when the news of my partying and choice to dramatically quit in Barcelona made it back from Spain.

That behavior, those choices in Barcelona were hard for me to understand. But for Meg they were bright, thick writing on a dark, dark wall. Neither of us was old enough for her to lay down on the tracks of the roller coaster I was on and hope to make it stop.

Thank goodness she didn't.

—⟞

CHAPTER 14

I NEEDED TWO MORE CREDITS TO earn a degree in mathematics. Granted, it wouldn't be a bachelor of science math degree. For that I would have needed to double up on upper-level courses again, and that had driven me insane. After quite a bit of soul searching I allowed that I would probably still exist as a human being, although decidedly second class, if I only had a bachelor of arts in mathematics instead of a BSc. It was not a decision I took lightly, and it weighed on me every day on the way to the lower-level physics class I took for credits to round out my "artist's" mathematics degree.

Anyway. I was so dejected from recently being dumped that I didn't want a lab partner. It looked like everybody was going to pair up without me and I would get my wish for reflective time in physics lab. When a third woman arrived late the first day, it was impossible to miss the 50 percent increase. This particular one would stand out as beautiful and explosively bright in any lineup, not just the tiny subset of chicks taking physics that year.

"I guess that means we're lab partners," she said to me with a moderately mischievous smile.

"I'm working alone. There must be somebody else you can find," I mumbled.

"Hmm. OK, suit yourself. Let me know if you change your

mind," she said as she picked up the lab assignment.

I thought about her a little after seeing her backside at the front of the next class. Not conversations about angular momentum, or terminal velocity. Thoughts that had the relationship starting around midnight and ending by the time the sun comes up.

Right on cue, she turned up to the next lab in cutoff shorts which looked to have been measured once and cut twice, a pushup bra and lowcut t-shirt, the closest thing to heels a girl could get away with during the day at Brown, and bright red lipstick. Ferrari red.

"I'll just be working over here if you get, say, *stuck*...working by yourself," she said as she sauntered past me. She smelled good. Subtle, slightly musky, or smokey. Something clicked, the *ahhooogah*! horn sounded and my eyes launched out of their sockets, as my feet started winding up with the "Yabba Dabba do" sound to run after the only one of us in the room who wasn't a cartoon of a physics student.

What the fuck do you think you're doing? said my head. *That road leads to one thing, and one thing only. You will be annihilated by another heart trampling.* "I don't care, it will be worth it," said a part of me I had never really thought of as wise before, and never would again. In fact, even that part of me was about to change drastically.

CHAPTER 15

⸙

I REJOINED MY FRIENDS ON THE Brown Sailing Team, and tried to find a rhythm again on the water. Things were going fine mid-semester, in studies and athletics, when my left testicle swelled to the size of an egg. I ignored it. For a few days. Denial, or hope it would go away on its own. Who knows what I was thinking?

At afternoon sailing practice, my good testicle, my swollen testicle, and I leaped to bring the 420 dinghy quickly around in a roll-tack. (If you roll the boat sharply and with perfect timing with your teammate, you can make a little extra wind when you turn.) The pain of the testicle suddenly hemorrhaging was like nothing I had ever known. It was impossible to hope it would fix itself now.

My race was no longer around buoys. It was to the operating table. We rushed in to the dock, back to Providence, and into the school infirmary. After a couple phone calls and some pain-killers I was on the plane to Los Angeles. My father's hospital in LA had a urology surgeon who had an open slot for surgery the next morning.

I woke up to a four-inch horizontal incision just below my tummy and a silicone prosthetic left nut that was bigger than my real one but slightly smaller than the removed ruptured mass.

The next thing I remember was asking what day it was, and how many days until the first race.

I had come second in the singles nationals as a freshman. I was second again sophomore year. Junior fall I took off. I was going to finally win the Singlehandeds senior year, or die trying.

"We'll start radiation treatment tomorrow," said Dr. Imbasciani, and my father agreed.

"How long is that course of treatment?" said my mother, the third person in the room and also the third doctor.

"About a month," said Dr. I.

"Okay, that's going to be pretty tough on him, but if it's what has to be done, we might as well get started," said my father.

So far, there was no indication that I was present. At least not to me.

"Will I die if I don't get radiation treatment?" I said.

Three heads swiveled toward the questioner, as if surprised there was someone else in the room.

"Well, Kevin, you won't die immediately, no. But if there is any remaining malignancy anywhere in your body, and we have no way of knowing whether there is at this stage, you put yourself at immense risk not undergoing prophylactic treatment immediately," said Dr. I.

My parents looked at each other with wide eyes of fear. *Where is he going with this? Of course we start treatment tomorrow. That is what is done. Everything to eradicate the illness.*

"What if there isn't any malignancy...downstream? What if you already got it all? Doesn't radiation then increase my risk of cancer in the future?" My thoughts at the time may not have been that clear or concise, but I got the concept across eventually.

"Well, strictly speaking, you are correct. But the literature indicates that the odds are high that we did not get it all. Radiation is the obvious, percentages-indicated next step," said Dr. Imbasciani in as dispassionate a voice as he had. I could tell he cared for his patient's future. I also felt all the gears and wheels turning in all three physicians' heads about what should be done and about how to convince me what was best.

At this stage I should say that I might be painting the three doctors out as bad guys, or at least as lacking compassion. That's not true, not at all. They all loved me. However, they also all came to the table with decades of a scientific world view which proposes most scenarios as essentially binary, a philosophy that implies one choice is better than the other in all but the rarest of cases.

Deep down, I knew I was a rare case of some sort. I also knew for a fact that if I didn't win the Singlehandeds in my last chance, I was going to die anyway.

"Can my incision withstand sit-ups and torsion two weeks from now?" I asked.

You couldn't hear a pin drop because all the air was sucked out of the room with the gasps.

"Well, I'm not entirely sure. I suppose we could figure out how to strap around your lower abdomen to try to best protect the sutures. Also pretty important to try to keep the area dry, and obviously clean," said Dr. I.

"OK. Can I ask you guys to please look into that for me? I'm going to the Singlehandeds, and I'll do whatever I need to do after that. Will the malignancy show by then if it's in there…in here?" I pointed to myself.

"It's hard to say. If we don't do radiation now, you will need to get a blood test every month, and I mean not ever miss even one, not one, and a CAT scan every three months. Otherwise, if the cancer is still there and we miss it, it will have too long to grow and spread, and your odds of survival will plummet."

"Roger. Got it. Every month. Anything else?"

"Kevin, I really think we should take more time with this. The race is still over two weeks away, and you've only been out of general anesthesia for a short time. Why don't we see how we feel tomorrow. Dr. Imbasciani, is there an afternoon slot Kevin could have for the first radiation treatment?" I don't remember if that was Mom or Dad, or if I made it up completely just now for effect. I do remember the feeling, and it would have taken words like that to give me that feeling.

Two years later, I would face a similar majority opinion alone, which would trigger a very similar feeling, when I decided not to bank sperm before they removed the second testicle.

CHAPTER 16

~~_6_~~

THE 1990 COLLEGIATE SINGLEHANDED NATIONALS took place mid-November on Gull Lake in Kalamazoo, Michigan. It was cold, and at least one morning we had to chip ice out of the one-person Laser sailboats before heading out onto the water. My memories are pretty vague. I guess I was on a sort of autopilot mode, what I would later come to call the (android me). The parentheses express how it feels to be on medication. Like your whole deal is just off to the side, or a step behind. Or a last minute addition to a long list, or a sort of explanation of your real self, because you couldn't explain yourself in the body of the sentence of your life. It's not *you*.

Head down, feelings shoved way underground, denial about anything upsetting, determination to legitimize by Achievement. There was a lot of athletic tape and a fair bit of pain, and the flash of anger then disappointment and drooping shoulders during the penultimate race when my hopes were finally scuttled by a competitor who handled the tricky lake conditions with more cleverness and resilience than I could muster that week. I came mathematically close to winning, but I failed and had to settle for second. There would not be another chance.

Here's what's so crazy about buying hook, line, and sinker into the Achievement Model of life and success: I was ashamed.

My family and friends were proud of me, some expressing astonishment that I chose to compete at all, much less very nearly won. But I couldn't hear them—not a sound of what they were trying to help me hear, to help me see.

CHAPTER 17

‿᷏

I GOT BACK TO BROWN WITH some coursework to make up and
some understanding professors. My friends made noticeable
efforts which I mostly pushed away. The only thing that felt right
was to call on my hot physics lab partner and hope she made me
feel better somehow.

I picked Amanda up for our first date in torn jeans—a
symbolic nod to her opening gambit cutoff shorts—a cable knit
sweater, my fanciest shoes, and a phony smile that I desperately
hoped would melt away eventually to reveal a real one. She
greeted me at her freshman dorm door with a very gentle smile,
bid adieu to her roommate, and we headed down the hill toward
the Providence River and a restaurant called Three Steeple Street.
She ordered The Mouse That Roared salad.

I ordered a bottle of chardonnay, showed the server my
legitimate ID, and assured him that the young lady was unlikely
to be participating in the consumption of alcohol at his reputable
establishment. He winked as he took away her glass.

I slid my wine slowly toward her side of the table. Our fingers
touched, and for the briefest of moments, there was the electric
thrill of newness, of doors opening, of whole worlds flashing
into existence which I couldn't imagine moments before.

For Amanda and me, it was a feeling that was at once

explosive, pure and simple, and at the same time already laden with pathologies. The primary one is healer/sick. In one of those uncanny things which Freud would have loved, Amanda would go on to consider the medical specialties of Emergency medicine and Pediatrics. My dad: ER Doc. My mom: Pediatrician.

We talked a lot about Amanda's father Stephen. The enormous stainless steel watch which dangled powerfully up and down her forearm with a loose band belonged to him. In the early nineties, watches that big weren't on every wrist you saw. Amanda pulled off the look, and her admiration for her dad made it twice as sexy to me. She got me to talk a little about the French Lit that I liked. We talked about our sisters, and then about our most embarrassing moments in high school. I went to a huge public school in Southern California, she went to an all-girls private school on the Upper East Side of Manhattan.

I invited her back to my place to listen to *Peter and the Wolf.*

Hey. I never said I wrestled bears in the wild in my spare time, did I? I loved classical music, and I loved fairy tales. Whether she did or not, she could tell I did. We closed the door to my little room in the off-campus house I shared with some really nice, rather quiet sailing team friends. We lay down on my futon and its striped flannel sheets. We started with fingertips and eventually found ourselves in naked, tender embrace. I still had bandages over my scar. We stopped somewhere between second and third base when I got self-conscious. I'll never, ever forget the empathy and optimism I felt in her understanding smile at that moment. I felt, just then—I truly believed—that everything was going to be OK.

I'm not sure Amanda had ever been shut down before. I was providing something new in her life: the thrill of the chase. So, I wasn't just taking, I was giving a little back. I got very good at conjuring crooked ways of telling myself this over the next few years.

—⟨⟩—

CHAPTER 18

I MANAGED TO PRETEND NOTHING HAD changed all the way through the rest of senior year. Nothing at all. I took my little orange pills because that was what I was told to do. It seemed to be working well enough to maintain the illusion of normal.

My scar healed, I got used to being a little asymmetric in my undies. Move along, nothing to see here. Everything still worked, thank Zeus. I prevented Amanda from getting perfect grades with various, highly gratifying diversions.

My stance of abstinence toward drugs and alcohol inverted. If they made me take establishment drugs, then surely I could choose a few recreationals of my own? There were late nights with fraternity brothers and Pink Floyd, smoke pouring out of the room like Spicoli's van. There were crisp spring days when I rode on the bike path to practice while the rest of the team drove the half hour down Route 136 from Providence to Bristol. We all trained hard together, then I rode back to campus.

I said a few funny things at parties now and then, and the Brown team went on to win the overall national championship for combined results of Varsity, Team Racing, Women, and Singlehanded championships. We wouldn't have won if I hadn't gone to the Singlehanded Nationals.

Somehow, though, things like that never kept me from feeling like a failure and a fraud instead of the successful young man people seemed to think I was. Maybe it was because I lost my mind. Maybe it was because I lost one of my testicles. Maybe, I could have handled one or the other, but I wasn't handling both very well.

I could vaguely recall the types of thoughts I had when I was a cocky teenager. But I couldn't imagine the feeling anymore, that the world was a safe and predictable place. Certainly not the feeling that it was a place where I belonged.

CHAPTER 19

ALTHOUGH I HAD FINISHED MY courses on time to graduate with the Class of 1991, I had unfinished business. Fall of junior year I fell in love with a twentieth century French author and filmmaker named Marguerite Duras. She used Beethoven's music in a lot of her movies and wrote about it a little too. I had always listened to a lot of classical music, but as I spun up on my way to trying to strike the sun, I got more and more into just Beethoven, until finally people had to ask me to turn down one of two pieces: the C Minor Symphony and the D Minor Symphony. They are also known as Beethoven's 5th and Beethoven's 9th. They both end in major keys after starting in minor ones. This just wasn't done until Ludwig did it.

I wanted to graduate from Brown with honors, which meant writing a thesis. It wasn't going to be a math thesis. Especially not on MEDS. Plus, I wanted to write about Duras and Beethoven. Their love letters to their contemporaries, and across time to me, seemed like one of the most real things I knew.

I stayed in Rhode Island the next fall. I got a little apartment in Bristol with a floor that sloped toward the futon. Some afternoons I sailed a one-person boat called a Finn. The Finn was an Olympic class, which seemed important. Also, it was cool to be learning a new boat.

Monday, Wednesday, Friday I brewed a huge pot of black black coffee and slugged it all, which cracked the lid of the MEDS just a little on the jar that my imagination was pickled in. New thoughts could sneak out for a short walk around the grounds.

Tuesday, Thursday, and Saturday I drank no coffee because the doctors told me that I risked triggering a manic episode if I used caffeine. I could steer clear of many things in life, but not coffee. It seemed like a decent compromise for the bipolar guy, to have a bivalent caffeine regimen. Long afternoons in the saddle on the bike or in the sack with Amanda, alternating with long afternoons on the water in the Finn, rounded out my days.

CHAPTER 20

⤶

I CAME UNGLUED AGAIN IN NOVEMBER. This time in Tokyo. I had pushed extremely hard to finish my French literature thesis before getting onto the plane, and I handed it in. Writing it wasn't that hard. What was hard was transcribing it from the hand-written fountain pen manuscript to typeset French with all the little eyebrows and hats above the vowels.

I'd like to say that I thought I was proud of it at the time—that would sound nice now. The truth is that it stumbled just over the line of sufficiency for not precipitating debilitating embarrassment. That's how I thought of it, anyway. Especially since the cancer, I was forever campaigning to stay on the good side of that line. A few months later, I was awarded the Ruth Electa Collins Premium for outstanding (senior male) work in French. There weren't many of us, but a win is a win, right?

About forty college students from around the country got on the plane at Logan International Airport in Boston to head abroad for the Japanese-American Intercollegiate Goodwill Games. At the awards ceremony, held at the Naval War College, the Japanese students all got on stage and sang a rousing hymn. It seemed important to compliment it with American goodwill. I took the mic and told a story about a man with no wife, a woman with no husband, and all their kids, and I started singing.

I think most of us were swaying arm-in-arm by the time the lady met the fellow and knew it was much more than a hunch.

They gave us goody bags on our way out. What could possibly go wrong with fifty bags of rice and fish-heads on a forty-five minute bus ride full of forty drunk American college students?

We had a day to tour around before getting back on the plane to the land of the free and the home of the brave. A few of us took the train into the hills to go temple-hopping.

$\curlyeqprec$

A LARGE THRUST OF THE "move along, nothing to see here, I'm an ordinary guy" attempts I was making included forgetting that I might be different from the other five people out for a memorable day. There was clearly far more sophisticated psychological sleight of hand going on behind the scenes to maintain that charade, but it's what I needed, so it's the message (I) told "myself". You can fiddle with the capitalizations, parentheses, and quotation marks but one way or another, we tend to believe our own lies and submit to our denials. I'm pretty sure there is scientific proof that doing so is an evolved survival mechanism.

I had just spent a year-plus straining to fake myself into imagining that I was nothing but normal. Looking the other way as I snuck my psychiatric medication past my thoughts and down my throat. Pretending not to notice how often I had to adjust my junk because my fake left nut was made of rubber and way too big.

I partied with the gang, but my brain responded a little differently to our frolicking. It didn't happen all at once, like flipping a switch or launching into a bad trip. Sure, I started acting a little off and saying some slightly bizarre things by the time we were back on the train into town. That just made me normal in the group. Didn't it?

One of our band of merry men was a tall, striking woman; let's call her Stella. We rolled into a high-priced area of restaurants, and she got a little group of four Japanese businessmen to notice her. They invited her into a fine restaurant for dinner, and Stella accepted with a crippling smile. Her five male best friends popped out from around the corner like a movie hitchhiking scene, and we all went inside.

We found ourselves in a private room in the back with our shoes off. The rice paper doors were slid closed each time a tiny, kimonoed server departed. The food was amazing. The sake was smoother than silk. When it came time to settle the check the men said, "No, no, impossible. Cultural exchange, English learning opportunity. Honda will gratefully gifting you this party time." We all looked at each other and shrugged. *Sounds good to us!*

And so, the high-grade sake in addition to the previous beers did not work on my (android) "restraining bolt" like Loc-Tite. More like the pneumatic guns they use to remove F1 tires in times measured in seconds.

CHAPTER 22

WE MUST HAVE GOTTEN BACK to the hotel near the port sometime around 3:00 a.m. I said goodnight to everyone in the lobby, headed up to my room to change into sweats, the team jacket, and sailing boots. Then I headed back down to the lobby and out the door. I found a basketball not too far from the hotel.

What are the chances? How did they know I would walk this direction first? Oh, they don't need to. They just put a bunch of balls out and if I miss them all, the Director re-tasks the troops until contact. How did they get so many red, white, and blue basketballs in Japan? Well, they've known I was coming here for a few weeks. Plenty of time. The Director must be so psyched to have Tokyo tech. I bet he would have done more in Boston, but was held back a few times by bad coms or missing camera angles. This show's like nothing the world has ever seen. Shoulders back, spine crowbar straight. Touch the top of your head to the sky. Smile. Not too big a smile, that looks cheesy....

I kept the basketball with me until well after the sun came up. I did a number of things that would have been unlawful any other day. Since all of Tokyo was actually now the movie set for the "The Kevin Show," the things I did were really just me doing my job. For a few more hours, part of me didn't trust that I was really the star of a show being broadcast to the world, but most of me did.

The untrusting self set out to prove it. He walked across streets in rush-hour traffic with his eyes closed. He found a worker's pickup truck parked up on the sidewalk at a worksite. It was unlocked, so he hopped in. *If this really was parked here for me to get into and drive around town so they had that footage, the keys would be above the sun visor just like they are for Arnold in Terminator 2.* The keys fell into my lap.

I drove around Tokyo for a couple of hours. I remain so tremendously relieved that I did not hit anything or anyone. I finally parked the truck as best I could and got out. I had somehow found the National Theater, so parking on the front steps of that made dramatic sense.

I left the keys in the ignition and walked. I eventually came to a building which felt right. Time to go inside. There were two rows of computer terminals visible through the window. I'm nearly certain now that I was hallucinating the sign above the door, which said "Genius School." I was bitterly disappointed that the door was locked. I knocked and waited, knocked and waited some more. Nobody came to meet me.

The next place which felt right to enter was open. Although the streets were eerily deserted, I had to get off them. The Director wanted me inside. I have incredibly vivid memories of the time inside that building. There was a basketball hoop and a big stereo setup with microphone and karaoke machine. I shot some baskets with my ball and then with the orange ones already in there, making jokes about whose balls were whose. I fiddled with the stereo for a while and played some loud music. The karaoke machine didn't seem to work. *Of course, they want me to sing original songs now!* So I did. I set the stereo up to record, pushed the triangle and the dot buttons on the cassette player/ recorder together, and started singing. I remember it being a brilliant blending of Bob Dylan, U2, R.E.M., Michael Jackson, and Madonna songs. It was important to stick with artists who were well known in Japan....

Karaoke-time was over. I found access to a pipe shaft and climbed down. That was where I was meant to leave my sailing boots, as far below sea-level as possible. Also my shirt. I placed them ceremoniously at the bottom of the shaft and headed into the Tokyo evening, wearing only sweatpants and a hidden scar.

CHAPTER 23

THE EMPEROR'S PALACE. MAGNIFICENT LANDSCAPING. I wandered around the grounds for quite a long time before finally being arrested. Not open for tourists. Especially not large bearded ones with bare feet and no shirt.

The little police station was comedic. It was obvious that they were getting very frustrated. There was definitely no playbook for this situation, even without the language barrier. I found myself back on the street, which to this day I don't entirely understand. It was dark now, I was somewhere in the middle of Tokyo, and I wanted to get back to my little hotel room. The only problem was, I didn't know what the hotel was called, or how to get there. I got on a bus and smiled at the bus driver. He nodded and gestured to sit down, closed the door, and drove to the next stop. Very cold air blew onto me, which meant I was supposed to get off. I spent a few hours getting on buses which felt warm when I stepped onto them, and getting off again when the signal hit my face.

I can still picture the looks on the graveyard-shift-commuters' faces. White man with scruffy beard, no shirt, no shoes. Not normal passenger. I found my way back to the hotel.

One of the coaches rushed me up to my room for a quick shower and change while he shoved my stuff in my bag. We were the last ones onto the bus. There was admirable patience and finesse. College athletes have partied hard before, and some had even come home past curfew. It wasn't Coach's first rodeo. Still, it probably seemed like I couldn't decide whether I was the bull or the clown.

There was a spot in the front, and Coach had me sit there and then had my teammate Virginia sit next to me for the trip to the airport. They put Bob Marley on the stereo. I cried softly to myself looking out the window. It was confusing being the most important person in the world while also losing the last scraps of my free will. I was grateful the Director had chosen to give me some time on the bus with familiar teammates and friends, and some of the bestest of all musics, before the next scene.

There was no way for the coaches to know how jumbled my head was. My neurons, and the pathways that were first laid down in 1989 got to a certain state of agitation that made the self inside my head believe again, truly believe, that he was the star of a worldwide show being broadcast live and taped for replay and international overdub. All my cues were conveyed real-time, by whichever medium fit best with the scene. Sometimes bus heaters or number codes on signs. Sometimes songs on the radio. Sometimes conversations I was not even in. All designed by very smart people with unlimited access to cutting-edge technology and vast resources. Unimaginable planning and execution. Except, it's what I thought was true.

The short-range reason for it all was to make money with product placement and advertising. The long-range vision, and the reason *They* had chosen me, was to Save the World.

At the Tokyo airport, when the script called for it, I was able to play the part of a college athlete about to get on a plane and go home. I was able to stand still, to listen, to smile and hand my passport over to the team leader for check-in.

The airport bustle became overwhelming. I stormed off the set, running downstairs to baggage claim, up onto the belt, and past the incoming suitcases. I dramatically leapt over the top of the little luggage train tractor parked near the chute and ran toward the biggest plane I saw. It was a 747, and it was only a few hundred meters away. I got all the way underneath it, between the main landing gear struts, when the police arrived. They did not mess around. They surrounded me, took me down with a flash of martial arts and martial law, and drove me away.

CHAPTER 24

꒜

I CAN'T IMAGINE THE PHONE CALL. I'll try anyway. Dad was probably at work at the hospital. It would have been something along these lines. I've never asked him about it. I don't know that I will. I worry that the memories for him are too traumatic, or disappointing, or both.

Dad, picking up: "Dr. Hall."
Overseas caller: "Dr. Hall? This is Coach Rosenberg."
Dad: "Yes?"
"Your son was arrested in Tokyo by the police. He got agitated at the airport, ran out onto the tarmac, and was arrested. He's being detained by the Japanese authorities."
"I'll be there as soon as I can."
"We're glad he's OK."
"Doesn't sound like he's OK."
"You're right, he's not OK, but he's still alive and as far as we know nobody got hurt."
"I see. Thank you."
Click.

It would have sucked to drop everything and get on a plane to retrieve your irresponsible and selfish son from a faraway land.

I know how I feel when I get called to meet the principal of my son's fifth grade class because Rainer has been involved in a boyhood situation on the playground. I think he should know better, and that I have given him all the tools and attention he should need to behave responsibly, and that it is frustrating that he doesn't, and disappointing, and annoying to have my day interrupted by something that should be under his control.

I also know I love him, and if there were anything I could do to make it easier for him on the playground, or in class, I would do it. That day, my playground wasn't just down the street. It was halfway around the world.

Imagine Dad's thoughts as I poured a huge cup of Coke over the top of my head and said "That one's for free(dom)," just as we were about to board the plane. *Product Moment.* Coke was, after all, the title sponsor of the show. I don't know if we were already flagged as risky passengers before that event. I don't know what he did to still get us on that plane. I imagine he found a way to get a stronger sedative in me, got me in my seat, and kept his fingers crossed. Livid.

We touched down at Los Angeles International Airport and went straight to Pasadena. I was admitted to Las Encinas Hospital. I fit right in.

It would have been a horrendous trip for Dad, on so many levels. Still, it's not quite the same as having to handle alternative scenarios, like a phone call which starts, "Dr. Hall. I am so sorry to tell you that your son is dead." Or, maybe, he had already played through that phone call over and over so that when it came, it wasn't so hard to hear.

The fact that he felt disrespected by my challenges last year makes me think it has never occurred to him that I have done a good job simply surviving with such an unreliable mind.

CHAPTER 25

~~

D ROOL. DISAPPOINTMENT. DESPAIR.
Group. Art Therapy. Discussion.

It's OK to succeed. You don't have to throw it all away on purpose.

Right.

Smoke break! Thank God for smoke break.

There was a race coming up in a few months, and my autopilot still planned for me to be there. This kept me thinking (in a drugged, foggy way) about the future. The singles boat I had been training in before heading off to sing karaoke in Tokyo had an ideal weight of about 220 pounds. I could almost call my psych ward overeating training.

I moved in with Mom in Ventura, California. Back into the house I had grown up in. Back onto the Pacific Ocean. Back to the gym, to sailing with the twenty-five pound weighted speed jacket. (Strap it to your shoulders and lean back. Now, slide off the edge of a bench until your knees just touch, and hook your feet under something. Stay there for twenty minutes. (You get five jump burpees for rests.) Next, row as hard as you can for twelve minutes. Back out over the edge leaning back for twenty, row for twelve. You've just done one Olympic Finn race. There's another one today, and five more days after that.)

The 1992 Olympic Trials for the Finn Class were in Newport Beach, California in April. My goal wasn't to win my first Olympic Trials and head off to Barcelona. Not after I jumped out of the boat two years before at the Pre-Olympics. It did seem like maybe a one-man show was better for me and for any potential partner likely to eventually be victimized by my instability.

I finished eighth in the Trials, and I even forgot to be disappointed or ashamed with that result. Something about Schopenhauer, and all man's misery coming from his inability to adjust his expectations. Becoming an outpatient only a few months before the Trials allowed me to set my expectations plenty low. So I wasn't miserable when I didn't win. It's a great trick.

CHAPTER 26

M OM TELLS ME SHE REMEMBERS the tone and desperation in
my voice when I called from Chicago to ask her to pick
me up at LAX. The last she knew, things were going great for me,
and I was headed to Long Beach to help at a training camp for
the 1992 US Olympic Team. Mom and I spent a difficult night
in a hotel near the sailing center, during which I made a big show
of flushing my MEDS down the toilet.

The next morning, I made an even bigger show of throwing
her wallet and car keys into the sea. That was when she knew
she wasn't going to be able to get me to the hospital without
Dad's help. He wasn't impressed.

I turned up early at the Alamitos Bay Yacht Club to get ready
for a long day in the sun. The full tube of white zinc oxide covered
my face and neck completely. Since the camera angle from the
left end of the bathroom was poor, I faced a bit to the right. I
spit three times on the counter and then placed the manuscript
of my thesis face-down with the ceremony of a Tibetan monk
putting the finishing grains on the holiest of sand mandalas. I
waved my hand over the page with a magician's flourish, and
lifted the parchment.

One word bled onto the counter: *L'amour*. Love. The last
word of my thesis. Proof. He knew exactly what I would do.

Nice work planning for this scene, Director. Great vision predicting everything, scriptwriters. Amazing work with the tech, to have the Word appear like that. Nice touch with the magician's flourish, Kev.

"Kevin, maybe it would be better for you to stay ashore today. Make sure the video equipment is ready for this afternoon's debrief?" said the Olympic coach.

"I'm happy to go on the water today. We're working mostly on downwind, right? I've already got my sunscreen on!" I said.

People giggled. Or, I made that up now because it makes me feel better.

"I see that. We're actually just going to do some long, boring upwinds. Julia has a new sail, and we need lots of photos of it on this mast. It would be most helpful if you make sure we're ready to look at video when we get back," said Coach.

Julia smiled gently, nodded. *He's right. You take it easy today. We're here for a whole week.* She pushed her boat in the water and headed to sea for the long day, without me there to help her train to win her bronze medal in Barcelona.

"OK. I'll be ready when you guys get back," I said.

They look confused. That wasn't the script. Hmm.

I wandered back toward the bathroom, waiting for the next cue.

There! On that far trailer. An Olson 30. There's no place more like home for me than a boat like that.

I scramble up the trailer and onto the deck. The hatch is locked, which I expect. I try it anyway. For the scene. (We need the beat of me looking up at the seagull and remembering to sneak in the back hatch.) I wiggle below the poop deck and crawl forward past the rudder post, aft bulkhead, quarter-berth, companionway, all the way to the front hatch. I open it and then look for my cue.

Yes! Nailed it. First try.

Both coolers are full of Coke. Not a few cans. Full.

I pop one open, pretend it's ice cold, and take a long sip. The camera in the back of the keel-stepped mast has me in profile as I exhale the orgasmic "Ahhhhh!" (which only a relentlessly marketed soft-drink can provide). I hold the super-smile as long as I can and then gasp for air. I turn with furrowed brow directly to the camera in the back of the mast.

It's warm. I wasn't ready for it to be quite so warm. I'll be ready for another take, in five.

I finish the Coke. There is a white zink pattern on the top of the can now, and a can-rub pattern on my melting face. I crush the can, cast it into the forecastle like a frustrated sailor might toss a broken harpoon. Leap out the forward hatch as if Ahab himself has called for all hands on deck.

Next I throw all the lines overboard. Sheets. Dock lines. Sail ties. Tails of halyards.

Tales of Ishmael.

Queequeg and I pass the time tacking and jiving until Mom and Dad storm onto the set.

On the way to Pasadena, I threw my magnetic travel chess set, along with both books of chess openings, onto the 710 Freeway. I flipped through and then jettisoned as no longer relevant, my journal of the past two years. I got out of the car at a stoplight and ran a few blocks as my parents drove along side.

Welcome back to Las Encinas Hospital. We've been expecting you.

Soon after arriving on the locked ward, I reacted badly to one of the paintings. I don't remember exactly what triggered me, but the Devil was behind the thick plastic screwed firmly into the wall over the Monet poster. I don't know why a painting with the Devil in it was put there to upset me. I guess the director wanted a set piece which had me tearing the Monets and Manets off the wall.

The plexiglass didn't stand a chance against a madman's rage.

A week later I was on a more open ward when I tricked the staff into stepping out of the little kitchenette. I swept past them, locked the door, climbed out the little second story window, down the side of the building, and strolled over to the rose garden. I smelled one big red rose before they put me back in the locked ward.

The art on the walls was fixed.

⤚ᴄ

MY WHITE KABUKI-MASK PERFORMANCE IN Long Beach prompted a change in my meds from lithium liaised with Prozac to the far more sexy-sounding couple Depakote met Wellbutrin. Him, a suave, fair-haired antiepileptic. Her, a purple-skinned antidepressant cum antismoking pill cum cash cow.

The medication I chaperoned now wasn't worse. So, my odds of struggling with compliance weren't worse, either.

While I had lived in Rhode Island, Dad sent me a subscription to *Money* magazine. It arrived every month, letting me know that he cared about me and my future. After my third manic episode, after leaving work to rescue me a third time, and as the third round of ambulance, hospital, inpatient, outpatient, and aftercare bills stacked up on his desk, Dad must have reached some kind of turning point in his thinking about what things he could do, or not do, to help me the most.

One of the tough-love choices involved forwarding all of the medical bills to me and announcing that he wouldn't pay another cent if it happened again. Another was to have me apply for disability income from Social Security. Any job I might have had in the last six months would have required over thirty days of medical leave. By the letter of the laws I was entitled to it, and the checks for the few months I received them helped a lot with debt that would have mounted even faster without them. Still, it was a confusing thing to have done. Part of me doggedly wished to feign situation-normal, even in the face of contradictory evidence. The rest of me figured that if Dad and the government both saw me as disabled, well, who was I to question them?

I moved back east for the summer of 1992. Amanda and I were still going strong, other than our odd, but somehow required, high-school-ex *booty-calls*. Maybe especially because of those. She would continue to tell me over the following years that none of the other boys wrote letters quite like mine, much less poetry. Her questions about my few other women were always met the same way: "She's not you."

I'm not saying there was no drama. Still, I never punched out one of her beaus, and she never boiled any rabbits. We were tethered together partly by the shared goal of my survival, partly by our intellectual parity, partly by the purest of laughters, and partly by just how well my wobbly bits seemed to fare with hers.

I made a little money coaching the top kids around Long Island Sound. I was housed by a generous and incredibly patient and understanding family. I raced my Laser around the Northeast. It was in the Laser that I had won the Youth Worlds, and now the Laser was also the newest Olympic class. It was the Laser that I had sailed for thousands of hours in high school, and it was the Laser Class that saw me undefeated in North America for nearly two years. In short, the Laser was the one thing on earth I knew would never betray me.

The next Laser World Championship was going to be in Auckland, New Zealand, in January 1993. I was going to train with a close Australian friend whom I had met and shared the medal stand with seven years earlier at the Youth Worlds. I believed that I had a shot at winning in New Zealand. For sure a good shot at the podium.

Off to exotic Australia, where I'd train for a few weeks with Adam, celebrate Christmas with the kangaroos, and then head across the Tasman to the Land of the Long White Cloud, bound for glory in New Zealand.

CHAPTER 2 8

‿๑

THE TWO-YEAR MARK IS THE first statistical hump in cancer
survival. After two years in the clear, the odds of survival
climb dramatically. I had been diligent, or prudent, or wise to
never miss a monthly blood test. Twenty-three clear tests since
my surgery, since my "radical orchiectomy, left side".

One of the tumor markers, called the beta hCG test, is
basically a pregnancy test. A man growing a little baby cancer
looks a lot like a woman growing a little baby sailor to that test.
The other test is called alpha fetoprotein, and it can also mean
you're pregnant or growing a little baby tumor. At what turned
out to be the two-year threshold, almost to the day, my test
results shot through the roof.

My sister drove me out Highway 126 toward Six Flags Magic
Mountain. Not too far from the amusement park was a place
to bank as many units of my own blood over a period of three
weeks as possible. I think I bled about eight liters into plastic
bags with my name on them. It was going to be major surgery.

I wrote letters telling friends that I was about to need even
more support than they had already given me. Something about
how if every dog has its day, where did I go wrong? The psychiatric
medication worked well over this period. While there is certainly
mental and spiritual stress in facing a biological health crisis,

it didn't trigger me to imagine I was in a magnificent land of guardian fairies.

The operation to remove my lymph nodes would take many hours. The lymph nodes are the blood's filter system, and if my markers had recently sounded the alarm, it meant I had some gunk stuck in those filters. The nodes needed to be cut out of there, pronto.

This time there was very little to discuss. I agreed with Mom, Dad, and Dr. Imbasciani about everything except the choice to be optimistic. I hadn't done anything wrong. In fact, I was ultra-healthy. Brown rice and broccoli, lean chicken and fish. Lots of water, lots of sleep. Fit as a fiddle. Taking MEDS like a good soldier. Mind a precise machine of quiet calculations.

Body revolting like a Parisian in 1789.

I didn't deserve cancer. Not again.

CHAPTER 29

⟶

M Y FAVORITE SYMPHONY during emotionally stable times is
Brahms's Symphony No. 2 in D Major. I read somewhere
that there was evidence that familiar, soothing music could help
the prognosis for major surgery success, despite the patient being
under general anesthetic. Dr. Imbasciani said he liked Brahms
well enough, and it would be no problem playing some good
music while he opened me from sternum to groin, tossed my
tummy and some guts into a plastic bag, flipped them out of the
way onto my folded-back abdomen skin and fascia, and scraped
out the bad guys.

Here's a crazy question. I was reading Robert Musil's *The
Man Without Qualities* at the time. It's not a super common
book. There aren't many English translations from the German.
The translation I had of Part One had a green spine and was
unmistakable. While it's true that doctors tend to have books
on their shelves, it's not that often you see Proust, or Joyce, and
especially not Musil in a doctor's office just sitting there. Except
this time. Except in Dr. Imbasciani's office. My question is this:
If the feeling that I belonged there right then, that everything
was going to be OK—if seeing that very rare book meant
angels were watching over me, and the magic helped me feel
connected and calm in the face of trying circumstances, did it

mean I was sick in the head?

That's the double edge of my exuberance when I spin up toward mania, attracting more and more connections. For the first 90 percent of the ride, the world becomes more fun, more interesting, more enchanting. More real, more the place I'm meant to be. Then, in the very next breath, a huge switch gets thrown and I'm stark-raving mad. A danger to myself and others.

Like Roberto Benigni says to Tom Waits in *Down by Law,* "the world is sad and beautiful."

In the case of *The Man Without Testicles,* I mean *Qualities,* on Dr. I.'s bookshelf, the "delusional" thought that it was put there "for me" was helpful and reassuring. I know I'm not the first person to wonder just "who" or "what" put "it" *there.*

There are lots of ways to look at it, and lots of names too. They range from biochemically induced psychosis, to spooky action at a distance, to tapping into the unveiled, entangled nature of the Universal Mind. Madness, synchronicity, magic, kismet....Late in his life, Carl Jung came around to deciding that what was true for him was quite simply what worked. It's taken me twenty-five years of trial and error, trial by fire, and endless internal trials by an unfriendly jury of my selves' peers, but the idea that "what's true is what works" has a certain elegance. Maybe C.J.'s way is good enough for me.

CHAPTER 30

⟞

I CAN PINPOINT THE MOMENT I could conclusively define Hell, and I was in it. I was furiously clicking my morphine drip button. I was still in a bit of pain, my thumb was raw from clicking, and Wayne's World was on the TV above my inclined hospital bed with the rails that are hard, but not impossible, to click down yourself.

The nurse came in and turned it off, because I was laughing so hard that I might pop out my fifty staples. The first big chuckles, she came in and told me to hold a pillow over my tummy and be careful. When the laughter escalated and echoed in the next county, she shut it down. I remember thinking *Great. Now I'm not even allowed to laugh. Talk about unfair!*

Amanda finished her junior classes that fall and came to California. She helped me lace up my girdle as tightly as possible so the fifty staples didn't pop when I tried to go for my first walk. From the front door to the driveway. The next day, all the way to the next-door neighbor's driveway. In my neighborhood, you could pass the sugar from one house to the next through the kitchen window, so it wasn't a big journey. Still, I got short of breath and energy after fifteen steps. The next day, two houses. By the end the week, we walked together to the end of the block.

Neither of us can remember exactly how or why we decided

to not speak to each other for a couple weeks after she left. I think it had to do with her being overwhelmed with sadness for me, with the heaviness of the situation, and with us deciding that a short break from it all while she was on vacation with her family in San Juan would be a necessary relief. No news is good news, sort of thing.

When we connected again, I was in indescribable anguish. I had spent about ten days telling my parents over and over that I would not bank any sperm, listening to their impassioned pleas about how I could always choose not to use it, and responding to them that that was precisely the point, that when it came time to choose not to use it I would have forgotten the pain and I would be selfishly passing a future of potential, or even likely pain on to my children.

There had been a whole lot of head scratching when all the lymph nodes came back benign two weeks after I got stapled fifty times after my retroperitoneal lymph dissection. No sign of cancer. It wasn't anywhere in the twenty little masses they had cut out in the operation of *Man without Qualities/Testicles* and Brahms's D Major Symphony fame.

I didn't think I should leave all the experts hanging for too long, so I went ahead and had my other testicle hemorrhage a few days after the benign results were revealed. Well, that explains it.

My second testicle was removed. Radical orchiectomy, right side. Now my surgical history rolls like poetry off the tongue: bilateral radical orchiectomy.

Nobody knows if a close examination of the remaining testicle before they unzipped my frontside would have shown any signs. I suspect that if the second testicle had announced its demise sooner, all that would have changed is the order of the operations.

I wouldn't have hated myself any less, if the arm of the upside-down cross on my body was carved into my flesh before the torso and not after.

CHAPTER 31

~~~

I F SOMEBODY WAS GOING TO need a bunch of surgery, we were relatively fortunate as a family (or maybe our fortune was well-engineered and well-earned by Dad). Employment at CIGNA hospital in downtown LA included insurance. It also turned out that just down the hall from where Dad saved lives in the ER, was one of the best urology surgeons this side of the Mississippi.

If the first prosthesis was about the size of a golf ball, the second one was the size of a tangerine. Something about recalls on the Dow-Corning fake boobs, so the only other company that made them had these. I'm still not quite sure why I never asked to see what they were proposing to put in there. Or even better, just chose to be Orin OneNut. Seriously, my ball sac was stretched tight by the new pretend manhood. Besides feeling like some kind of hunchback down there, it meant that chafe was now a very real, ongoing, daily concern.

As soon as I could think straight and walk all the way to the donut shop and back, I got help from a friend who used to babysit me and Sis. He was now one of the top salesmen for Toyota in Ventura County. He and maybe even the dealership somehow helped me take out a new-car loan, somehow, and I bought a brand-new white Toyota extra-cab four-wheel drive pickup. It all happened pretty fast. I dreamed it up. I got me, myself, and I together, and it was unanimously agreed that a brand-new white horse was necessary to survive. Damn the future, damn the torpedoes, I was headed for the open road.

I put roof racks on top of the matching cab cover to be ready for skis or a Laser. My uncle helped me install an aftermarket cruise control from Sears and Roebuck. I put thick carpet padding and lush beige carpet inside, then I peeled out of town the second the license plates arrived from DMV.

I remember a sureness to the whole process, an ease and nothing-is-going-to-stop-me vibe. Maybe I was getting the other kind of "sick". Whatever you call it, I was glad to have had that happy juice flowing through me after they took my second nut, and not some black bile of doom.

I stopped for two weeks to visit my aunt and ski timidly in Aspen. The tight girdle and very ginger skiing on the wide groomed boulevards of Snowmass wasn't nearly as risky as sitting around hoping the good times kept rolling all by themselves. There was no way they could in Ventura. Staying there would be all too familiar and too close to reeling, confused, distraught family. Too close to home, and too sad.

I attended a ski workshop taught by Aikido master Tom Crum, called the *Magic of Skiing*. My Aunt Martha was one of the instructors, and she hooked me up. Big time. It was about breathing from Center, skiing from Center, and saying Yes. There is nothing better I could have done in this world. I took Tom's signed book, *The Magic of Conflict*, with me everywhere I went, for months. Tom is on a first name basis with the Dalai Lama, and I chose to believe a teeny tiny part of their peace and wisdom flowed out of the autograph ink and into me.

The gentle high and positive energy that had poked its nose above the medication while I was gliding down the slopes wore off quickly as reality set all the way in. No balls no more.

I was really scared I wouldn't be able to handle another down time. Scared, like Virginia Woolf in her last letter to her husband before walking into the river with rocks in her pockets, scared.

I left my skis and my MEDS in Colorado, and Amanda and I drove back to Providence together in the pickup while the antimanic downers slowly but surely worked their way out of my bloodstream. It didn't seem like Amanda was on a need-to-know basis for my decision. I was doing her a favor by keeping it secret....

Reality became more poignant when the first big needle for my hormone therapy went into my ass. No testicles means no testosterone. No testosterone no good. It would be years and years before my bi-weekly shot wasn't a major emotional affair, calling up all sorts of questions which furiously whirled around things like "Why me?," "What did I do wrong?," "When will it ever end?," and "Maybe I should just end it myself now, if it doesn't matter what I do or how hard I try or whether or not I pray or sing or win races or write beautiful love letters or light candles in a daze."

Humans are really good at pattern recognition. Along with reason, and the ability to back-stab without being found out, we excel at pattern recognition. The pattern I was coming to recognize is that God had it in for me.

We are also really good at empathy and compassion. My friends back in Providence were there for me in so many ways. Zack organized a big party where he and Scourge sang a song they had written. It went "Lift your head up high, your friends are all around..." Stella made me a flag of a bright sun. People brought books, and mixed tapes, cookies and videos, and most important, hugs and patient ears. I don't know what I said, or if it even mattered. What I remember is other humans, sitting close to me, and listening. I remember the looks of pain and sadness in their eyes, and being astounded and moved by the way that same look included hope. I had run out of it. My friends carried it for me until I was ready to hold it again myself.

CHAPTER 32

⟿

WHEN WE FIRST RETURNED TO Providence, I had moved into a tiny alcove of Zack and Richard's place, not far from where Edgar Allen Poe used to wrestle his demons and tinker with his medicines and work his magic. We put up some bookshelves which left just enough space to walk from Richard's room past the books, to the living room. We hung a Laser sail from the ceiling and called the place behind it my room. I couldn't have asked for a better trio of allies than Richard, Zack, and Amanda.

I added some double vodkas to the MEDS-flushing-out program, in case that helped. I was desperate for a change more aggressive and more fundamental than the things you might say when a friend asks "Wassup?". I needed to change *who* I was.

I wanted the self I knew back, the one that rejoiced, and was moved by music, and loved art, and adored books, and laughed purely. That self was not in town when the Depakote was around. His pathetic, zombie twin brother (Kevin) didn't have the spirit, the chutzpah, or the will to carry on with a mind in a cage and a body forever playing mean.

Within a month of moving in with Zack and Richard and devotedly trying to fit into Amanda's junior year, the MEDS were ancient history.

Cross my heart, I was literally trying to survive when I

stopped taking MEDS in Aspen. I hoped the music, and maybe even a few angels would come back. I needed them to return right away, because gray-painted (Kev) just wasn't going to make it much longer. Simple as that.

I used alcohol, and coffee, and increasingly, both. Late nights out. I was all about anchors-aweigh. As in, get them away from me. I offered Amanda a focus of increasing fascination. Then I got just plain weird.

I don't remember piecing together much of a narrative for my days and behaviors and choices. More like flitting from one twinkling thing to the next as I bounced around little private stories driven by whatever coincidences and patterns I could recognize or conjure up.

I did irresponsible things like leaving a candle lit in my room when away from the house, and repeatedly changing the music back to the Chili Peppers at parties with ice hockey players who wanted to listen to AC/DC.

I created connections which were strong for me then, but I might not necessarily see now. I read and wrote and ranted. I walked around Providence looking for miracles. Finally, the script flipped all the way and I was back on the studio lot. The Director put his headset on and tasked the troops. Everyone in my life "became" actors again, playing roles and spouting lines to manipulate me to give a good show to the People. Meaning, everyone on planet Earth.

Strangers with earpieces were fed information and lines to encourage me to go here and there. The cameras linked back to the mothership, and I was everywhere. It didn't worry me that I couldn't find any pictures of myself or catch a glimpse behind the curtain. These were professionals running the show, after all.

Philip K. Dick's first published hardcover is called *Time Out of Joint*. It is similar in theme to Robert Heinlein's 1941 short story called *They*. Compliment them both with Thomas Pynchon's *The Crying of Lot 49*. The scope of the conspiracies in the three stories differs, but the creepiness does not.

That's all just relatively recent fiction. The truth is much stranger. Viktor Tausk, a disciple of Freud, wrote a paper in 1919 about patients who thought they were persecuted at a distance, by enemies with technologically marvelous machines. "Influencing Machine" is the name Tausk used, and it has stuck.

The first recorded clinical description of an "*Influencing Machine Delusion*" was published a hundred years before the delusion was named. In 1810, John Haslam had a patient in Bethlehem Hospital (also known as Bedlam), named James Tilly Matthews. He wasn't just a Welsh tea-broker and architect. He also believed he was being controlled by an "Air Loom": a large device akin to a pipe organ, which played the mind instead of music.

He thought French agents put a magnet in his brain which allowed them to control him. He signed himself "James, Absolute, Sole, Supreme, Sacred, Omni-Imperious, Arch-Grand, Arch-Sovereign...Arch-Emperor." And I thought I had gone big telling people my address was "Kevin Hall, New York." I guess I'm not the first one to this party after all.

Tilly's Air Loom has captured imaginations so much that a full size model was built based on Tilly's drawings. It was installed in the Laing Gallery in Newcastle, in 2002 and has been exhibited elsewhere since.

What's new in the twenty-first century is that the technology available to persecute us is now up to the task of constant manipulation. Ubiquitous surveillance and directed influence via controlled media are utterly plausible.

Doctors now agree that this makes the delusion "nonbizarre".

⟳

CHAPTER 33

A MANDA WAS THE ONLY ONE I thought might be outside the conspiracy. I drove my truck into the courtyard of her dorm, the newest building on the Brown campus at the time. Then, I pulled the fire alarm to get her to come down.

"C'mon, we're going to Bermuda," I said.

"Now? Don't you think we should maybe pack?" Amanda said. She knew all about it, but she had never seen it up close and personal. She had never seen this look in my eyes.

"They have new clothes for us when we get there. Let's go, the plane leaves Logan in two hours," I said.

"Let's just park the truck and maybe go for a walk first? Get a pizza or some ice cream? Both?"

"Not hungry. Driving away in fifteen seconds. With or without you."

She could tell that I was serious, and that unknowable things hung in the balance.

We drove for an hour to Boston and then out toward the shipping docks. We blasted through a locked gate. I saw a company logo twisting itself to fit my psychotic narrative. I stopped the truck. It was the middle of the night. I tried the door, somehow knowing it would be open. It was unlocked.

I'm reading you Houston, see? I found the door first try.

Then, right there, in the little access cupboard just inside the front door—which somehow reminded me of the shaft in Tokyo where I had left my sailing boots—was a child's stuffed animal.

That doubly confirmed it; there was no way I would have found that so quickly unless *They* put it there, for me. I was 100 percent positively definitely on air again. I got back in the truck, threw the stuffed animal at Amanda, and called her a spy and a traitor.

That'll ratchet up the stakes for the scene a notch. That was right, wasn't it? What? We need higher stakes? Got it. How's this?

I ceremoniously aimed the truck at the freezing water of Boston Harbor, glanced at Amanda as I revved the engine three times, and then floored it. We accelerated through third gear.

If they've set up this scene, they're ready for this. There are divers in the harbor. They are ready for us to hit the water. They'll save us.

Luckily, there was a huge drop off the loading height before the final run to the edge of the wharves. We launched off it and crashed down. The impact startled me enough that one of my selves decided I wasn't supposed to drive into the harbor after all.

I was supposed to drive to Logan Airport.

That's right, the flight leaves in an hour. I'm sure the truck will drive fine, because they reinforced it last night while they were setting up this scene.

It drove fine. We parked the truck in short term parking and headed inside the terminal to the United counter.

"Two tickets for the flight to Bermuda. First Class," I said.

"Which flight, sir?" said the end-of-shift-weary woman behind the counter.

"The one which leaves in an hour," I said with confidence.

"Oh no, not in an hour sir. The next flight to Bermuda leaves in the morning. I think about eight o'clock. Let me see…"

"No. It definitely leaves in an hour. Check again," I said.

"She has the flights right there on her computer. We can

come back first thing and get a ticket on the morning flight," Amanda said. "Why don't we go get a nice hotel room nearby and see if we aren't happier in bed than we are standing here?"

"OK. Yeah. Let's do that."

We checked in like newlyweds. I might even have carried her over the threshold. I'm sure the wedding jeans were off in no time.

We're supposed to smoke a cigarette now. They want us to smoke a cigarette, but they didn't leave any here. Weird.

I snuggled into Amanda's shoulder and pretended to go to sleep. Ten minutes later I was standing in the doorway, telling her she better please hurry up, we were going to miss the flight. She hurried.

I didn't bother with traditional parking. In fact, I pulled up onto the sidewalk in front of the revolving doors, got out of the truck, and headed inside the airport toward the check-in desk. Amanda did not. She headed the other way, and recruited the policemen she had seen on the way to Terminal B.

After a little tour of the Emergency Room at one of the Boston hospitals, I was off to world-famous, Harvard-affiliated McLean Hospital. They told me James Taylor had stayed there, thinking that might make me feel better about it. I have since learned that David Foster Wallace did too. He was at McLean roughly a week before I landed across town for my first psychiatric hospitalization back in 1989. Granted, at that point he was very *down*, and I was very *up*.

The choices I made that night, and in the days leading up to it, were made in that strangest of mental states which is both me and also not me. It was my body. No question. And I, Kevin Allen Hall DOB 9/11/69, am responsible for all that happened. No question. At the same time, there was little continuity between the behavior and the human who had lived 99 percent of the time in my body for the twenty-three years before that night.

There was, however, perfect continuity between the delusions in Boston 1989, Tokyo 1991, Long Beach 1992, and now Boston 1993.

What a lovely quartet.

CHAPTER 34

_ℒ_

AMANDA HAD TO PUT THE trauma of a car crash, of sexual favors to try to soothe me, and of calling in the police to come take me away all behind her and try to get on with her junior spring semester. My friends had to hope this was the last time. I can't imagine the various mixed emotions in my family, but I presume they ranged from glad I was alive to disappointment that I had again "chosen" to renounce my future for the sake of indulging in a manic high.

That simple, unilateral perspective—primarily held by Dad but existing to some degree for everyone who knew me—was the elephant in the room for years to come. Maybe still is. It sounds pretty straightforward, if not just a little old school: Bad Choice (to stop meds), Bad Consequence.

Maybe it's a little *too* simple. Maybe it's not reasonable for a young man to ask every single thought to line up like a battalion of air-tight rationality soldiers so they can fight the good fight for that gold watch. Because those troops still have to keep barracks in a head that happens to sit on the shoulders and share a body with a heart full of passion and poetry. My head and my heart were clearly both answering to a soul in tremendous pain.

Somehow, when things aren't going well, my soul seems to stand between head and heart like a resolute mom on Saturday morning, arms outstretched to meet the necks of two noisy nine-year-olds fighting over one iPad.

As I started over with a pattern I was becoming too familiar with, of waking up disoriented, drooling on myself from the strong sedatives and anti-psychotics, and the crushing despair as reality set in, I had to hope this was the last time. The problem was, I had no evidence that it would be.

Au contraire.

CHAPTER 35

⤳

THE WEEK BEFORE I THOUGHT the Show was sending me and Amanda to Bermuda for a sort of a retreat and practice honeymoon, I had taken a job as the coach of the University of Rhode Island Sailing team. They didn't have a big budget. In fact, my salary would be the University matching whatever the team could raise with car washes and bake sales.

I took my first week off work while I tried to get my head back on straight. There can still be ice in the boats mid-March, and it was a cold winter. Surely I was doing everyone a favor keeping us warm and dry a little longer?

I didn't do as great a job coaching spring semester as I might have done before losing my second nut and my mind for the fourth time. My heart was in it, but I'm not sure I was as competitively oriented as I should have been. I was mostly all about focusing on the process, and living in the moment, and noticing the way the light reflected off the ripples at sunset. Or, sometimes, just taking in the sea air with our deepest selves. All that stuff has its place in life, but it might not be on the start line of the qualifiers for the Nationals. We didn't qualify.

I don't know how much people did or didn't know about my little reality wrinkles. I've never asked. I wish I had done a better job at my first grownup role, but oh well.

CHAPTER **36**

꩜

I FREAKED OUT ON AMANDA ABOUT our relationship after my
Mom's wedding the summer of 1993. My feelings were so
jumbled it wasn't funny. Part of me was like "I'm not ready
to be married! We need to end this! There's a whole world out
there, what are we doing? We're so young...." Stuff like that.
Meanwhile, the other part of me was all "I'm such a loser and
you deserve better so I will save you the trouble of ending it, and
I'll just be a dick so you can always know you always stood by
me." Amanda took it, whatever "it" was, really well.

Conveniently for both of us, I had made a good friend on the
URI team. Tara and I ended up doing a lot of racing together that
summer around New England in a new little two-person design
called a Vanguard 15. Amanda lived on Long Island with her
family and hung out a lot with an older man who treated her the
way she deserved to be treated. I was jealous as fuck of Joe, but
the dispassionate me knew it was best for everyone. Tara could
not have been any more kind and compassionate than she was.

I tried really hard to stay on my MEDS. I tried really hard to
find reasons to live. I tried really hard to buy into the idea that
because I had been successful, I could be successful again if I
just did what I was supposed to do and was patient. I tried really
hard to believe and to feel that made sense, and was exactly what

I wanted. Was all I had ever wanted.

I took little orange pills which were downers to keep me from going up too far. I took little purple pills which were uppers to keep the downers from pushing down too far. My spirit was trapped between collapsing walls like the ones trapping Han Solo and Chewbacca, Luke and Leia in the garbage masher on the Detention Level. Nowhere to move. Slimy monsters coiled around my legs. C3PO not on the other end of the coms to tell R2 to make it all stop.

Drinking enough rum & Coke turned my brain back on and the pain back off enough that I could pretend I had something to live for. For short spurts of time. Alcohol is a depressant. Coke is a stimulant. Sound familiar?

Not enough stimulation.

Maybe the bright lights and havoc in New York City will do something positive. Something life-affirming. Something worth it. Something Real.

I pulled into the middle of an intersection on the Lower West Side and stopped the truck. Got out. Pissed for a good long time on the left front tire. Cars honked. I gave them the finger and kept pissing. Got back in. Drove to Grand Central Station. Pulled up on the curb right in front of the doors. Left the engine running. Walked in my Birkenstocks down to a pay phone and dropped a quarter in. Dialed the number by heart.

"Birkenstock head office, may I help you?" said the perky woman who picked up.

"Mr. Mann please. The one in marketing. I have an appointment," I said.

"Yes, yes of course. You must be Mr. Hall calling? From New York?"

"That's me. Kindly put me through."

"Thank you Mr. Hall. Ringing you through now," said Perky Pat.

"Mann speaking," came the strong voice.

"George, Kevin here. How are things?" I said.

"Not too bad, other than the worry that you haven't seen your way clear yet. But you've called, which means you've come around. Right?" Mann said.

"I have. I thought about it a lot, and I checked with legal. You can launch the campaign. I got them to set it up so that we start now. With this phone call. I have a little surprise for you guys too. I think you'll like it," I said.

"Wonderful. Great news. You won't regret it," Mann said.

"I bet your sales pick up by close of business today. Watch this," I said.

I let the receiver dangle. Took off my right Air Jesus, placed it next to the phone. Took off my left Birkenstock, placed it toe to toe with the right one. Picked up the dangling receiver, placed it on top of the leather sandals. Nodded respect at my newest living-sculpture-live-advertisement. Turned and bowed to Grand Central Station. Walked back to my truck. Got in. Closed the door, engine still running. I was just about to back into the street when a man burst out the door and ran toward me. He held my Birkenstocks, waved them at me frantically, with a proud look. He tapped the window with one of them.

"I—" catching his breath, "I thought you might want these back. You really should keep them, in case you want to walk around the city later," the man said. He is caught up in being Good Samaritan. He doesn't register the frustration and disappointment in my eyes.

"They're not mine anymore. They're supposed to stay right there, where they were. Forever. They're for everyone now. Everyone needs shoes. Thank you, I know I can count on you to put them back where they belong. Good day," I said.

I shift into reverse and give him a look which says, *Please don't make me run over your toes backing out of here.*

∞

I drove my pickup onto a college campus in session for summer school. I threw all my worldly possessions onto the campus green and walked into a calculus class with my wicker picnic basket, saying I was "waiting for Amanda." Only problem was we weren't going steady.

Cops to ER. ER to inpatient. Inpatient to drool. Drool to be patient. Be patient to Start Over.

Amanda and Tara overlapped a couple times during visiting hours at the mental hospital in Amityville on Long Island. I remember the red Mickey Mouse shirt I wore. Thinking it was perfect. Sitting on the shower floor, letting the water soak Mickey right through. Letting the water run down my face, down the back of my neck. Wishing it would rinse away the shame and despair. The embarrassment and disgust. The pain and uncertainty. The questions. All the questions. Please, just wash them all down the drain.

CHAPTER 37

⤳

THE WORD THE DOCTORS WANTED to make sure I understood during this fourth stint in the loony bin was *kindling*. With each successive manic episode, the chances of another one go up dramatically. The content of the delusion gets embedded, making it harder and harder to avoid identical psychotic, delusional thought patterns. Essentially, the grooves of neural pathways get wider and deeper with use. The slippery sides and deeper bottoms to the bobsled runs of our delusional thoughts begin to conflagulate each time the brain clicks out of consensus reality and into its own version. Smaller and smaller "signs" become "proof" until just a glance, or a bird chirping, an ad for toothpaste, or a Dolly Parton song on the radio all mean the same thing: the whole world is in on it.

Less scientific but more real to me was the fact that with each successive manic episode, my friends found it harder to stand by me, my family found it harder to know what to do, and my model of life got more rigid. Unreliable Mind means wreaking havoc and consequence. (Reliable mind) means an android that looks just like me lives out the days remaining in my body. Perfect consumer. Solid citizen. Nobody home.

My new shrink and I agreed that the path I was on had poor odds of me celebrating a twenty-fifth birthday. Well, he thought so and I didn't have the energy to disagree. In fact, I didn't really care. Checking out, all the way out, sounded like a good solution. Albeit a permanent one.

Depakote is a front-line treatment for epilepsy. Dr. Lipshutz fished around for ideas, for hooks he might be able to use to connect with me. To his credit, he eventually sold me on taking pride in sharing with Dostoevsky an alleged disposition for brain waves akin to those of frontal lobe epilepsy. Manic-depression and epilepsy might not be the same thing, but they must have something in common if the same medicine works for both. At least, according to the biochemical model they must....

Dr. L. sold me on the compassionate use of humane medication to help handle the stress and challenges of our day and age. He encouraged me to forgive myself. He said it was very hard for even his wellest patients to stick with the medications all the time, meanwhile staying completely away from all drugs and alcohol.

He said I really had been through quite a lot in a very short time.

CHAPTER **38**

‿ᴥ

I GOT A JOB AT COFFEE BEAN to supplement my coaching income
during the fall semester. I had the payments on the truck, I
had medical bills that my father had decided I needed to handle
myself if I were ever going to learn, and I had an expensive habit
of buying classical CDs. My parents had given me the entire
Mozart Collection for my twenty-first birthday, which I loved
very much. The only problem was it didn't match my moods
very well those days. I found myself gravitating more toward
the enormity and pathos of the Russian composers, primarily
Rachmaninoff and Tchaikovsky. There was always Beethoven,
and sometimes a good middle ground was later Brahms.

The barista job was a solid plan. I felt more like a wooden
penny than a million bucks, but I had to show up. I got there
at 5:00 a.m. and turned on the lights and put the baked goods
in the ovens. I started brewing the coffee and checking the sugar
and napkins. I tried to come up with the greatest tip jar sign of
all time. I didn't come up with "Just the tip, please," but I sure
wish I had. (Kevin) didn't feel like smiling inside, but (he) very
quickly figured out that there was a remarkably strong positive
correlation between the cheer (he) served with the coffee and
bagels and the tips that landed in the jar. This was by far the best
experience I ever had with "fake it 'til you make it." There was

money on the line, and I needed it.

I was able to sustain a mask of joviality and humor until about ninety seconds after counting out the tips with the other morning barista, clocking out, and grabbing my keys to head out the back door. By the time I was buckling my belt in the Toyota 4x4, I was one step this side of suicidal. The next day was the same. And the next.

A few days before driving into New York City to "accept my Birkenstock contract," the radio had been getting really oppressive and bossy. The DJs kept talking straight to me, even when I changed the station. I suspected that was probably *wrong*, so I stopped using the radio and played my cassettes. The problem was, all my mixed tapes had been tampered with. For example, *they* put Beethoven's 9th "behind" an R.E.M. album. Yikes.

Now the only way to stop the escalating paranoia coming out of the tape player was to plug it up. Sometime during the summer, Amanda or Tara had left some tampons in the glove box. Perfect.

In retrospect, it's a great little personal case study:

The devious, psychotic-me was desperate for some fun. (I) had a tape with a recording of the 9th over which I! recorded R.E.M.. I! discarded the memory of having taped over anything, and then I! destroyed other evidence, like tape cases. Finally, psychotic-me went to the trouble, to the level of detail, of removing the previous label which said "Roger Norrington conducting...."

Once all the "evidence" is completely erased from history, the new "reality" is air-tight. I, and (I), find the tape and wonder when *they* stole it to re-record R.E.M. with Beethoven's ghost for the backing track.

Just to fuck with us, or is there a message we are supposed to find? Play it over and over. Parse the passages and the pauses. Finally, decide the transmission is only meant to confirm megalomaniacal status. There will be scene instructions soon.

Copy. Roger. Wilco.

I usually had a couple hours between Coffee Bean duties and sailing team practice. Every once in a while, I would find Amanda sitting on the doorstep of my little bungalow. Sometimes she brought me a flower and a hug and turned around and left. One time she stayed, and we cried together, and the feeling passed into me, from the place where we first met, that everything might just be OK. It was a lot of responsibility for a young woman, and as much as I hated to say it on account of either of us, it sure seemed like she had my life in her hands.

After about a month of lots of coffee and not much Amanda, I was so worried that I decided I should probably admit myself. I saw a doctor in Providence who was really hard but also fair. Didn't tiptoe around my fragile ego. Said I could certainly check in to inpatient, but he didn't think I needed to. He thought I had proven I knew how to be tough before, and it was time. Fucking fight a little harder, kid. If you're up for it. Or, I'll just call right now to keep the last bed here open.

It was gutsy, his play. I can only imagine the lawsuits if I had transcribed it all just before hanging myself. But, he was right.

If I ingested a ridiculous amount of caffeine, for a short time my synapses could jump over the tar pit of my MEDS and feed stale breadcrumbs to my hobbled imagination. For an hour or two, I could elicit tiny little mind games, happy little connections here and there. A very subtle letting go. A trust in some flow. Implausible things from different spheres would come together at the intersection that was (me). Catch them quick because caffeine is not a slow-release, long-lasting, patented cocktail. It comes on, it works, and it goes.

Anyway, those things made me feel "right place, right time." Even when, or especially when most of the evidence suggested I was a walking, talking embodiment of wrong place, wrong time. An accident waiting to happen. (In fact, that's exactly what I was for Halloween that year. Banana peel on my shoe, pot with the handle pointed outward strapped to my chest, electrical cord dangling in the water of the pot, and broken condom hanging from my beer cup. Invisible third cancer hiding, probably in my pineal gland or my spleen. Inevitable fifth breakdown tucked right there, behind my ear like one of James Dean's Chesterfields.)

Look. Synchronicities made me feel safe. Connected to something bigger than my pathetic little problems and my cosmology of preordained, targeted doom. I had come to need those moments of conjured wonder. I had come to really rely on them for Meaning. The medication shut them all down. It sure seemed like the taking of all the MEDS was just trading the risk of burning up for the quiet, devious danger of slowly but surely freezing to death.

CHAPTER 39

⤴

I DECIDED THAT I NEEDED TO learn to live without the crutch of my sailing successes. I decided that if there was a real me hiding behind the frosted windows of psych meds, he/it was also hiding behind the idea that as long as I achieved results, I was OK. The contrapositive being if I didn't achieve results, I was not okay. My status and self-worth were so intertwined with racing sailboats that it was impossible to tease out what was really "me", from ME, and (me).

My Aunt Martha had always been supportive. I felt the least judged with her of anyone I knew. I had done well being in the mountains a few years previously at Dad's. And Martha thought she might be able to get me an interview about a job teaching skiing. I was a decent skier, but I had always been an inspired, natural teacher and coach. (At least when I was sane).

I was even a good teacher the spring at the University of Rhode Island. The only problem then was I think I was trying to teach embracing of the moment, or catching butterflies of the divine. It didn't translate directly to winning of the race.

When the fall season concluded in late 1993, I left my entire safety net in Rhode Island—lover, best friend, mistress, buddies, and boats—and headed for the hills. They all needed a break from me. I had been chafing every loop in that net.

My year in the mountains, teaching skiing, working at a bookstore, and writing when I wasn't sitting by the river, was perhaps the most important thing I have ever done to survive. I occupied the bottom rung of the totem pole in the ski school. Nobody knew or cared that I had ever seen a sailboat, much less won a world championship in one. I found, eventually, that I could talk to people, that I made them laugh, that sometimes the things I said made people think and even consider their own lives in a new way, so much so that they thanked me later, or even wrote to me about it.

Once the ski season ended, on the way to work at the bookstore, I would sit quietly on the same rock for an hour. Every day. Rain or shine. Exuberant or depressed. Alive, or just pretending.

My commute was downhill all the way into town, and there was a little branch of the river that passed under the road just before town started. I'd lace up my rollerblades and do turns across both lanes, listening for cars and pushing pretty hard. I never had even a near-miss of an accident. If you go fast enough, and the pavement under your wheels is hard enough, the mind has to stop thinking about this and that. Then the air glimmers a little and tastes better, and the self just is.

Reflecting on that time now, I believe that skating fast downhill, and then sitting quietly, made for a divinely balanced pair of ways to be centered in two different states of being. I think if I didn't spend six months doing that, I probably would have gotten cancer again before long. I still may, but it has got to be good for the body and soul to live so purely from center.

CHAPTER **40**

⁓

I HAD FOUND A DECENT RHYTHM with the MEDS toward the end of my time in Aspen. I personally tweaked the plan a little. Instead of taking one upper and one downer in the morning, and doing the same at night, I popped the uppers at breakfast and pushed the downers when I brushed my teeth after reading Rilke in the twilight. It made more intuitive sense to me, and my body/mind/soul knew that for certain it was not any worse to do it that way.

Probably the most glaring thing about my entire past, given my diagnosis, is how little I interacted with psychiatrists as an outpatient. I was able to get prescriptions for the medications from anyone in my family except my sister. Right or wrong, it remained unsaid that getting my candy from family was better than me not going to shrinks and not having medication either. I just couldn't face the psychiatrists' offices. The scheduling and breaking and rescheduling appointments. The approved art and magazines in the waiting room, the little white silent doorbell button. The glances at the clock when it was about time to go even though I had finally started to talk and was about to make progress. Avoiding all that was a big part of pretending nothing was wrong. Pretending as much, and for as long at a time, as humanly possible.

∞

When I applied to Brown, it was infamous for being a place where one could literally "major in comic books," design one's own Independent Concentration. Amanda didn't major in comic books. She earned an honors degree in the philosophy of modern physics. She was all about the questions themselves. The big ones.

After she graduated in the spring, she headed north to Vermont, where she led youth bike tours. She came out to Aspen once that summer. We hiked through the wildflowers and talked and held hands, but it was strained and I wasn't super bubbly. I didn't get very many letters from her, and it was hard to reach her on the phone. Part of me knew exactly why, but I had gotten damn good at denial.

So at the end of the summer, I hedged my bets and headed home to California. Dad was going to take over the truck payments. He could use it and I couldn't afford it (maybe now I realize he said that he could use it, to try to take the sting of another failure off my shoulders). So, if nothing else, I needed to drive west for that.

Amanda flew out to visit. She had cut her hair very short, which for some reason was disorienting and alarming to me. I was very fragile, remember, and that was a big change to the look and feel, if you will, of one of the few constants in my life. Maybe the only constant.

It seems preposterous to me now, but that is with the mind and heart I have now. Then it seemed like she had done it on purpose to upset me, to push me and knock me over a little. I didn't understand why or how she could do such a thing.

We went sailing out to Santa Cruz Island for a few days and had a nice time under the stars at night, hiking on the island during the days. Our moments together were tender but not passionate. We talked about me moving back east. I could do lots of writing, pay a little rent, and she could finish her thesis. I could have a regular schedule. We could cook healthy food together. Sip wine quietly, occasionally. Get really into loose-leaf tea and maybe cut back a little on the coffee. We could see how it went.

The day before we were going to get on the plane together to execute the plan, Amanda maneuvered me into a sitting position on the couch.

"There's probably one more thing we should talk through before you come east," she said. Honestly. I was in such denial I had convinced myself that I didn't know what was coming. That it couldn't be *that*. Maybe she wanted to have the laundry and cooking rotations organized and written down. Maybe she wanted to make sure I understood that it was absolutely not going to work for me to try to sleep with her sister, who would also be living with us. Maybe she wanted to know if I had strong feelings about VHS or Betamax. I hoped it was the last one, because I did.

"Sure, OK. What's that?" I said.

"I spent the summer with a guy. He worked in the bike tours too. We shared a cabin, we—"

My head exploded as my world caved in. It was overwhelming because it wasn't limited to what we were talking about, or to potential implications of the simple news that she was a young woman with certain needs, wants, and desires and a self of her own, who had been far away from a young man she cared about, but who also came with desperate needs and astronomical wants and confused desires and very little sense of his own self.

The news triggered my entire backlog of failure, of inevitability, of the repeated pattern of defeat. Just, exactly at the moment that I had finally gotten all the way upright on my own two goddamn feet.

I had been so optimistic, really about everything, when I left Aspen with an incredibly sturdy body, strong heartbeat, and quiet soul.

Not fair. Not fair not fair not fair that my shitbird fuckbox of an excuse for a brain wouldn't let me get on with life. Wasn't two cancers and three Bedlams enough? It was that last one, that really cost us. Took her away from me. Because that's what happened. I needed so much, she needed something else. I will always need so much, that she will eventually need someone else. Not fair.

I was too panicked to move. To say anything. To be mad at her, or to wonder what I could have done differently. Or to even wonder what the news she was telling me meant about my future. I stared blankly, as far away as open, unblinking eyes can.

"I still want you to come live with me. I still love you. This was just something I had to do. I hope it will make more sense to both of us, one day," she said. I felt like I was ten feet underwater with concrete boots.

And yet we got on the plane together. I moved in. There was a lot of passion for a while. We were together, we were broken up. She was off to visit summer-guy Stu, I had found a hot squeeze on campus. Amanda said I could bring her over if I wanted but didn't mean it. I almost did but changed my mind at the last second.

We bumped along, deafening silences and loud banging alternating just like the tender moments and harsh words. It wasn't pretty, but it wasn't boring either. I thought the fight-and-fuck sex was good up until then. The last week we were together, both got ten times better.

Amanda drove me to the airport and stood next to me while I got my seat assignment and checked my duffel bag through to Paris Charles de Gaulle Airport. We stood and embraced, maybe for the last time in our lives.

She said, "I love you."

"I know," I said, and I turned to go away. This time for real.

CHAPTER 41

⤙

I TOOK THE TRAIN SOUTH FROM Paris to the Mediterranean and set up camp in Antibes. The provisional plan was to look for work on a large sailing yacht. I hoped to sand or varnish wood, or polish stainless steel, or lift heavy things. Anything to work with my hands, think as little as possible, and simply not fail.

I spent a lot of time at the Picasso museum, I wrote page after page, and I wrote love letters to a woman I was supposed to be figuring out how to let go. I struggled to be angry at Amanda.

I saved my anger for the world when not one but two final interviews with captains had them decide I was "overqualified". Something about how they had seen my type before and they knew me better than I knew myself and I would quickly get bored and jump ship in the next port and it just wouldn't work out. They didn't even seem sorry, just a bit annoyed that I had taken their time. I remember thinking something along the lines of *Are you FUCKING KIDDING ME?* As if I needed any more evidence that the world has it in for me. I can't get a job, because I'm *overqualified?* Thanks a whole lot, Asshole (looks at sky).

CHAPTER 42

⤚∽

I HOPPED ON A TRAIN TO the north end of the spectacularly
beautiful and quaint Cinque Terre region of Italy. Cinque
Terre, on the rugged portion of the cost of the Italian Riviera,
means "five lands". There are tiny ancient fishing villages nestled
in coves at the bottom of steep, rocky cliffs. Where the cliffs
aren't too steep, the land is terraced, mostly for olives. When I
visited, there was a path along the coast from one region to the
next, although in places it was poorly marked and marginally
passable. I walked and walked and walked and thought too
much and thought too much and sometimes thought just a little
less. A film of the inside of my head while I walked would show
a square wheel spinning and spinning in diarrhea.

Eventually I got to a thought that started coming every
hundredth rotation. Then every tenth. Then fifth.

My feet hurt. My legs hurt. I can't believe I'll never see
Amanda again. The stars are out.

I should just jump.

My boots are too loose. I should stop this time to switch
shoulders with the duffel bag. Amanda did the right thing. I
can't even give her kids.

I should just jump.

It's just going to keep happening. It doesn't matter what I do. Life on meds sucks. Life off meds will surely lead to death.

I should just jump.

What about my family?

I should just jump.
I should just jump.
I'm going to jump.
I should jump.
Going to jump.

About to jump.

I think now that this is what happened: my rational mind played a very clever trick on (me). It had calculated that I was unlikely to actually die in the full-moon night if I fell from where I was. As the conversation got more and more ugly in my head, my subconscious dredged up from its still-functioning depths a feeling of potential excitement and thrill and newness. Subconscious was fully onboard with the plan for something exciting and new.

My mind knew I had to sell it pretty well. I couldn't fake it so badly that it was clearly an inauthentic suicide attempt, so it had to seem plausible *in the instant* that "I" or (I) or ("I") or i had in fact decided to jump, and chosen to jump, and jumped. Plus, as the stress mounted in my head approaching the acting out of my final scene, I remembered it had to be good for the Director, too.

Mind was pretty sure I wouldn't die, but Self was definitely sure that pretending to try was worth the risk of being wrong. Besides, how would I know and remember I had been wrong? I'd be dead, so I wouldn't know. Error problem solved.

But I have chosen. Whatever happens, I chose it. Me. I am doing it. Not God, not Illness, not Ambition or Failure or Fate. Just Me.

It wasn't a layup jump. It was a nonchalant *here goes nothing.* Then the flash as the situation passed a one-way cusp.

I more or less hope you've calculated gravity and friction and bouncing bones right, but I'm not even sure that I hope that. I think I do. Do I?

Then the thoughts stopped, as it became clear to all parties that there was nothing under my feet. Adrenaline, attempts to orient and reconcile sensations, sights, sounds, acceleration felt in my gut. The sound of my silent scream changed to snapping branches and sliding scree.

I got so beaten and sliced up tumbling through the brambles which finally broke my fall that I felt something I hadn't felt for a long time. An immediacy, an energy and urgency. As I tumbled, I had time to think, *No! Dammit! Actually, I do want to live. Well, I'll be—* Granted, it was born of pain, but it was something new, something that I had ultimately caused (as opposed to having it done to me), and something that intensified when I finally dragged myself through the sand and into the sea.

I remember the full moon, I remember the sting of the salt in my many wide open wounds, and I remember thinking that this must be better than nothing. I didn't know how, and it wasn't the kind of feeling that lends itself to words very well, but there was a truth to the moment my forearm-length, calf-length, and quad-width gashes, along with cougar-scratch gouges across my torso and down my back, hit the salt water. The truth was that I was sure of exactly where I stopped and the rest of the world started. The edge of that boundary, where my pain met the Mediterranean Sea, was part of ME. Nobody else. Nothing else in the universe. My pain. Me.

The adrenaline of the fall, the burning inside and out, had

broken all the way through my MEDS. Every last layer of them. Reptile Kevin wanted to live. Left-brain (me) was more for it than (he) had been in a very long time. All because I thought, as I tumbled down the side of the cliff, that I had in fact calculated badly, and I was really, finally, going to die.

I suppose I was lucky not to get infections. I got in the salty Med twice a day and spent the rest of the time writing. Before too long, the writing was about forgiving myself if I couldn't do it, couldn't manage to stay alone in Europe. I had gone into Genoa, Italy to try to find the Ministry of Agriculture and hook up with the apple harvest. Too late. I asked if I could help fishermen repair their nets in exchange for something to eat. They were worried I couldn't tie good knots. Finally, I called my mom in tears and said I had better come home, that I was afraid of what I might do if I remained alone. I didn't tell her about my trial run.

Calling Mom was brave. Because it was—in my eyes at the time—admitting defeat. Piling failure on top of self-inflicted wounds into which I was choosing to rub hot, jagged salt. I might have been walking barefoot uphill both ways on broken glass too. You know, the kind that gives you tetanus.

⤙

CHAPTER 43

ONE OF THE THINGS THAT I had to show for my time in Europe was a lot of writing. Personal writing, letter writing, poems, plus all the stuff, gone forever, that didn't make it after getting written and then torn up in disgust. A few things keep trying to shine through. One is that deep deep down, double-agent undercover, a small ember of hope was still there. Between the lines, it was there. Two was that part of my intense pain about Amanda is that I had wanted to, and truly, deeply believed that I would one day, raise a family with her. The third thing was that I very much loved the ocean and sailing on it, in a pure way. Above and beyond the competition and my vexed relationship with it, I loved to muck about in boats.

I haven't spoken to them about it, but I imagine everyone in the family breathed a large sigh of relief when I announced my plan to move back to Ventura and sail my Laser every day with an eye toward the 1996 Olympics. I would be in one place, with family, training physically, sleeping regularly, and I would be much less likely to brood unbecomingly.

Mom could check up on my meds ninja-like in the night. Sis could call without it being crazy-long distance. Dad could help shop for good deals on car insurance and power tools.

I got a real job. Arguably my first and last real job, but there it is. The application didn't have a part about history of mental illness. I was able to tick the "no felonies" box.

A company called Behavioral Science Technologies was expanding into French Quebec, and I helped a little with translations and early client contact. The job was in Ojai, about thirty miles into the hills behind Ventura. It's a very special, arty little community with a lot of history that includes people like Aldous Huxley and Krishnamurti. I got up at 4:30 a.m. and rode my bike to work, where I stayed until noon. Rode my bike to the gym back in town where I lifted weights and then swam a few thousand yards. Then I went sailing until dark. Then I ate. Then I slept.

Was I healthy? Yes and no. From a systems analysis standpoint, I took my medication at the same time, twice a day, every day. I took my biweekly testosterone injections without ceremony. My body fat was well down into the single digits, my resting heart rate was somewhere between the high thirties and about forty-three depending on the week's training. I was logging lots of hours on the water, getting sailing fit again, and finding a little bit of rhythm.

A few months into this regime, I got a personal trainer. I don't remember our first date. I asked Annthea to marry me by the end of our first month together. She was a little older; she was very fit and very kind. We had fun. Doing things. Bikes, beaches, movies, training, more training, more movies. We married in December 1995 at the San Buenaventura Mission. I don't think I told her I was a nutcase. I honestly can't remember doing so, if indeed I did. She didn't tell me she could act like one sometimes either.

We moved from a tiny apartment to a slightly bigger one. Then, my grandad died. Grandad Harley was a self-made restauranteur in Rockford, Illinois. He had an honest laugh and a real twinkle in his eye. He had a habit of telling fun little one-liners. They were funny without fail, at least the first time he told them. "I teach karate," he would tell me out of the blue, "…and five other Japanese words."

Annthea and I moved into his old house. Dad and Uncle Allen helped with a clear financial arrangement with no down payment. It would have been a lot harder for us to play house so soon without Grandad passing away. I'd rather have lived in a cardboard box for a year and had another few days with him. Not a mean bone in his body.

Annthea and I got a golden lab puppy. I rented thrillers and sci-fi and mowed the lawn and we made love twice a week. Not quite hole-in-the-bedsheet style, but much closer to that than what I was used to. It made me sad even as I needed it more than not.

I call them my Android Years. There were no electric sheep in my dreams, no burning need to light candles, or sing, or stand naked in the rain, arms outstretched and smile to the sky.

But. I was "healthy". And. I was on the rails of a train that had a nonzero chance of arriving one day at the opening ceremonies of the 1996 Olympics in Atlanta. Which means I was OK. Right?

I put "Chase a Dream" on my fundraising letterhead.

CHAPTER 44

~~⌐~~

M Y FIRST REGATTA BACK I finished fourth in a strong field that
included all the sailors I would have to beat at the US
Olympic Trials. Later that summer, I convincingly won the North
American Championships. Just one little problem. Testosterone
is a banned substance. It is the testicles that manufacture testosterone
in a human male. I had none.

The endocrine system—as in testes and ovaries, thyroid and
adrenal gland—also helps regulate moods. Even in dudes.

You might be most familiar with the female hormonal system
and occasional, subtle hints of mood variance. In any case,
biweekly testosterone cycling was not on the list of the top-five
ways to help stabilize moods for men with bipolar disorder.

I wish I could tell a quick story about the support I got from
the muckety-mucks for their twice-disabled Olympic hopeful.
Or about the five-inch thick medical file and six months' lead
time culminating in a medical dispensation to compete despite
my slightly modified physique. I really do.

Dad was an especially big help during this time. I learned
who I was supposed to contact at the United States Olympic
Committee and asked them what they required. They said
everything except the empty champagne bottle from the night
I was conceived. I sent them everything (including the bottle,

which I finally found wedged in an alley between a drain pipe and a beer tent in Germany). Then we waited.

We waited a month, and then another month, and then we asked if maybe they had received our petition and information. We waited another month and finally got a response. The response was that it was the "consensus of the medical committee that a waiver could not be granted." This later turned out to be false. The doctor who wrote that letter acted unilaterally, but anyway.

We tried more letters, some phone calls, and eventually got something very helpful. The United States Olympic Committee told us it would ultimately be the International Olympic Committee's decision. So we started over with the IOC in Lausanne, Switzerland. We heard nothing. Two more months of nothing.

This all struck my father as terribly unjust. He gets shit done when there is an apparent absence of justice. Although things like bureaucracy, benefit of the doubt, patience, unique challenging case, etc., etc. had sounded appropriate for a while, Dad put the effort on a far more proactive stance and enlisted the help of the American Civil Liberties Union. There were a few meetings so they could wrap their heads around the situation. They sent a few letters to the USOC and the IOC. We heard nothing.

Time to try something new. My friends would tell me after the Trials that they thought I should have waited until I had won to worry about the eligibility issue. In hindsight, that is probably true. At the time, the logic was that the Trials were in April and the Olympics were in July—August. There simply wouldn't be time to sort it all out in that short period, so it had to be done beforehand. Of course, if I had known that it would take a front page article in the *New York Times*, right at the top, the entire top half of section A1 (Clinton got the other half for I-don't-remember-exactly-what), plus an appearance on *Good Morning America*, to get the USOC/IOC to call back, I would probably have known to wait until after the Trials to start the whole thing.

The IOC called the very next day and said they had been *working very hard* on the case, Mr. Hall.

I did get to meet John Updike in the makeup room at Good Morning America. I doubt he remembers me, but I don't blame him.

CHAPTER 45

⟜ら

THE SAILING EVENTS OF THE 1996 Atlanta Olympics were held in Savannah. By the time I was made to spend two weeks giving blood in Los Angeles, while my competitors kept their schedules and training at the venue the month before the Trials, competing in the Trials was only ever going to end in tears. I wish it had just been tears. Instead, on a downwind leg in moderate breeze and big waves, when it became clear there that there was no way I was going to win, I nearly drowned.

There's Nick rounding the bottom mark in second. Andy right behind him. I'm here in what, eleventh? Nine more points this race and—

First abnormally large inhalation. First abnormally big hull oscillation.

Six races to go. Twenty-three points down on Nick and nineteen down on Andy. Plus Mark—

Second and third inhalations, increasingly large and closer together. Second and third rocks of the boat, increasingly large and out of control.

Even if I gain all those points on Nick, an average of what? Five points a race roughly? Every race? That leaves Andy at 4.5 and Mark at 3.8 and—

Fourth, fifth, sixth, seventh breaths each bigger and closer together than the last. Shoulders starting to heave with them. Mast swinging back and forth in the sky like a metronome for Rimsky-Korsakov's "Flight of the Bumblebee."

Oh. Oh no. Oh fuck. I can't win. Impossible kind of can't. I've lost. I am lost. I am—

SPLASH.

I capsized and fell in the water and continued hyperventilating but now some of the oxygen I needed to breathe had hydrogen attached to it.

I had to be rescued. Annthea jumped in and held onto me. Used her strong legs to egg-beat the choppy water and keep both our heads up. She was a bona fide trained lifeguard. She was probably actually saving my life. This was for sure a very different kind of urgency to the stinging salt in the Mediterranean. This was the out-of-control-my-universe-has-exploded-like-Alderaan kind.

On the way back to the dock with wife and coach (how did we all get back with a coach boat and a sailboat and a broken sailor?) I had only one thought. Failure. Failure to get waiver to compete with no balls, failure to win and make the waiver relevant, and now failure to even be able to finish a race. Plus failure not to crack in the face of all that.

We got to shore, people expressed care and concern, and I couldn't shrink small enough as we left the venue and got me home to hide under the covers that night and not eat or talk or even cry. Just hide.

Surprisingly, I woke up the next morning with the weight of the world lifted from my shoulders. Now that it was impossible to win, there wasn't much point in worrying about the results. I went out on the water and won the first race of the day and placed third in the next race. The remaining races I sailed with some dignity and decent results. There must be a fantastic sports-psychology lesson in there somewhere....

This was my Trials self-debrief: more experience, more

character building, more proof that I am a total loser and God's little seagull friend is never, ever going to stop shitting on my head just for fun.

I don't think it was discussed, the idea to add some anxiety medication to the mix. If I had been offered a pill that they told me would help at this point in my life, I probably would have taken it. If I had been offered cyanide and an apple, I definitely would have.

‒⁖‒

CHAPTER 46

I HAD KNOWN MORGAN LARSON SINCE early youth sailing. He was NorCal, I was SoCal. He sailed doubles and had lots of friends; I was a dorky loner. After the 1996 Olympic Trials, he was looking for a couple good men for a month of racing in a cutting-edge boat called an Australian 18-foot skiff. The tour was in the south of England, and it started in a few weeks, and would I like to go? The third on our team would be a younger, very talented sailor (Mark) who had finished third, two places ahead of me in the Laser Olympic Trials.

It was a fantastic opportunity on a number of fronts, and off we went. There were some great times on and off the water, and I realized that although I had achieved success in singles sailing, I really liked small teams, and I was good at it. The responsibility to teammates was probably good for me.

I might have been the only one who brought his wife on the tour. It seemed like we all had fun together, but I'm afraid now to ask. Racing hard, or fixing broken masts with Morgan's dad late into the night, or complaining about how the helicopter camera's downwash had capsized us else we might have won that race, was our UK pro tour.

One night, a few weeks into the four-event circuit, one of the Australians had two young English lasses on the hook.

He convinced them that he was chief "shooer" at Sydney International Airport. As in his job was to shoo the kangaroos off the runway. After I finished half of my second beer, my wife of six months Annthea steered me out of the pub and home.

I wanted to see Charlie D. close the deal. Instead, I got angry at the world that I couldn't party with my friends. However, avoiding an episode while on tour was more important, and Annthea helped me remember that.

(I can't help but imagine that the stories got even better after we left.)

I did some other racing with Morgan on the professional circuit in bigger boats in the format known as match racing, which at the time was like the minors for the America's Cup. We did well for such a young team and had more good times on and off the water.

I continued my status as a twenty six-year-old person with a mental illness and no testicles who had never faced either of those things. I continued to pretend they were nonissues. And I continued to get away with it, for a little while longer.

CHAPTER 47

_____&_____

THE NEW OLYMPIC CLASS FOR the Sydney 2000 Olympics was called a 49er. It was basically a scaled-down, two person version of the Australian 18-foot skiff Morgan and I had already started to master. We launched our campaign for a gold medal in Sydney by tying for the silver at the first-ever 49er World Championships (the boat didn't exist the year before). We lost the tie breaker at the 1997 Worlds to the other American team, the McKee brothers from Seattle. They were both already Olympic medalists, but with different partners.

The 1998 49er World Champs were in Bandol, France. One of the races was so windy and rough that we capsized five times, and then broke our mast on the last turn into the finish. If we had pulled off the gybe, we would have won the race. Instead we crashed and the mast broke, but we were so close to the finish that we drifted across the line, still in second. The rest of the fleet was decimated; centerboards straight in the air above upside-down 49ers strewn across the Mediterranean like a disorganized graveyard.

The broken mast was a setback. Directly related or not, I went out all night before the final day's racing. I drank lots of red wine, cavorted and courted in French, and spun my brain up enough to override the MEDS. Then, we went out and sailed a second, a first, and a third in the final three races, backing up our first Worlds bronze medal with another one. Part of me has always wondered whether it was a fluke, or instead if maybe (I) knew exactly what "I" was doing. Did I bring Me back on the field for the big game by flying us over the MEDS? Do not try this at home, but as I become more experienced with it all, I tend to favor explanation number two. I knew what to do to achieve my best possible performance.

Besides the big night and the incredible last day's results, and besides the amazing crème brulées I devoured all week, my other big memory from that event is driving around and around a roundabout one afternoon, saying "I'm being spontaneous!"

Morgan and I traveled and trained some more and then earned our third bronze in a row at the next Worlds, Melbourne '99. I'll come back to the story where I grabbed the mic again at the awards a few chapters from now.

CHAPTER **48**

⟍⟋

THE MUSIC WAS LOUD WHEN MOM ARRIVED. I didn't hear the first round of knocks.

There were eighteen CD cases spread neatly on the floor. I heard Mom's knock when I took the R.E.M. *Green* disk out after listening to "World Leader Pretend" for the third time in a row.

"Hi, Kevin. What song was that one? I liked it," Mom said.

Sure you did. What else would they have you say?

"It was the wrong one. Hang on," I said, leaving the door open and running back to grab the disk in column two, row two. "I think it's supposed to be this one."

Mom closed the front door behind her. Sat down on the couch. Waited. Tried to get a bead on the laser level in my eyes. Counted the changes in direction, the double backs and splitting trains of thought as I picked the next compact disc and nudged in the tray.

"What's this one called?" said Mom.

"I think you'll like it. Female vocalist. Natalie Merchant. It's called 'Wonder.' "

The strong, bouncy, C# major guitar intro, the mellifluous voice, the hope. Mom smiled.

This should be fucking vinyl. How do you cut out in the middle

131

of a song with a record-scratch with a fucking disk player. Fuck.
I fucked this up.

"Reach into my head to / steal the glory / of my story—"
Now!

I cut the power on the amp and the CD player both, just to make sure.

"Sorry Mom, wrong song."

"That's OK. She has a pretty voice," Mom said.

"Yeah. Yeah, she does. Here. This one is actually the right one."

I played "7" from Prince's *Love Symbol Album*. Full volume. I still love the opening voicing.

Next was Jethro Tull's "Skating Away." Then Pink Floyd's "Wish You Were Here." Then Nirvana's "Lithium." Then "Lithium." Then "Lithium" again.

(The only reason it wasn't Alanis Morissette's "Front Row" is that I was six months early with this performance. *Supposed Former Infatuation Junkie* wasn't released yet.)

It's not Mom's favorite, the Nirvana one. She did sense that I was trying to stay home. That I could be halfway to Tijuana by now, if one more butterfly had farted in Bangladesh.

Mom sensed I was trying to communicate.

Trying. I'm trying. I think she can tell I'm trying.

She tricked me into showing her what I was working on in the office on the computer. She knew the stimulation of the music was not attenuating the accelerating release of dopamine.

She said the ambulance would be here soon, did I think I'd like to go with them? She begged me with her eyes, with the eyes of a mother, not to run. I stayed.

In the ambulance with the big dudes in white wearing too much aftershave, I started flipping back through the past couple weeks. Did I stop MEDS? I don't think so but I'm not sure. I mean, I don't think I stopped the MEDS. But I didn't definitely not. I didn't mean to, if I did. Honest.

Did I drink a lot? No, not really. Didn't write much. Didn't sail much. Didn't fuck. Didn't surf. Didn't hike or bike or run or read. What the fuck have I been doing? Where did this storm come from?

Fuck. If I haven't done anything wrong and it still happens, I'm really fucking fucked.

One infuriatingly frustrating thing about psychiatric medication and acute psychosis and their interplay, is what happens to memories and to one's memory in general. I don't remember Annthea visiting me at the hospital, though I'm sure she probably did. I don't remember us talking about what happened afterward, though I'm sure we probably did. She was consummately there for me.

I often hear stories about things that sound like they were amazing, or moving, or crazy good fun, and I sometimes say, "Wow. I wish I had been there!" only to learn that I was there. Look, I know everybody has certain things they don't remember, and some nights are just blurs. I know that people who have diabetes have to take insulin, and bipolar is kind of like a pretty similar chemical imbalance in many ways...

Neither of those things helps me. Because I also know what it's like to remember, at least in useful large chunks. I'm talking about years missing. And I can remember what it's like to trust my mind, and to trust the world. I know I used to. It was a long time ago now, but I remember.

⤶

CHAPTER 49

I HAD FIGURED OUT SOMETIME DURING the honeymoon two and a half years before that I was married to the wrong girl. After a couple years as a husbandry droid, I couldn't take it anymore. I suppose the eighteen-card CD shuffle was one of the final transmissions:

Ground control to Real Kev. Ground control to Real Kev. You're not living. Pretensions on.

Hey, so man I gotta be straight with you: You're going through the motions. Society's motions. Your parents' motions. TV and magazine motions. Promises of perfect potions. Can't be your game. Sure ain't your race. No name. No face.

Get out of there quick, out of wedlock. Out of spiritual gridlock. Out of drydock. Get out, you soft-cock!

You're getting sick. The deep kind. The kind you can't ever fix. The kind that involves time. The kind where you look up thirty years later and say, woopsie daisy. Thank you for playing. Maybe your next life, kiddo.

I landed in a locked ward not too far from my house. I started over with the drool and the slow climb back out of the gutter that I was by now all too familiar with. The best part about that joint was the way smoke break was announced. The fantastically warm and friendly orderly who announced my daily tobacco bliss had lungs big enough to address half the county from the mountaintop. He did a lot of different things during the day, but he seemed to really live for two words. They burst out. With pride. With joy. With hope and understanding, with humility and compassion. With a tiny and not-at-all overwrought touch of levity: *Sssmmmmoke break!*

Yes.

I expedited my timeout by starting to pick up butts at the end of smoke break. By clearing everybody's tray at dinner. By doing my emotional evaluation with honesty double-time, triple-honest. I smiled. I beamed. That's what they wanted. That's the biggest box that needs the X.

Smiling hurt like having my eyes splayed open with rusty coat hangers and being made to watch violent TV for twenty-four hours might hurt. I did it anyway.

I was out of there in no time.

Just to punctuate the point that I was living someone else's life, I made the mistake of seeing Amanda for a beer on my way through New York a few months later. We sat quietly across from each other in the LaGuardia bar, clutching our Heinekens for dear life until they were warm. We talked about her med school challenges, about the sailing, and finally she asked about my wife Annthea.

"She's not you," I said. Amanda's eyes lit up with something like the light of ten thousand stars, and she looked to me to see if there was any more where that came from.

"She never was. She never will be. I'm still in love with you. It's not actually that great for my marriage, to be honest," I said.

Fortunately it was soon time to board my flight home. Unfortunately we kissed first and my knees dropped out from under me and time stopped and I wanted nothing more than to stay the night. If not forever. Fortunately we managed to talk ourselves out of it, but not without another kiss, and then a colossal conflict of will. We walked in silence to security.

We exchanged letters. Mine was long and measured and tender and honest. It ended with "Please forgive yourself for the way things ended a couple years ago. Because I don't know if I can forgive you for reopening my heart to our love for each other—What am I supposed to do now?"

Amanda's letter was similar to mine. But, it included this: "I would not be true to myself if I did not say that a piece of my calmness has come from knowing somehow that we will be together again. It may be next month, it may be three years, but it is a knowledge that springs from deep, where laughter is born…So, no, I am not finding peace very easily these days. For all the resolution and the closure our meeting brought, it has also opened a door that I'm not sure I know how to close, or want to. Our tears that day and the warmth of your sigh in my ear are the realest things I've ever known."

We talked once more on the phone, and then I broke off all communication. She sent a few letters, Mom told me she called. I couldn't handle it. Plus, I was training for the Olympics. Having an emotional affair with the woman I loved wasn't the regimen proscribed by my personal trainer (wife).

CHAPTER **50**

～⌒～

A MANDA TOOK A CLASS IN medical school called Healing and
Madness. One of the assignments was to write two poems.
(I know, right? Doctors writing poetry? Shutthefrontdoor!)
This is what she wrote a year after we saw each other at
LaGuardia. She sent it to my friend Zack, in case he ever got a
chance to show it to me.

Amanda Rosenberg
Reaction Paper - Healing and Madness
May 5, 1998

~~HEALING~~ MOURNING

He used to write poetry.
And when mania seeped in through his pores,
out flowed the sweet liquid of hope.
In the hours when all Others relinquish
imagination to reverie,
his percolated
boiling in pockets
rising to the surface
escaping

unopposed
by the ~~atmospheric~~ pressure keeping ~~Others~~ us meek.
And it is painful,
the poetry
stuffed with doubt, fear, childish frolic,
pinpricks of poignancy.
Poignant for ~~the audience that is~~ us, ~~pure~~ agony for him.
His breath, his touch, the way he tied his shoes
was passion.
It preceded him into the room and lingered
in the air after he'd gone
belted down with leather and brass
on black rubber sheets,
lying in a pool of urine.
Genius

He doesn't write poetry anymore.
But he is HEALTHY
He dreams, with caution
He feels
very little
The ceiling is too low to stand up straight,
the floor rises to meet his feet
too soon.
And he is preceded by a vacuum
left by a passion teased from its roots by a sexy little pill
that promised a future
but went down with the past.
It weighs on him, just like us,
the atmosphere.
And he, too, is meek.
Imagination, once again
the realm of reverie.
Madness

it is a gift

it is a plight
    this kind of sight
this kind of mis-dys-piss-function
    fine filaments running across space
cobwebs harboring the eggs
    threading eyes of time, expanding and
of deviation.
    collapsing with the rise and recoil
and it is by will and righteousness
    of breath.
that honor be reserved
    and it is only by chance that
for the tides of custom and
    the space fills with air and

not poison.

CHAPTER 51

I STILL NEEDED SOMETHING CONCRETE TO allow myself to break my promises to Annthea. You know, go ahead and fail at marriage and throw another casualty on the growing mass-grave of my past.

As Annthea and I raised our golden lab, Jessy, together, it became clear to me that we wouldn't make a good parenting team. Let's just say our styles were too different. Maybe my wedding vow wasn't ironclad in light of that new information. Maybe there was an out clause around parenting incompatibility. No? OK, what about how she accidentally misrepresented her age? This came to light when when we filled out the paperwork for the US Sailing Team health insurance plan sometime in 1997. At that point, the biological clock of my wife seemed like an important thing to know within, say, five years.

Anyway, Morgan and I were in Sydney training. Just the boys. Two years in a row, we flew from Los Angeles on the 10th of September and arrived on the 12th after crossing the International Date Line during the fifteen-hour flight. It's unclear whether my birthday, being the 11th, happened those years. It was definitely possible to feel younger in Sydney.

Morgan was working the accent and the small-town surfer charm and coming home every other morning having been someplace new, each smile bigger than the last. I was insanely jealous. What the fuck was I doing married to one girl, in love with another, when I could be out in Sydney as a wingman with a legend? Oh well. I had gotten a lot better at knowing all of my various limits in all of the various directions, and running a wingman program has a certain risky sound, looking at it now. I'm sure it was for the best. Still....

There was a massive party for Black Flys sunglasses. A few bands, piercing and tattoos available on the spot by top artists, drinks that glowed, girls in leather dancing in cages, boys doing flips off the walls and climbing along the ceiling hanging upside down. And that was just the stuff I noticed.

There was nowhere I would rather have been that night. My wife of three years was landing in the morning to be with us for the rest of the tour.

I decided on a whim to get my head shaved to a cue ball shine. While I didn't consciously predict the fallout, who knows what my subconscious would say if we could ask it? When Annthea arrived at the boat park as we were just about to launch and head out for the day's racing and saw my hair, she *completely* wigged out: "What have you *done*? How could you *do* this to me? Why didn't you *ask* what I thought first?" and on for about a minute of rave that only certain women carry the capacity for. I knew I had what I needed. A sort of peace washed over me. It was not caused by an entirely rational sequence of events. It was maybe a little contrived, but now it *felt* right to end it.

Maybe Amanda cut her hair after Aspen so I knew to do this...
Seriously?
Why not?
I told Annthea calmly that we would be heading out to race now. When we got off the beach I said to Morgan, "Shit. If she doesn't like me now, when I can still *grow* hair, how's it going to be when I'm old, fat, and bald?"

Morgan conveyed—in the most subtle and gentle and

diplomatic yet still somehow clear way that he is world famous for—that I had a good point, and it didn't seem like I had been that happy with Annthea lately, and that yes, in fact he had kind of always thought that she had an exceptional streak of unpredictability.

"Why the hell didn't anybody tell me before I married her?"

Cricket. Cricket. Cricket...

What was anybody going to say? *I know you're basically suicidal, and need this marriage on the rebound from Amanda, and it seems like a great idea to you now but think about the future. Does it really make sense?* No F'ing way anybody was going to say that.

I had to figure it out myself. Thank god we had gotten a dog.

After Crowded House's amazing farewell concert at the Sydney Opera House and then the spectacular New Year's Eve fireworks over Sydney Harbor, Annthea headed back to her personal training clients in California. Morgan and I hitched up the trailer and headed down the West Coast and around the corner to Melbourne for the 49er Worlds.

What? It was actually the East Coast? I knew that. Sometimes I think I can move mountains.

CHAPTER **52**

⤚

A T THE AWARDS FOR THE 1999 49er Worlds in Melbourne,
when Morgan and I were on the stage to accept our bronze
medals, I grabbed the mic. I thanked Julian Bethwaite and his
dad Frank, for designing and building the 49ers. I continued,
"Grandad used to say a couple things to me. One was, 'If this isn't
nice, what is?' The other was 'Thanks for bringing me along.'"

I'm not sure why Grandad said I was the one bringing him
along, but it makes me feel good to think about and write about
now. I turned to Morgan and said, "So, buddy. Thanks for
bringing me along." There was applause.

I'm doing it right.

We all had a pretty big night. In order to keep me from
heading into town by myself, which a small conference must have
determined was Not Good, my teammates and friends ended up
choosing to bar the door to my room with the biggest sailor
they could recruit. Just when that started to fail because I had
a lot more adrenaline than he did and maybe more endurance,
the backup plan to enlist the help of a friend of a friend to try
to keep me distracted and in the house was actioned. She might
have had more endurance than I did.

I remember walking around in circles in the morning
trying to apologize to absolutely everyone about absolutely

everything, and one of the guys saying, "It's OK. You're among friends." Those words, at that moment, could not have landed better or helped more.

However it came to pass, I came back down, the cameras were turned back off, and Morgan and I got on the plane to head east from Melbourne to New Zealand.

Morgan and I started our new jobs in Auckland with an America's Cup team called AmericaOne. I rode in on his coattails as his partner in the 49er. After a couple weeks of work, there was a big team party. During last call, I wandered alone into town. Somehow, I got to the top of the Oracle building. Pin-balling off the crazy angles of the inside of my mind was the idea that I was supposed to jump just like Michael Douglas did in the 1997 movie *The Game*. The Director was testing my faith, and it would make a really great scene when I jumped and they caught me in the huge airbag with the target on it. *Look how much he trusts the Universe!* the audience would say, applauding.

The reason I didn't jump was not because I talked myself out of it, or came to my senses. Rather, I didn't jump because I got distracted, so I forgot to. Just as I was about to lose my footing once and for all, a huge seagull flew nearby in front of me, and then landed near the center of the rooftop. I turned around and stepped down off the ledge to try to look it in the eyes. I've called plenty of things angels in my life, but that there bird was the real deal and still is, as far as I am concerned sitting here today.

CHAPTER 53

⤚⟞

THE NEXT AFTERNOON I HITCHED a ride south out of town to the Sweetwaters music and art festival. Sculpture and dance, pagans and trance.

What a beautiful twilight.

Listen. Music.

Elvis Costello! I ran there, nudged my way forward, and lost myself.

Thank you, Director.

Elvis played an encore and the show was over and the crowd dispersed and I stood in the open field. Under the stars. Alone.

I got the late-model Nokia cellphone out of my pocket. I had seen it in a window in town that morning, and I had to have it. The Veruca Salt way. "I want it, and I want it *now!*" But, I didn't stay long enough to open an account and get a SIM card. Just wanted the snazzy hardware.

I tried to make a call. Nothing. I pushed codes for secrets for God into the number pad. Nothing. A big guy came up, offered me a smoke, asked if he could borrow the phone to make a quick call to his mum.

"Sure," I said.

"Thanks, bro," he said. He slid the sexy silver cover closed, open, closed, open with his thumb. He tried to dial. Nothing happened.

"I think something's wrong with it. Maybe you have a friend who can fix it?" I said.

"Uh, OK. Yeah, sure, OK. I'll see if I can get it fixed for us," he said, slipping it in his pocket before I changed my mind.

I can still picture him telling the story to his mates at the bar: *I thought I was trading a smoke for a call. Turns out, this tweaker was so gone he traded my cigarette for a mobile phone. Far out! Right?*

The scene fades before I learn whether one of his friends tries to make him feel bad for taking advantage of me. Little do they know it wasn't my money in the first place; I was just sharing the Love. The Director was paying.

Teepees and witches' cauldrons, bio fuels and geodesic domes. One of the best trance DJs in the Southern Hemisphere. I wandered around the huge tent looking for the best sound.

Around 4:00 a.m., three women wearing Kabuki masks and long flowing grass skirts and nothing else moved imperceptibly slowly across the stage below the rave screen. Even sober I could appreciate the artistry in that.

Some percentage of the dance crowd was on Ecstasy. I was on water. Nothing else. Not drugs, and not my MEDS.

You're supposed to crawl across the stage like an alligator when the women are done. Get around backstage and get ready.

The six foot, four inch transvestite who greeted me just inside the entrance to the backstage area didn't recognize me.

"Honey, you can't be back here! Let me just walk you back out," she said, taking my arm. Rather firmly. They had seen lost souls before, and he had probably had them ruin an *I Will Survive* routine. Not this time.

Hmmm. I was pretty sure I was supposed to go backstage. Guess not. Which means I'm...

This thought coincided with bumping into one of the huge cables which held our end of the tent tower up.

And so, I decided I needed to see the sunrise first, which

meant getting as high as possible above the earth, which meant climbing hand over hand up the long diagonal three-inch diameter cable. Halfway up, I swung my feet up and crossed them, hanging below the cable and shuffling the rest of the way. This wasn't a camping pop-up tent, it was a full-size Barnum and Bailey's big top.

Unfortunately, backstage was at the west end. Fortunately, there was a way to hold on and traverse the peak of the tent between poles. Unfortunately, it was a long way down.

Fortunately, I was fearless and my balance and poise were jacked. I got past the east peak and found a little spot where I could sit down. I sat. Right on cue, the sun peaked above the horizon as I drank in the first deep breath of morning. It couldn't have been timed more perfectly.

OK, um, wow. Wow. Wow! How did They do THAT? How did they know I would take exactly that long to climb and cross the tent? How do they know what I'll do?

The sun cleared the horizon and the rays fanned out into the new morning. I breathed.

The camera shot from behind me boasts a perfect silhouette of a modern monk in synch with the sunrise, floating on a cloud of tent top. Nice work, Kev. (You're welcome, Director.)

The halo of God's long streaks of hair reached over my head and across the sky.

Breathe. In. Out. In. Out. My heartbeat slowed way down. The bright sun got brighter. The colors around me sharpened, met each other with more finesse along their boundaries. Blended where they were meant to blend. Contrasted where they weren't. The birds stopped chirping willy nilly, and sang a purposeful chorus. I was Home.

My attention smash-cut to the escalating noise of the crowd below me. The megaphoned uniform requested that I please descend. Now. Out of peace, into handcuffs.

Oh boy, is this going to be fun. They always use their best improvs for the cop parts. Geronimo!

I climbed down to applause. Loud, ringing applause. I am 100 percent certain I did not make that up just now for effect. I remember the visuals of a sea of hands clapping. Too elaborate to hallucinate.

Fantastic Abbot and Costello conversation with first the medics and then the police, as I desperately tried to convince anyone who would listen that the situation was that I *hadn't* taken any drugs. We finally got to the point where one of the policemen went for humor and said as he guided my head into the squad car, "Tell it to the judge."

Jail. A few people looked scary, but in the huge public holding cell, all that really happened is we swapped stories. I have no idea what I said when it was my turn, but I do remember thinking *Damn, some of these guys can spin a bloody good yarn!*

Really Big Guy finished his story with this one, to wide grins all around:

"It wasn't a static environment…"

I wonder how they'll choose to translate that one into Spanish?

The psychiatric hospital wasn't too far away from where the team was staying. One of my most resolute friends visited me as often as she could get away from work. I learned later that Sarah also lobbied extensively and tirelessly on my behalf during the two weeks I was absent. She somehow convinced the brass that I would get myself and my shit together and prove to be a valuable asset in the near future.

I arguably owe my entire career to Sarah.

CHAPTER 54

᷈

I T WAS CLEAR FROM MY hospitalization in Auckland and the
discussions while I spoke freely and was still lucid that the
stressor that precipitated the triggering of my coping mechanism
of mania was my failing marriage. In other words, I went crazy
because I needed a divorce.

Annthea wanted to come to New Zealand to rescue me. It
would surely have been very hard for her to hear from my family
that doing that might not be the best use of her time. I had
already thrown my wedding ring in the fountain at the Aotea
Center for the Arts downtown. The only thing left to do now
was get home and hand her some papers and hope she didn't
know any spells to turn me into a newt.

I got home from New Zealand and put my bags down. I
didn't really hug her back. She asked what was wrong, so I told
her we were, and that it had to end. She was surprised, then
angry, then terribly distraught. She started tearing the art off the
walls of our home, which caused some glass to shatter. I tried to
hold her and get her to stop before she hurt herself.

It was a very intense afternoon. There was no time for any
emotional baggage, or second-guessing, or pity. I had to restrain
her so she didn't cut herself up. She's very strong. It was such a
confusing feeling, holding her so tight to protect her from the

reaction to the news that I was pushing her away forever.

I found solace in imagining a certain beauty in the symmetry. A year before, she held me the same way as I reacted to the news that my Olympic dreams seemed to have pushed me away forever too.

Annthea and I hammered through the incredibly painful and humbling process of sorting ownership of stuff. I gave Annthea the car and all the furniture, wedding gifts, and tchotchkes we had collected. I committed to helping pay for her to finish her masters degree in kinesiology. It was an odd commitment to make since my income was so tenuous (travel and equipment tend to eat up the Olympic Committee grants about as fast as they come in), but it felt right.

I was glad when my mom told me that Annthea is healthy and happily remarried in Ventura.

CHAPTER 55

T HE SOUTHERN HEMISPHERE SUMMER CORRESPONDS with the Northern Hemisphere winter, and vice versa. In fact, my Kiwi boss at the ski school in Aspen spent her summers in the Southern Alps, skiing in New Zealand. We were coming into summer in California. We trained in Los Angeles Harbor until October, then shipped all the equipment and personnel across the Pacific.

I eventually got promoted on the America's Cup team from just spy to also head coach (head of a coaching staff of one). Spy duties were about reverse-engineering the opponents' designs from pictures and data. Spies were allowed to be two hundred meters from an opponent's boat, but no closer. While their sails were down, I'd have a chase boat driver with a range finder circle the enemy while I took hundreds of photos with the power-winder cranking on the camera. With those photos, we could figure out exactly how big their sails were, which allowed us to also figure out how deep their keels were. I was made to believe it was a matter of international security.

Once the boats started sailing, I'd take notes on the conditions, on their sail codes and techniques, on new design features, and we'd shadow them to record their performance. All of this info would go into a huge game theory matrix to try to help us optimize our design parameters relative to the fleet.

Of course, they were all doing the same thing, which made the whole exercise of dubious value. It was still a lot of fun.

After being on the water all day spying, I'd stay late into the night culling and distilling all the information on the opposition that was available from all of the previous races, plus the day's TV footage, plus my own footage. I transferred it onto about five minutes of video, and I came up with one or two points to consider regarding the strategic strengths and weaknesses of tomorrow's opponent.

I'd do the same careful distillation and editing of the footage of our own maneuvers and show it to the crew too. It was best to let them work out what to do with it. My biggest value to the team was probably the "dead horse" call I made every once in a while when the conversation started going around in circles, and the next stop was deciding whether it was about blaming someone in particular, or not blaming them but instead deciding it was all their fault. Most of the time, the call to stop beating the dead horse helped things remain constructive.

Occasionally there would be helicopter footage of the decks of the superyachts out watching the races, and the camera would zoom in on some spectacular bikinis and whatnot. I'd always make sure to lead the debriefing with those clips. Sailors are sailors, after all.

For the coaching, I would do detailed analyses of start strategies of the other teams. With computer tracks of each team, I could get right in there and pick each decision apart. I'd present my theories to the afterguard, the brain trust. You know—the guys in the back of the boat. The ones who didn't touch any ropes.

None of this work required physical balance and coordination, creative leaps, epiphanies, or God. The MEDS didn't bother me too much given how recently I had seen the risk of tampering, given how close I had come to ending my career just after it started. Also, I had started to figure out how to "drink responsibly".

CHAPTER 56

I HAD LEARNED MY LESSON WITH the previous Olympic Trials and the IOC. This time, I stayed on top of their required regular testosterone-level tests and focused on my training. Things were going well. Morgan and I were on track to prevail at the two-man 49er Olympic Trials in six months, if we used all our skill.

At a low-pressure race following a training camp in Long Beach, California, in April 1999 I came off the rails again. It really upset me to face my failed marriage, even though I "understood". I believed in promises, and I had made one.

I didn't stop my medication. However, I started drinking pretty heavily. Lots of the water of life (the Gaelic early-days name for whiskey), lots of vodka too, in a short time. Nights out. Up early to train. Extra coffee from being out late.

It was pretty clear that I was in trouble when Morgan and I were racing and I started to believe that *they* had rigged the entire Los Angeles and Long Beach Harbors with whirlpool-making devices so they could keep pushing us back in the fleet every time we got into the lead. I didn't express this in so many words to Morgan at the time, but it would have been obvious to him that I was a few sandwiches short of a picnic.

I was agitated, he didn't know quite what to do, and while I didn't jump off the boat before getting back to shore, I was

Kevin A. Hall

pretty confused and not much help getting the boat onto the beach and the sails down. 49ers are very light and powerful; they don't sit docile by themselves just off the beach. They want to go like a horse in the gates. I basically kept opening the gate and kicking the horse, while Morgan tried to wrestle the boat out of the water and handle his fear that his Olympic dreams were bolting out of the pen along with my sanity.

I just walked away that day and got into my grandad's big beige '76 Cadillac Coupe, the one you could fit a king mattress on the front hood. The one with the shocks like butter and the fingertip power steering. Whitewall tires. Vinyl top. The one I floored toward a T intersection along the beach, hit the breaks at the last second, and somehow—I really don't know how—ended up on the center-divider grass island, perfectly parallel to the shoreline, perfectly perpendicular to the road I had been on, perfectly perched with about a foot in between the wheels and the curbs on both sides.

Even in my condition, I was stunned and knew I was lucky to be alive. I remember getting out of the car, still trembling, and walking away from the open door toward the beach. I left the radio blaring.

I remember being incredibly relieved as I walked that I didn't hit anyone with the car. I remember my face in the pavement and my arm behind my back before I even noticed the shadows or sounds of the policemen who came to get me off the street.

CHAPTER 57

⟋⟍

D ROOL, silenceanguishguiltsadnessGroup. (Welcome back,
Mr. Hall!) There was a grand piano at Las Encinas Hospital
in the main meeting area. I shared some smokes with a musician
who tried pretty hard to stay on the DL, but after hammering out
a version of "Somewhere Over the Rainbow" that brought tears
to my eyes, one of the other patients leaned over and whispered
that he was the bass player for Nine Inch Nails, or maybe it was
drums for The Smashing Pumpkins, or rhythm for Rage Against
the Machine. Everything was mixed up in my head, but I am
sure he was an otherworldly musician in a band I had more than
one album from.

Annthea agreed to our separation. California has a cooling
off/reconsider period of one year after the application for divorce
is filed. It would be another half a year before it was finalized.

So Annthea was out of the picture, but now I was worried
that Morgan would be the one asking for a divorce. It was
devastating to think about, on so many levels. It was all I could
think about.

I was probably going to be in for another week, but I was
allowed on hour-long leaves with family. My sister brought by
a portable CD player and some American Spirit smokes to look
forward to, and which I could use to pay people back. I never

really understood why the cigarettes felt so natural in there, when I didn't smoke. It's just what was done, I guess, and anything that gave the illusion of connection was a good thing. Plus, sharing smokes isn't an illusion, it is a connection.

Dad took me to a used CD shop nearby, where I got Hole's *Celebrity Skin*, K's Choice self-titled album with the very haunting song "I'm Not an Addict (that's a lie)," and, well, Cher's new album *Believe*. There, I said it.

I met some amazing people during this time in, and we shared our fears and our grief openly, in a way that is very rare and incredibly powerful. I still carry the understanding of the depth of the bonds I felt while inside during those ten days.

CHAPTER **58**

THIS TIME WHEN I WAS released, I went for a very different exit
strategy. I called Amanda the day I got out. She got on an
airplane from New York the next day. I have never been so
nervous in my life. I imagined we might both just *know* the
second we saw each other when she got off the plane. But what
if we didn't? What if the carpet at Gate 26 (this was pre-9/11,
when you could meet someone at the gate), or the feng shui of
the plastic plants, or the announcements about the white zone
came between us that first moment?

She set down her bag and we looked at each other. Into each
other. It was reverent, even a little somber. There weren't huge
smiles. But as the space between us reduced to nothing, the
feeling was still there. The rightness, and the calmness, and the
thrill and the hope.

The desire wasn't far behind, but we had a bit of a drive
in Dad's Ford Taurus before that would be anything to worry
about. We didn't really talk much the whole hour in the car. We
were just pleased, if not relieved, to be together again. We didn't
really talk much for the first couple hours we were in the house
either. It was all brand-new and spine-tinglingly exciting. It also
felt like we had never been apart.

157

WHILE I WAS HANGING WITH Dorothy but we couldn't find my red shoes to click together, Morgan had set about canceling our plans to train in Germany and Finland with some top teams. He probably went surfing, made some fish tacos with fresh cilantro and lime somewhere warm and had a few beers, and looked out at the sunset and wondered how he ended up with me and not somebody else, somebody who actually turned up for the hard work and steady day-to-day moments it would take in the homestretch to the Trials.

We eventually went to Europe and did a few minor events. We were out of synch. I was hungover from the extra MEDS and the disappointment. Morgan had to pretend it was no big deal that I had let us down.

In the fall, we moved to Saint Petersburg, Florida. Zack came to coach us and support me metaphysically. Amanda and I exchanged letters and mixed tapes, cookie care packages and encouragement. Hers for my sailing, mine for her medical school.

Showtime. The US Olympic Trials were in November, and the lead went back and forth a few times in the twenty-one races. We put together an excellent event. The McKees, with the experience and confidence of a gold and a bronze medal between them already, sailed even better. They had never beaten us in international competition, the entire three years, other than winning the tie breaker at the first Worlds. Not once.

The US Trials were different. It was a much smaller, much weaker fleet than the international fleet the US would face at the Olympics. International fleets were more like American football or ice hockey, tight, fast, rough. The smaller domestic fleets were more like European football. Open, long, patience and finesse. Only one team in each division goes to the Olympics in sailing. We had nothing to be ashamed of, even if we weren't going to Sydney. Jonathan and Charlie, who remain good friends if not also mentors to us both, went on to win the bronze at the 2000 Olympics and then to win the next World Championships in convincing style.

I described the feeling of losing the Trials as tantamount to staring at the ceiling in the next room, with paper-thin walls, while your best friend fucks the brains out of the girl you've been in love with since you were seventeen.

As soon as the 49er was packed up and put up for sale, Morgan and I headed back to work in New Zealand together. The guys on the team didn't seem to think any less of us because we weren't going to the Olympics. Chin up, they said. No big deal. It rang a little hollow coming from our teammates who had already won their medal. What everyone stressed was that the beer would taste just fine again tomorrow....

Probably the closest I ever got to an Olympic medal came a few months after the Trials when one of the Spanish sailors, the reigning world champ, told me at a party in New Zealand that he was "very sorry for me and Morgan, but also very relieved for himself" (that they would be facing the other US team at the Games and not us). I know, it's a little oblique. The Olympics are about the striving and the participation. By extension so are the Trials, according to the Olympic creed. But at that point, it was best for me to take what I could get in terms of validation.

Santiago's words gave me a sense of accomplishment and pride, although I couldn't really show it to my dad, or put it in the bank.

Our America's Cup team lost in the last race of the Louis Vuitton Cup (the challenger selection finals) to the Italian team Luna Rossa. At that point I didn't have a very high profile in the sailing or handbag cup communities, so I'm pretty sure my two breakdowns during my first America's Cup job were kept within a relatively small group. I came out of the 2000 America's Cup cycle with a reputation for hard work, and for a clever but still practical approach to the game.

I remain grateful to Sarah and to the management of AmericaOne for giving me a second chance.

CHAPTER **60**

⁓

AMANDA AND I WENT CAMPING in Vermont after I got back from New Zealand in late March of 2000. It rained for two days straight, so we hid out in a Motel 6 just off the highway. The first night we watched some reruns and she caught me up on medical school gossip, and her thoughts for a specialty. The second night we got seriously drunk. She gave me a really funny look and then said, not quite slurring, "Will you marry me?"

I was thunderstruck. I didn't say anything. Fortunately I didn't have to as she passed out not long after proposing. It gave me time to realize, after looking around the hotel room, including behind the curtain in the shower, that her "you" could only mean *me*. I was the one she was asking. There was nobody else there.

I gave her a very meek yes when she came to, but it took me a long time to actually get her a ring. As she tells it, we bought the first one with her mom's credit card, and she bought herself the second one with my credit card. She might be right. The point is that it was hard to imagine she hadn't thought long and hard about it. I could rest assured she knew exactly what she was getting into. My profile was glowing, if I may say so myself: Fertile? Nope. Sane? Sometimes. Job? Sort of.

Oh, but I did know how to ask her, in French, whether or not she cared for Roland Barthes. (In fact, she did. Modern Culture and Media was one of her favorite classes at Brown.)

We got married about a year later, in April 2001, at the Brooklyn Botanic Gardens. The cherry blossoms were in full bloom. The air shimmered to match my heart. Only one of my good friends could make it; the rest were away training or competing, and I didn't have any friends who didn't sail, which sounds sad to me now.

The only weekend my mother-in-law, Babs, could secure at the Brooklyn Botanic Gardens for "her daughter's wedding" fell during the biggest sailing race within a month either side of the day we got married. My sister, Kristina, was my best man.

It was a beautiful setting and a beautiful wedding. However, Amanda had asked the musicians to play Tchikovsky's Seranade for Strings in E Major when she walked down the aisle. They assured her that they knew it, and again assured her when she double-checked a week later. While the enormous videographer stood in front of me so I couldn't see a thing, Amanda had to decide whether to begin walking when the band started ripping through Vivaldi's Four Seasons. Wrong song, played waaaaaayyyy too fast. She let the rest of the party get nearly to my end of the aisle. I tapped the videographer on the shoulder and asked if he might perhaps take up another position. Any position, so that I might see the bride walk down the aisle? He acted like I was out of line, harrumphed and trundled over to a new vantage point, where he would shoot Amanda grabbing her father's arm and basically running down the aisle to match the music.

It was the right way to do it. Anything else would have looked ridiculous and awkward in its attempted defiance of the situation. True to form, and just another reason I will always admire her, Amanda grabbed the situation by the…horns, shall we say, and carried herself with dignity. Plus, she only had to keep it up for about six seconds because that's how long it took her to walk from the back to the front.

Our lady rabbi looked down at my red shoes and smiled. It was my one, my only conceit that day. She thought they were great. In a Jewish wedding, bride and groom each hold their index fingers up while they say their vows. We wrote our own, and we alternated through a range of seriousness. My favorite promise was that I would continue to leave the toaster to pop itself up after removing my toast, which drives Amanda crazy to this day. My favorite promise of Amanda's was that she would learn to sail if it's the last thing that she does.

The finger up is to show everyone there, and to remind yourself, that basically you know what you're doing. You're involved, you're aware, it's definitely what you want. When I fart, and Amanda can't believe it can possibly be so loud, I say, "You had your finger up." When she buys shoes, and I say I can't believe they can possibly cost so much, she does the same.

And after all, it's better than putting a different finger up at each other.

CHAPTER 61

⤴

WE HAD JUST REACHED CRUISING altitude when the man in the seat next to me finally pushed the call button. He wouldn't play chess with me. He wouldn't talk about Nietzsche or Y2K. He didn't even care that Brad was about to marry Jennifer.

"I'm sorry, but could you please find me another seat? I really need to work," said my neighbor in the window seat.

"The flight is completely full, Sir," said the flight attendant. Addressing me she said, "Can I get you anything?"

"Yes, please. Two testicles, an Olympic medal, and a Sprite," I said.

Grimace. Eyebrow raise. Phoney baloney smile.

"Ice?" she said.

"No thanks."

She came back with two other attendants, handed me the Sprite and a cup, and said, "When you finish that, I can get you something else."

The attendants watched intently.

An hour of antics later (in and out of my seat, in and out of the lavatories, attempts to help the flight attendants serve the meals), I was sitting in First Class in the center of the cabin, where there was a solitary big chair. In the seat to my left was now a very strong-looking fireman. On my right was another large citizen. Maybe it was the tight gold choker necklace that I had told the attendants was a shock collar for when I went off script that got me promoted to First Class.

I was the first one off the plane in New York. The handcuffs felt good. They were in the script.

I didn't even have a view of the Van Wyck Expressway, at Jamaica Hospital.

CHAPTER 62

THE NEXT AMERICA'S CUP CYCLE, from 2001 to 2003, saw the inception of a new team from Seattle called OneWorld Challenge. It was natural for Seattle's double-medallist brothers to be recruited in the first round. Morgan also got snatched up by the team quickly, and I eventually found myself wearing the same jersey and cap as a gaggle of old friends and nemeses. The substantial paycheck was exciting, and Amanda and I did a great job of living well below our means.

An opportunity materialized in front of me that I seized. The team didn't have a first draft-pick navigator yet. I tossed my hat in the ring. I suggested that my pilot's license and math degree were relevant, and that I could learn to reboot Windows twice.

It ended up being a great fit and a perfect role for me. Not so much because I had all the answers. It was the team around me. Mark Chisnell is still a household name in navigator circles, and he was recruited not too long after I was. He was half of the story of my success as a racing navigator at OneWorld. The other half was Nobu Katori, a Japanese naval architect and self-taught software developer. Mark, Nobu, and I designed new racing software from scratch, with no legacy deadweight. It was designed to be powerful and flexible with a bare minimum of touch-screen keystrokes, so that I could also contribute to powering the winches of the boat by grinding on the pedestals as much as possible.

Amanda and the other Cup wives used to have the kids "grind with Daddy", by turning their little bikes upside down in front of the TV during the broadcast of the race. They'd spin the pedals with their little hands, just like we did on the boat to turn the winches.

Our team came out guns blazing, going undefeated in the first round robin. We went down in equally blazing flames. We lost in the semifinals to Larry Ellison's Oracle team. They earned four points for four wins. Our final score was negative one. Our team was penalized an entire point, plus a monetary fine, for allegedly stealing design secrets from another team. Our boat did look a lot like Team New Zealand's, but maybe that was because our head designer used to be theirs. In any case, that aspect was well above my pay grade.

CHAPTER **63**

M Y MEDICATION REGIMEN SEEMED TO be agreeing with me well
enough. One thing that for sure helped is that I changed my
injections from biweekly to weekly. Why didn't I do this sooner? I
was led to believe that I would essentially be starting over as a new
applicant with the World Anti-Doping Agency if I changed my
therapeutic use regimen. Changing the dosage is changing the use.
It was too risky.

Anyway, once a week meant twice as many pinpricks. Twice as
many injection bruises and crampy feelings in my ass. But, smaller
mood swings at the beginning and the end of my cycle.

Testosterone is awesome! Day after shot day, I can push bigger
weights at the gym, pull harder on the rowing machine, think
smarter and faster, access wider vocabulary with greater ease, carry
optimism and paradox, contradiction and hope in my heart side
by side, and the old fella might as well be made of rock. I suppose
my temper is a little shorter, and the idea of punching someone is
less remote than usual, too.

Emotionally, the end of the cycle feels a lot like a minor
depression. Lethargy, apathy, slower wit and less interest in tits.
Physically, it feels obvious.

I still cared about my childhood Olympic dream, but I had to find the right boat. After a false start in the especially expensive two-man Star Class, I decided to go back to the Finn. It was getting tough to justify the Olympic quest. My career path was unlikely to be impacted drastically by a medal because I had found my niche already. Pay to go sailing and stall my career, or get paid to go sailing and advance it? Not a straightforward decision for a newlywed.

Jumping into the Finn a few months before the '92 Trials was looking like a great move now. Lots had changed, but I had logged a few good hours eleven years earlier. Maybe this was meant to be.

Amanda and I had saved a little money, which allowed me/ us to take delivery of a 16-foot Olympic Finn dinghy in Holland in May 2003. As all boat owners come to learn, buying the boat is the cheap part. Running it is what really costs money. With all the important events in Europe, my boat ownership was no different. And, I needed to fund my own coach and equipment because as a latecomer, I was unranked in the United States.

Dad's philosophy is that the check for the funeral should bounce. He decided it was most effective to give me and Sis our inheritances early. She put hers into her new business, which is still growing every year.

I put mine into equipment, travel, and coaching. I hoped that one day the investment would pay off with a (very-expensive-and-elaborate-to-order) leather jacket with five rings on the back, and breakfast in the Olympic Village with my wife and the Romanian Gymnastics team.

But truly, the money was a huge help, and it left us with half of the debt we would have had at the end of the campaign.

It was extremely windy in the Netherlands, the country

below sea-level, in the late spring when I took delivery of the new boat. Medemblik, Holland, is just one lonely dyke away from the North Sea. I was still at least twenty pounds too small for the powerful Finn. It was a little like coming back to the gym after a few years off, throwing two big forty-four pound plates on each end of the bench press bar, and then just seeing how it feels to try to get it off your neck by yourself for two hours.

It was demoralizing enough to make me wonder what the hell I was thinking. I nearly sold the boat back to the dealer at the end of the week. Surely I didn't need to be humiliated that badly in an activity of my own choosing. Not only that, but it's not like Red Bull was lining up to sponsor me. It was expensive just putting my toe in the water.

I did a few of the European events in the early summer. Amanda joined me for an adventure in Maarstrand, Sweden. There was one light wind training day before the event, and I was completely on the pace even though my setup was still out of whack. I made the mistake of thinking, *I can do this.*

CHAPTER 64

⟍o

A MANDA AND I WANTED TO start a family. I hadn't banked
sperm, so there were two choices for us: sperm donors and
adoption. We started on both while we wrestled with the choice.
We chose an organization called Friends in Adoption, based in
Vermont, and we attended their three-day orientation. Open
adoption means you meet the birth mother, sometimes months
before the baby is due, and build a relationship with her. It's
admittedly an unusual relationship. The rules of engagement are
confused and cautious.

First off, she picks you, and she picks you because she likes
the brochure you made about who you are as individuals and
as a couple, about what kind of parents you think you'll be.
Pictures of happy dogs and big extended families, or sunsets and
ski vacations…your choice what you include, but her choice
about what feels right for what can only be a harrowing and
ultimately very brave decision to give up her baby. The hope
that the child will have a fortunate life—which the birth mother
might remain unable to provide—is based on lots of things.
Ultimately, the choice requires faith.

The orientation is, well, disorienting and pretty demoralizing.
Most states have a cooling off or grace period, during which the
mother has the right to change her mind and take the baby back,

even if baby has already gone home with the adoptive parents. I think it's a good law, but talk about hard on a young couple as brand-new parents.

During aspiring-adoptive-parents orientation, we saw video after video about how painful it was for families to have babies taken away from them when birth mommy changed her mind. The families would take baby home to newly painted nurseries with handmade cribs and elephant mobiles hanging from the ceiling, baby monitors and blankets that Nana knit. Then, before the week or the month was up, everything would change in an instant, and they'd be worse off than when they started. So painful to watch.

Amanda and I understood where the agency was coming from. It was a real possibility, and if a couple went into it blind and it happened to them, there's no telling whether they'd ever recover. We held each other close in the little Vermont bed and breakfast, and talked late into the night about what we might do if we were fortunate enough to be matched with a birth mother one day. What we might do if we had to decide whether to take baby home right away or wait out the thirty days.

We both felt, pretty strongly in fact, that we would take the risk of heartbreak over leaving baby in the hospital to be without a home for the first days and weeks of his or her life. We got our background checks and home studies done, gave fingerprints and blood and urine and medical files, and submitted to multiple physical exams. We submitted tax returns and numerous letters of recommendation. Basically, everything except a firstborn.

We decided to disclose my history of mental illness, which was an agonized and painful decision. It's not on the second page of the manual: "If you suffer from mental illness, don't worry about it! Nobody cares!" At least, I didn't find it there.

I can't imagine how I would feel now, knowing I am a good daddy 98.6 percent of the time, if we had been denied the chance to be parents together because I had a label tied to my big toe that said "Very, very large imagination, feels music in his soul, cries at movies." (That's not what the tag would have said. It would have said "History of mental illness. Bipolar disorder. Petition DENIED.")

We signed the final papers to get in the line, wrote (tax deductible) checks to the agency, and other checks to help pay for the advertising that the agency does to let pregnant women know about Friends in Adoption. We chose to support ads placed in the Northeast and hoped a brave woman would call and pick us.

SIX MONTHS UNTIL THE FINN Olympic Trials. I put the thought as far back in my mind as I could that it was only a matter of time until the inevitable pattern repeated and something went horribly wrong in my life. But it was still there, and I could always feel it, that horrendous monster beneath the bed. Lurking. Waiting for just the right moment to pounce.

It was a pattern I had internalized more as a feeling, and the closer I got to something I really wanted, the stronger the feeling got. I faced it every single morning, sometime around when I washed out the huge cup for my protein shake and headed off to the gym. Every couple of weeks, I stared at myself in the mirror and told myself to just start getting ready for it because I was already overdue. Might be my sanity. Might be a new cancer. Amanda might figure out she's made a big mistake. Or, God might go easy on me and just send the bus to run me over.

Don't think. Just set about achieving simple goals: gain about fifteen pounds of muscle; figure out how to tack and gybe; how to start; how to go upwind and downwind properly in a boat that's famous for having bailers to let the blood out the bottom along with the water.

One of the biggest things I learned in the 1996 Trials (besides how humiliating it is to have a mental breakdown in front of fifty peers) is that starting and upwind are important, but when the racing is in open water with waves, downwind is where the big moves are made. It's sort of sailing's equivalent of golf's "drive for show, putt for dough." Basically, you can hike your nuts off upwind and gain maybe twenty-five meters on a twenty-minute leg. Or, you can get better at staying in the zone and flowing downwind, catch two more waves than the next guy, and gain a hundred and fifty meters. Like many sports, the harder you push it, the faster you go, but you might crash. Because the Olympic Trials only come around once every four years, it's pretty hard to practice in match conditions. There's just no way to simulate the pressure of four years of your life being justified (or not) in a week's competition.

Anyway, back in 1996 my starts and upwind were solid. I was arguably the fastest or at least the strongest upwind once the wind got over about twelve knots. The problem was that was only half the race. Downwind, especially when I started losing confidence, I tightened up. Boats blasted past me on either side, riding the waves while I dawdled along in the troughs like I was dragging the world's biggest jellyfish behind me. It's a terrible feeling. The harder you try, the worse you do. Yoda tells Luke "Do. Or do not. There is no try." Well, at the '96 Trials in the Laser, I seemed to often be stuck in *"do not,"* and badly at that—with no way of lifting my anchor off the bottom.

I would cover that weakness for the 2004 Trials and turn it into a strength. The Finn Trials were going to be in Fort Lauderdale, Florida. Amanda had started her ER specialist residency at the University of Maryland Shock-Trauma Center, one of the top programs in the world. No surprise there. We looked all around the greater Baltimore area for a modest place to live and finally ended up assuming the mortgage to a beautiful little one-room cottage in Bowie, Maryland. We took over the payments and the keys from none other than Tara of the summer of '93 overlap of ladies fame.

As we signed the papers and took the keys, I had the briefest glimmer of "too good to be true". The house really was perfect—no closing costs, big yard for the dog, and so well built.

They set this up. It's the only thing that makes sense. What am I supposed to do? I don't see any clues or cues...

Fortunately, it was gone almost as quickly as it came.

Not long after moving in, we got a very exciting phone call. We were matched with a birth mother! She was about five months pregnant. She picked our profile, and the agency asked us to consider contributing to her medical care. The checkbook was out by the end of the phone call. She was due some time around the Olympic Trials.

Amanda and I agreed that Southwest Airlines would be our new mutual best friend (it was just a little early to put our child-to-be's tummy mummy in this category), and we mapped out a schedule through the end of the Trials. We bought the airline tickets online together, and I packed up my boat, sailing gear, and blender, my movies and music and some wedding pictures. I put System of a Down in the CD player, turned it up all the way and ripped the volume nob off, and headed for the cultural mecca that is Fort Lauderdale, Florida.

I found a tiny little apartment nearly across the street from the race venue. I found a (male) personal trainer to work with at the gym. And then, I stopped my psychiatric medications.

CHAPTER **65**

I COULDN'T TELL AMANDA OR MY family. I just knew that I wouldn't be able to live with myself, I mean literally not draw breath, if I looked back on the Trials and decided that I had lost by a whisker, by a point, by a couple of missed waves, by a pattern on the water that I would have seen without the psychiatric medication onboard.

The MEDS were never good for my athletics. They made music dull, but they also made my reflexes slower and my balance forever slightly off. It feels a little like trying to use a mouse that's turned sideways on your desk. You can do it, you can learn, but you will never, ever get your high score on Missile Command unless you were born with a sideways mouse in the first place. Besides reflexes and balance, the meds reduce my ability to be unconsciously/subconsciously attuned with the patterns of the wind-shifts. Finally, the MEDS seem to make my vision narrower, and unquestionably they lower my confidence. They really suck.

Risky? Yup. Foolish? Time would tell.

I made some promises. I promised to be in bed by ten o'clock every single night. I promised to avoid even secondhand alcohol. I promised to limit my coffee intake to one a day. And I promised to read for at least half an hour every night. Reading

176

provided one of my best early warning signs. If I was reading and kept getting derailed to research something or write something down, the next stop was for the whole world to start glowing, for everything to become interesting, not just the connections that popped out of the pages of the book.

Right after the gentle glimmers of beautiful hypomania start to become a warm gleam, I'm always only a bunny blink away from the glow worms in my mind becoming one giant sand worm. Next, and it's always the same, comes the heat of being swallowed by the sun.

The really bright lights always come on. As in, the Director calling in stereo from inside the moon, from beneath the waves, and from the earwig in my ear: "Lights! Camera! And...action!" Those lights.

Even if I thought a show about a sailor with no balls was unlikely to sell, I'd be force-fed lines and stage directions, and my free will would swim away like Free Willy.

I had to be careful and disciplined up in there. I had to promise myself that if that started happening, I'd put my restraining bolt back in.

CHAPTER 66

I KEPT ALL MY PROMISES. From mid-October until the end of the
Trials in February. I watched, like a hawk, the weather outside
the house and the seasons in my moods.

There were two directions for strong breeze in southern Florida
in the wintertime. The northeaster and the east-southeaster.
The NEer makes the route from Fort Lauderdale to Miami a
downwind course. The SEer makes the trip north from Miami
downwind. Either way, there are big waves. Off Lauderdale,
the wave patterns are almost always confused. The Gulf Stream
currents and the entire Atlantic Ocean are just off the South
Florida beach. The ever-changing wind directions as the cold
fronts roll through almost weekly play a part too.

For an Olympic hopeful who would be racing in those
waters, there was no substitute for logging hundreds of hours
sailing downwind in them, pushing to catch an extra wave. It
took practice, days and days of practice, to find the extreme
edges of how tightly to carve turns. To learn whether one more
"pump" (our version of rowing with the sail by fanning it to
create extra wind) will get you on the wave or it's better instead
to save energy and stay smooth, getting ready for the next one.
This is all stuff that we've all been doing all our competitive lives.
The difference for the 2004 Trials in Fort Lauderdale, was instead

of rather regular patterns that have a rhythm, the seas there had the specific constant of chaos.

I was confident going into the Trials. My equipment was really organized, and I knew it inside and out. Charlie McKee, who had been my coach nearly twenty years before when I won the Youth Worlds in Greece, made time to be away from his family to coach the Trials.

And Amanda was there the whole time to help knock down the spikes and fill in the valleys of a ten day competition. I couldn't have asked for a better support team.

Two days before the Trials started, we got a phone call from Friends in Adoption. No easy way to say it. The birth mommy went AWOL after getting the money we sent. Maybe she just changed her mind? No, actually she was running a scam. The agency learned later we were her second victims. It happens. Not that often, but it happens. Try not to be discouraged....

We had to very quickly forgive ourselves for having our hopes and our wallets duped. Rats. Rodents of unusual size, actually.

THE FIRST TWO DAYS OF the Trials were windy and wavy. I stunned the rest of the field by coming out of the blocks to win the first four races.

Putting the entire fleet on the back foot made the rest of the week a lot of fun for me and a lot of stress for them. One of the best moments of the event came in the fourth race. It was the second race of the day, so we were all tired. One of my main competitors for the Olympic spot rounded the last turn with a comfortable lead into the short final leg. He aimed for the low end of the finish line and went for a smooth style with what's called "two to one" purchase on his mainsheet. Less load, but also half the stroke when you pump, like rowing with a short oar.

I came around the last turn fully in the zone. It's in the back of your mind somewhere, quiet and calm, the idea that you will be leading by the finish. Sort of a warmth of confidence, a presence. It's not a thought. At least for me, when I'm sailing really well, I'm not thinking *Grrrr, I'm gonna catch that guy and pass him.* You just know. "Balls to bones," as the Oracle says to Neo in *The Matrix* about knowing whether or not he's in love, or knowing whether or not he's The One. (OK, silicone prostheses to bones in my case, but whatever.)

I stayed on the big chain ring, one to one, direct link to the sail. Long oar. I aimed higher than the guy in front of me. More potential speed, much higher workrate, less margin for error with steering.

The legs push into the lower back. The shoulder pulls hard on a straight arm, mainsheet wrapped around the wrist to prevent any slippage, like a strap for a 330-pound deadlift. Then at the end of the stroke, to make sure to launch down the wave—which gives more speed at the bottom turn to line up the next wave—the arm gives a quick snap to finish the pump. Everything slowed down around me. It was like there was a golden path laid out on the water and all I had to do was steer to keep the bow aimed down it. The sound of the spray shooting away from the boat had distinct elements, not just a general quality. I didn't look over to see how my gain rate was; I didn't look up to see how far the finish line was. I just *knew*.

It would have been a horrible feeling for Mo, when the gun went off before he got to the finish, meaning someone else had gotten there first. When I looked up, his whole body slumped with the disappointment. Right then I knew that there was one less guy to worry about for the rest of the week. In fact, right then I knew there was only one guy to worry about for the rest of the week, and that was me. If I used all my skill, stayed present, and made wise choices at the big moments, it was completely in my hands. For the first time since sophomore year of college, I believed that I'd get to keep what I did for the rest of the week.

I trusted myself and I trusted the world.

I made some mistakes over the next eleven races, but I also had a few really inspired moments. I won five of those eleven remaining races, and I secured my spot on the US Olympic Team with one race to spare. I could sit out the last race and still win. Some people choose to do that. Job done, it's been a long road. Get into the harbor and get the boat on dry land. Get out of the cold wetsuit and into the hot shower as soon as possible. I don't have a problem with that, it's just never been my style. I looked forward to enjoying the final race, knowing there was no pressure beyond what I put on myself. I set a personal goal of sailing the entire race completely present. I won by half a leg.

I'm glad I gave myself that moment because the next six months were going to get rough.

CHAPTER 67

THE FIVE-INCH THINK MEDICAL FILE that I submitted to petition the IOC in 1995 had grown quite a bit as a case file. There were lots and lots of blood tests over the years. They kept showing the same thing. I never had unusually high levels of exogenous testosterone in my body. And, I still hadn't spontaneously grown new testicles.

The US Sailing Association assured me that they were on the case too now that I had earned a spot on the 2004 US Olympic Team. I wasn't a medal favorite, but I had won my Trials by the widest margin of any of the eleven US classes. If Athens turned out to be a light, shifty regatta and I had a magical week, who knows what might be possible. I wasn't delusional, but I was good in light shifty breezes and stranger things had happened.

∞

Amanda has always decided what she wants and then set about achieving it. Becoming a mother was no different. The signs seemed to be telling us that adoption wasn't our path, at least for now. Also, I didn't want to be the reason she one day found herself looking back and wondering if she had totally blown it, missing out on pregnancy and birth. It seems so primal, and human, and

182

part of the cycle of life, and yadda yadda in a reverent way. It seemed like we might end up with tinges of regret or resentment if we didn't try to get pregnant. I had to put theoretical, left brain fears about Baby being "hers, not mine" aside and flip through the sperm donor profiles sitting next to Amanda, page by page.

It was one of the most unsettling spiritual experiences I have ever had. On the one hand, I was sitting next to the woman I loved, and had always loved, and had dreamed about, written about, talked about starting a family with. On the other hand, some part of me was viscerally reluctant to stand aside while another man had "relations" with my wife. Maybe that sounds ridiculous. All I can say is the feelings that come from the old, reptilian part of the brain, which was forged and was already quite evolved long before "Me Tarzan, you Jane" years…those feelings didn't seem to have taken the day off.

Look, I can quote all the books, and Pastor A and Rabbi B and Guru X and Medium G. *A family is a family no matter how it got started; the child is born of your love, not your intertwined chromosomes, etc., etc.* The words are really great, they're hopeful and noble and warm and have a certain truth. My lot in this life is that all the other shit, the stuff Jung made a career exploring, and artists commune with on the good days, and crazy people can't keep inside if their life depends on it, well, I wear all that on my sleeve. And my sleeve was saying, "This really fucking sucks, choosing a number which is written on a vial which is full of stuff made in a few minutes by some kid who needed money and had a strong right wrist and a good magazine." I'm just saying.

The good news is that some of the profiles were hilarious. Our favorite "Tell us a little about yourself" essay had one donor writing that he was "really honored to be able to give like this and help some people out and he really wanted to make a pungent [sic] difference in this world." We still laugh today. Every so often, one of us will say something like "Hey, sorry I forgot to pick up the dry cleaning and the milk. I'm just really busy over here trying to make a pungent difference in the world, OK?" Extra points if you manage a stinky fart too.

Our all-time favorite, which still comes up a few times a month, concerns the question of "Do you like animals?" Answers ranged from "Not really, I hope you still pick me," and "I think dolphins are really cool, they're so beautiful and smart and just inspiring, really, and one time I got to go to Sea World with my uncle and feed a dolphin a little smelly fish right out of my hand but it bit my hand and well I still really like dolphins though…" to this one: "Do you like animals? Yes, ducks."

For some reason, Amanda and I both found that excruciatingly funny. No other animal would work. Try it. Yes, aardvarks. Doesn't work, trying too hard. Yes, salamanders. Same thing. Yes, porcupines—not quite. Yes, this, yes that. Nothing packs the pungent punch of "Yes, ducks."

In the end, we chose vial #3606. I have a real love-hate relationship with that number and any numbers with a similar ring. Mostly hate. They represent what I do not. What I cannot.

We took delivery of the little swimmers and headed off to the land of stirrups and turkey basters. A doc did the deed while I pretended I was thrilled. Just being honest. I promise I can concoct lots of other, far more flattering sentences to describe my feelings, but that was how I felt.

We waited. It's not exactly like sitting by the oven while the muffins rise and the timer tick-tocks and finally dings, but there's a certain related hope and expectation. I headed off to Athens for the final lead up to the Olympics. To my childhood dream coming true.

⤴

CHAPTER 68

I T WAS A BUMPY RIDE, the Therapeutic Use Exemption waiver
for the Olympics thing. The title of its file folders at home is
"The Hassle" (Folder 1, Folder 2, …). There were five weeks to
go until the first race of the Olympics, and I still didn't have a
waiver. I was required to be at a lab every morning for something
like ten days straight to give blood, at precisely the time I would
have been at the gym. Why this bloodwork was necessary now,
and the last nine years of tests wasn't quite enough, I will
never understand. Way back in the ACLU days, Mr. Rosenbaum
had a great line about the most generous explanation being
"bureaucratic insensitivity". I was beginning to have a hard time
evoking that as the most likely explanation, and I was starting to
get pretty cynical. Finally, Amanda couldn't stand it any longer.
She saw me collapsing, she was disillusioned, and she was getting
mad. She sent a letter out to the press. The press dug around the
story, and exposed a few misrepresentations of progress (there
was no progress).

The clock kept ticking, counting down to opening
ceremonies. The only thing that had changed since the front-page
article in the *NY Times*, since I went on *Good Morning America*
in 1996 and had a chin wag with Joan Lunden, was I had
qualified to represent my country at the 2004 Olympics. I tried

to keep it up, that chin, but it was getting hard. I reminded myself of my days in Fort Lauderdale, when I thought the wisest thing I could do was a lot like what Friends in Adoption urged us to do—imagine and prepare for the worst, but quietly, timidly hope for the best.

The phone did ring. Amanda was coming to Athens in another two weeks. She had just gotten back from the doctor's. We were pregnant!

I basically collapsed in sadness. When it was hypothetical that we were making a baby with the help of someone we'd never met, much less had a few drinks with, it all sounded pretty great. When it was staring me in the face, the thing I couldn't do, it felt completely different. Combined with the trip to the lab to again give blood—so that some bureaucracy could maybe, but maybe not, tell me once and for all that I was "OK enough to join the rest of the Olympians, despite my differences"—Amanda's news was ten parts happy and exciting, ten million parts rubbing my face in the fact that I wasn't a man.

I recently watched a movie about Stephen Hawking called *The Theory of Everything*. He had it pretty rough. His body played some very mean tricks on him. For sure. And wow, what a mind, and what resolve, and what loving support, and what a triumph of the human spirit. His last words in the movie, after the confirmation of his theories and after turning down the Queen's offer of knighthood, were spoken by the computer voice after he typed them in. The words were about his children: "Look… what…we…made."

Something happened to me with those words. Faraway pain, and then something very new. Something I had never felt, or allowed myself to sit with. I have spent twenty-five years trying to downplay, to be OK with, to label as no big deal, what is, in fact, kind of a big deal. Amanda squeezed my hand on the couch, knowing exactly what I was thinking about. Popcorn slipped between the cracks in our little movie room as I finally decided once and for all that it's OK if my ancestors do feel a little disrespected.

Hey, so, I already speak words all the time like "Look who we love with all our hearts and all our might," and "Look at the curious and beautiful little creatures who bring us so much joy and occasionally little tests of patience," and "Look how wonderful it is to have a family together after all we've been through," and even "Look what we started, what has been brought together in this world."

But not "Look what we made."

Hawking's words (or the ones in the script of the movie about him, to be precise), helped me to forgive myself for having such overwhelmingly strong feelings about knowing I will never speak them.

Maybe if I had banked sperm, I would have forgotten all the pain later, and Amanda and I would have used it. Or, the scientists might have figured out that neither cancer nor mental illness is actually hereditary. Vial #4202, say. Use it or lose it.

Maybe it would have worked. Maybe not.

Knowing Rainer and Leo and Stevie now, I can't imagine anything else but what I have done. What *we* have done.

CHAPTER **69**

I WAS THE SECOND MEMBER OF the 2004 US Olympic Team to walk into opening ceremonies. *Runner-up Flag Bearer* was my official title. I still haven't made complete peace with the fact that I was only voted runner-up. Maybe I should be very proud of that. But the part of me that bought into all the media about my story of overcoming adversity, and heard the ACLU lawyer Mr. Rosenbaum's words ten years beforehand about how instead of the IOC barring me from the Olympics, they should have me carry the flag…well, I really, really do wish it had been me. And I'm ashamed of those feelings. But that doesn't erase them.

I still sort of imagine that if I could answer the question "How did you do?" when people ask me about the Olympics (and I know damn well they're only talking about the result and not whether I sailed with dignity, or was present for the whole event, or earned and maintained the respect of my peers, or even just played fairly the whole game (even when no one was watching))…well, I imagine that if I could say, "Er… I was one better than midfleet, BUT! I!! CARRIED!!! THE!!!! FLAG!!!!! INTO!!!!!! OPENING!!!!!!! CEREMONIES!!!!!!!!" that I would, in that moment and forevermore, truly believe I am a good person. That I have value in this life and on this earth, and that God and his mean, dirty ol' seagull had finally stopped shitting on my head.

It says it right there, inside my uniform for opening ceremonies, in huge, lovely white letters on the navy-blue background of my team swacket [sic] (A "swacket" is a blazer-cut jackety thing but made out of what is essentially high-end sweatshirt material. Swacket. Really fun to say. Pretty fun to wear, at least around the house as a smoking jacket. Just don't let your kids or spouse or friends see you, and make sure the paparazzi aren't outside).

"The most important thing in the Olympic Games is not to win but to take part, just as the most important thing in life is not the triumph, but the struggle."

Here's the rub. I felt this discrepancy deep down, long before I ever got to the Olympics. Ever wonder why the only sports they televise in the United States are the ones we have strong chances for medals? Smell a rat yet, if it's supposed to be about the struggle?

Fuck participation and struggle! I want my medal!

CHAPTER 70

❧

THE MORNING OF THE FIRST race of the Olympics, I was supposed to meet a representative of the World Anti-Doping Agency at the US Sailing Team dugout near the boats at 9:00 a.m. Blood would be drawn and it would be tested while I was out racing. Fine. Whatever.

My phone rang at 5:45 am. We had all gotten team phones to keep in touch; slim little Motorolas or whichever company decided to spend marketing budget to be affiliated with all the hype around higher, faster, stronger. I remember it going down something like this:

"Is that Kevin Hall?" said a voice I didn't recognize. I rubbed my eyes, looked around the room, found a clock. *Wha?...Huh?*

"Uh, yes."

"There's been a change of plan for this morning's blood test. You need to come to the main stadium to be tested. Try to be there by 7:00 a.m."

"What? Why? The plan is to meet at the team base at nine so I can go racing from there."

"The plan has changed."

I didn't find out more details. Instead, I threw the phone against the wall. The main stadium is closer to the Acropolis than to where the boats got pushed into the Aegean. I was hysterical.

The phone shattered into many, many pieces. It was actually very satisfying.

But, it meant the phone number of whoever had just called and woken me up was no longer available in *recent calls*. Amanda tried to calm me down, but at this point well over a decade of seagull shit was now in my ears, in my eyes, and in my mouth, causing me to lose my footing, just fucking everywhere. I really didn't know what was going on. It didn't make any sense.

I do realize that I'm writing about something that is occurring in a context of tremendous fortune and privilege. I don't need reminding, I can hear the lilt of disdain in my own ear. *Poor Kevvy-wevvy gets a little bump in the woad of his wittle wace in his wittle boat in his wittle game. Poor, poor kevvy. Hey. Try dealing with something that is actually a big deal, and not just a little challenge for some privileged dude in some race in what is officially called "Games".*

It's a good thing there were no actual cameras recording the wake-up-call tantrum. That's for sure.

CHAPTER 71

I AM PROUD OF ONE THING about the Olympics. It's not really about the Olympics, actually. It's about respecting my commitment to Amanda, and to our future, and to this life, and to understanding that I had no choice but to compete with an albatross around my neck and a sideways mouse. The medications did their job. The Director was quarantined by the time the milk was going on the museli.

I never got an explanation for what the change of plan was all about. I still don't know how the truth would have helped anyway.

I knew it was going to be stressful at the Games, and I knew there was a chance of some funny twists and turns. I didn't imagine being woken up before 6:00 a.m. the morning of the first race and told I had to drive away from the water, but hey maybe I wasn't paying attention. Anyway, I had gone back on my medication right after the Trials, and I stayed on it right the way through. And it's taken me a long, long time to get there, but sitting here today, I'm proud of that.

I thought about going off a few times during the summer I lived and trained in Athens, to be able to feel the wind on my face again, to have the spring back in my step, to take the parentheses away from the person that was (sailing). But I didn't

192

do that. I stayed the course. I promise you, it's harder than it sounds. Even with so much at stake. Even with fifteen years of growth and practice living with manic depression.

That doping phone call only made sense to me—either back then or even now as I write this—in my personal, alternate reality. In the psychotic world where *they* were fucking with me to make for a good show. There was no other universe in which it made any sense. Seriously.

I finally calmed down and pretended everything was OK. Sadly, the real me, and even most of (me), missed the experience of the Olympics. When reality gets hard to explain, my choices are to shut down or to ride with the Valkyries and hope for the best. I shut down that morning and watched from two steps behind myself as my body put my boat in the water, raced, and took it back out. I basically looked up ten days later and found I was at the medal ceremony.

I was looking over at my family, who were looking at me and wondering why I wasn't sitting with them. I couldn't tell them then that I felt immolated in shame. Shame that I had placed eleventh. Shame, that I had failed. Again.

I finished one place better than midfleet, I beat some great sailors, some of whom were bigger and stronger than I was, many of whom were competing in their second or even third Olympics. But, I was so ashamed of my result that I slunk away from Mom and Dad, wife and sister, to sit with my coach during the ceremony.

The medals were handed out to the three people up on the podium, the only three who could justify the air they breathed with solid proof, while the rest of us struggled to exist.

Some part of me knew that the only thing for it, the only one, was to hope for laughter. I knew Coach Luther had a better chance than anybody of making me laugh, somehow, about something. And I needed nothing in the world more than to start laughing at the whole thing, and especially myself.

I remember thinking this:

All these years "building character," you'd think I'd finally have a little, and be able to call on it at times like this and do the right thing and just sit with my family over there. Fuck, I can't even do that. Could I be any more pathetic?

Hey, wow, great, I've just added another layer of failure and guilt and shame to the already tectonic layer I'm operating with at baseline. Is there synchronized shame-spiraling in the Olympics? I'm good at that! Who needs a partner?

CHAPTER 72

Amanda and I had some incredible adventures after Athens. We got on a ferry headed away from Greece toward southern Italy to be tourists, and I tried hard not to look back. I drank a lot of Chianti and she drank a lot of Pellegrino. We sat by the pool and read trashy magazines, we slept in 'til the afternoon. I thanked Amanda, over and over, for all her support. She told me not to be sad or angry about the Olympics and my experiences there, and that one day she was sure I would be much more proud of it all than I was right now.

The one little results-oriented moment I had occurred on the last day. Like the 1996 Trials in the Laser, I had nothing to lose anymore. I was free, you might say (though it would be a stretch).

While a win in the race might have put me in the single digits in the final standings, there was something far more important. I was basically tied with my future boss going into the last race. Grudge match of the century. (Match first. Grudges would be coming soon enough.)

I woke up and put one foot in front of the other. I listened for the quality of the sound of the water as my boat first splashed in that morning. I hoisted my sail feeling, really noticing, the thin, no-stretch line cutting into the back of my hand, did my warm up and made my tactical plan with a smile, and came blasting off the line to round the first and second marks in the lead.

I found a hole of no wind by the third leg and slipped back a few places. I don't remember what place I got in that, or any other race. What I do know is that I beat my new boss, and nobody could take that away from me. If it ever came down to a pissing contest onboard at work during the next four years, and I didn't like where things were headed in the bullshitting, all I would have to do is say, "*Uh, Athens much?*"

First stop after Italy was Marseille for my first race with Emirates Team New Zealand. Their paycheck reflected the fact that I was now a first-round draft pick navigator, one of a handful in the world. Their playbook had me holding what's called the "short sheet" around the first mark. It allows the big winches to be used for the new spinnaker going up while the old genoa is waiting for enough hands to wrestle it back on deck as it comes down. Being cautious, although it was setup for me when I got there, I thought I should double check it. It was wrapped the wrong way! I spun it off the winch, reloaded it properly, and held on. The only problem was that it had been loaded correctly. Now I was holding a rope attached to a huge sail that was helping pull a twenty-five ton racing boat through the water. I had two choices. Let go, or try to hold on.

Team New Zealand had a nickname around the harbor: Team Tough. It was pretty obvious what I had to do. I held on. The skin ripped off my fingers and palms, and I went back to my spot with the little wireless touch screen to hope nobody noticed. The adrenaline wore off just before the finish. It was starting to really hurt. I asked if I could maybe see the medic boat. By the time I was transferred there were cameras shooting the scene. My hands looked like they had been run under a very wide-blade circular saw at a depth just high enough to miss detaching the fingers from the knuckles. It hurt. And, I was sure I was alive.

I could already hear the ribbing I would be getting at the bar. *"It's great you're so tough and all, but it's not a good sign that you can't even figure out which way a winch turns. We were looking for a navigator with a brain…"* It would be a perfectly legitimate concern.

CHAPTER 73

WE GOT BACK FROM EUROPE about a month after the Olympics and headed to the hospital that afternoon for the checkup on the baby.

Amanda knew right away. The image was only just coming onto the ultrasound screen, but with her training she knew something was wrong long before the look went south on the tech's face. I knew pretty quickly too, from Amanda's face. By the time the tech looked at us, she figured out she could skip the first round, the pity and the *"There's no easy way to say this"* part. Amanda's tears were quiet and brief. On the outside. If her insides were anything like mine, we were going to need each other like never before. The anguish is hard to describe. A little for myself, a lot for Amanda. I can say that I didn't have any trouble believing the dead fetus was real. Medicated me could still be plenty sad, and he was.

I don't remember having conscious thoughts about it, but based on discussions we had before deciding on using vial #3606, part of me must have been relieved to know we wouldn't be half-biological parents. Fear of weirdness about a baby being "more Amanda's than mine" was a feeling I had at times during our discussions about options for starting a family. I find I don't get to pick and choose all my feelings so that I only have noble

198

ones of which I am proud.

Amanda threw herself into the last year of her ER residency program at the University of Maryland Shock-Trauma Center in Baltimore. I tried to organize as much as I could around the house before I moved to New Zealand alone and left her to the 100 hour work weeks and the Baltimore winter while I sailed around in the sunshine in the Southern Hemisphere summer.

We contacted the adoption agency and asked them to activate our status. We *possessed* a bunch more viable embryos, maintained them at the right temperature, paid for the storage, and passively imagined them as part of a potential future. But the decision was natural and mutual to go back to adoption. It was like I was getting the phone number to call the agency and then heading to the phone while she had grabbed the phone on her way to looking up the number. There was literally no discussion. We were definitely meant to become parents by adoption.

Plus, Amanda isn't known for her patience, and although we both wanted a child, having made the decision, she wanted one *now*. Things can have a funny way of working out.

Our brochure was picked by a birth mom in New York, who was six months pregnant with a boy. Choosing a name was really easy and went in much the same way as our decision to call the adoption agency back. We both wanted to call him Rainer, after the German poet Rainer Maria Rilke, whose transcribed poetry and letters had figured as a big part of our correspondence during the early years together. In Rilke's *Letters to a Young Poet*, he writes to a young man about trying to be calm or at peace with not having answers to all the questions in his heart. "Try to love the questions themselves," Rainer Maria writes. It's a great way to look at the world if you can pull it off.

We chose Rainer's middle name after my paternal grandad, Harley.

I was not the only father pacing against the clock that night at the hospital, hoping baby would arrive in time for the tax deduction. This was definitely one of those sublime-and-also-profane circumstances that reminded me that to be human often means simultaneously holding contradictory, or at least very incongruous, thoughts and feelings.

Rainer Harley Hall arrived in time for the write-off. He was born at 11:49 pm on New Year's Eve, 2004.

CHAPTER 74

⤚⤙

I HAD TO GO BACK TO work in New Zealand about a week after Rainer was born. While his birth mother could change her mind up to a month later, there was no law against leaving town with him in the meantime. Amanda got his passport in record fashion and got on a plane to Auckland as he turned three weeks old. I had long days on the water, then came home to our little miracle.

We both went all-in, meaning we just didn't think or talk about the dreaded possibility, or count down until the thirty days were up. I felt grounded in a way I never had before. More than just becoming a good defensive driver, things slowed down just a little and gained a kind of frankness. Real life.

We still send Rainer's birth mom pictures and a letter via the agency every six months. We talk about her, and have pictures of her on the fridge, and sometimes it's a little confusing for Rainer, and even for us. Not too long ago, one of Rainer's friends at school came up to me and said, "Rainer says he's adopted!," expecting me to say, "What? Really? Well, he's not." Rainer looks like a mix between Amanda and me. To an uncanny degree. You can see where the kid was coming from.

It's much harder to suppose that Rainer's younger brother Leo came from a physical union between me and Amanda. His stunning, six-foot tall birth mom is black. Leo is lighter than she is and very handsome. We started the paperwork for a sibling right away after Rainer was born.

Amanda and I each have one sister. You could describe both our families as somewhat square: two parents, two children, four chairs at the dinner table.

We both hoped for three kids and five chairs. We wanted the chaos and the overload of a bigger family. Careful what you wish for is all I can say now.

Leo's middle name is Edward, from Amanda's paternal grandfather. He is named Leo after the man who taught me how to sail when I was five, Leo Robbins. So far, it is Leo who builds the model boats after school, who only draws boats, who is the first to see a new ship on the horizon, and who can't wait for Sunday sailing in his little shoebox junior boat called an Optimist. Sometimes I like to think that there are connections all around us that can never be proven (whatever that means), but exist nonetheless. Because we say they do. Because they feel True.

CHAPTER 75

⤸

THE OTHER SAILORS AND I stood in a small group in our
stepping-out clothes. We sipped rum and Cokes and chatted
as we overlooked the harbor of Cagliari, at the southern tip of
Sardinia. Our fourteen-sailor "Mean Machine" team had reason
to celebrate. We were crewing for an amateur owner-driver. The
team that beat us was all pros, and had been together for years.
Us, (Pro-Am) vs. Them, (All-Pro). Like me and four LA Lakers
almost beating the 2007 Boston Celtics, we were only two points
off winning the TP-52-foot-boat Audi Medcup event.

I bought my round and swaggered back to the group of
fellow navigators. I passed out the drinks. We talked mostly shop
and a little shit. Loosened-up, hair-down Kevin started running
the conversation through the *it's happening again* filter while
(Kevin) tried to maintain that was very unlikely.

"He really is amazingly quick to figure this stuff out," said
one of the guys who writes his own code for weather modeling.

"I think the next release is coming any day now, isn't it?" said
another boffin who builds his own instrumentation.

"How do you know it's not already released?" I asked.

They looked at me a little funny. I see I've mis-stepped.

That wasn't my line.

"I mean, what if there's a quiet beta that we don't know about yet? Wouldn't it be cool to get on that list?" The guys smiled.

Good enough recovery.

"I just don't know how he keeps up with the day to day, with all that responsibility on his shoulders," a third sailor said.

"Must be kind of weird, doing all those interviews and stuff," weather-guru said.

Why are they talking about me as if I'm not here? Unless… unless this scene is supposed to trigger me.

I looked around.

Perfect venue. A hundred places for cameras, they must have been put up today while we were out racing.

"It's not that bad," I said, and I turned to run.

I ripped my Olympic watch off my wrist, and my wallet out of my pocket, and threw them as far as I could. I stormed away from the bar, angry to be put on the show tonight.

I wanted to just hang out with my friends without being bothered. Just this once. Too much to ask? Maybe I've got it wrong. Need a test.

I slammed my hand down on top of a cactus, really hard. Everybody looked for a split second, then went right back to their conversations as if nothing happened.

That only happens if they were expecting this, and the scene is supposed to move on.

(Otherwise, surely this is the part where the hot Italian "nurse" arrives and asks if Ima Okaya?)

I continued away from the party and down the marble steps. Some friends caught up with me.

"Everything all right, Kev?" said the biggest guy on our team.

"Yeah. Sure. Anyway, don't need my watch or my wallet anymore. They're so fucking heavy to carry around, know what I mean?"

One of the guys started playing guitar. Maybe that would soothe me.

How the fuck does he have his guitar with him here?

They told him to maybe fade out "Hotel California" and pick a different song.

We eventually made it back to the boutique hotel with a tumultuous combination of cajoling, kicking and crying, screaming and playing possum, carrying, pushing, and pulling me. All the while I was ranting and raving saying "Show me the money. Don't you think it's funny?"

We maneuvered in fits and starts up the stairs toward my room. I complained at every light fixture, "It's not fair!" (Meaning the breathtaking beauty of the interlace of the patterns on the walls, the incredible geometric designs of light bending through eighteenth century crystal chandeliers, was smothering me in sublime magnificence. It wasn't fair to overwhelm me with awe like that.)

Please Director, make that stop. I'll say my lines, but those light patterns are debilitatingly, sensation-overloadingly, soul-annihilatingly Beautiful.

I presume that my friends didn't know what I meant. They probably figured I was angry that I couldn't go out with them to the disco. It would have been much easier to explain back then.

We got into my room and Sarah asked me which pill I was supposed to take.

"The purple one," I said. "In the round tin."

"Which tin?" Sarah said. (Both tins were round.)

"Dunno. We tryin' to go up or down here?" I said.

"Maybe down for now? Why don't you put some music on?" Sarah patiently recommended.

There were two or three other able-bodied witnesses at the door. There was no way to fit through the window. I was here for a while. I looked in iTunes on my laptop.

Perfect. They can tell the story for me.

So ya / Thought ya / Might like ta / Go to the show…

Pink Floyd's "In the Flesh" played through, followed by "Mother," which only got a half billing before "Waiting for the

Worms," which got cut to "The Trial."

There we go. Leave it there.

"The purple one, Sarah; I need the purple one."

She showed me that both tins had purple ones, which I, of course, knew.

"What happens if we just take them all?" I asked.

"Not tonight. Which one of these is the morning one, Kev?" Sarah's voice was familiar and soft and warm and patient. The British accent gave it a small air of authority.

Sarah held up one tin and raised an eyebrow. Morning? This one?

I pretended I didn't understand.

"In the morning you take espresso if the dragon didn't get you overnight when you put your head on the pillow. So. If you can figure out which pill I'm supposed to take with that info, I'll do it. Otherwise, I'm outta here," I said.

Now, my morning tin has a dragon on it, and my nighttime tin is from Trader Joe's. It says "Espresso Pillows." Weird, right? Which is it? Buzz you up or lay your head down for to sleep?

"Kevin I can't tell from your riddle. You already know, though, don't you?" Sarah said. She was still hiding her fear and impatience, but not by much now.

"The purple one. I'll take the purple one. Because that means I took the red pill and the blue pill, which puts me right where I want to be. Capisce?"

She might not be as big a Matrix *fan as you, dude. Give her a break. Just fucking take the pills. It's not that hard.*

"Pillow. The night one is the pillow." I said.

She handed me the open tin with all its promise of dying wind.

"The Trial" stopped playing on my laptop. I started the song over.

"How many do you usually take? Should we take an extra one?" Sarah asked.

I grabbed three of the big ones and chewed them. It tasted

revolting, they're not made to be chewed. The bitter immediacy, the wrongness of it jolted me for a split second.

This. Here. This disgusting taste. This is real. Feel it. Know it. Own it. You don't want to learn how Sardinians treat their mentally ill.

One of the senior members of the team changed his flights to accompany me to Zurich, where I would get on the plane alone to New York, and he would head back to New Zealand. As we got in the cab to the airport, I bummed two cigarettes, stuck them both in my mouth and lit them, rotated them each forty-five degrees off axis like cockroach antennae, and sucked hard. The glows were real. The smoke in my eyes, was real. I caused it. Me.

This is really happening.

There is no show.

I am going home.

In Zurich, I bought Amanda a Gucci bag. It was on sale. For twenty-five hundred euros. I wanted to buy another one, but my guardian talked me out of it.

"She'll love this one. If you get two, she'll think you have no idea what she likes," he said.

I trusted him.

The flight home from Zurich to JFK was terrifying. I played little games, with magazine pictures and puzzles, with movie cuts and album titles, with folded pages of my books, pen and paper, this and that.

Meanwhile, (I) played much harder games with the person having a helluva lot of fun. The one who felt good about life. The one who knew everything would be all right. (I) had to tell Him, that He was full of shit. That it was all in his head. That He would deeply regret bolting from the stable. Could He please, maybe just try to watch just one movie and keep his seatbelt fastened? So we can get home to our family?

The rum and Cokes and wine and smokes resurfaced, and

I had to puke. But, I had just promised (myself) to keep (my) seatbelt fastened. So I reached down for my shoe and hoped it all fit in there.

Amanda's hug at the airport fixed me. I said I was sorry. I made a mistake. I forgot I was different. I forgot I'm not allowed to have fun like everybody else.

"The kids can't wait to see you, Daddy," she said.

CHAPTER 76

I HAD A STEADY-AS-SHE-GOES YEAR AFTER buying the Gucci
handbag. Coming so close to landing back in the hospital
reups the vigilance. In September 2009, I got to the end of the
season with Emirates Team New Zealand, and I wasn't sure I was
doing what I was supposed to be doing.

We had won four of the five grand-prix events of the Audi
Medcup circuit in the team's TP52 boat. I performed consistently
and especially well whenever the pressure was up. The whole team
was really tight, and we even had some fun. We won the season
by a country mile and celebrated the last night. I chose a night
of club soda and lime. I knew I was already running plenty hot.

A few friends from other teams asked me, over fine canapés
at the awards party, if I had signed to stay on with Team NZ. I
had made a point of ensuring that I had returned every single
company USB stick and paperclip to the boat before the party,
but I wasn't consciously ready to articulate that I had made up
my mind to move on. I changed the subject.

I felt some wildly varying, intense emotions during the
thirty-hour flight home. One of the things I cued off, a sign if
you will, is that the entire team but me was upstairs in business
class on our sponsor Emirates Airlines. I was in the middle of the
four-across of row fifty-eight, right behind the lavatories of the

new Airbus 380. It smelled like a crystal-ball metaphor for their plans for my future with the team.

Another thing that disrupted consensus reality for me was the little bag which held our eye shades and earplugs. I had a feeling it was exactly the same size as my 60 GB iPod. It fit perfectly. That's no big deal. What was weird, was that it had a tiny hole in exactly the right spot for my headphones, so my iPod could be in the closed bag with my headphones still plugged in. It was too weird to be anything but a *sign*.

The flight attendant came by and told me I couldn't sing out loud after I sang this line: "I can't love you / because we're supposed to have professional boundaries." (From Alanis Morissette's song "Front Row" on her album *Supposed Former Infatuation Junkie*.)

By the end of the flight, I was certain I was supposed to be an artist, not a sailor (I won't bore you here with all the little epiphanous proofs that kept adding up.)

I got home to New Zealand, and I quit.

The team had been good to me and my family all the way through. (For example, I was kept around on a retainer when the whole professional circuit was on something like year-long league strike the year before.) What happened was, at the end of the season, I asked to know a little better what they were thinking for my future. I must have been hoping to hear something else, so I put feelers out to other teams. Technically, my contract had ended as I stepped out of the Economy cabin in Auckland.

I also said I really didn't know what I wanted to do, and that I "might take up oil painting." I'm pretty sure I meant writing, but I was going for dramatic effect. In retrospect, I could have handled it all better.

There was a little voice hiding way in the back of my skull— behind the stack of unused folding chairs, behind the nondairy creamer and the little red and white plastic stir sticks and the stick-on name tags and the blue magic marker almost out of ink—that didn't want to be a professional sailor anymore. But the rest of me, the (me) who had gotten used to the steady income that was more than my dad made, and the cool uniform with the name-brand logos, and the status at the bar or dinner parties, well he wasn't about to let that mousy voice from the back be heard. It would take me four more years and a lethal accident to hear that voice again.

I didn't go buy any paints. About the time I should've or could've been looking for a pen and paper to start trying to write again, a new Swedish team, Artemis Racing, called to see if I might come and help run the entire performance and instruments department. I headed off to Spain to meet my new colleagues.

The campaign for the 2013 America's Cup with Artemis was a fantastic fit for me. I was hired as a member of the sailing team, and also as cohead of the Performance and Instruments Department. Managing a group would certainly bring new challenges. We had over five hundred channels of data to generate, calibrate, graph, and distribute to the designers and sailors.

Normally being fully funded from inception makes for quite a strong team because you can get straight into designing and building prototypes, and training with the full support of trainers, physios, etc. We were able to start sailing with the first AC72 wing in the world. We got a handful of valuable days on the water, a little bit of data. Then the wing fell down, broken in three pieces. Miraculously, not only was no one hurt, but the thing folded back and forth like a giant accordion onto the deck of our rule-skirting French trimaran. We towed in and started rebuilding it right away. We got really good at fixing poorly designed parts that broke.

After a year of being told by designers that the data which

our department was producing was all wrong, the designers eventually recanted. Maybe their Finite Element Analysis (FEA) models did have one or two insignificant, unforeseeable errors. Although the relentless insistence that the data was completely wrong eventually subsided, it was too late for my psyche. I took it personally. My self-esteem free-fell like an Airbus without wings.

Unfortunately for Artemis, the America's Cup is not a boat-repair competition.

CHAPTER 77

IN AMERICA, YOU'RE NOT ALLOWED to specify a sex when you apply to adopt a child. You get whichever little person the adoption stork delivers. By the time Leo turned one, Amanda and I both knew that we wanted our third child to be a girl. That meant that, if we were fortunate enough, we would be adopting from overseas. China allows the choice of a girl and even has lots more girls than boys looking for homes, but doesn't allow a history of mental illness. Other countries do allow it, but want the adopted child to be the parents' first child. Russia was the only country where we had a shot of finding a daughter. We got the very, very large pile of paperwork done (well, Amanda got it done, and I signed when I had to) and sat by the phone.

Six months later, a day I happened to be home from working with Artemis overseas, the phone rang. Amanda picked it up. Listened. Nodded. As I tried to read her face, it was clear something was up, but I had absolutely no idea what. Good, bad, I couldn't tell. Mostly she looked shocked.

"They want to know if we can be in Moscow by the end of the week," she said matter-of-factly. The thrill set in for her about the same time I finished processing her words. Wow. Already. Buckle up!

The only thing we were strong on was that baby sister—about

whom we had been talking for a few years with the boys—not be older than her brothers, that she not disrupt the birth order. Besides that, we were specifically hoping for *not* a newborn. We talked about baby sister with the boys often and for years. How she would be with us one day, but we didn't know when. Rainer, age five, said, "Cool." Leo, three and a half, said, "That will be so great! Then we'll have to get a mini van!"

We would still have been delighted if the bundle on the doorstep ended up being brand-new, but we both felt like we had been there, done that with the bottles and the diapers and the screaming in the middle of the night.

When I swap war stories with the fellas, my experiences raising infants are pretty different to most of theirs. Sometimes they lament being out of honey for the hot tea they'd make for their wives. Or they'd try to express how difficult it was to know that the best thing was for them to go back to sleep, that mommy and baby would benefit most from daddy's snoring now so that he could be alert the next day. No sense both parents being up all night and cranky. Imagine the emotional strain, knowing it's best to roll over!

It was assumed in our family that boys can feed a newborn from a bottle just as well as girls. So a fair way to decide who gets up in the middle of the night for the feeding is to look at who has recently worked the night shift in the Emergency Room, and pick the other person.

The agency we were working with told us they could help us get a visa in time to enter Russia at the end of the week, so we should book our flights immediately. It sounded ridiculous. It sounded impossible.

(Heavy accent) "You drive to New York. You go corner 42nd & 7th. You go there 10:00 a.m. You hand your passports to *Boris*. Boris meets you. He will have green shirt. You come back to same corner two days later. At 10:00 a.m. You have visa."

Are you kidding me? We hand our passports out the window

on 42nd to a guy we never met called Boris and then cross our fingers and hope we'll see him again? Amanda and I looked at each other, shrugged, and said, "OK. We'll be in the 1990 black Volvo wagon. See Boris tomorrow."

I don't know what we would have done without our nanny Gaylene in our lives. Yes I do. We would have panicked many times. We were hooked up with her by a mutual friend the first time Amanda came to New Zealand with Rainer. Gay was interested in doing some nanny work, and she was interested in some travel because her three kids were out of the nest and dispersing away from New Zealand. We could promise some travel. Gay got on the plane with Amanda a week later and squeezed into our little hut in Bowie, Maryland with Amanda and Rainer. She became a big part of the family over the next seven years. She lived with or very near us in Maryland, in New York, in New Zealand, and in Spain. It's wild to think about how much of the life we have now has been made possible by Gay's care and love for the boys and for Amanda and me. The boys, aged seven and five at this point, stayed with Gay in Spain while Amanda and I went to meet their (maybe) new three-year-old sister in Novocherkaask, near Rostov-on-Don, in the southwestern corner of Russia.

Five days after the first phone call, we sat just pushed back from the Aeroflot gate at JFK waiting for nasty weather to pass. The flight attendants had short skirts, which was nice, but they were bright orange and dill green, which kind of killed the Russian-girl mystique for me. There were all sorts of great accents and smells and great people-watching before we even left JFK.

We were met at the airport and taken to Rostov-on-Don, where we spent the night in the Hotel Don Plaza. The women's National Chess Championship was also at the Don Plaza. Another day, I might have tried to watch a few games; some of the women in there might be as smart as Amanda. Some might be as beautiful. None were both.

We were picked up by Natasha and drove another hour and a half on three-lane roads with a passing lane for both directions in the middle, which amounts to a full scale, state-sponsored game of chicken. I had experienced it before on the way from Athens to the ferry port. It takes some getting used to. Valium might have helped, as long as you measured the dose in kilograms.

We arrived in the early August afternoon and put the little blue paper slippers they gave us over the tops of our shoes. This became something we got better at over the next few months, but never quite used to. We got a brief tour of the orphanage and then waited in the head doctor's office. A little girl in a red dress with round cheeks and a bowl cut of jet black hair was led in by the hand. She was almost four years old, and I fell in love with her by the time the door closed behind her. *You* will *take me home*, her subtle smile, her eyes, and her spirit hollered.

Her name was Nina. Her birthday was coming up in a few weeks. September 11, the exact same day as mine. You don't say.

This is meant to be, if anything ever was.

I pushed Nina on the swing for an hour, "Yishyo, Papa!" she said with nearly every push. Again! Wrapped firmly around her little finger in five minutes flat was Papa.

My spiritual feet were firmly on the hard Russian earth as my heart soared next to Nina's.

We both deserve this. This is right, and real, and true. Maybe everything really will be OK.

Nina played with the little teddy bear we brought. We blew up balloons, and blew bubbles, and just hung out. She was pretty interested in Mommy's handbag and all the shiny things in there. We had brought pictures of Rainer and Leo to leave with her if we were allowed.

The plan was to come back in a month or two—depending on various rubber stamps coming from various back offices—to visit her. Then we'd visit the judge, plead our case that we were capable parents and wait somewhere between ten and twenty more days for the final paperwork to clear. That was the level of precision Boris's friends in the motherland could provide.

Over the next few months, during two more stays, we would be getting to know the Don Plaza Hotel very well. The dill on just about everything edible. The Hypnosis (pronounced GIB-nose) Gentleman's Club downstairs, which advertised with flyers on every floor of the hotel. The towels we wish we had stolen with the exotic Cyrillic letters.

Just before Halloween, we again left Rainer and Leo with Momma Gay and flew to Rostov to see Nina. Our liaison Natasha drove us back and forth and all around to drop off paperwork. Sometimes we went in to the ministry or small back office with her and other times we stayed in the car. After a week of that, we met with the judge and told our story. Natasha translated. My eyes were wet when I described the day we met Nina, her little red dress and jet black hair, and how I fell in love with her as she walked confidently through the door.

We went back to the Don Plaza for more dill, and we waited out the ten more days of bureaucracy.

Then our new daughter joined the family that had been looking for her since the moment she was born. She had watched for four years while other, whiter kids—with smaller medical files—left one of the fourteen beds in her room empty. If we hadn't found each other, she would have started over in a matter of weeks in different state digs. She would have had to try to explain to her new older friends, and to herself, why her parents hadn't found her yet.

It breaks my heart even as I know the story jumped to a

different trajectory with our days together on the orphanage swing-set.

We left the hotel in Rostov for the last time and went to get Nina. It was early November, already freeze-the-tops-of-your-ears-off cold. We were told that the orphanage would be reassured if we brought lots of warm clothes for her. We stuffed her into a new snowsuit from the underground department store in Rostov, wiggled her little hands into mittens, and pulled the wool hat over her head to just above her bright green eyes.

The whole staff had become very fond of her. She was bursting with life. No way to hide it. There were tears and long waves good-bye, kisses on her cheeks and forehead, and more kisses. More waves. We made our way to the car, turning around to let Nina blow more kisses back to her first family, with the feeling that unspeakably amazing things had happened in impossibly magical kingdoms for us to have found each other.

It was November 11, 2011. 11/11/11. A little bit like with Leo and the sailing, I chose to see good omens, or meant-to-be-ness, or magic, or Love, in the fact that Nina and I shared the same birthday, and she was coming home on such an auspicious date. I don't actually care if you can't prove it has any meaning. It does for me. It's a powerful feeling. It comes bounding through the door ahead of all the conscious thoughts and the mechanistic reductionism like a frisky, happy puppy with huge paws getting his first taste of the yank-back of a chain-link choker-leash.

It *feels* like magic, or Fate. Somehow, without evidence, it still feels *true*. Like competing in the zone feels true but is pretty hard to explain. Like falling in love feels true but is pretty hard to explain. Like making love and having time stop, is true.

Nina knows the boys were both adopted at birth. Some nights before lights out, she mixes it up a little. Instead of asking for water, or saying she has to go pee again, or asking can we *please* read one more book, *please*, she opens her heart.

"Why did it take you so long to find me?" Or even harder to hear, "I don't know if I really belong in this family. Why don't we have a picture of my birth mommy, like Rainer and Leo do?"

You can't demur with a seven-year-old. Amanda and I answer her with the truths we have. *We don't know how to get a picture. We don't know where your birth mommy is. We don't know if she's still alive. We will look for her, together, one day.*

We look Nina straight in the eyes, trying to keep our own fears at bay, and hold the hug close until she's ready to let go.

CHAPTER 78

AMANDA AND I WERE RELIEVED that our daughter's name was Nina, which we loved, and not Svetlana, which is also beautiful but not as much our style. We gave her the middle name Stevie, after Amanda's father, Stephen. He died the year before, suddenly and unexpectedly, and it was devastating.

Stephen was, quite simply, the best. Quiet but remarkably intelligent, understated but extremely funny. A good soul, an old soul. He was a great father to his daughters, and husband to his wife, and a great father-in-law to me. I never felt anything but support and a wish to know me, to really see me, from Stephen. We miss him as intensely today as ever.

We wish Stephen could have known Nina. The two of them share a purity in their love for life and an unmistakeable at-homeness with themselves that is very rare. They would have been peas in a pod. It would have been magical to watch them giggle, or plant tomatoes, or play the memory match game, or just look up at the sky and point to the cloud that looked like an elephant.

Stephen, we think of you all the time. We have a little bit of you with us in Stevie every day.

The kids like to remind their mom when she gets sad that "Grandpa is here, right here in my heart, Mommy."

Leo had been on the plane to New Zealand at exactly three weeks old, just like his brother. Nina missed that tiny tradition by a few years. No matter. We were required to live in New York for three months with her because she was adopted by an American couple who lived there. We had pretended to live in New York when we adopted Leo, but we actually lived in New Zealand.

We again pretended to live in New York with my mother-in-law when we adopted Nina, but we actually lived in Spain. There was admittedly a tiny bit of stretching of certain truths and omitting of others. In the case of our children and the lives we hope to share with them, we sleep fine at night with the sense that the ends justify the means. Please don't tell on us.

We couldn't get Nina a US passport until she spent three months on US soil. We homeschooled the boys, or rather we got help with homeschooling by taking them to somebody else's home—while Amanda worked an occasional shift at the Southampton Hospital on Long Island, and I did as much of my work from the basement as I could, instead of onsite in Spain. We took one day at a time with Nina.

Amanda just happened to speak second-year college Russian, which if you knew her wouldn't surprise you at all. In fact, she studied Russian because Stephen had.

Still, it somehow surprised me again every time she spoke to Nina. Amanda's Russian meant that Nina's first few months with her new parents and her crazy brothers and her Nana were about as natural and smooth as any of us could ever hope for.

Later we would move to Berkeley, California, and Stevie would stand up on her desk in class and say, "My name is Stevie now. Please don't call me Nina." She hadn't known a word of English two years before.

CHAPTER 79

⁓

UNFORTUNATELY, BREAKING THE ARTEMIS WING-SAIL just north of Valencia in May 2012 was one of those bad omens that no matter how hard we tried, we never got away from. The builders on the team burnt the candle at all three ends to get the wing in the air for what was essentially an arbitrary deadline. We were the first team to put an AC72 wing in the air. And the first team to break one.

(I would later hear from designers on other teams that it was obvious from the pictures on our own website that it would break. That it would twist itself to death: the ball position—the rotation axis of the front element—was too far forward. They could tell this from their desks, looking at a Facebook photo. Why couldn't we tell it from our own dock?)

We relocated with the team to San Francisco in July after a year of training in Spain for the home stretch to the America's Cup. My family and I settled in Berkeley to continue prepping for the 2013 Cup. The first AC72 catamaran we built—the big, red "AR1"—suffered damage the very first time it touched the water, long before a wing or sails or even the sailing team went near it.

During a towing test, before any water had splashed over the bows, the forward beam cracked. The forward beam of a catamaran is like the chassis of a car. Everything rides on it.

There were more delays before our first sail. Instead of being the first team to launch, like we should have been with our budget and schedule, we were the last. We got some good days on the water in San Francisco Bay, but the speed record for our team remained with the old French trimaran, with its tattered cloth sails and rust stains on some of the bolts.

The new design, with the custom titanium pieces, with the huge wing and the latest carbon fiber cables, with all of our cutting edge computer-model-indicated upgrades, took over a year to overtake the top speed of the venerable old French trimaran with the built-in ashtrays.

The team planned one last sail before putting patched-together AR1 (aka Clifford the big red dog) aside as the spare boat and focusing on the new boat. Not long before that, I took Rainer and Leo up to the Lawrence Hall of Science in the Berkeley hills. We learned about structures. Roman aqueducts, bridges, cathedrals. On the way home, Rainer said, "Daddy, shouldn't your front beam be an arch like the other teams' are?" If only our designers had known what the Romans did....

The second boat, referred to as "the blue boat," would incorporate everything we had learned watching the other teams. There would be no sparing of attention to detail, right down to the hue of blue. Some major modifications needed to be done to the new boat. As things stood, our competitors were going to be flying over the water on hydrofoils, and we were going to be plowing through it. We would be lucky not to be lapped.

Back in October, Oracle had miscalculated the complicated loads on the flying foils and forward beam. They "stuffed the bows" and pitch-poled, lifting the sterns of their catamaran fifty feet in the air while sailors clung by their fingertips for dear life.

The wreckage of the capsized AC72 racing cat was swept under the Golden Gate Bridge by the strong outgoing tide. The Oracle sailors sustained major bruises, various cuts, and a few broken ribs, but the feeling in the America's Cup community was that they had all but cheated death. What had been on all of our minds for a long time was now on YouTube.

Haunted by the video, I took extra care at home with the kids and at work with the team during early 2013 making sure all my ducks were in their respective rows. I doubled my focus on the five hundred channels of data, which seemed to me to be all-important for safety. The hard facts made it easier to keep (unhelpful) emotions or (disastrous) flights of fancy away during this time.

May 9, the very last day that AR1 was scheduled to be sailed, we started a maneuver called a bearaway. It's the most dangerous part of the race, when the boat is at maximum power and the wind changes from pushing the bows up to pushing them down until the forces rebalance. I got a bad feeling in my gut, an instinctual premonition that this bearaway felt different to the hundreds of others I had done. I started moving toward the center of the boat early in the turn. The leeward bow went underwater, and it did not pop back up like it should. It just kept diving. The back of the boat rose into the air, and I held on for dear life and braced for the wing slamming the water.

The impact wasn't as bad as I expected, but there was a sickening noise of inches-thick carbon tearing away from bulkheads, tearing apart at tie-rod joints. It sounded like being inside a thousand year-old redwood as the rate of fall accelerated after the last whack of the super-ax-hacker.

Later review of the photos would show that there was no wing-hit impact. Instead, the front beam, the one that had suffered damage the first time the boat got put in the water before it had even sailed, the one Rainer thought maybe should be an arch, had collapsed.

Andrew Simpson was a very, very good man. The best kind of guy, the kind who lifts everyone in the room with his knowledge and his enthusiasm and his pure heart. I helped pull his lifeless body from the water. It was a horror none of us will ever forget.

We all respond to trauma a little differently. When we got back to shore, I kept walking around in circles for a while saying "We'll have to postpone the team BBQ, again. We'll just have to postpone it again…" over and over. We had tried to have one a few times in the months before, but it kept getting canceled as we had to push to try to cover new delays or new breakages. Somehow that was all I could think about.

My friend Zack called from Connecticut because the crash was all over the news. The helicopter footage of the wreckage was dramatic. It was good to hear Zack's familiar voice.

The following week the kids performed in their school musical. I had to leave. All I could think about was how Andrew would not get to do this. Ever.

Months later, some mornings I would put Coldplay's "Fix You" on, and I would look out at San Francisco Bay at the hole in the water where Andrew's life was extinguished. A choir sang that song at his funeral, and I kept putting myself through it, over and over. I would keel over in anguish, and the kids would give me a hug and ask me if I was crying because my friend was dead.

After witnessing that a few times, Stevie drew me a picture. I'm looking at it right now as I write this.

She said it was me and my friend.

We're both smiling.

There's a tiny yellow sun in the corner.

I started drinking.

CHAPTER **80**

⤷

D ESPITE THE ACCIDENT AND THE now even more compressed time line, and despite the fact that lifting the blue boat out of the water on hydrofoils would put new, unknown-to-our-team loads on our flat front beam, the team decided to press on with the new boat and all the modifications to make it fly above the water like the other teams' boats.

I looked at our poor track record with complicated structures holding up their first time out. I looked at our goal. Artemis wanted to demonstrate resilience in the face of catastrophe by getting this new blue boat, which was not originally designed for flying loads, to the start line by the first race of the qualifying rounds in a few months.

It didn't feel right to me, and I realized I wasn't going to be able to contribute to the effort if I couldn't believe in it. At the time, I struggled deeply because in my mind, true courage would have been to take the time to really figure out what went wrong. To look at the event the way airlines and operating rooms do when they have an accident. System-error and human-error textbooks suggest methods for learning from and preventing accidents, by expanding the discussions away from one discreet moment or root cause.

Amanda attends a weekly meeting called MnM. Stands for

Morbidity and Mortality. Someone's dead, could we have done better? It's not "Who killed him?" Rather, is there any way on God's green earth we can think of now, creatively and together, that we might save the next person whose case presents like that of the recently deceased?

I started researching that stuff nearly a year before the accident. I had a bad feeling, and I hoped by learning things I could make it go away. Maybe even prevent what it was about.

They were not my words, but it was said for months before the accident that somebody was going to die on the red boat.

CHAPTER 81

T HE SAYING "loose lips sink ships" refers to what goes on down at the docks and especially later in the bar, when sailors might speak a little too freely about the boat they crew on. The listener—often the one buying the drinks—can sometimes use the information to great advantage. I never kept my mouth shut at our meetings. To a fault, I am quite sure. I was going to be shouting against a gale if I stayed at Artemis and said what I thought.

The stress of remaining near that whole scene, and the potential consequences of not being able to reconcile all the conflicting data in my various levels of perceptions and understandings, was not a good life choice for me and my family.

It would have been hard enough without the additional risk of biochemical-mental-spiritual volatility. While "self-medicating" with alcohol isn't ideal, it was better than jumping off the Golden Gate Bridge or raving to the media about my perspectives on the crash.

I had two choices. Change what I thought about the whole thing, or take evasive action and steer well wide of the jutting, flaming coral reef marked clearly on the almanac of my upcoming days on the team.

Exposed stress.

It was an unsettled time for our family. We had the kids in private school. In fact, we were crazy. When we lived in Spain, we had them in a British school. You know, to try to keep their schooling in their native tongue while in a foreign country. Once we moved to Berkeley, where the kids were "settled," we thrust them into a Spanish immersion school. Amanda and I both believe languages are good for brains, and practicing for the SATs can wait.

Escuela Biligüe Internacional is an absolutely fantastic school. The kids loved it there. Quintessential Berkeley. Gluten free, but not tuition free.

Just a month before the crash, we had also made a bit of a gutsy call to buy a house. It felt right. So we did it. A few months later, we had private school payments, house payments, somewhat expensive tastes, and I decided I needed to change careers. Amanda was working hard splitting her time between two jobs, but my income had figured as part of the equation until then. We were worried about what might happen if I dropped out of the pro sailing game for long.

What I really wanted to do was be as good a father to the kids as I could, now more than ever after staring life's capricious fragility in the face. And I wanted to be a decent husband.

I was facing many of the same feelings I remember having when I got cancer, summed up best by the reminder to not take anything for granted.

Feelings about re-prioritizing, which a health scare is cliché for causing, but like so many clichés, that one has real teeth. What was really important? Could I imagine myself looking back in twenty years? Would I feel regret if I dedicated my life and time and energy and heart to winning a stupid silver cup, but missed my kids' birthdays and graduations, and never made it to a friend's wedding? Surely the Holy Grail of sailing would more than make up for it. Right? Wouldn't it?

I would probably regret it a little. As we all know, life is nothing if not a long series of tradeoffs. But did I even know who I was anymore? Had the past twenty years of my life been about not knowing what else to do, or not having the courage to do what I really wanted? Finally, who the hell is this "I?" Could I ever even know, if he was essentially living in the (parentheses) of psychiatric medication, still rolling down the lane of life with the kiddie rails deployed so he'd have a better chance of knocking over some little striped pins of plastic Achievement?

About six months before the crash I was pretty worried about how we did things at Artemis. I often muttered, and occasionally said out loud, that "We should treat this more like an airplane with our families onboard." I strongly considered resigning. While I didn't know how to handle my concerns about the data, I believed that the team would be even worse off without me at that point. Because I was the head of a complicated, ever-stressed-for-time-because-our-turn-to-install-our-equipment-was-always-last department, I felt like I'd be letting over a hundred people down if I walked out. Maybe their families too.

I'm not saying I was doing an irreplaceable job. Hardly. I'm saying that I was keeping my fingers in a few dams that I understood the best, and new fingers wouldn't be able to get in those holes overnight.

The job I was doing didn't match the way the team wanted to do things by June. They didn't ask me to leave, but they did remove my authority without a matching removal of responsibility.

I resigned. It was a very difficult decision. For me and for my family. I was probably hammering a nail into the coffin of my America's Cup sailing career. I was probably shutting off the tap of steady income on a large, ongoing professional team. We don't send resumés around at the elite level of sailing. It's all word of mouth. The word was obviously going to go out that I was a quitter when things got rough.

I was encouraged by some teammates to just quietly collect my paycheck and ride it out from the sidelines. That's how I knew who knew me and who clearly did not.

My last day of work was in the middle of June 2013. June 16th, to be exact. Bloomsday to me. Halfway through the sixth month of the calendar year for those of you who don't raise a Guinness for Poldy on that day. For Leopold Bloom. The dude who rescues Stephen Dedalus from himself half way through *Ulysses*. Easy for me to remember, but I really wasn't sure what the sign meant at the time. The signs weren't singing and dancing for me. Not just yet.

CHAPTER **82**

ONE OF THE THINGS I wrote to Dr. Joel Gold as we corresponded about my psychiatric history for a case study in the book written with his brother Iain called *Suspicious Minds: How Culture Shapes Madness,* was that I had "learned my lesson and now that the stakes were so high because I was a father, I'd never go off my medication again." I had meant it when I said it. One hundred percent. But now, after coming so close to being killed because I was still literally chasing a silver cup, it felt like all bets were off.

I had been describing—or trying desperately to convey—to Amanda the sense that I had been feeling like a fraud for some time, when I discovered David Foster Wallace's story called *Good Ol' Neon.* It starts "My whole life I've been a fraud. I'm not exaggerating."

The story goes on to reveal that we're learning about a suicide, as told by the recently deceased, who had been a year ahead of David Wallace in school, and who David had always thought had it all figured out. There are some hilarious scenes with a psychiatrist, there's a great description of what it's like to be exuberant and have everything flash its interconnectedness, but mostly there's a sense that it is really hard to know what it's all about, what it's all for. And that success doesn't help the protagonist in that story with a reason to live.

I found myself not long after the crash in a beautiful house, with a beautiful wife and children, asking myself *Well, how did I get here?* and the much harder question, *Where am I going, and what if I don't ever get there?*

With the rigorous, step-by-step lines of a mathematical proof, I convinced myself—the person who that day sat and wrote it out—that I had convinced my selves, that the answers were invalid if "I" who was "going" and hoping to "get there" wasn't really *Me*. I wish I hadn't burnt it, I'd like to read it again now. It called the MEDS into question, along with everything else I could think of that I used to prop myself up. No wonder I burned it. It proved I was a fraud.

Like the Tin Man looking for a heart, like Philip K. Dick asking over and over about identity, humanity, and reality, and like David Foster Wallace searching for a spiritual compass after the staggering success of *Infinite Jest*, I had to know. I often wish someone had taught me the trick of remembering to forget that Achievements aren't enough. At the very least, it would help me relate to Dad better. But even on medication, me, and (me), myself, and (myself), I, and (I), that consortium of identities and behaviors, knew that for me, it wasn't enough.

I went off my MEDS, started getting up at four in the morning to write, started drinking even more, and told Amanda it sucked to hear she didn't like the new Kevin, but that it was finally the real me. It nearly cost the entity in this body his marriage.

Amanda maintains, and I'm finally starting to believe her— after a year of couples' therapy—that she wasn't actually saying she had one foot out the door. It's taken me well over a year to begin to understand what she was saying when she told me that she had to find the strength to know that she and Rainer and Leo and Stevie could "live without me if they had to." She meant that if things continued to degenerate with my stability and behavior, she had to permit herself the thought that she would rescue herself and the kids.

She meant, also, that she had begun to prepare herself for the worst. For the phone call to come down and identify the body.

I started work as a consultant with a small group trying to marry OpenSubdiv, the Pixar open-source animation code, with engineering software designed to handle the compound curves of cutting-edge composite structures.

I got to go to the NASA Ames Research Center south of San Francisco and help present some ideas. I remember getting a tingle when, unsolicited, the NASA visionary to whom we were presenting told me during very candid, informal chitchat before the meeting that 1. he had just returned from Burning Man (#cool!) and 2. he had just retaken the Myers-Briggs test. He was still an INTP. I too had just retaken the Myers-Briggs. I too was still an INTP. He had a huge, hand-written reminder in his Eistein-messy office: "Perfection is the Enemy of Good Enough".

Anyway, the Myers-Briggs test is an evaluation that some companies and teams use to help people gain insight into themselves and each other. The test is based on the pioneering work of Carl Jung, about the various components of our psyches and ways we relate to and perceive the world. The continuum most people have heard of that Jung essentially invented is Introvert—Extrovert. There are three other pair axes: Sensing—Intuition, Thinking—Feeling, and Judging—Perceiving. Every human has elements of each of the eight ways.

My preferences are for Introversion (over Extroversion), iNtuition (over Sensing), Thinking (over Feeling), and Perceiving (over Judging). It also says that INTPs are marked by a quiet, stoic, unassertive, and aloof exterior that masks strong creativity and enthusiasm for novel possibilities. Their weaknesses include poor organization, insensitivity to social niceties, and a tendency to get lost in abstractions.

My test results suggest that I am just over the line in each of the axes. That maybe one more question answered the other way and the self who (I) know best, the (one) who has spent most of the past twenty-five years under the influence of Depakote, might be an ESFJ. That is, if he weren't the boy in the bubble with the popped-balloon heart.

Maybe even extremely E, and extremely S, and extremely F, and some kind of J. (I'd really like to have taken the test just after climbing down from the rave big top in Auckland at sunrise.)

Now that I wasn't sailing, would my life be any different without the medications? I had some historical evidence in front of me to refer to.

It would probably be different.

There's a very good chance I'd be dead.

Still, it was hard not to wonder if (as the Italians say) I couldn't somehow "have the wine bottle full, and the wife drunk." *Avere la Botte Piena e la Moglie Ubriaca.*

Forget cake.

CHAPTER **83**

⎯⎯ᧁ⎯⎯

A FEW MONTHS AFTER I STOPPED going to work with the last
place America's Cup team and started trying to hide how
much I was drinking, life inside my head was getting really, really
fun. I had about twenty books going. I stayed up late watching
Amanda Palmer videos. I found an old Atari on eBay, and a
VCR at Goodwill for five dollars to convert the RF signal and
get it to work on our huge plasma. Space Invaders with a proper
subwoofer—now that's some daddy-sized badass!

Things started Happening. It's hard to write words here and
give you the creeps like I got, but I'm going to try anyway. I think
with some luck on my part, and some suspension of disbelief on
yours, the words might provide a tiny spec of insight into my
version of mania. The stuff we say has to do with certain special
substance highs, or synchronicity, or madness.

I don't have any answers. Zip. Zero. Zilch. That's not my deal,
just like it wasn't Rilke's. I used to drive the guys on the team
crazy in design meetings and tactical debriefs both, asking oblique
questions that I thought just might lead in a roundabout way
to a little epiphany, a tiny step forward, or even God-willing, a
breakthrough. The questions were always somewhat hard to frame,
so by the time I got to the question mark in my voice, things were
pretty convoluted, and people tended to say things like, "Uh, so,

what are you proposing we *do*? Do you have a *solution*?"

Maybe one of the reasons I chose to scuttle my America's Cup career instead of shutting up and sucking up is that there's just no place for poets. No time for questions that don't have an answer related to saving time, saving money, or proof it will make the boat go faster.

I'm getting more and more comfortable with that not meaning that I'm defective or a bad person, just maybe needing additional varieties of teammates in part of my life. Or, maybe it just means I'm too scared to stick it out, stick with it when it starts to seem repetitive but in fact represents the opportunity to more closely approach mastery. Probably, it's both.

Right, back to the Happenings. Again, I won't be able to make you feel anything close to what it *feels* like. Find the most compelling words ever written about exuberance, about the moment (with or without substances) that you know that you're "jacked-in to the mainframe," or the feeling that your marrow is connected directly, positively, concretely, irrefutably to that of Lucy (the pile of bones that seems to prove that we stood up before our brains got big and not the other way around).

Find the most compelling words about eternity, or about the center not holding. Universes in grains of sand. Royal, infinite space in a nutshell. Tygers and fearful symmetry. They all dance around something which, in a sense, "by definition," defies thought categories and language structures. The stuff *just before* the split between being, and not being. The stuff surrounding the whole inside/outside deal. The stuff that eschews what we call *before and after*.

Sorry. I keep getting sidetracked, but maybe that's the point.

∞

In my experience it is very rare to hear a movie soundtrack on a classical station. Very rare. As in, I never had in my life. Sure,

I have the London Symphony Orchestra *Star Wars* soundtrack (John Williams conducting) on vinyl. I've never heard it on a classical station. Anyway, I made the family watch Steven Spielberg's *ET* with me. The next morning, driving the kids to school, what comes on but the John Williams soundtrack to *ET*. The theme is unmistakeable. Daa DAAA, da da da da Daaa daaa...My skin crawled just a little, but only briefly, and not really that consciously, and I turned it up a touch. Weird, but no big deal.

Maybe you've been singing along in the car before, and flicked the radio on to find the same song playing. Still no big deal. Imagine doing that but finding the radio is playing the song at exactly the part you are singing. Slightly bigger deal, but yeah, still just coincidence.

Who says the Meaning Police don't, by an ironic twist of fate, unwittingly create additional meaning around a synchronicity? Precisely by the mechanism of all the energy they spend trying to refute each particular instance of enchantment.

Maybe, God looks for all those little energy flares, loops through time, and tags those moments with extra meaning.

I'm just saying, the people who are positive that's not true are not necessarily wise.

They might be smart, but that doesn't mean they're wise.

Or right.

⤶

CHAPTER 84

I'M A PRETTY BIG *Alice's Adventures in Wonderland* fan. It sits there on the shelf, and every once in a while I just have to see something. I had put it on the shelf when we moved into the Berkeley house six months before, and I hadn't taken it down yet. One day, I grabbed it and flipped to the Pool of Tears bit. Later that morning, I got an e-mail from the Salvador Dalí society, advertising the edition of *Alice* Dalí did in 1969 with paintings for the twelve chapters. (I was born in '69.)

This time it felt more like a *real sign* than the ET music. I decided, or ((evaporating parentheses)I) decided...*we* decided, that we had to have it. *They* were sending messages again, testing my faith, to see if I was ready and willing to go back on the show, or they were going to have to force me with more aggressive signs.

Amanda knew that I was struggling, but we never discussed my medications or drinking. We had long since identified that the parent/child and doctor/patient roles we had in our relationship since the very beginning (me the child and patient), were not ideal. However she did it, Amanda stuck to her role as friend and confidante and didn't parent or physician me. It would have required that she achieve and maintain some clever denials to not bring up my MEDS and drinking day after day. However, one extremely insipid thing about being a person with bipolar challenges, is that I remain extremely lucid and convincing—if not a little temperamental—right up to the point where I am, most definitely, not.

The better I feel, the sicker I am getting. It's hard for a partner to know exactly where in that upward trend to jump in and say something like, "Hey, it seems like you're really happy and life is really fun for you. We should probably get that checked out, because we both know that means something is terribly wrong."

Amanda wasn't that impressed that I haggled the Dalí dealer down from $9,500 to $9,000. More destabilizing of our unraveling relationship was the sense of betrayal and loss of trust that accompanied my unilateral decision to send along the credit card number.

The conversation might have been something like this (it wasn't actually recorded, as far as I know):

"I knew if I asked you, that you wouldn't understand, and you'd say no," I said.

"How do you know I'd say no?" she asked. Fair question.

"Well, do you want to get a Salvador Dalí *Alice in Wonderland*? I've bargained them down to only $9,000."

"No, I don't. I love Dalí as much as the next wife, you know that. But it's not a great time to be buying art. You might have noticed, you, uh, quit your job recently?"

"I did? Really? How do you know buying this piece isn't my job now?"

"Kev, that's ridiculous."

"So? Maybe that's the point. Maybe the only way *they* can be sure I understand is if I do something ridiculous. Anyway, it doesn't matter. The charge already went through."

"I just wish you would have asked me first."

"But we just said you would have said no. What's the point of that, if I had already decided?"

"But I didn't say no, because I didn't even have the chance.

That's the point. Things like this, we're supposed to do together."

"But we wouldn't have been 'together,' it just would have been this discussion before I sent the credit card instead of after."

"In which case, it's not this discussion, is it? It's a different one, with the possibility of a different outcome."

"You mean with the possibility of what you think is right and what you believe in, not me."

"It has nothing to do with believing in something…."

"It has *everything* to do with believing in something!"

We were on our way from LAX to Legoland in the rental SUV. About this point Rainer leaned forward and asked, "Are you guys fighting? What are you talking about?"

"Daddy and I have different opinions about something, Luv," Amanda said.

"Yeah, she thinks I have to do life her way. Well she's wrong."

Amanda's look when I said that definitely reached me, in the real world. The one that kids either do or don't feel safe in, the one that—when they're talking to their therapist in twenty years—either makes them want to be more like you, or instead makes them want to define themselves in opposition to you. Until that look, I thought we were playing the scene beautifully, the part where the parents have a heated discussion on the LA freeway that the kids are forced to witness, but that ends with the parents both conceding a little and then hugging and saying, "*I love you.*"

Good job. The kids now have a model for working through differences and ending up in a hug.

That's what the Director set up, brilliantly by the way, by putting the Dalí book "on sale" on my computer the moment I pulled Alice off the shelf.

Amanda had probably only needed to practice her lines one

more time, which she must have done in the lavatory on the plane from Oakland to LA, to make sure the conversation kicked off in the right direction.

But wait! That look, the whole *Kev, the kids. We can't do this to the kids…*look. There's just no way she could play it that well. It had to be real; *that was real.* This isn't the show, this is real life. I'm yelling at my wife in front of my children. I have to get my shit together.

Unless…unless…oh, of course! That was the natural next beat for the scene. Of course the mom gives the dad that look, the scene was about protecting the children in the first place. I was about to blow it. I was about to play the tortured-artist rage *dad. The look was just on the contingency plan list, and she nailed it. She absolutely nailed it. Damn, she's good.*

I sat on my hands and looked out the window. *Something's wrong. Oh, that's right. I remember now. I'm not the center of the universe. There is no show. Get it together.*

CHAPTER 85

M Y E-MAIL DINGED. THREE DAYS prior to our family reunion kickoff, I had gotten out the Russell Crowe movie called *A Beautiful Mind.* It's about John Nash, a mathematician who earned his PhD at Princeton in 1950 with a dissertation on non-cooperative games. The work was ahead of its time and has since been named The Nash equilibrium. He earned the Nobel Prize in 1994 for his core ideas from the '50s . The story is close to my heart. Not because I'm smart like that—I'm smart enough to know that I'm not—but because I feel deep empathy for all the wrestling he had to do inside his mind to keep the angels and demons who sat on his shoulders most of the time from ruining him or completely ruining his family.

There's a great quote on the back jacket of Sylvia Nasar's incredibly researched and written biography of John Nash: "How could you, a mathematician, believe that extraterrestrials were sending you messages?" the visitor from Harvard asked the West Virginian with the movie-star looks and Olympian manner. "Because the ideas I had about supernatural beings came to me the same way my mathematical ideas did," came the answer. "So I took them seriously."

Another mind that I imagine to be similar to mine in some ways is that of Philip K. Dick. PKD's imagination and brain chemistry forced him to trust the voices, to believe in them, and to write about it. That was his only out, and he wrote and wrote. His *Exegesis* is a fascinating, looping, Gnosticism vs. Holy Spirit vs. *What if they're the same thing?* thousand-page musings, recursive and expansive both. That takes a certain courage that I positively admire.

Are the voices real? They sure are when they're talking to *you*. As real as anything you've ever known. Pushing them away doesn't seem to work so well. It's more like you have to invite them in, make them tea, ask them to tell you all about it, nod and listen, and finally come through the teatime with the ability to say, "I believe you; what you say is very compelling and makes pretty good sense. But, I also believe this other version over here, of what is Reality. That's my wife. Those are my kids. They aren't actors. They're real. They really, really are real."

Then why doesn't it seem like it?

CHAPTER **8 6**

⤳

A MANDA AND I COOLED DOWN from our discussion of my adventures with *Alice in Family Financeland* while she drove on toward Legoland. The kids each had a device in the back. I scanned the palm trees and the trash on the embankment ice plants, the auto dealerships and the Walmarts, the billboards for ambulance-chasing lawyers and the latest Will Smith movie.

I had felt the vibration in my pocket that says "new e-mail message," but I waited. Ants-in-my-pants, London Falling. I waited. For the delay to pass the decorum test. It proves I still had one foot on the real side of the fence. Amanda and I still shared a space together. Our two solitudes were still touching, but only barely. I was still aware that particular space had rules, had guidelines that expected certain things from me. We were still trying to negotiate further understandings, and I was on standby to do my part. I waited for it to be completely clear that nothing was likely to be put into that shared space by either of us, anytime soon. Then I pulled out the e-mail.

I had been writing quite a lot for the previous few months, ostensibly to start hacking away at a novel. Mostly, it was to find the surface of appreciation for how much craft and plain hard work must underpin any successful art, and to work hard enough so that I could hope to one day scratch it.

245

I was used to training for my sport, and I knew which skills needed to be stronger and which could be maintained. With storytelling, it wasn't like I didn't know whether to bench press or do squats first. It was more like I needed to figure out where to go to get a starter set of arms and a rental set of legs so that I could just touch the bench and see the squat mirror. That was step one. To be aware of how far away from even really starting I was.

I had put the word out to a few friends in a few circles that I was looking for a writing coach, someone to help me wrestle some concepts I had that I thought were decent premises into something vaguely recognizable as a story.

The feeling I am about to try to describe is as otherworldly as anything I've ever known. I appreciate that part of it is the whole "when a person is in love, he is loving the energy of the loving, and the object (woman, music, man, art) is sort of a place to direct that energy." It's probably a state recognizable on a brain scan, and the objects of infatuation might range from Greecian Urns to, well, ducks.

Still, this was my brain, and my channels were pretty wide open. My biochemistry was back to "au naturel" without the MEDS (unless you count coffee). A furious string of what I felt were very strong coincidences compressed themselves quite close together in time.

The ET music on the radio and the *Alice* book were relatively simple to illustrate. There were impossibly many others that don't merit your time but were all similarly disorienting and disturbing, amusing and wonderful and magical and wow. Texts, subtexts. Meta-texts and meta-dialogues, hyperlinks and hyperspace. All localizing in the nexus of nodes of nexuses that was ME.

So, we were driving down the freeway. I was staring at my forearm where I had a new tattoo, and I was thinking about the scene in *Beautiful Mind* where Nash is in the top-secret levels of the Department of Defense, and Ed Harris has the isotope clock for entry codes implanted in Nash's forearm. It's brilliant storytelling. At that point in the movie, we are right there with poor Nash, deep in his delusion. I could just about read the name tag on the fifty-star general briefing Nash/Crowe.

The e-mail that was burning a hole in my pocket had the subject line, "Hello from Victoria's friend." Victoria is a family friend in Berkeley who hosts great dinner parties. At a recent party, about twelve of us sitting around the dining room table had already made good use of the wine cellar when Amanda somehow got me to admit that I was trying my hand at storytelling. (Victoria has been a successful screenwriter for years.) I sheepishly described a little of my project, getting excited for a moment, then lost all confidence and stared, marooned with embarrassment, at my shoes.

Amanda announced with directness and enough dignity for both of us, "Kevin's looking for a good writing coach. He's serious about this, not just fiddling around until he decides he's ready to get back on the water." Victoria and her husband were both immediately supportive. In fact, everybody was. I was confused. The little boy in me was braced for being told that trying to write wasn't very responsible, and it wouldn't support the family. Echoes of my father saying that the fact that my French thesis had won an award was nice because luckily it came with a $200 prize, which I could actually use.

Victoria said to leave it with her, she couldn't promise anything, but she'd see what she could do. Two weeks later, an e-mail arrived. Just as I was climbing aboard my spaceship on the way to Legoland.

Subj: "Hello from Victoria's friend."

This is how it starts:

How nice to "meet" you. Congratulations on working on your book. Everyone does have a story, but not many have the guts to sit down and work it out on paper. Good for you.

By way of introduction, I come from the world of film development where I ran Oscar winner Akiva Goldsman's production company at Warner Bros....

Akiva Goldsman wrote the script for *A Beautiful Mind*. Hello, *VERTIGO*. To whatever extent I had been maintaining one foot in the consensus reality door, that foot was removed by this moment, this psychosis or delusion or dream, or VALIS or karass or synchronicity, or coincidence, or angels. Or Whathaveyou.

Not just, like, can't quite feel that foot because my leg fell asleep or because I've been hiking in the snow for six hours. More like *vanished. Nothing below the ankle. Not a ghost limb, not an outline, not the frayed end of a residue shoelace. What foot? What exactly is this thing you seem to call "foot?" I don't know from "foot."*

I was flung, I was falling, falling down the good ol' rabbit hole, commenting to myself on things getting curiouser and curiouser. The next thing that happened, and that happened every time before, is a very distinct *click*. It's the click of the script flipping.

Not unlike the clapperboard in old movies, or maybe the digital clapper now. Sight and sound synchronized. Except "sight," equals Me, and "sound," equals the Universe. It's a one-way, trap door. The click is the latch closing behind you on the gate back into sanity.

On the other hand, all of a sudden (the French "Tout d'un coup" is better), Everything Makes Sense. Every Memory Fits. Every Moment Was/Is a Stepping Stone. Everything Will Be All Right. The Pain and Suffering Were Part of a Bigger Plan. *I'm exactly the person that I'm supposed to be.*

And for the rest of the trip into Legoland and through the

intervention and back to Berkeley and finally on to the horse tranquilizers, I was on camera, and everyone, as in Everyone, was watching ME.

Kevin Hall, Earth.

Use that address, because your letter will find me.

And, the thing which makes it extra hard to understand why it's wrong, that it's false, is that (me) is nowhere but nowhere to be found on the set. Locked out. Written out. All the way out.

The character arc from prior episodes—a little like watching *Boyhood* but starting when I was in college and ending now that I'm a dad (and with my dad driving a Ford Taurus, not a Shelby Cobra)—still had me bouncing back and forth trying to decide which version of reality was the real one. Which one would still be there even if I stopped believing in it. And as much as I knew and loved my family, when I got to the bottom of the rabbit hole, they all became *They*.

For example, in my mind, while the kids are "at school," they're not at school, they're being trained and drilled on their lines for different situations, to make sure they know how to keep the story going: *We need Rainer to throw a tantrum now, otherwise Kevin will stay too relaxed and start to question the reality of the cameras and the show. We need something just implausible enough that his emotional overload gets him back on track. We have to get to that Red Bull product placement scene by the end of this sequence....*

Most people have had at least one or two little glimmers of something uncanny enough to merit the tag "other". A déja vu that is overwhelmingly powerful and creepy (Science can sort of explain them, so no big deal. Time discontinuities and/or pattern high-level hierarchy in brain signals.) Or, say, bumping headlong into a friend from a former life, someone from your Midwestern hometown, about whom you were just thinking.

Just that instant! But, you're both in Reykjavik, both to interview members of the cast of *The Secret Life of Walter Mitty*, and wow isn't that amazing! (This one is of course explained by the law of averages. Every day it doesn't happen the odds of it happening go up…Really? Is that like every time you throw another heads the chances of getting a tails goes up? Rosencrantz? Guildenstern? Any thoughts? Oh yeah, they're dead.) Or finding a book that was a childhood favorite, and that you have been looking for year after year, right next to the book that your new boyfriend told you to check out at the used book store…Whatever, the point being those little moments, those little tremors which cause us to fleetingly think/feel: *Wow. Maybe there are things we don't completely understand or have equations—or even questions!—for.* Those feelings can come through loud and clear, thick and fast, and be interpreted as *real*. As irrefutable.

Think of John Nash saying his thoughts of messages to him from outer space came to him the same way as his groundbreaking math ideas. We're obviously not willing to say the extraterrestrials put the math ideas in his head. No, they were conceived through the free-will-choice of pursuing them, through training up of intelligence, and some luck. Ghosts just aren't real. Not *really* real, anyway.

But once you're down the rabbit hole, there is no inside vs. outside, no outer space and aliens vs. my own head and its own thoughts. Everything is so connected, the boundaries are so far gone, that it feels like the whole world, which is *for* you, is also talking *to* you, and, well, *is* you.

Now the more of these little moments you have, the deeper the neural pathways get. The more predisposed you are to think that way. And the sooner the next creepy or cosmic occurrence will drop you into one of those crevasses. Each successive episode pushes the record player needle deeper into the groove of the ever-softer LP that is your spinning brain.

A gush of dopamine by the train of evolution that rewards

the organism for recognizing a pattern that might lead *to* a herd of bison or *away* from a sabre-tooth tiger lair.

In the case of the delusional mind, the pattern wouldn't exist without me noting the convergences and being moved by them. A big part of the kinship I choose to feel and imagine with James Joyce and Philip K. Dick has to do with how open they each were with their amazement and reverence for coincidence as a legitimate mystical stance.

(I spent two days at the PK Dick Archives in Fullerton, California. One of his project folders is labeled "The Day the Gods Stopped Laughing." It's full of reverence for synchronicity.)

Another pair of mystics with scientific street cred which should figure in the conversation are Carl Jung (who coined the term synchronicity) and Wolfgang Pauli (one of the early twentieth century's greatest physicists, from whom Jung got ideas and drew courage in his own work). In 1930, Pauli hypothesized the existence of the neutrino. Twenty-six years before its existence could be proven. (In 1956, it was finally discovered/proven by experiment.) His mind worked just fine, thank you very much.

Incidentally, the name *quark*, given by Murray Gell-Mann to the fundamental constituents of the nucleon (as in up, down, and strange quarks) came from *Finnegans Wake*. Anyway, so there I was. Since this isn't a neuroscience or particle physics book, I'll get on with the story.

Like the *ET* music on the radio, like the chances of an *Alice's Adventures in Wonderland* rare picture book coming on the market and into my inbox and my life the very day I pull the book down off the shelf, this *Beautiful Mind* /potential new writing coach occurrence felt way too unlikely to be simple chance. It's not about thoughts. It's not about some long, traceable linear chain of action/reaction, cause/effect.

Sure, evidence of entanglement *seems* to be in your head—but there are no devices by which it can possibly dissuade your heart. Feelings are just plain stronger than a thought. This vertigo felt like there was a guiding hand that made it happen. Felt like the same old immersion in paranoia, or maybe "pronoia" (when it seems like things keep lining up and it hasn't gotten double-overwhelmingly scary yet), which I had experienced in the past, but not in the past ten years. And, it felt like coming home. Like I was finally, after a long time away fighting a war as a drone for some evil capitalist overlord, I was finally home and able to drop my sword and my armor and just be myself again, naked in front of my Destiny. The instant I got to the part in the new email that said "Akiva Goldsman."

I was back on the show. And,

hey, this is the first time my entire family has been on the show with me. Cool!

‍⸝‍

CHAPTER 87

C HECK THIS OUT. It is from Joseph Campbell's *Mythic Worlds, Modern Words: Joseph Campbell on the Art of James Joyce.*

"...his psyche drifts toward the quest for...loving experiences —pleasure, rather than the fierce disciplines. As a result of these kinds of experiences, the person's self-image is lost. And the characteristic result is a split self-image, which is the beginning of schizophrenia. The individual imagines himself to be the outcast, the clown, the fool, [a Fraud?]; and at the same time (on another level, more secretly) he imagines himself to be the desired hero, the one who is going to set right not only his own life, but the whole world. Prominent in the mind of the schizophrenic in this context are the images of world kingship, the divine king at the center of the world, and also savior images."

Campbell is talking about the schizophrenic as a person in touch with his subconscious and about James Joyce as a person who's art sought over and over to reconcile this split. Joyce's daughter was schizophrenic. He was very close to her. When I read those words, it's pretty clear that Campbell is also talking about me. It's a strange loop indeed when you start meditating on the idea that you are the same in your insanity as everybody else....

If there were a punctuation mark which means "exclamation mark plus ellipsis", it would go there.

The reason I had initially written to Dr. Joel Gold and told him about my past, about first having Truman Show Delusion in 1989, is that I was desperate to feel less alone in this world. At the time, I had a great job. An amazing family. It didn't matter. They weren't enough to whitewash Fraud and Alone.

I reached out to Dr. Gold because I saw a news item about Truman Show Delusion that felt like familiar territory. I checked it out, and I felt like I was looking at myself in the mirror. I felt like Truman Burbank, drawing an astronaut's bubble around my little head with a bar of soap, and adding the two antennae and looking up at the heavens. I had even, one time, said to the "camera," "That one's for free," just like Jim Carey does once he's become sure that something is *happening* around him, and he's pretty sure he's got a grip on it. I had also walked across the street with my eyes closed, which is a scene in an early-draft script of *The Truman Show*.

That Joseph Campbell quote, and things like this, are staggering to me. Consider. The mind is one of the most complex (if not the most dynamic) systems known to us. Chaos theory suggests that the most subtle differences in conditions can have massive consequences (this is sometimes called the butterfly effect). Insanity, according to current neurochemical theory about the brain, results from the brain's systems becoming more chaotic. Shouldn't there be as many scripts for insanity as there are complex brains? Surely we have infinitely varying initial (memory) and biochemical (brain state) conditions?

Yet, while each of us is sent down the rabbit hole a slightly different way, most of us end up in roughly the same place, give or take the technology of the day, the culture of the decade, the Zeitgeist. Most of us end up with some blend of delusions of grandeur, paranoia of persecution, and conviction that we've found, grabbed, and pulled back the curtain.

Now.

That. Blows. My. Mind.

Ask anybody. Ask Heisenberg. Ask the Cheshire Cat. Unlikely doesn't mean impossible. That's what kept going through my head when the (responsible me) tried to get the "True-man me" to reject the fantasy that the whole wide world was watching me on TV.

I'm just trying to say here that when the script has flipped, it feels like you've called God's bluff, and with your whole soul, you defy him to disprove that the arrow does in fact point the other way, that what is happening is an unpacking, then unfolding, (re)-discovery of Fate.

CHAPTER 88

I T WAS MY IDEA. I really wanted to get the band back together. There was still a little boy inside me that wanted it to be me and Sis, Mom and Dad. Off to Disneyland, to Space Mountain to see if I'm finally tall enough and to get a new Mickey Mouse hat to add to my collection. Mom and Dad would get along on our full-family reunion at Legoland. Surely. Mom gets along fine with Dad's wife Sandy, and Sis is always so good at smoothing things out if there's a little bump. Dad would do his best. You know, suck it up if there was a little tension.

We met Mom at Baja Fresh. Leo and I especially, but really all the Halls, love burritos. Going to Baja Fresh in Ventura was the closest thing Mom and I had to a regular visit after I moved out from my childhood home and in with my first wife, Annthea. I always ask for a water cup, which is small for a cup for water, but about the right size for a small cup of salsa.

Over my Burrito Ultimo with cilantro and more cilantro, Mom's fish tacos, and Amanda's woes, we caught up on the minutiae of the trip down from Berkeley: They gave the kids extra pretzels on the plane. Stevie sat next to me and had lots to say looking out the window. Rainer finished another Harry Potter. Leo drew another catamaran. Kevin can't wait to see the life-size Lego X-Wing, and are you sure you didn't find all my original Star Wars stuff yet Mom? Mom's Prius is about to turn 100,000 miles. The beach house needs a new roof.

After the kids had (sort of) eaten their lunches, we got the iPhones out and sent them to the park bench outside, under the palm tree in the strip mall with the KMart and the liquor store, the nail salon and the computer repair center. Amanda had to get it through to Mom in code. I don't know if it was an eyebrow raise sequence, or kicks under the table, or maybe just a few quick words when I headed to the bathroom to drain my forty-ounce Coke so I could start on another one.

When I came back out, Mom's look had changed ever so slightly. A super-subtle tinge of sadness, of the helpless despair of a mother who can't protect her son from a pain that nobody can see or touch, that doesn't show up on an X-ray or a blood test. The hug was extra long, even calibrating for the few months since we had seen each other, when she came up to Berkeley to support us after the crash.

I rode with Mom the rest of the way to the Days Inn close to Legoland. Same blanket to protect the backseat of her immaculate Prius, same little trash bucket with the sandbag ears to hold it between the front seats. I don't know what Amanda and the kids talked about, or if they did. I sort of imagine them blasting *Frozen*, and Amanda trying to laugh with the kids about when the snowman loses his butt, yet having a really hard time finding anything very funny.

We were supposed to all go out to dinner, but Sis's flight down from Eureka missed the connection in San Francisco, and so Dad and Sandy waited all afternoon at the airport and weren't up for dinner with the gang.

My mom and my family went around the corner to a place that looked like it would be great, ersatz homemade pies and good meatloaf. The food was terrible. But they had great menus with Dora to color in, and enough crayons that the kids wouldn't be fighting over the only purple one. There was mac 'n' cheese jealousy from the cheeseburger group.

For a little while at dinner, the Director gave me a break. Maybe it was being with Mom, and watching the kids color. Maybe it was the one and a half glasses of wine being just enough to cap the caffeine from the Coke, but not so much as to loosen the screws again. I remember it being a nice dinner for me and the kids. Move along, nothing to see here.

The other group had meanwhile checked in. We said quick hellos and agreed we should all get some sleep for the big first day at Legoland. Dad proudly announced that he had gotten tickets for everyone. We made the plan to meet at breakfast.

Reconstituted scrambled eggs and heat lamp bacon, or turn-the-paddlewheel Raisin Bran and Fruit Loops, or both? How much is too much cream cheese on Leo's bagel, anyway? Is there at least a Starbucks on the way, this coffee is *disgusting*. We all knew the drill. Mom had already looked it up. The Starbucks was a one-exit backtrack.

Sister Kristina had gluten-free organic food for my nephew Blake, age nine. When he isn't hacking the CIA's computers, he's mashing the Grieg and the Schumann A minor piano concerti with a Grateful Dead double-bootleg. Rainer can't get him to wrestle, Leo can't get him to draw sailboats, and Stevie can't get him to practice handstands with her. But they love each other like only cousins can, and when the four of them are on the same server in Minecraft, working together to get some new armor or to defeat the zombie vampire pigs, it's magic. It's really, really special. I can sit there for a long time and watch them, pretending I'm reading, and feel like I'm a good dad and everything's going to be OK.

We arrived at the amusement park, and I was palpably more excited than any of the four kids. All the logos and bumper stickers on all the cars were talking real loud, as we made our way toward the entry gates. Their symbols stood out as if embossed, and they glowed and danced for me, despite being 2-D and inert in the real world. They interlocked with other symbols on nearby cars, and with Led Zeppelin albums, and Celtic Legends, and my Dungeons and Dragons Mage's Spellbook, and probably also some Keanu Reeves movie with Tilda Swinton playing Gabriel. They were alive, and they spun a narrative which is all brand-new and as old as the trees, full of soul and über-clever. The most succinct name for everything that was going on is "the voices." That captures part of the situation, but it doesn't convey just how fluid it all is, and what an unpredictable magpie, out for shiny things, I became.

Calling them "the voices" is something the sane people do from the other side of the latched gate. To me, once the script has flipped and the latch has caught, they're not "voices." They're just reality. Plain and simple. God's honest truth.

There's just no way to know whether or not "the voices" are coming from "outside."

Belief = Reality.

The voices urged me to put my name down for the tour of the time-share. It's perfectly modeled in Lego bricks just *outside* the entrance to the park. Just sign here. I could tell my family was annoyed, but I didn't understand why. Didn't they want me to pause, to give the Director and the show his product placement, so everyone in the family would own one of these little units by the end of the day as a bonus for making sure I stayed tuned in, on point, hit my lines? Didn't they want a nearby apartment of their own so that next year they had a good place to crash when the "Relive the Legoland Day" celebrations went down? (At which I would have to appear to sign autographs and maybe make a cameo on stage with David Byrne)? Didn't they realize how much I was doing for them? Even though I didn't love all the advertising stuff, I wanted to do it for my family.

I guess they didn't. My family remained annoyed, and it was time to move on. Amanda basically gave me a countdown, the one that always precedes a time-out for the kids if they don't get their ship together. I responded as Mommy wished, and we got to the turnstiles, got our tickets scanned and our hands stamped, and headed on in.

I was saving the battery on my Google Glass. They were a hangover from a special project at Artemis. I spearheaded the project, but I also paid for it with my own money in case it flopped. The sky-blue Google Glass was *mine*. Make a movie of my life, from my point of view. #Cool.

Amanda took a picture of me wearing them under my straw Quicksilver fedora, and posted it on Instagram: #midlifecrisis. Little did either of us know just how well I was going to own that hashtag over the next few days, then weeks, then months.

CHAPTER **89**

THERE'S NO MISTAKING DAD WHEN he's disappointed in me. There's the time I knocked the motorcycle over into the convertible 1962 Porsche Speedster, skateboarding in the garage when he had told me specifically not to. The time I took the job looking after his forty-foot boat and the next time he came to use it he basically tripped on the pile of used condoms. The time he and Mom came and picked me up from a 1992 US Olympic Team training camp where I was supposed to be coaching but went bat-shit crazy on a land-locked boat instead. The time I didn't sit with the family at the medal ceremony in Athens.

It's a look I know well, and a look I am certain I already pass on to my oldest son when he lies about forgetting his homework, or the money he stole out of its (former) hiding place in James Joyce's illustrated *Dubliners*, or he trips his sister and says it was an accident. All those things have the common denominator of being *avoidable* with a little better judgement or a little more care. Maturity. They all demonstrate a measurable lack of maturity.

For Dad, what was starting to go down at Legoland was no different. The doctors had told me to take 1000 mg of Depakote every day, for the rest of my life. I took 700 mg, for years, during which time I represented my country in the Olympics, won two races in the America's Cup final as navigator, and devotedly provided for my family of seven (counting the two cats). Right up until I pulled my dead friend out of the water. Right up to the point where it became clear that my athletic career (on the field) at the pinnacle of my sport was coming to an end as I aged out.

Right up to the point where I was so shaken and confused and angry and alone and tired of the rat race that I had to know: if that TrumanKev guy is my true character, what is my fate?

For Dad, the moment I stopped taking the MEDS was a choice, a lack of will, an alignment with the shades of morality that seem to say, "*I might make a mess, but there will always be somebody to pick up the pieces, and I am owed that.*"

I see where he's coming from. I really do. And the discussion gets really hard, and subtle, and dicey from here. It's probably especially hard for Dad because there's no history of mental illness or suicides or even alcoholism in our family. I just happened to be this way, but I don't even have a long genetic tree full of shaded squares and X'ed out circles to show that I was always going to be at risk for melting my own wings. Since it's not in my genes, I must *really* be choosing to allow this to happen. (Oh, and about those genes. You really should have banked sperm, Son. It's *my* progeny too, you know.)

I've been reading a lot of amazing memoirs lately, primarily about the different perspectives of living with addiction and schizophrenia. Each one wrestles with the highly charged but razor thin fence between force of will and power of illness, between choice and compulsion. Some might say between "good" and "bad," but you won't find me among them.

"There is nothing good or bad but thinking makes it so." Hamlet says this right after telling Rosencrantz that Denmark is a prison for him, and that he could count himself king of infinite space, were it not that he had bad dreams.

For those of us with neural risks, whichever route may have been put before us to seduce us into the dungeon, whichever route we may have stumbled on to emerge from a thicket of simple celebration or commiseration only to pitch headfirst into the roaring rapids of glass and fire, it's all about bad dreams. About feeling so isolated and lonely, so disillusioned and confused, so optimistic with no supporting evidence, so pessimistic with the history of mankind to back it up, so fraudulent and uncomfortable taking up space in a room or taking air from the sky, so utterly wrong in our own skin, that waking life is terrifying, and feels more like an impossibly bad dream, more purgatorial, than any nightmare ever did. And it sure seems like the only way to wake up from it is to look for the ghosts we feel might be our best friends. The ones in books and stories where the hero isn't just trying to graduate from a Porsche to an Aston Martin to prove he's legit. The stories where people mean what they say, and do what they say they will. The stories where fathers accept their sons for who they are, and are proud of them just for putting one foot in front of the other day after day, no matter how crooked the path. The stories we think we can climb into through the picture frame on the wall, if only we just get our brains to work slightly differently.

And a lot of it is right there. Control. What we *can* make happen. If we can't get the world around us to change, and we're wise enough to realize that it never will—at least not in a time frame and manner that will soothe us enough—there is another, obvious strategy. Change ourselves.

I don't know what I want. All I know—and I know it balls to bones, is that I don't want the spiritual-sensory-deprivation-chamber-life I have right now. Not how I feel right now, and, much worse, not how it must be now and forever if nothing changes.

They say insanity is doing the same thing over and over and expecting different results. Well, if I get up in the morning sober, or with my restraining bolt on, and the world is just as lonely and scary as it was yesterday, and I tell myself don't worry because tomorrow when I get up it won't be, doesn't that make me insane? Don't I demonstrate my sanity by pushing off? Don't I show I get it by admitting that the world may not change, but I can? To the extent that the world is what we make of it, and the world is how we imagine it and see it and process its signals, PRESTO! I've just changed the world. *I* did that.

For however long, it becomes something other than the prison I am so familiar with. What it is now doesn't matter. Has absolutely nothing to do with it. All that matters is that it's different. The damsels *have* to be fairer, and the trolls *have* to smell better, and the wine *has* to come further up the cup in any other dungeon, right? Surely that must be right. God just wouldn't make a world where that's not right. He just wouldn't.

The only problem is that I haven't just changed it for me. Although I think I have control at the beginning of the motion to alter reality, very soon afterward, as in pretty much immediately, the bus is being codriven by an illness, and the illness is much, much stronger than Odysseus's will, and the giant has a thousand eyes, not one.

Now, I understand that the timeframes all vary. It can happen with the first hit of crystal meth, or it can happen slowly and insidiously over years and years of Wild Turkey, or it can happen when you go off your MEDS, sooner or later. But for all the differences those branching paths have, they are all roads for humans, and they all lead to the same place eventually.

So where do we look for this hope that we're seeking? Hope requires love, and love requires patience, and patience requires trust, and trust requires faith, and faith requires, well, more Faith. And when your family stops believing in you and your friends are long gone, and the money's run out and the hospital bills are mounting and a truck goes by and splats a muddy puddle that gets in your eye and extinguishes your very last smoke, when hope's just a word that maybe you've seen, or sometimes you've heard—well, there is **one thing, and one thing only**, for that: You fall back on your addiction, choosing the poison you know over the agony of being buffeted along in life's torrents to slam into rocks or be held under by an eddy.

Unless you count suicide. Then, there are two.

CHAPTER 90

THINGS WERE GETTING MESSIER by the hour at Legoland. I would tell my family that I needed to go check something out, and we'd make a time and place to meet back, and I would wander off, making up stories in my head, marveling at the beauty of the Lego models, and of the trees and the little boats that went around an amusement ride with little guide rails, the beauty of the uniforms of the Legoland employees, and of all the different kinds of strollers, of the plastic lunch trays and the life-size X-wing fighter, of the trash cans and the trash itself. Everything, every thing I saw, every sound, every thought and memory and idea for today and vision of the future, they were all beautiful.

I was doing the scene now about how badly the overlords of advertising have us by the short ones when it comes to kids and the shit they want us to buy for them. Here we finally are, having saved up for two years for the family vacation to Legoland (it took us a little less time, but in the scene in my head, my family had been looking forward to this for twenty-four months, and made sacrifices to save enough to be there). The kids are excited, and jacked up on the energy of the amusement park, the thrill of seeing all this stuff up close in real life, and they want a souvenir. And it's just not a very rational decision the parents get to make, is it? It's all tied up with emotions and basically whether or not you love the kid. If you don't buy him the biggest Lego set in the store (which guards the exit like a dragon of capitalism), well you must just not love him as much as the parents in the next line love their kids, right?

I stood in the corner of the store, stood really still, and sang at the top of my lungs. Sang Alanis Morissette's "That I Would Be Good." It imprinted on me when I was in the bin in Auckland in 1999, and it never left. Not my head and not my soul. I played it for Amanda when she came back into my life later that year. And, our wedding dance was to that song. For a few strung-together split seconds during the wedding dance, even all medicated up, the cameras rolled on Amanda in white, on me trying not to step on her toes in my red shoes. I've never told Amanda that, but I think it's plenty interesting. Brain chemistry, or glimpses of divinity?

I stood in the back corner of the store, holding the Sydney Opera House Lego Set in front of me, and I sang. "That I would be good...even if I did nothing." It's not that long a song. I'm sure the family was relieved (and the fellow shoppers definitely were) that it wasn't "Stairway to Heaven." C'mon, Director. I can't do better than that. I *want* that Lego Set!

I just helped you sell a thousand of them. Callers are standing by! That more than pays for mine.

It became very clear that Amanda didn't love me, because she wouldn't buy the Opera House for me. (Later, when I spoke to Rainer about the whole thing, and what it was like for him, he said, "It just seemed like you were a kid that day Dad. A big, little kid. And, one who wasn't getting everything he wanted." He couldn't have been more on point.)

Eventually, it was pretty clear that decisions were being made around me about whether or not I would respond to requests to please leave quietly with the family. I finally jumped into the middle of the conversation.

"Look if we're trying to organize an intervention for someone in the family, let's just be straight up about it," I said.

"Hmm?" Amanda said.

"I'm ready for my intervention. Let's go after seeing the 4-D Chima movie," I said, proud that I managed to advocate for all five kids. (Rainer, Leo, Stevie, Cousin Blake, and Kevin). "Then we'll get started, OK?"

I'd like to think that was me doing my best, and doing pretty well.

CHAPTER 91

WE GOT BACK TO THE Days Inn and my brother-in-law, Uncle Bud, took all the kids. Four kids, one small hotel room. Sugar low, amusement park energy crash, Dad acting really weird and a little scary. I'm told they listened to a lot of Bob Marley, and they built all the small Lego spaceships that we bought on the way out of Legoland.

Just before the meeting, I checked one last thing on my iPhone.

"What's that?" Amanda said.

"Oh, nothing," I said.

"Doesn't look like nothing," she said.

I was checking to see if my life insurance policy was paid up.

I took up position on one of the queen beds. Dad sat in a chair opposite me, Kristina next to him, Mom next to her and Amanda sat on the other bed. I'm glad I couldn't see her very well. It was breaking my heart that I was breaking her heart and tearing down the world we had built so devotedly together.

It says on the inside of my wedding ring "The love that has graced our lives." It's from a Cowboy Junkies song that goes "And there in the silence they search for the balance between this fear that they feel, and a love that has graced their lives." There had been fear, and love, then fear and love over the twenty-four years we had known each other, and the twelve and a half we had been married. We had started to find a balance, sometimes in silence, sometimes with all three kids screaming at each other, sometimes all five of us singing the Sublime song "What I got" with the windows down. This, now, was all fear, all the way around the room. The love was there too, but it's hard to feel it with so much fear.

Dad wanted me to understand that when I chose to become a father, I embarked on an unspoken contract to provide for my family and to not fuck up.

Mom could tell I was really hurting, and really trying, and I could see the pain on her face that she couldn't make it all better with just a hug. Sis, well, she comes into her own at times like this. She used to go to Guatemala and buy up all sorts of clothes and handbags and bring them back and follow the Grateful Dead around in her VW van, selling the colorful clothes and bags and grilled cheeses (and I'm not sure if there was anything else) out of the back of the van. She had seen one or two bad trips in her day. She had felt connected to the universe and to the vibe and the humanity around her as the beach balls bounced around the stadiums. Later, we would talk about how much of a breakthrough it was for her to see me that way. She realized that we were a lot more alike than she had ever imagined, that we were both all about the connections, and the opening of doors, and the questions, and the feel of it when that stuff all rolls around in your belly and your heart.

Un-illogical modalities of the inimitable.

Amanda had it tough that afternoon. She loved me fiercely, truly, madly, deeply. She also loved the kids and would do anything to protect them. And it was looking like I wasn't going to be a very good daddy, for some period of time. I interrupted our discussions at one point to ask if I could go next door to my room to get my book. There was reluctant agreement. I'm sure there was also fear that I would bolt and never come back. Dive off the first bridge to splash onto the freeway, or hitchhike to

Mexico. They would not have been unwarranted fears.

I came back almost right away, hopped up on the bed, and began flipping absently through *Every Love Story Is a Ghost Story*, D.T. Max's biography about David Foster Wallace. I had stayed up all night to finish it, underlining more and more as the pages passed. I read in the bathtub with a blanket over me, while Rainer slept in the bed in the "intervention room," and Amanda, Leo, and Stevie slept in the next room. I knew David Wallace had committed suicide, but I didn't know exactly how old he was, and I didn't know it was on September 12th. He was forty-six. I had just turned forty-five. That scared me.

Rainer slept on his back, with both arms straight out. I had never seen him sleep like that before, and as far as I was concerned, he was showing me that he knew I was being asked to be the second coming, and he supported the plan, and he just wanted to make sure I knew that my own son was there for me, arms on the cross that was a Days Inn scratchy bedspread.

This is what I said to my family:

"It's different. You all want to believe it's no different, but it is. You have to be in my shoes to know how it feels. To know that once you strip away all the bullshit and it's time to stand and deliver your seed to the next generation, well you try facing that kind of failure. I feel like a machine made to put little pills in little bottles, made for exactly that, and, well, there aren't any pills are there? I can tell myself I'm just like all the machines in all the rows next to me, but that's a lie. We all know it's a lie. It's a lie to try to make me feel better, and to make you all feel better. Guess what? It doesn't help. Not if we're honest. Which is what this is about, right here, right? Being honest. Well, I'm here telling you that until you see what a failure I am through *my* eyes, you will never understand how hard it is sometimes…"

Well, what do you say to that? I still think it's shit that words can't touch. What if I just decided it was OK for those feelings to be real?

CHAPTER **92**

MOM SAID SHE COULD COME BACK to Berkeley with us to help with the kids while I had my *time out*. I agreed with the unanimous call to check myself in. I drove with her to the airport. I asked if I could please smoke, sitting in the back of the Prius. She said no. I turned my Spotify up. I listened over and over to Eminem's "Slim Shady": "I'm Slim Shady, yes I'm the real Shady, All you other Slim Shadys are just imitating…"

We flew back to Berkeley without much incident other than me being a little distracted, not unlike a little kid who sees a stuffed animal in the next check-out line over and forgets to tell Mommy he just wants to see how soft it is. We landed, drove up into the hills to the house, put the bags down, got the kids snacks, I gave them big hugs good-bye which maybe they didn't totally understand, but maybe they did, and we got back in our own Prius and drove back down the hill to the Emergency Room.

I cried the whole way. The (me) that really did make a commitment to be there for my family was letting them, and himself, down. I wanted to go back to how it was before.

However, I needed to know what would happen if I found a way to keep myself together but take less MEDS. Not none, less. (Argue about whether I should have said "fewer" on your own time, please). Or maybe different ones? Is Depakote the only kid

271

on the block for people like me? What, exactly, does it mean, this "people like me?"

What if I risked a little more? What if I risked failure? What if I let my heart see the open road instead of continuing to hang a sign over the front of it like storm shutters that said *"I've Achieved! I have stuff, lots of stuff, which proves it!...Ergo, I'm OK. See me here, I am of value, I matter, I count, I not only own this spot that I'm standing on, but I deserve it, and you better watch out because I sort of think I deserve yours too because I'm clever and I'm shrewd and ruthless and it's kill or be killed and guess what, I'm the one with the lightsaber. Don't make me force the point."*

What if? Because that, there, wasn't the droid I was looking for, to be.

If I hadn't been raised an atheist, I would say I'm looking to be closer to God, and to serve.

CHAPTER **93**

I MAINTAINED A PRETTY GOOD SENSE of calm and of humor with Amanda when the tears finally stopped. The admitting folks were relaxed at the ER. I showed them some little magic tricks with my Lego necklace, how to bend and rotate and pass it through itself so it looked just like the design on my NASA shirt. Which, it sure seemed to me, looked like a sperm in elliptical orbit around a sun, or was I the only one seeing that? One of the admitting nurses asked about my Google Glass, which I was wearing again.

He got more than he bargained for. I definitely had fun. He was a good sport.

Once the paperwork was done, next stop was around the corner to lockdown. They handed me my gown, and I changed and slumped onto my creaky bed in the corner of the sterile room. My window had a look out onto the street.

I was pretty disruptive the first two days of Group. Mostly the passive disruption of somebody sitting in the back flipping through a magazine, when the group leader needs him to join in to have a successful group. I didn't want to be in any groups, and I didn't want to talk about anything. I just wanted more food than what they gave me at lunch, and I wanted my old friend the smoke break. Why do some old friends only seem to show up when you're far from being at your best? Worse, some old friends mean you're back in with the wrong crowd.

I took my downers and hoped for the relief that would come with sleep. I only got up three or four times the first night, which isn't bad. Polished stainless steel with a few scratches doesn't make the best vanity mirror, but it was clear when I looked at myself that I was sad and disappointed, and a little confused about how I got there. Not like which way the ambulance drove up Shattuck Ave., but more "Where did this really start? Where, exactly, did I go wrong? What really set me off to land me here? Or was it always just a matter of time and my number was up?"

I had nightmares about the crash. I had dreams about meetings with all sorts of structural diagrams and, like, Dalí-esque crutches with long shadows holding up parts of the boat as it was rolled to the water.

I kept flashing to Rainer sleeping on the hotel bed with his arms directly out and clinging on to that as confirmation or proof that the story in my head was correct. I tried to read, anything, but I couldn't yet. That happened every time, and it was disorienting and infuriating every time. A lifetime of improvement with patience doesn't get you ready for living with a brain inside your skull that is no longer able to do something as fundamental as reading.

Day three, up on the patient white board, I saw "Name Risk" next to my name. That worried me, I didn't know what it meant, but it seemed really important. Then I saw him. His name I mean. I saw his name. Two rows below me. Another Kevin. He must have been watching me because just after that he sidled up, all scruffy red beard and cradling a big book, and he said, "You're the other Kevin," and he held his hand out. I shook it, but in a pathetic, dead fish, wet noodle way. It's weird to try for a firm handshake then watch yourself end up with that. He gave a gentle smile. *Hang in there; it starts to get better soon*, his eyes seemed to say.

"Do you like Stephen King?" Kevin asked, holding up the big *Dark Tower VII* hardcover with the great gunslinger and the roses on the cover.

Gunslinger and roses...hmm, let's see : Guns n' Roses, G n' R, Patience...Patients...Paid Shunts...Laid Cunts Made Runts Frayed Stunts. I need a Blunt.

"Love Stephen King. Have you read the whole series? Cool," I said. "I haven't yet. Is it OK to read backward?"

"Yup," Kevin said. "Look. I'm almost done with this one, and I'm supposed to leave today. I'd talk to you more right now, but I want to finish it so I can give it to you."

"That would be so great, man. Wow, thanks. Thanks a lot. OK. OK. Can I get you a coffee or something?"

"Just keep Betty Bible over there away from me; she doesn't seem to be able to leave me alone, and I've had enough of Elijah for one day," Kevin said. He smiled, the one with the wink and nod and twinkle as if to say, *Yeah, our friends and family might think we're a little loco, but they should see this dame wandering around muttering holy Scripture, bumping into walls and asking if she can kiss us. Now that's crazy.*

Sometime that evening, Kevin handed me the book, and we told each other good luck, and I never saw him again.

When your channel is wide open and all the information in the galaxy seems to be pouring in and you can't organize much of it around any stable paradigms, something as concrete as *Them* choosing to give you a little break and a little hope by sending in an actor to pass you just the book you need to be reading right now, and having that character given your name, for comfort, to reflect yourself and see yourself's near future as represented by him walking out the door...well that was compassionate of *Them.*

∞

I came down pretty quickly. Within a couple of days I was docile and going through the motions in Group, I was sharing my food when people seemed to really want the Salisbury steak, I was cleaning up the mess at the coffee station when the same feral woman missed her cup with three packets of creamer and about seven packets of sugar. I offered to pour it in there for her, but then I noticed her hands weren't really shaking.

"It's not for my coffee. Shhh. I shouldn't tell you this, but that's how they get in your head. Through the sugar and creamer. Nanobots. So I pretend. I pretend to put it in my coffee so they don't know I'm on to them, but I miss, see, and they can't tell that's on purpose, and so they leave me alone. Oh, oh, I see you already swallowed some. Or was that milk? Did you find real milk? Where? Where? Don't let them in. They never stop…" and with that she walked away, presumably in search of milk for an uncompromised latte.

I asked to have a different shrink assigned to me. The easiest way to put it is that the first one was too perfect. By the book, all the exact right questions, into the details of exact blood levels, wanting to start working on my support-net plan even though the need for it was a ways off. Was there anything on my mind that I thought my family should know? Did I appreciate that the competitive world I lived in was a real echo-chamber, that it was easy to lose oneself in a hall of mirrors of quest for outside validation?

You don't say.

Just like they had rewarded me for good behavior and sent an angel of sorts in Kevin, my new doc was way better. Not only that, but they told him to say that he had done his residency with my friend Dr. Gold. That really perked my ears up. Nice detail, subtle, easy to implement, but guaranteed to achieve a strong positive reaction from me. Really good bang for buck.

Promote that researcher/script writer.

(Did I mention Dr. Gold was my year at Brown but we didn't

know each other? We didn't meet until I wrote to him at age forty-three about Truman Show Delusion. The dude who named the private movie in my head lived just down the hall from me the first time the cameras rolled up there.)

Just like sending in someone "named" Kevin, having my shrink cast as a friend/protégé of Dr. Gold's was a *sign*. My version of reality *was* right. Otherwise, how could something so unlikely happen?

Why are they having me do scenes in a mental ward right now? I'm sure the viewers have had enough of this set piece. Plus, Jack Nicholson and the silent Indian did it way better than I'm managing.

I remember Rainer, Leo, and Stevie coming to visit me. I remember the day Amanda brought me a little headphones radio. (No cords.) I remember trading juices for chips, and arguing about the movie on movie night, and listening to a woman tell me how terrible she felt that this had happened again. She really hoped her husband didn't leave her this time. But he said he would, he really would she better believe it, if it happened again. She really hadn't seen it coming. Did I know what she meant?

I remember finally getting out of the hospital. There is a tiny element of relief, of accomplishment and progress at getting past the symbolic and real gates. There is a huge element of internal panic: what if I can't keep it together, and this is just the beginning of a new cycle of troubles? What if the stress from this means I have cancer again? What if people hear I cracked and decide that the reason I was so strongly opposed to the blue boat at Artemis is that I was crazy? What if I never feel anything again? What if Amanda wants a divorce now? What if this is it? Me and Sisyphus, sharing a hill and a boulder until the end of time. What did I do wrong? Why me?

There's still only one answer:

Why not?

On the really good days, a meek voice manages to disagree with "Why not?"

Instead, it tells me, "Because *they're* prepping you for service."

Interesting.

CHAPTER **9 4**

⤚

F AST FORWARD A YEAR, AND we're back to the day before
Thanksgiving, when I asked what the Legoland time had
been like for Dad, or if he wanted to talk about raising a son
with mental illness. I'm still wrestling with his words, and I fear
I always will, no matter where I happen to find myself on the
whole forgiveness continuum:

"I felt disrespected. I couldn't believe I had to waste a
thousand dollars and a week of my life to be a part of that."

A few months later, after some deafening silences between
us and some seriously cryptic transmissions, Dad stated plainly
in an email that Legoland was hard on him because I had let
Amanda and the kids down.

That read as a slightly different perspective than what he had
told me in person at Thanksgiving, when it was about how much
he felt disrespected and how much money and time the week
cost him. I don't remember the kids coming into it at all back
then. Maybe after sitting with it awhile, he wasn't that happy
with that self-portrait and figured I needed to be reminded of my
responsibilities, and while he was at it, reminded that I should
maybe finally try to "do the best I could."

Good call, hadn't thought of that.

Dad's e-mail infuriated Amanda, and you just don't want to do that. Here's what she wrote back from the new public library in Devonport, New Zealand, looking out over Auckland Harbor while two washed-up old America's Cup boats sailed past with heaps of tourists onboard. Right around the corner from where Lorde cut her teeth on wedding rings in the movies.

Her subject line: The Doctor Weighs In.

Dear Gordon,

I hope that it is OK that Kevin forwarded me your recent e-mail exchange. Kevin and I do a lot of talking, about all things, but in recent weeks and months a fair bit about the relationship between you and Kevin and how it has changed form and content over the years, how it informs Kevin's parenting, and how it relates to where Kevin is in his personal spiritual journey. I feel at this point I would like to participate in the conversation, specifically because your last communication appears to speak on my behalf and I would like to take this opportunity to speak on my own behalf.

In your last e-mail you write about your experience in Legoland. If I understand correctly, you expressed the idea that, for you and Sandy, the upsetting part was not how it affected you as Kevin's father, but how it seemed to be affecting me and the kids. While I recognize that you and Sandy love me and the kids, and want to spare us all from harm or trauma or upset and all the repercussions those might entail, you never asked me what my experience was like. You never asked me if I thought Kevin was "doing his best," as you put it. And it leaves me with the realization that you really don't understand what our experiences of Kevin's mental illness have been. And that is simply because you have never asked, either of us.

As you accurately pointed out, once Kevin and I reunited in 1999 (and even at times during our earlier college relationship) his struggles were our struggles as a family and no longer your responsibility. And as a family we have thrived. We are a loving, tight, resilient clan of five. We laugh and we cry together. We fight and we make up together. We adventure and we explore and we learn about the world together. We wonder at the brilliance of the stars, rocking with the waves anchored off Rangitoto together, and we eat ice cream on Sundays together. We cook and run under the back yard sprinklers, we play Monopoly and we clean our rooms. We ride bikes and sail Optis and do math homework and struggle with learning to read together. We wonder if we are making the right life decisions and we dig splinters out of the kids' feet when we told them to wear shoes. We argue about using the iPhones too much, we have family movie night on Saturdays together. We wonder about birth mothers together and ask how we found each other and what makes us a family. We learn and forget Spanish together, and try new foods that we like and some that we don't. We pick up towels off the floor constantly and we feed the cats together. We fix broken washing machines and empty the dishwasher together. We sit in silence on the swing together and play music too loud for the neighbors and dance in the living room together. We mourn the loss of my dad in an instant, and wish we could have been together instead of oceans apart when we heard the news. Together we watched my mother waste away to nothing and take her last breath. We held her hand and wished it weren't so, and wished we could have done it differently together. We miss the mints she used to give the kids and we remember planting tomato plants in the back yard with Grandpa together. We talk about the not knowing and the knowing and all the not-so-sures together. We read Harry Potter together and watch Youtube videos and look things up on Google when we want to know about snakes or the moon or why boogers are green or what whales sound like. We walk on the beach together feeling the same sand beneath our toes, and we stand awe-struck at the sunrise over the soothing skyline of Rangitoto volcano every morning, and pretend we are surprised it's still there. And we are thankful together.

We are a family, and that is what we have done with the challenges that we have been presented. That is what it looks like for a family, just like any other family, to grapple with the questions and marvel at the beauty of the world. Except we have done all that, and more too. We have borne witness to one of us strapped to a gurney in a mental ward, and we have not been sure how to answer the question of "can I bear to wake up again tomorrow," and we have had to discover what it means to be oneself in the face of mind altering medication, and we have wondered every day how to show the kids that to be human is to falter, but we will catch each other when we do. And through all of this, through twenty-five years of gut wrenching self exploration, we are stronger and more in love and more at peace than ever before.

And so you wonder if Kevin is living up to his responsibility. I ask you, what responsibility is that? When music sounds so beautiful it brings him to his knees, he wonders if he is sick. When food tastes good or his laughter comes from his belly with an honesty that can't be faked, he wonders if he is sick. When words come easily, when thoughts and ideas and connections flow with ease and simplicity, he wonders if he is sick. When names are on the tip of his tongue and strangers remind him of movie stars, when books delight him and movies resonate with his soul, he wonders if he is sick. When he picks a layline with ease or senses a wind shift before he can see it on the water, or rejoices in the bounty and beauty of the sea that has loved him all his life, he wonders if he is sick. When he is happy, he doesn't marvel at how wonderful it is to feel at peace with the world like the rest of us get to do. He gets to wonder if he is getting sick. So you ask about responsibility, and I would answer you this way. Yes, he is meeting his responsibilities. He is meeting those responsibilities whether he is happy or sad, sick or well, manic, depressed or somewhere in between. His only responsibility is to himself. Because the only real achievement worth anything at all is self-knowledge and self-love. And from that, everything else follows. And the part that is not evident to you, is that Kevin's life-long struggle for self love is what is keeping him alive— keeping him here as a father and a husband. And god knows we need him here. It is messy and it isn't always kind, but it is honest and it is essential. Because after all, he is alive, despite his body and his mind's best effort to destroy him. He chooses life, every day, every morning he gets out of bed, and every minute he puts one foot in front of the other. And he does it with grace and honesty and integrity. And one of the only things missing is the love of a father who accepts him for who he is and respects his journey without wondering if he is "doing his best."

And if you need to measure it in terms that are more familiar to you, the facts are equally astounding. He has provided for his family with consistency, hard work, and determination without fail. We have three beautiful, intelligent and curious children who love him without bounds. He has a house with no mortgage, the respect of his peers and wider sailing community, and a growing fan base in the literary one. He is an Olympian, and world champion, and a published columnist. He is an A list navigator, and coach, his peers being counted on one hand, more highly paid than almost any other because of his unique mix of math skills/computer skills/talent/artistry/fairness/integrity/humanity. And he writes words and stories, essays and commentary, articles and love letters, with clarity, craft and beauty.

So, in the event that you had asked me, I would have answered you with a resounding NO, the kids and I do not feel let down. We are lucky to have a man such as Kevin as our father and husband and friend.

But of course you would already know this, if you knew him.

With love,

Amanda

D AD STILL SEES MY MANIC EPISODES as "indulgences," as me choosing to have fun at everyone else's expense. And, obviously—as he always has—as avoidable with even a half-speck of consideration for others and exertion of some trivial amount of willpower. It just shouldn't be that hard for you to take your meds, Son.

Recently, as in a few months after her letter, Amanda gave Dad an hour and a half on the phone to either backpedal, or add addenda, or highlight the subtleties of his view and suggest that perhaps they sound a bit black and white when put that way. He didn't, and he won't, because he can't. So be it.

Kafka wrote a long letter to his father saying he agreed that the difficulties between them weren't his father's fault. But, um, well, didn't that maybe perhaps mean they also weren't young writer Franz's fault, either?

I forgive Dad; it just brings me full circle to the point that it's pretty hard on our relationship. I love my father, I will be there to hold his hand when things start to go really quiet, but I can't afford to beat myself up anymore. My "indulgences" have been hard enough without adding layers of guilt about a failed relationship with Papa.

Wait a minute. Here I am, with all the love and support of a wife and kids, a mother and sister and friends. Here I am with a roof over my head, employment, hobbies, books, challenges, and joy. I even know my father loves me in his own way. (What does that even mean?)

Here I have been all these years, doing something sort of pretty much like "doing my best." Even excelling (why was that so hard to say?)

Over there's my dad. He's educated. Hell, he's actually a recently retired doctor. And he sees the manifestation of my psychic pain as me choosing indulgence. Like it's fun. Like things were going super duper hunky dory until I spinelessly indulged myself. Like I had a choice.

Choice. My dad, of the doctors' Hippocratic Oath, could choose to see my ups and downs as part of a larger struggle. Could choose to see that my self-loathing and isolation and anguish have their own, sovereign existence in this world. Could choose to believe that I am doing my best to live with those very, very, very real demons.

And if he isn't ready to do that, he could choose to face his own fears instead of asking me to carry them.

∽

CHAPTER 96

ABOUT SIX MONTHS AGO, I changed my medication for the first time in nearly twenty years. We were settled back in New Zealand. The kids were in a great public school a short walk from the house. Amanda was back with good friends at Auckland Hospital. I had some modest opportunities to coach, or to navigate professionally a few times a year.

We were in a position in the family to take the risk.

It started out really bad. The new shit (Lamictal) seemed to rush into my brain like a shot of cement. It shut me right down, scary down, not-get-out-of-bed down. Bad Thoughts down. There's a complicated transition regime, and it's necessary to follow it precisely. My body didn't break out in a rash, which is one very dangerous risk of the transition. It sure didn't seem like I was headed into space anytime soon though.

We stuck with it.

The problem was, the new stuff bolstered the old stuff, so in effect I had three helpings of downers onboard. Once we could be sure the new stuff had taken, and we came off the old stuff, things started looking up pretty quickly. Music sounded pretty good. Colors came all the way back. Laughter became involuntary again, instead of cued by context.

Anger crept near.

A very short temper arrived.

I had never really had a temper before.

(For the record, by no means does this does prove that the biochemical view of mental illness is the whole story. It does seem corroborate strongly that it is part of the story though.)

Things didn't used to bother me outwardly too much. I was the steady guy, at home and on the team. Kids screaming in your ear as they spill apple juice on your new laptop? No big deal. Shrug shoulders. Smile and ask them to finish their juice at the table, next time, please. That's life.

That's life on my old MEDS, at least. Muddy veneer over wood-paneled daily life. Nothing to turn off.

I didn't need any temper-type coping skills for the past twenty-five years, because there was nothing of short-fuse consequence. Sometimes the veneer wore a little thin, is about all.

Honey, could you please hand me the medium brush? The one with the soft bristles? I'll just touch this little thin spot up over here....

All that time on strong MEDS, the metaphysical and spiritual fireworks were inside. War on myself. Stalemate. But, inside.

Now that music sounds wonderful again (I hear all the parts again. I hear harmony voicings in my head, which I'm sure is not unusual for musicians, but for me it is new again since before my first breakdown.) I want to sing. Sometimes I need to sing.

Sometimes I can't write fast enough.

But now, I can stop anytime and just breathe if I choose to.

The kids drive me fucking insane. Parenting, apparently, is actually quite hard. Discussions with Amanda, apparently, can get quite difficult and heated.

The kids also bring me truer joy. Stronger hope. Greater reverence. Deeper gratitude.

Amanda and I are starting over in some ways, more at home in others.

∞

I knew something was wrong when I looked at the floor in my office. The marble table top was shattered in twenty three pieces. There were gouges on the floor where the sharper bits had landed. The legs were upside down.

The last thing I remember, see, is that I was on the couch with Amanda, and we were trying to work through something. We weren't connecting. There was no connection. It was uncomfortable. I said something that landed badly. She said something else that set me off.

Reptile me was in a really bad way. This was unknown territory for me. It seemed like maybe she was not safe, I was not safe. We were not safe.

I watched from three feet back as my body got up from the couch, rushed out of the room and down the hall into my office, considered sweeping everything off my desk, respected my work (somehow), and instead overturned with unbridled aggression the table we had bought together in Valencia.

The one with the rounded wooden corners and edges.

So Rainer didn't cut his head.

Uh…um…er…I've just been violent. Really, really violent. At home.

That wasn't me.

Really, buddy? Who was it, then?

Guess what. No free lunches. Getting my passion mojo back comes with a price. The price is that I was there with broken shards at my feet in a forty-five-year-old's body. Three kids, mortgagey stuff, marriage work, midlife disorientations and unravelings…and a nineteen year old's coping skills. That's when I went on MEDS. That's how old emotional me is now.

I think as I write this a few months later maybe I'm, like, twenty-nine-ish. Maybe.

But, my heart is younger than it has been in a very long time.

⟜

CHAPTER 97

I'VE HAD ONE DREAM THAT I know changed my life. In the
dream, I was lying in bed, staring at the ceiling. The lyrics
to Bob Dylan's "Tangled Up in Blue" scrolled along up there
like heavenly karaoke. For the record, my favorite Dylan song
is "Visions of Johanna," but this is a true story about a dream.

Fade into the song, singing along:

All the people we used to know
They're an illusion to me now
Some are mathematicians...

Then the words were blanked out. Redacted, say. They were
missing. I kept singing, in my dream.

(Some are carpenter's wives
Don't know how it all got started
I don't know what they do with their lives)

The words came back, keeping time with my singing. Dreams
are good that way.

Me, I'm still on the road...

I woke up.

I shared my Dylan dream with Dr. Dodd, my Jungian analyst in the Titirangi forest south of Auckland. He asked me what I thought my dream meant, and I stuttered and mumbled, grunted and fumbled, then tried for some bullshit Foucault. Maybe it was Baudrillard. Never mind.

Dr. Dodd said, "I see. Well, could it also perhaps be your own blank canvas? This open space between the words of this other artist?"

Wow. Go on.

"You have lived like the mathematician, you have worked with the data, with your struggles to bring order to your own life."

Got my attention here.

"What if that blank space is for you to fill in yourself? Your blank canvas, with your true self. Maybe the 'True Man Show' movie is even deeper than you thought. Maybe you need to brave the open road if you want a blank canvas. Hmm?"

It definitely wasn't a dream about finding the next boat out of Nantucket.

I had been trying to decide whether I needed to hurry and get my career back on track before it was gone, or stick with writing and writing and writing until it was done. One problem. I had no idea what "it" was.

I was driving Amanda insane. One day, I would tell her that I planned to write until it was done, this story I was trying to bring to life. About a crazy dude who thought the world was out to get him. Except it actually was.

Hopefully within ten years, I'd say. It only took James Joyce ten years to write *Portrait of an Artist as a Young Man,* I'd say. (Uh, does it worry you that Jimmy J. already knew what he was doing? she gently but firmly pointed out.)

Long as it takes. That's how long it will be until I go back to paid sailing.

(I had been at it for well over a year, the writing. The wastebasket was full.)

I know, I know. All about the process. Keep on learning, keep on striving. Process doesn't put food on the table. You don't get a medal for participation.

I was failing again. Precisely half of me lobbied relentlessly:

You can't afford to fail again, but...fear not! I have just the thing! Go back to the safety of what you know. It's who you are. It's what you do. It's inevitable.

(Plus, you love it, right?)

You were just going through a phase, a funk, after Andrew's death. It's time now to honor him. Stop grieving. Get back out on the water. Time to move on. Check your medication supply. Hey, you know that there's this great alcohol-free beer brewed by Guinness?

Phew. Problem solved. Can almost smell the check in the mail. Book the vacation to Vail.

Then the next morning I was a writer again. Beans and Rice, that's all BB King and Ella Fitzgerald needed.

That night nope, I'm definitely a sailor. Final final. Signing off. Sorry about all this. I better hustle for some work before they forget about me out there.

Sailor. Writer. Sailor. Writer....Oh, wait.
Father.
Son.
Fuck. Bad Son.
Darn.

I had tinkered away in January with what became Chapter Two of this book. Then I started making phone calls to sailing contacts. Sending e-mails. Panicking. Sure the sailing world had already forgotten my name. My last result. My skills. My talent. My great sense of humor (personality? work ethic?) Goddammit.

I had the dream, and Dr. Dodd told me I had a blank canvas.

February 19, I wrote the first chapter of the book you are reading. February 27, I wrote the last sentence of the first draft. The final few chapters took a while after that, but it was clearly time to love the questions themselves.

My question now is:
If I were again a young artist
And back I could go
Would I paint a different picture?
Not if I don't try.
Could I imagine a story in which I forgive myself?
Not if I don't try.
Does it matter if anyone reads it?

Cricket. Cricket. Cricket...

CHAPTER 98

MY FRIENDS WITH GOLD MEDALS keep them all different places. Some keep them framed behind glass, spotlit in the entryway. Some keep them in sock drawers. They used to tell me about that, about the sock drawer, and I used to want to punch them right in the face.

It seems like you only get to say it's "no big deal, the silly old thing just lives in my sock drawer anyway" once you actually have a medal. Until then, the conspicuous coming up short is all there is. It's a really big deal. Finders keepers, losers weepers.

I've had all my trophies buried in a box in the basement until very recently. I refused to use them as crutches, although sometimes I wish maybe I had every once in a while. I might have leaned on the bottle a little less.

As I get older, the silver cups and the plaques, the medals and the leather wastebaskets, represent more to me than little triumphs. They also represent the trying. Just like it says in my swacket. I've put a few trophies back on the mantlepiece. They look relaxed up there now.

As the races recede and I can't taste the champagne spraying around the stage anymore, the memories of the people and the places grow stronger. The 49er worlds in Bandol, France, where they claim crème brulée was invented. The race in Sweden where the sun only dipped below the horizon at midnight, and the wind was so weird that the instruments claimed we never tacked. The whistles and roars tumbling through narrow Spanish cobblestone streets when Messi scored a goal in the World Cup. The warmth and honesty of the handshake of congratulations that the German boy gave me in 1986, leaping out of his boat at the end of the last race to swim over to mine. The heartbreak but also sincerity I felt giving the same handshake to the McKee brothers in 2000.

As the competition fades away, the medals in a sock drawer make more sense. They aren't who I am. But I can still put them in a warm, soft place. And, I can still daydream about a parallel universe where I didn't get cancer and go crazy quite so many times, and so I stood on the podium. In that daydream, I would also understand that true strength and courage meant I knew I was worthy before the doves were released at opening ceremonies.

Recovery from surgery goes better if you start out fit. Recovery from Achievement-Is-Who-I-Am is far more elusive. For one, it's not considered an *illness*. It's dangled—and has the aroma pumped out of all the vents like Southern fried chicken—as the path to health and happiness. There's nothing wrong with it as long as you never, ever question it. Once you do, brother, be ready for a storm.

The gift of receiving a health scare to reprioritize, is that there's time—and even unanimous license—to take a look in the mirror and wait for a truer reflection. The masks just don't come off on their own. They only come off when we risk it all. When there's no other way.

It's beautiful here. Joyful, and terrifying, and beautiful.

CHAPTER 99

Hamlet, the dude, is famous for his "To be, or not to be…" soliloquy.

Hamlet, the play, is revered in part for its staggeringly clever use of the "play within a play". (Prince Hamlet tinkers a little with *The Mousetrap* to surprise his fratricidal uncle into unmasking critical information: the ghost of Hamlet's dead father is telling the truth.)

My favorite lines in *Hamlet* are spoken by the Player King:

"Our wills and fates do so contrary run
That our devices still are overthrown.
Our thoughts are ours, their ends none of our own."

Maybe it's OK if I feel as though I'm in a play sometimes. Maybe it doesn't mean I'm sick.

Maybe it's OK if my devices are occasionally overthrown. Maybe it doesn't mean I'm crazy.

Maybe it's OK to feel that I have some kind of Fate guiding my life, with synchronicities and vertigo and Enchantment.

Maybe I can believe in magic, and still leave plenty of room around me for Reality.

Maybe I don't even have to go make peace with my imagination's days in the dungeon. I can just write my story, on a blank canvas, from here.

Today is May 9. It is the two-year anniversary of the crash, of Andrew's ascendence to a place beyond dreams.

I woke up early this morning and got back to David Foster Wallace's *The Pale King*. My eyes came to the words "East of East Saint Louis." Before the sound of the second "East" hit my brain voice, a song took over in my head: "and you're East of East Saint Louis, and the wind is making speeches, and the rain sounds like a round of applause…." The lyrics are from Tom Wait's song "Time" on the album *Rain Dogs*.

It was like it came from Outside. The song took over. Inside my head, I had been reading a book. Now I was singing. "…his invisible fiancé's in the mirror…."

The jolting directive to rewind the tape to last night stung me like eighty-eight amps to the collar of a great dane.

You sure you're not north-north-west here, my friend? Fifty mg? Did you take your 50 mg of Lamictal?

"Yes."

Night before?

"Yes."

Night before?

"Oh. Twenty-five milligrams. Just twenty-five."

The next pack of MEDS had sat that night, dutifully obtained from the pharmacy, in the bedroom while Amanda slept. She had a night shift coming up in fewer than twenty-four hours, and I didn't want to wake her.

Did you drink yesterday?

"I had one beer in the late afternoon, after jumping with the boys on the trampoline for forty-five minutes straight. We all took our shirts off. Rainer commented that he had butt crack sweat. It tasted really good. The beer, that is. The beer tasted good."

Are we sick? Am I sick?

(…)

(…)

NO. I am not sick. I am alive, and I am part artist, and this is my life, and I am a world leader (pretend). But I am not sick.

Maybe being a person with bipolar dispositions means being forced to acknowledge the sacred duality that is life on earth, to such a degree that it sometimes overwhelms. Maybe our role is to act it out, so nobody forgets that there are more things in heaven and earth than our philosophies and science.

We all have experience with dueling realities of some sort in life. A concert in Europe, where the people standing next to you in the bullring are American. From your state. From your town. You have a close mutual friend who lives in Rio now, and you both spoke to her that very morning.

You ask a buddy to recommend someone for your next tattoo. Meanwhile, you get a random friend request on Facebook and end up hitting it off in a fun chat. The referral's name comes through that night. It's the same as your new FB friend's.

You call somebody out of the blue for no reason, and she says she had just been thinking of you when the phone rang.

These glimpses can be hard to wrestle into the same world as the sweet mundane of laundry, homework, and traffic.

Society, self. Results, process. Material, spiritual. Head, heart. It's a long, looping list because it is.

Maybe it's stubborn to believe it's about reconciliation.

Maybe that's the wrong game.

Learning to gently hold all my parts together is how I want to practice my role.

I can use the whole palette and still color inside the lines.

My ghosts don't have to demand revenge. They can write me in and out of scenes, depending on the day.

I'll be ready, bright lights or not.

Black Sails White Rabbits;

Kevin A. Hall

GRATITUDE

There are many people to thank. There are many, many stories of my gratefulness to tell. You will find them all at

dewpoint.us

Thank you for being a part of my story. Our story. OUR story.

15230136R00184

Printed in Great Britain
by Amazon.co.uk, Ltd.,
Marston Gate.

TRANSGRESSIONS

Erotic Stories

Anastasia Fleur

Red Heel Press

To V

CONTENTS

HROTICA

"**W**hat seems to be the problem?"

"It's Joel in Accounting," Julia said. "He keeps making … comments."

Clare studied the woman sitting across from her desk. She didn't think she'd seen her at the office before—Clare was sure she would remember someone so striking. In a swift, barely perceptible once-over, Clare assessed the woman in entirety, scanning the parts of her that she could see. She wore a blue silk camisole that hugged her contours perfectly, from the full breasts with just a hint of cleavage showing, down to the small waist. The black trousers she wore might as well have been leggings, they were so form-fitting. And perhaps they were. Clare couldn't keep up with what counted as "pants" anymore —though she certainly appreciated them on the woman for all that they revealed—slim, muscled thighs crossed casually, a foot bouncing in stylish leather flats. Clare noticed the scent of cinnamon emanating from her—from a recently chewed piece of gum?—which made the woman appear younger somehow than she probably was. Clare guessed in her late twenties.

"What kind of comments?" Clare asked.

"Sexual," Julia replied, her eyes flashing dark and dangerous at Clare, which was enough to force Clare's gaze downward, as if merely the mention of the word sex implicated Clare somehow. Or had the woman noticed her staring?

◆ ◆ ◆

Julia had never encountered a more attractive HR manager in her life. She'd seen Clare a few times since she started at the office two months ago, but had never spoken to her before this, and in an office with almost 300 employees, she was still putting faces to names. Mostly Julia had stolen glances from her cubicle down the hall as Clare paced back and forth past her open office door while she made phone calls. But Clare was even more attractive up close—her beauty impossible to ignore, like a soft slap in the mouth. And such a surprise. She was utterly feminine, somehow made more so by the maroon necktie she was wearing—a full-size one, too, not one of those skinny hipster ties Julia had been hoping would disappear ages ago. A gold tie clip held it in place, and though a clip also held her hair back, a few strands had broken free, framing Clare's face in a way that made her seem windswept, like a Victorian heroine pining on the moors. Though Julia knew essentially nothing about this woman, she seemed so unlike other people she had encountered in HR. Indeed, Julia thought Clare seemed as if she would be just at home here as she would running a small, feminist, anarchist bookstore.

Julia openly appraised the woman sitting tall behind the large, messily organized desk, the dark hairs that fell in soft waves about her face, the eyes that seemed to change with each shifting of the light—from blue to green to grey and back. Right now they appeared blue, but not the icy kind, the aloof kind. No, to Julia they appeared to be the blue of flame—the hottest part of the fire.

Even though Clare was merely sitting, pen poised to take notes on Julia's claim, she radiated sensuality. The hairs on Julia's forearms prickled as she allowed herself to wonder briefly what the woman looked like under the maroon tie and tight button-down she wore.

But as Julia let her mind wander so, somewhere in her awareness, it registered that Clare had asked her a question. "Hmm?" she said, snapping back to attention and away from her daydream.

"If you don't mind, Ms. Dawes, that is, if you feel comfortable—I'm going to need you to elaborate on the specificity of these sexual comments…"

Clare felt oddly flustered. She removed the cap from her pen, looked at it as if it was an unruly pet, and then put it back on. Clare made sure to keep her face and voice in an expressionless tone, but her hands, which she now folded on her lap, out of view, were shaking. She couldn't stop herself from registering again and again the striking brown eyes of the woman before her, which seemed to flash at her like a dare. *What was this sensation? Was it fear?* Clare had never been anything other than the pinnacle of professionalism, so why did she feel as if she was engaging in something *inappropriate*?

And why couldn't she figure out what to do with her hands?

"Well," Julia started, suddenly shy to repeat the filthy words that Joel had taunted her with—not in front of this beautiful woman, at least, whose undeniable allure caused her heart to hammer in her throat. "I don't know that I can say it out loud."

"I understand this is difficult for you," Clare said. "But you should know that during an investigation like this we try to keep things as confidential as possible. You will not be punished or retaliated against in any way. Coming forward is a protected activity. We also have a zero-tolerance policy for unwanted sexual contact at this company, and I will do everything in my power to help you. I just need to know exactly what happened."

Comforted though still feeling timid, Julia surprised herself by rising from her chair and leaning forward over the desk, which, Julia noticed, was littered with sticky notes, half a cup of congealed coffee, a philodendron plant, and an inspirational quotes calendar, of which today's read, "Don't just think about it, *be* about it." Julia felt both embarrassed and endeared by this sudden knowledge of Clare, and nearly retreated, but Clare's impassable, mysterious face compelled her forward, so much so that Julia was now leaning entirely over the mammoth desk, inching toward Clare, pressing her elbows flat against the desk to steady herself. As Clare did not move from her position, and because the desk was bigger than Julia had anticipated, she beckoned Clare forward with a whip of her head. Clare hesitated a beat before placing her shaking hands on the desk and leaning toward Julia's clavicle.

From here, Clare noticed the soft down of Julia's neck, hair as white and fine as confectioner's sugar, even though the rest of Julia's hair was dark brown. In a voice barely above a whisper, Julia spoke softly into Clare's ear, her lips so close to Clare's face that the heat of her body sent a thunder clap straight down to Julia's center.

Clare listened to Julia repeat the string of lewd comments that Joel had said to Julia, struggling to stop the flood of sensation that Julia's lips had awakened in her. *Focus*, she chastised herself, *You have a job to do and it is not ogling a woman in need of your help!* And yet, she could not stop herself from registering the soft peaks of Julia's breasts as she leaned over the desk—low-hanging fruit, literally!—the impressions of which were now firmly embedded in her mind and would not remove themselves.

The litany of filth continued as Clare warred privately with herself, and when Julia's lip brushed the soft fold of her ear—accidentally?—Clare let slip a brief, throaty moan, "Unh."

"I know," Julia replied, still inches from Clare's face. Every hair on the back of Clare's neck stood at upright attention. "Isn't it horrid? I even told him I was gay, which I thought would be a deterrant, but it seems it only bolstered his advances."

"That is horrid," Clare agreed, breaking with her usual, impartial script. Then, she snapped to, remembering herself. "Thank you for telling me. I know it isn't easy to come, I mean, to talk about something like this. Openly."

When Julia sat back down in her chair, Clare was relieved, as it allowed her to recover from the warmth and smoldering nearness of Julia's body, and a respite from the brief brushing of Julia's lips that had set Clare's particles jostling. "I'm so sorry that happened to you—it's awful," she said, thankful to have enough wits about her to form coherent sentences. "Rest assured that his behavior is entirely unacceptable and will not be tolerated at this company, toward you or anyone else. Is there anything else I need to know?"

Julia struggled to come up with something—*anything*—that would allow her to stay in the beguiling woman's presence for a little while longer, but couldn't. She was tongue-tied and more than a little turned on still from the brief glimpse of Clare's long, graceful neck and the sweet, animal scent of her she had just encountered when she leaned in close to her ear.

Julia felt desire cloud her throat as she rose from her chair to bid Clare adieu, and as they clasped hands, she allowed hers to linger in Clare's for a fraction of a second longer than propriety allowed.

The pleasure and heat and memory of this brief encounter would stay with Julia for the rest of the day and well into the evening, where she freely allowed her mind to wander over and over again the details, the impressions, the proportions that had so shockingly bewitched her.

Who is this woman? she wondered.

◆ ◆ ◆

The following week, when Julia walked past Joel's desk on the way to her own, she was startled to find it empty. Even his nameplate had been removed, only a ghostly, sun-stained outline of it remained outside his cubicle wall.

Had her complaint worked? Was she finally going to be free and able to do her job in peace? A thrilling lightness moved through her as she sat down at her cubicle and opened her laptop, where a company-wide email from the CEO greeted her. It was about Joel's departure, though there were scant few details as to why. Julia scanned the email " … blah blah … thankful for his service and dedication … blah blah … wish him luck on his next enterprise…"

Horse shit! She thought, wanting real answers, and knowing precisely the enchantress who could provide them.

Julia peered her head over her cubicle wall, craning her neck down the hall to the office Clare occupied. Her door was open again and Julia could see that she was talking on the phone. When Clare glanced up briefly and saw Julia's eyes upon her, Julia swore she saw the corners of her mouth flicker into a smile before looking away. Julia smiled in kind, almost involuntarily. She typed a message to Clare.

Subject: Case Update
"Does this mean what I think it does?—J"

Two minutes later, Clare responded:

RE: Case Update
"Unable to discuss details at present. Tonight? At 1221?"

Julia's eyes widened. 1221 was the gay bar near their office. Was Clare suggesting it to convey her sexuality to Julia? Or did she choose it because she knew no one at the office would likely be there, and, hence they could talk openly? Regardless, Julia was thrilled, both to learn more about what had happened with Joel and to spend time out of the office with Clare. She did a little dance in her seat, hoping no one would inopportunely walk by, as she typed: "I'll be there at 6pm."

It was only as Clare walked into the bar that evening that she realized she was nervous. Except she didn't actually "realize" it —she looked down at her hands and saw that they were shaking again. She shoved them in her coat pockets and out of view, making her way to the end of the small, dark bar and ordering a vodka gimlet.

She turned to the bartender: "Make it a double, actually." She cracked her neck from side to side and hopped a little on her feet, as if she was not about to meet a colleague for drinks, but instead ready to begin her UFC cage match.

The place was filling up fast, as the after-work crowd streamed in, removing blazers and backpacks, loosening neckties and replacing laptop cases with pints of beer. Clare managed to carve a space out at the bar that could just fit two people as she waited for Julia to arrive.

Why was she nervous? *There is nothing improper about meeting a coworker*, she told herself. And yet, she felt as if she was getting away with something. It didn't take long for Clare to remember the wild charge of Julia's lips against her ear and the heat that moved through her when Julia did so, desire coursing down and down and down. Clare shook off the memory and stood up straighter, telling herself, *It's just a drink. She's just a coworker. It's fine. I'm fine!*

When Julia entered the bar at 6:02pm, the sight of Clare struck her again like a volt of electricity. When she found Clare's face among the crowd of bar-goers, tucked beneath a slew of bears and queens and flannel femmes, Julia felt stunned, unable to take even a single step forward. But then she saw Clare smile, and found the resolve to make her limbs obey her. Clare wore tight, green plaid pants that showed off her long legs and tiny waist. A black button down, sleeves rolled to the elbows, top buttons unfastened, revealed the slightest swell of her breasts. And her dark hair was down, its shiny waves loose and giving off an air of wildness that contrasted with her perfectly set features.

Julia pushed her way through the throng of happy-hour bodies and wedged herself in the small space next to Clare. They were close enough to kiss and Julia found she did not know where to look. She focused on the side of Clare's neck, inhaling once again her brisk biology, a musk that smelled like September, something ripe and red and warm. Julia was feeling intoxicated already, though she hadn't had a single drink.

"Sorry I'm late," Julia said, breathless, cheeks flushed. "I've been up to my tits in expense reports."

Clare's mouth opened slightly at this, but nothing came out. She shut it.

"Am I allowed to say *tits*?" Julia said, interpreting the silence and mouth agape-ness on Clare's face as shock. "You won't report me?"

◆ ◆ ◆

Clare couldn't tell if Julia was joking or not, so responded earnestly, "Oh, I'm not on the clock now. Please feel free to discuss breasts as much as you'd like." Then thought, *Christ, did I just say that?*

Thankfully, Julia laughed. "My kinda gal," she said. "Speaking of tits, gonna try and fail to get the gay male bartender's attention for a drink. You good?"

"I'm good ... great actually," Clare said, surprised at how much she meant it. As Julia chased after the bartender a few feet away, Clare watched Julia's face. There was something so young about her, her movements and gestures. She did not walk, but rather, bounced. And unlike Clare's guarded demeanor, Julia seemed so open, so undisguised. An innocence emanated from her, which is possibly why her casual swearing felt so jarring to Clare. When Julia came back with a manhattan, three cherries skewered on a bamboo pick, Clare smiled again.

"What?" Julia asked, wedging herself once more into the space. Clare registered the unbearable nearness of Julia's body to her own and felt herself flush with heat.

"Three cherries?"

"A bonus for the bartender making me wait so damn long. Plus," Julia winked, "I once heard that things should always come in threes, for good luck."

"I'm pretty sure that's death—deaths come in threes."

"Is it? Fuck! Quick, take one then."

Julia held the skewer up to Clare's mouth. Clare paused for the slightest moment, before parting her full lips, which circled, then vanished the soft red fruit.

As she chewed, tasting the sweet burn of the whiskey-soaked cherry, the sudden intimacy of the moment caused Clare to demure. She tried to change the subject to something she hoped would be more neutral, realizing only after she said it that it was both a signal and an invitation. "All of my ex-girlfriends are whiskey drinkers."

◆ ◆ ◆

"Are they now?" Julia delighted in this information. So Clare *did* like girls. Now all Julia had to figure out was if she liked *her* in particular.

This would prove to be difficult to maneuver, however. She couldn't casually hit on the HR manager, could she? Wasn't that, like, five kinds of wrong? And when she herself had just submitted a harassment claim! This was going to be trickier than she anticipated. And then there was Clare's scent, casually debilitating her while they stood, the soft fabric of their elbows touching.

Julia tried to distract herself from her arousal. "Why do you think this place is called 1221?"

"I was wondering that, too," Clare said, placing her foot on the rung of the bar stool near Julia's thigh. Julia noticed it painfully, resisting the urge to lay her hand upon the muscled contours of it. The allure of Clare drew her like a magnet. She clutched tighter to her drink. Julia had never felt so exhausted from NOT touching someone! *What is going on with me?* She wondered.

"I bet the internet knows," Julia said, punching the question into her phone. "Aha ... it's, oh, that's disappointing. It's just the address."

"Not a very good story."

"No, I was hoping it'd be something like: In 1221, the first glory hole was invented. And today, at 1221, we honor that hole and every hole that has found a similar path to glory."

Clare laughed. "Let's definitely tell people that. It's a *hole* lot better."

"You did not."

"I did."

Julia raised her glass to Clare's and together they cheered. "So," Julia flashed her darkly shining eyes at Clare once more, "tell me. Tell me everything. I'm dying to know."

Clare considered Julia's words and felt at that moment that she could tell Julia *everything*, the darkest contents of Clare's soul, the triumphant and brilliant and strange recesses of her beautiful, perverse mind—anything to keep Julia's gaze upon her as it was in this moment. It was only when Clare realized Julia was expecting her to say something that she came to.

"Oh! Joel. Yes. Turns out he had a rap sheet a mile long. Not just at this company but several priors. I can't give you gory details, but let's just say the man has an appalling history of harassment."

"So it wasn't just me?"

"Far from it. The CEO had no choice but to let him go. He was a lawsuit waiting to happen, or several lawsuits."

Julia squeezed Clare's hand suddenly, in a fit of excitement. "Well, that's both the worst and best news I've heard all day!"

The pressure and warmth of Julia's hand sent another wave of arousal through Clare. She sipped her drink to steady herself, longing to know what other parts of Julia might feel like in her hands.

11

"I can't believe it," Julia continued, whether she was aware that she was still holding Clare's hand, Clare didn't know. But then, Julia let it drop. Clare took a sip of her drink reluctantly. "In the past, whenever I've complained, either nothing happened or the harassment got *worse*! Like, they knew they could punish me for speaking up. You're a goddamn hero, Clare Korikov."

Clare's cheeks burned bright at the sound of her name on Julia's lips, but she said, "Just doing my job."

"And a damn fine one at that," Julia said. "You seem surprised though. Are you?"

"That a beautiful woman would get harassed? Sadly, no."

It was Julia's turn to blush now. "I meant are you surprised that men are trash, ones like Joel at least." Clare tucked a wave of brown-black hair behind her ear and looked down at Julia's engineer boots, the scuffed leather toe looked like it had some stories to tell.

Clare stammered. "Well, no, I can't say I'm surprised by *that* either. Forgive the assumption—"

"There's nothing to forgive," Julia said, no longer looking at Clare's neck, but staring straight into her eyes. "You are very attractive yourself. But surely you must hear that all the time."

The blood pulsed in Clare's temples. This was quickly veering in a direction that was entirely out of her control. She didn't know if she liked it. And yet she very much did like it. She scanned her inner filing system, trying to remember every code and bylaw from her extensive career, to make sure she wasn't doing something improper. Yet, the desire coursing through her had its own ideas of what was *proper*. Besides, she soothed herself, it sure seemed that the attraction was reciprocated.

Still, Clare was unsure how to proceed, and the slight buzz from the gimlet only confused her further. She decided to restrain herself. She must not let Julia's allure get in the way of her professionalism.

As Clare gave herself a silent pep talk, a man precariously holding four beers elbowed her on his way past, spilling some of the amber liquid on her shoes, releasing its yeasty perfume into her nostrils, and forcing her body even closer to Julia's. The bar was packed now, the air smokey and thick, conversations pulsing and roaring, an animal scent emanating from so many bodies releasing the tensions and anxieties of the work day. Soon they would be scissoring whether they wanted to or not. (Which, reader, you should know by now, they obviously did.)

As Julia tried to ignore their perilous, maddening closeness, she couldn't help but notice a thin sheen of sweat glistening on Clare's neck. She longed to trace the line of it with her tongue. But she resisted. It was too soon, wasn't it? Too uncouth? Though, even with the crowd pushing them closer together, Julia could feel Clare's desire pulling her in like a celestial body in orbit. And it did not help matters that she had a perfect view down Clare's shirt from where they stood. Julia struggled to not survey the swell of Clare's breasts against the softly clinging fabric as they talked, but it was damn near impossible.

And then, as the tension pulled tight as a bow string, this happened: Clare set her empty drink down on the bar, reaching across their bodies, unintentionally sweeping her hand against Julia's breast, where she watched the nipple harden and rise to her touch. In this small, accidental gesture, something was unleashed inside Clare. The pleasure was so acute, in fact, that she couldn't help but do it *again,* as she pulled her arm back, this time very intentionally brushing against Julia's breast and watching Julia's face register the sensation, the intimacy, the *intentionality* of the touch. As she did so, Clare swore she could feel Julia's pleasure in her own body, the soft sigh of it radiating along her spine, her hips, and down into her cunt, which pulsed intently and rhythmically, like the hammering of her own wildly beating heart.

She looked once more into Julia's face, a devious half-smile disarming Clare. Julia had not moved away from her touch. Indeed, she had leaned into it. Surely this was a sign? Clare decided to be a little bolder, to press, as she had wanted to earlier, her thigh against Julia's thigh. Again, Julia did not move away. Far from it, Julia's leg pushed back against her own, the muscle and bone and skin pressing softly together now, nodding their perfect, wordless, animal approval.

That's two, Clare thought. *If she gives me one more sign, I'll kiss her.*

As she thought this, Julia ran her hand through her hair. Clare noticed that Julia seemed fidgety, unaware of what to do with her body in so small a space. Was she nervous too? Anticipating? Holding back?

The conversation continued, despite the wildfires tearing through each of their bodies. When Clare noticed that a strand of Julia's hair had become mussed and tangled, she saw an opening for her third and final test.

"May I?" she said, reaching her hand out. "You have a rogue strand." Julia nodded, but before she had a chance to respond, Clare grazed her hair and ear with the tips of her fingers, smoothing and tucking the hair back into its proper place. Julia closed her eyes dreamily as Clare did this, keeping them closed as Clare's fingers reached the arc of her lower earlobe, where they rested now against Julia's neck and cheek, and still closed when Clare leaned in and kissed her long and full and hard on the mouth.

Momentarily stunned, Julia's mouth twitched slightly, as if it had encountered flame. She let out a low moan before kissing Clare back, the force of her lips and tongue sending wild pulsations down the length of Julia's body, down to the tips of her toes and back. Her hands went to Clare's breasts, almost unconsciously, cupping them firmly in her palms before she realized she was doing it, feeling the soft pull of Clare's nipples against her thumbs.

The push of the crowd sent their bodies still closer together, every part of them touching that could—knees and thighs and hips, torsos and breasts and lips—each woman forgetting where they were or even *who* they were, responding only to this bestial hunger, the indelible ache of connection, of grasping, of a need so raw and pure and true it didn't have or require a name.

And then, in the span of no more than a minute or two, Clare remembered herself, her responsibilities, and pulled away. She had been too caught up, too beside herself, and now the authoritative part of her brain tugged at her. *This woman came to you for help, not a quickie!*

"We shouldn't," she managed to whisper, turning her head away from Julia's hotly probing mouth. But Julia then found her neck, kissing along the line of her jaw, her ear, the muscle leading to her shoulder. Clare's hands trembled. She struggled to find the part of herself capable of saying no in this moment, in the face of this enormous, exquisite appetite.

"Wait," she said, gripping the sides of Julia's face in her hands. "We can't. It's not right."

"Nothing feels wrong about this," Julia said, finding Clare's lower lip once more and gently nibbling on it.

Clare groaned again. The lustful side of her said, *She has a point.*

But the responsible side countered, *Think of your job. Your duty. Your integrity. You're playing with fire, Clare.*

Yes, but I'm also taking a keen interest in the … welfare of my employees!

She warred thusly with herself, until finally, achingly, responsibility won out. She grabbed Julia's wrists and held them away from her body. And then, when even *that* gesture of restraint felt unbearably hot to her, she let go of Julia entirely and moved herself as far away as she could.

"I'm sorry," Clare said. "I have to go."

"Wait!"

But she didn't. And before Julia could grab her things from beneath the bar, Clare had vanished into the crowd and into the uncertainty of the night itself.

The following day at work, Julia was hopelessly distracted. Each time, she tried to make eye contact or catch a glimpse of Clare, Clare looked away. And when they happened upon each other at the coffee pot, Clare actually turned and ran from her! Well, walked briskly, but Julia got the message. She knew Clare was avoiding her, she just didn't know why. Maybe Clare knew she would not be able to answer Julia's questions, at least not in any satisfying way. Back at her cubicle, Julia noticed that Clare's office door was shut, and spent an inordinate amount of time staring into it, trying to will it to open.

Then finally, slightly before 3pm, it opened. As two of their colleagues exited Clare's office from a meeting, without thinking,

Julia leapt from her desk and ran down the hall before the door could close on her. Flushed and a little breathless from running in heels, even low ones, Julia entered Clare's office, shutting the door behind her. Startled, Clare greeted her by standing up from her chair.

◆ ◆ ◆

"Julia, I can't—."

"I think I at least deserve an explanation," Julia said, continuing to step closer, more tentatively than her bold entrance, but still purposeful, striding around Clare's desk until their bodies were, once more, mere inches from each other. The familiar heat knocked against Clare's ribs. Her heart pounded; she felt as if at any moment, her limbs would detach and float away from her body. *What do you do to me?* Clare wondered, almost accusatory.

"I'm sorry," Clare said.

"I don't want your apologies." Julia stepped closer still. She saw Clare's searching, changeful eyes and felt her breath, which came out in short, staggered bursts.

Clare tried to retain her sense of conviction when faced with the agonizing emotion in Julia's eyes and the wall of desire that barreled down upon her in Julia's presence. She knew she would ultimately fail, but continued to listen.

"Don't tell me I imagined it," Julia said, "this feeling, not last night—not right now." Julia lay her hand gently against Clare's cheek, where the heat of it coiled down the length of Clare's spine.

Clare steadied herself. "You didn't imagine it."

Clare closed her eyes against the soft of Julia's hand, moving her face into the comforting curve of it. When Julia's fingers lightly brushed her lip, she opened her mouth, and kissed the tips of

Julia's fingers, tasting the skin and wanting more salt and more heat and more *more*. "Last night, I behaved ... inappropriately," Clare tried. "I shouldn't have—"

"I want you inappropriate!" Julia's voice came out high and strange. She almost didn't recognize it. She took a breath, trying to calm the pack of wolves running through her heart, before continuing. "You did nothing wrong. I wanted everything that happened to happen. I want you. If you'll have me."

Julia placed her hands on Clare's hips and pulled her closer. Their faces were a whisper away from each other's—all either had to do was tilt her chin slightly...

And just then, a knock. As loud and as unwelcome as a fart in an elevator.

"*Fuck*," Clare said. "My 3 o'clock. You can't be in here."

They both looked around the small office, quickly assessing that there was nowhere for Julia to hide.

Except. Well.

Clare pointed downward. Under her desk. "Are you serious?" Julia asked.

"I wish I was kidding. Now go, and don't make a peep if you don't want to get me fired."

The face Julia made while contorting herself under Clare's desk, as large as it was, was unmistakably irritation, but underneath that, a rebelliousness. Clare wondered what such a look portended, but she shoved the thought from her mind as she positioned her legs in the only place they could go, around Julia's lithe and supple body, the skirt she wore hiking up dangerously to accommodate the tight arrangement.

Another knock. Louder. "One second, Benjamin." The warmth of Julia's face so close to her thighs left Clare slightly dizzy. She needed a moment to catch her breath. "Okay, come in!" She said, a little too chipper, as she felt Julia's hands move to her bare knees, the skirt fabric riding a tiny bit higher up her thighs.

Clare gritted her teeth.

"I have those files on workers comp you asked for," Benjamin said.

"Thank you. Have a seat. Do these include the addendum on claims administration standards?"

"They do," he said. "Along with the most recent regulations from the EIA."

"Great."

Benjamin lay the documents in front of her on the desk as Julia's hands began to sweep higher and higher along her thighs, pushing her knees outward, as wide as they would go under the desk, creating goosebumps along the path they traveled. Clare inhaled sharply, yet she kept her face as impassive as she could.

Her eyes blurred as she scanned the words, her mind surprising itself as she said, nonplussed, "I'll need you to check on the CDI's reimbursement of expenditures. Make sure it complies with what's listed in Section 3700.A."

"Yes, ma'am."

Tension gripped Clare. Her knuckles whitened, though her face revealed nothing but stoic calm. *I'm doing it!* She thought. *I'm pulling this off.*

And then Julia pressed a single finger against the thin layer of fabric at her crotch, which Clare knew was wet already, and only became wetter when Julia increased the pressure there, slowly teasing her clit. Julia then pushed the underwear to the side, and drew a wide circle along Clare's opening, tracing the red, wet length of her—her outer and inner lips, her clit and clitoral hood, and the dark tuft of hair that framed everything—in a slow, agonizing movement.

Clare's hips bucked forward involuntarily when she felt Julia's hot breath on her inner thighs, and she bit her lip to keep from crying out when Julia's tongue made a slow, wet arc from the base of her cunt up to her clit and back down.

Sweat pooled in her lower back as Benjamin asked her questions about the documents. The stupid documents! How could she think about anything when Julia's tongue was teasing her into oblivion? Clare's jaw clenched so hard it popped, as Julia's tongue continued to make its agonizing ascent around her sex. The muscles in her thighs tensed and released as her body began to roar toward orgasm.

Clare begged silently for Benjamin to please go away now—for this meeting to be over with! Her answers became shorter, more terse, and soon devolved into near grunts and half-nods. And yet, he droned on. Thankfully, he seemed not to be able to tell at all that Clare was drowning Julia's face and lips and cheeks with her desire, soaking her chair as her own mouth tried to remain curiously placid, calm, pleasant even.

And then Julia briefly ceased her movements with her tongue, affording Clare a small measure of relief, only to then slip one—no, two—fingers inside of her. At this, Clare did cry out, unable to stop herself.

Upon seeing Benjamin's raised eyebrow, however, she regained some semblance of composure, "Ohh-hh," she stammered, "that reminds me, you'll need to make sure this includes supplemental workers and their dependants."

"Right, I forgot. This is why they pay you the big bucks, huh? You're the best."

As Julia worked her tongue and fingers slowly in and out of Clare, pleasure flaring all through her body, her skin and nerves and particles and synapses, she knew she would not be able to last much longer. Her insides clenched, her face began to redden. The pleasure was quite literally dismantling her and only mounting higher. She was suddenly thankful to have the desk to lean on for support.

Then, finally, blessedly, Benjamin appeared to be stacking up the papers, getting up from his chair, and yes—yes!—heading to the door. But the crazed smile from Clare that greeted him as he placed his hand upon the door knob gave him pause. She froze in panic, wondering if he could see Julia's feet under the desk, or the subtle, agonizing, rocking movement of Clare's lower body under the desk. She waited, breathlessly, until he said, "You know, I've never seen anyone so excited to talk compliance before. You're really passionate about this stuff, huh?"

"UH HUH," Clare chirped, teetering on the knife-edge of this fiery, all-consuming need. "Would you mind closing the door behind you? I have a UHHN client that needs my attention."

"You got it, boss. And will get these edits back to you by EOD."

He closed the door behind him and Clare lost her composure entirely. Feral with need, she gripped Julia's head under the desk, pressing Julia's face hard against the molten heat of her desire, hips tremoring, biting down on her own hand to stifle the frenzied groan that came tumbling out of her as she came.

Melting into a soft sigh of expletives, she dropped her forearm and head onto the desk, as wave after wave of convulsions rippled through her. Spent, sweaty, hand clenched in a fist of Julia's hair, which Clare did not let go of, until finally she did, softly, slowly, releasing Julia from her grip. Clare rested her head against her desk as the final riptides of pleasure carried her out to sea, until the only part of her capable of movement was her own mad heart.

It took Julia a solid minute for the feeling to come back into her legs and hands, which tingled both from being cramped under the desk and from the delicious trespass they'd just gotten away with it. Clare lifted her head from the desk when Julia emerged, a smirk as wide as the Grand Canyon on her face, blood surging to her cheeks and forehead.

"You beautiful motherfucker," Clare said. "I can't... I can't..."

"...believe how hot that was?" Julia offered, kissing the corner of Clare's smile, half laying on the desk to reach her. "You can't believe how much you enjoyed that?"

Clare nodded, reaching her hand up to stroke Julia's face. Upon seeing Julia bent so perfectly over the desk, so sweetly, Clare was flooded once more with desire.

"Don't move," Clare said.

And so she didn't.

Not when Clare rose from her chair and stood before Julia, not when she began kissing her way down Julia's shoulders, her spine, the soft valley of her lower back, and she certainly did not move when she made her way down the even softer sloping of Julia's heart-shaped ass. Her hands were like beautiful thieves, moving and discovering and capsizing every ounce of Julia's flesh. She didn't falter or fumble—her hands knew precisely where to exact the most pleasure, the most teasing, expansive pressure.

With that same deliberateness and dexterity, Clare lifted Julia's hips up to undo the top button on her grey dress pants. The stretchy fabric yielded easily, and within moments Clare was pulling down the zipper, and then tugging further still as the fabric slid down Julia's thighs and around her ankles. Julia's hips arched off the desk, feeling the cold rush of air on her bare skin mingling with the fever of her ardor, but Clare appeared to be taking her time, *relishing* her, delicately trailing her fingers down the backs of Julia's thighs, stopping just below the wet, swollen folds that begged for attention.

Pressing her face close to the fire, Julia could feel Clare's breath so close to her dripping, pulsing sex, and shuddered. Deftly, Clare backed away again. Julia swiveled her neck around to see Clare removing her shirt and bra. She took in the indelible round-ness, the full fruit-ness of her exquisite breasts, nipples firm and standing at attention, for only a moment, as Clare beckoned Julia to turn her gaze forward again. Julia did so reluctantly, and then she felt Clare's breasts and nipples painting their way up Julia's thighs. When a nipple grazed the slick wet silk of her sex, Julia groaned. This leisurely teasing had Julia on the brink of hysteria.

Bringing her face close once again, Clare traced a circle around the edges of Julia's opening with her tongue at the same time as she slowly drove her fingers inside it. She didn't stop at her clit, but kept traveling upward, teasing the skin of Julia's taint and the other tight center of her ass that came alive with each lapping of Clare's tongue. Alternating these movements, tongue and fingers entering and yielding and sucking and soothing, Julia felt her nerves fraying, a ferocity surging through her. She shut her eyes tightly, trying to grasp every sensation, knowing she wouldn't be able to hold on much longer, before galloping over the furious edge of orgasm.

But then, just as Julia was poised on the threshold of glorious collapse, Clare rose once more from the desk and stood slightly behind Julia. Julia heard a faint swish of fabric falling—Clare's skirt?—and a startled moan escaped her when Clare pressed her cunt against the hot iron of her own. Julia lifted her hips higher off the desk to greet her, to touch as completely, as firmly, the blooming, wilding spiral of her sex as was physically pos-sible. The muscles in Julia's thighs contracted violently as they slid back and forth together, with Clare's low groans becoming louder and more savage.

There was an unbearable urgency to their movements now, each thrusting of their hips became an offering, a seamless, wordless unity, as tender as it was frantic, as reverent as it was animal. When Julia came moments later, Clare held onto her hips, to keep as much of them touching as possible as she rocked and moaned and coiled into a fuse of luminous electricity, and holding on further still as the convulsions radiated through Julia's skin and out into the air, in an ecstatic procession of tumbling, tenuous, neverending light.

◆ ◆ ◆

Stillness now as the storms between the two women became a rumble, then a whisper, then a faint echo. Julia peeled herself from the desk, legs wobbling, as she attempted to stand. Clare helped steady Julia—and herself—though her legs were also shaking so much she almost couldn't.

"That was..." Julia tried.

"Yes," Clare agreed, unable to form coherent thoughts, instead smoothing the sweat-sheened hair near Julia's forehead and breathing in the thick, pungent smell of their fucking that now filled the small office. "It certainly *was*."

Julia pulled Clare tighter to her, pressing her lips against the firm line of Clare's jaw and the small scar that Clare felt self-conscious about and hoped Julia wouldn't inquire about. "What happens now?"

"Now?" Clare repeated.

Clare kissed her way along Julia's face, the slope of her red cheeks, her button nose, and down to the perfect bow of Julia's lower lip, where she lightly sucked at the flesh there. "Now, we put our clothes back on, we make sure our hair does not look as if we've just performed enviable feats, and you walk out of here, head high, gaze steady and neutral, as if nothing untoward has happened. And once you are safely in your car, you may collapse in a heap, as I intend to do."

"And then what?" Julia pressed on, taking Clare's hand and kissing each fingertip. Clare remembered herself once more, remembered that Julia was technically her subordinate, that what they were doing could very much get them both fired, and became fearful suddenly that this would be the last time, the only time, she'd have the chance to touch Julia in the way she so desperately wanted to.

Clare knew that they were breaking so many rules already. She didn't know how they could possibly sustain this—she only knew that she *must*.

THE CONCERT

I t's nearing midnight. Since noon, I'd been listening to band after band play in the swelter of the desert heat at an out-door music festival I looked forward to all year. But now, the heat is almost breaking. A stiff wind bristles through the black cotton dress I'm wearing over a blue and green striped bikini. The breeze caresses the hairs on my neck like a hand. Or several. I close my eyes to feel the sweet of it a little more, and sigh.

The bikini was my outfit from earlier in the day, when the sun roared to 110 degrees and the sweat stair-stepped down my spine. The noonday sun in the desert is no time to be pressed against a thousand sweaty bodies in a crowd, but midnight is almost manageable. It has to be because the headliner is coming on soon and I am not about to miss it.

I've waited all day and all night for this.

My friend and I have a strategy to get to the front row. We'll start to push our way through the crowd from the left side—by the merch vendors and guys selling hot dogs from a steaming cart—30 minutes before the band is scheduled to come on, which will give us plenty of time to find the small pockets of air between bodies and twist our own through them, inch by inch, row by row, until we are mere feet away from the make-shift fence that keeps the crowd from rushing the stage.

Our plan works. We're right there.

A line of security guards stands, arms folded, between us and the stage. The lights go dark, perfect timing. We've made it. I throw my head back, inhaling the secondhand smoke that hangs in the air, and smile. And as the band comes onstage, and the first growls of electric guitar swell, a new tide of bodies joins ours, cresting like a human wave through the hot, dry air. I quickly lose sight of my friend in the tumult, kiss two fingers and hold them to the sky for her, knowing I'll catch up with her after the show, and settle in to enjoy the music.

The stage is still dark when the opening notes of my favorite song ring out like a distorted hymn. The singer's voice booms and ripples as if she's in water, something sweet but clotted in the throat, and the hum of the bass guitar joins in, then the fleshy, thundering drums. The chorus of sounds sends a current through my whole body.

As her voice rises and falls, carrying my sighs up with it, so too do I feel my body being carried closer to the stage, the crowd pushing, pulsing with a life of its own. Something sharp digs into my ribs and I wonder whose elbow or beer bottle it is, but can't see anything through the fog of bodies. I wince and try to ignore it by watching the singer, her feral beauty. From this close, I can almost taste the sweat forming on her forehead already.

She grips the mic like a fever, and I sing along with her, a feeling of abandon and excitement falling from my lips. I watch as she stomps around the stage, hair falling around her face, black leather pants straining as her hips move to their own internal rhythm. The crowd has pushed me closer to her. I'm five feet away now. Close enough to see a metal gate corralling the crowd in, keeping us from mobbing the stage, and a row of security guards behind it, standing by, waiting, arms crossed.

27

It's then that I notice him. Someone pressing against me from behind with far more force and specificity than that of the general crowd. Two hands go to my hips and I feel the fabric of my dress bunch ever so slightly, a sliver more of thigh now exposed to the breeze made cool by my sweat. The pressure of his hands on my waist and the skittering pulse of the music set my synapses vibrating. I close my eyes, inhale the musk and dust and pot smoke swirling all around like a devil wind.

The hands clutch my waist, and tip my pelvis slightly forward. He pushes firmly against my ass, his intention as hard and unsubtle as a cliff face. In the rush and swell of the music, and the singer's high-lonesome voice, my flesh turns into a living drum and I find that I don't mind anything, not this stranger pressing against me or the heat or the throng of bodies tightening like a fist around me.

I keep my eyes on the stage, pressing slightly back into him. My shoulder blades meet his chest, and I welcome its hardness. The unmovingness of his body in the shifting sea of bodies anchors me and I feel safe, somehow. I dare not turn around, not that I could, pinned as I am by the crush of the crowd, the hands and hips and torso locking me in place. My breath catches as his hands leave my hips, make their way up and up, fingers grazing the periphery of my form, past the slim hollow of my waist, the taut rise of my ribcage. He stops here, hands at my ribs, and in this pause I understand a request is being asked of me. *Keep going or stop?* I place my hands on top of his, feeling the thick cords of his veins, feeling their enormity compared to my own, and move them slowly upward. He pulls the blood to the surface of my skin as his fingers trail pass, like the moon to a ravenous tide, stopping, finally at my breasts, which are full and aching to be touched through the thin fabric. He presses them, gently at first, his thumbs making slow circles until the nipples rise and harden. I let out a gasp that is quickly lost to the booming cries of the music, but he hears it. Or if he doesn't, then maybe he feels it, as his touch becomes bolder.

The dress and bikini prove to be too much of a barrier for him, and in a frenzied rush, he finds the opening at the top of the dress's plunging neckline, reaches into my dress and bikini top with one hand, and cups my breast underneath the fabric, kneading it roughly. The pads of his fingers are calloused, and I wonder if he is a musician. His hand is slender and strong on my bare skin, and our sweat mingles. The possession of the act causes me to pitch my head back against him again for a moment. His chest is as steady and hard as his desire and my thighs tighten against my cunt, as if to hold every ounce of pressure there. Every ounce of pleasure. I can't tell how wet I am in this heat, but suspect I'll find out soon enough.

My gaze is still locked ahead of me, on the stage, the bright lights, and smoke. The singer's sweat traces the air in a wild arc as she bellows and moans, the dark hair framing her face wet under the bright lights of the stage. I shake my head violently to the undulations of the beat, nodding, wordlessly, *yes yes yes yes yes*.

The stranger's hand remains clasped to my breast, fondling it more gently now, playing me like an instrument, while the other one travels down, fingers clawing at the side of my dress, inching the fabric up, slow as sunrise, each sliver of skin exposed to the air bringing with it both trepidation and excitement.

He stops to linger on the soft crease where ass meets thigh, each inch of trespass a chance for me to stop it, to put on the brakes, to say *that's enough*. But I don't. I don't stop it. I move my dress up for him. I help him along, guiding his hands to trace and cup the firm roundness of my ass, until the entirety of the lower half of my dress lays bunched above my waist. Ordinarily I would feel self-conscious about being so exposed, but the crowd and the night and the song and the large body of the man behind me embolden me, make me feel a little cocky, and a little crazy.

The song builds, frantic now, choking to a crescendo as he slides the fabric of my bikini bottom to the side, feeling his way into the cleft of my cheeks with his fingers. My back arches and my legs go wobbly when the tips of his fingers find my entrance, which is, as I had suspected, slick with wanting, with desire, and anticipation. As he slides inside me, plunging slow and deep with his long, slender fingers, his head tips forward toward mine, and I feel his breath on the back of my neck, warm and cool, at turns. The slight, sour taste of beer hits my nostrils as he removes his fingers from my wet cunt, which is now dripping with need. I want to cry out, to beg for their return, when I feel his hand move again, pulling the teeth of his zipper down. There's no way I could have heard the zipper over the loudness of the concert, but I do, I do! The shrill, metallic sigh of it sends a ripple right through me, and then his cock, which is warm and firm and eager.

The drums escalate, a feral rhythm matches our own wild pulsations, snare and bass and ride and hi-hats warring as he finds my opening once more and pushes easily into me, slick as I am with sweat and desire. He takes his time to fully penetrate me though, hands on my hips, fingers digging at my hip bones, pressing a little further into my cunt, and further still, his shallow thrusts gaining speed and momentum along with the galloping beat, until the full length of him is inside me. The night goes black. I am lost in the music, the soft slap of our skins, the agonizing pleasure of him plumbing the depths of me. Sweat slides down my spine, cunt red and swollen and filled and spilling like champagne.

During the song's stampeding build, the instruments go quiet, save for the throaty drag of the singer's voice, who chokes out the words like hot blasts of exhaust fumes from a semi. This sends the throng into a new bout of madness and I find myself crushed once more by a wave of bodies, my joints cracking and lungs struggling to take in air.

As she sings, our eyes lock, and I feel her stare as intensely as I feel his cock inside of me. She is looking at me and only me, as if my desire for her is as glaring and plain to read as a billboard. And perhaps it is. She places the microphone back on the stand and, with one hand, undoes a single button of the loose, light blue shirt she's wearing, soaked in sweat. The crowd erupts in a fury of hollering. And then she undoes another button. And on and on, each hint of her flesh revealed sends the crowd into a furor. She smiles when she reaches the last button, hovering, teasing us, teasing me. Pausing, she runs a hand through her drenched, shaggy hair, and shakes the sweat from it, sending a spray into the still, hot air. And then, she whips off her shirt, revealing a slender, androgynous frame, her small, pert breasts framed by a black leather chest harness, metallic studs glinting, and two black Xs criss-crossing her nipples.

The notes unspool in her throat, her voice cracking from the strain and the heat and it's enough to make me come then and there, just hearing her voice, something desperate in it, animal, her longing a thirst for salt that can never be soothed or satisfied.

And then she balls the shirt in her fist, winds her arm back, and throws it into the audience, the blue glint of it arcing as if in slow motion right at me. I reach my hand to the sky, sending a silent prayer toward any and every god who might be listening, and feel the cool wet fabric graze my fingers. I catch it. I catch it! I can't believe it. Holding the garment as if it was a life preserver, I place it against my neck, feeling the cold miracle of it on my bare skin. Inhaling the sweet, musky scent of her, I feel as if I might die, as much from pleasure as the crush of the crowd.

But I do not die.

Pain and pleasure meld furiously over and through and inside my flesh as the man pushes harder and faster, and the crowd pushes harder and faster into me. Her voice, too, catches speed, begins its agonizing climb up the mountain once more, and the

31

guitars join in, the bass, the drums, the handclaps and roars of the crowd, all of them tiny rivulets flowing into one gushing, thrashing river. Flowing into me. The man grabs a fisttful of hair at the nape of my neck and tugs my head back, so that suddenly I am faced with a snarl of stars, so many of them, you never see stars like this in the city. Their light has long extinguished, yet is reaching me just the same. The beauty of the riot of stars above and the riot of stars pushing all around me causes my vision to blur, the pressure between my legs as hard and acute as a diamond.

She strides into the final coda at the same moment I feel the shiver and clench of the man behind me, gripping and loosening and palpitating as his lust comes tumbling over that frenetic edge. The pressure in my cunt erupts and my own release comes like a deep, mournful, perfect lyric.

I barely have time to enjoy it, though.

A rogue arm flung against my windpipe sends the air out of me and my knees start to buckle. The crowd is engulfing me. I will be trampled if I can't stay upright. Before I am about to go down though, I feel the steady arms of the man once more, holding me, lifting me up and over the crowd, above the metal gate, where a security guard catches me and escorts me out of the mob, away from danger.

I take one furtive glance back at the crush of bodies, the singer's shirt held tight in my hand, and wonder who he might be. No eyes meet mine as I walk through the cleared path leading away from the stage, tugging the hem of my dress down, and feeling the remnants of a thousand fires heating me everywhere at once.

IT'S PEGGING SEASON, MOTHERFUCKERS

T hree dates in, Sara discovered she was dating a submissive man. Not only that, but a masochist to boot. She didn't know quite how to feel about this sudden, new information from him, being most comfortable with the submissive role herself, and unsure whether she could simply or easily snap out of it. Would it be possible to snarl at a man she barely knew and tell him, "Get on your knees, slut!"?

She tried saying it a few times half-heartedly in the mirror, but her command came out sounding oddly polite, more of a suggestion than an order.

Later that evening, over happy hour drinks at Oddjob, she asked her friend and sometimes-lover Renata for advice on the matter.

"The answer is simple: Peg him," Renata said breezily, as if she were remarking on the weather.

It was an uncharacteristically hot day in San Francisco and even indoors Sara sweated in her sundress, which was short, Rorschach-patterned, and showed the taut, muscled ridge of her thighs as she shifted, legs crossed, in the bar's worn, leather booth.

Renata watched Sara furrow her brow, even as she looked down and away from her. Sara's cheeks reddened. "I've never done that," she said, covering her mouth as she did so, as if even uttering the words somehow indicted her in the act.

Renata smiled, and sipped the fruity rum cocktail sweating on the table in front of her. "I'll show you," she said. "It's easy."

Sara's hand went to the back of her neck. Her heart raced—she swore she could feel the muscle beating at the top of her spine. With her other hand, she traced the rim of the drink in front of her, some bourgie lavender concoction that the cute bartender had talked her into ordering even though she hadn't wanted it. She still ordered it, of course—because she was submissive! With her index finger on the glass, she felt the perspiration dot the pad of her finger, and transferred the cold liquid to her forearm to cool herself.

"I'll teach you," Renata said. "We could even do it together, if that's something you both might want."

"You want to peg my submissive boyfriend with me?" Sara's eyes darted to Renata's, palms sweaty.

"You're right, it's silly. Forget I asked."

"No, no, I'm intrigued." Sara took a long pull from her drink, the citrus and lavender hitting her more intensely, the effervescence tickling her upper lip. She thought of her most recent ex-boyfriend, Pablo, who played video games for 7 to 10 hours a day. How bored she was with him. How she longed so fervently for even the smallest dose of his attention that once, when he boiled hot dogs for dinner, she swooned. There weren't even buns. Or forks! She ate the hot dog with chopsticks, dipping it into a puddle of ketchup, like a lunatic. And still she swooned at this miniscule gesture of romance, of care-taking. Compared to that, what Renata now offered was quite possibly the most exciting thing that had ever been set before her. She scooched closer to Renata, the outsides of their thighs touching in the booth, heat meeting heat. "It would be like a team effort?"

Now it was Renata's cheeks that flushed. She had just been complaining to Sara that the only propositions she'd received of late were threesomes, and she was beginning to resent the assumption that her lot in life was as a sexual sandwich filling.

And yet, here she was, offering herself to Sara and to a man she'd never even seen. The idea of pegging a straight man excited her terribly, however. She hadn't done so in years. The last was an old friend from college, whose face she delighted in smashing against the mattress as her hips ground him to glorious dust from behind. How thrilling to be in control, to *fuck* instead of being fucked, to hear the roar and slap of their skins as she thrust in and out.

The thought of pegging a man with Sara excited Renata even more so, and caused a shock to move through her, the flame of it gathering itself in her core and spreading outward in large ripples. Renata pressed her leg closer to Sara's in the booth, unsure suddenly if the moisture gathered at the apex of her thighs was from the heat or the flame her thoughts had ignited in her.

"Yes," Renata said, "a tag-team effort! If one of us fumbles or falters, the other will be right there, encouraging, helping, ... and high-fiving."

Sara laughed. She could easily picture Renata high-fiving her during sex. Though they had only hooked up a handful of times, Renata had such a playful demeanor in bed that put Sara at ease as much as it turned her on.

"What does he look like?" Renata asked, shyer now, and shocked a little bit by her previous boldness. Renata hadn't met any of Sara's lovers, except Pablo, and while he was nice enough, Renata was not attracted to him at all. In fact, Renata mostly preferred women. What if she had just promised Sara something she couldn't actually deliver?

Sara scrolled through her phone until it landed on a man's Tinder profile and held the glowing screen to Renata. He was a bit white-bread, but there was a wildness to his eyes that appealed to Renata, and a boyishness. He looked like a butch teddy bear, with a crooked grin and hair askew.

"He wind-surfs?" Renata gazed admiringly at his muscled arms in the photo, picturing how they might look if he was on his knees, deltoids sloping down to biceps, muscles taut with holding himself up, and smiled.

"Is that what it's called?" Sara said. "I always think of it as 'extreme sailing.'"

The night wore on. The heat did not break in the city and neither did the heat building between the two women. They hadn't slept together in ages. When Sara was dating Pablo, they became strictly friends. But now that Sara was single again, and full of desire, she found herself uncertain how to break the friend barrier once again. To talk about sex was one thing, but to put the moves on someone was quite another, especially for a submissive like Sara.

Drinking helped. As the cocktails flowed, the women found any excuse to touch each other—hand to knee, outer thighs pressed tighter, a cheek resting on a shoulder—a meeting and a breaking away, testing the waters, seeing if the other would pull away first or put a stop to it. Neither did. The slight friction of these small touches brought a tingling sensation to the areas where their skin met, as if their skin alone had the power to transform these innocuous areas into erogenous zones. Wanting to test this power further, Renata clasped her hand in Sara's—and again the tingling occurred, a current sparking, the wheels set in motion. Who knew where they would stop?

With these tiny points of contact, thighs and hands touching, starting bonfires inside her, Renata wondered, what might a third point produce?

Renata leaned forward and kissed Sara, tracing the soft circle of Sara's mouth with her own, feeling all the synapses fire down her spine, through her pelvis, and out of her toes. Her body was now a gauntlet of desire that Sara seemed to be operating at whim. How had she done this, and so swiftly? Renata pulled away briefly, wanting to admire her friend and sometimes-lover more fully. The two were somewhat oddly matched—where Renata was short, dark-skinned, and curvy with voluptuous hips and curly hair she couldn't quite subdue, Sara was tall, pale, and possessed a runner's body—tight, muscular, and tense as a bow string, with small breasts that did not require a bra.

"You're a marvel," Renata said. "Do you know that?"

Sara's eyes shut tight. When men told her she was beautiful, she expected it, but when Renata said it, she felt unmoored, transformed somehow. Like a cicada that had been waiting 17 years underground might feel breathing its first shock of sky. Her neck flushed with red, her breath came out ragged, and in a blur of motion that seemed to surprise even herself, she pulled Renata onto her lap and kissed her all the harder. Renata shuddered as Sara's hand clasped her waist, holding her in place like a toy. She felt like a toy, light and limber and radiating a goofy grin from the surprise of what was supposed to be just another Tuesday evening drink with a friend.

"There's a top in you yet," Renata said breathlessly, as Sara moved from her lips down to her neck, lapping every last trace of salt from its surface. Renata let out an open-mouthed groan as Sara's tongue dipped briefly into the hollow of her clavicle, and her hand reached up and cupped her breast, fingers open in a slight V to gently clasp the nipple, feeling it harden through the fabric.

"Come home with me," Sara said, her voice breathy and bright.

It was almost 2 a.m. The bar was about to close and both women had to work in the morning. Renata traced the line of Sara's firm jaw with her finger. "I want that so much," she said, "but not as much as I want to take my time and fully devote myself to the pleasure we both deserve."

Sara sunk a little, her lip curling into a half-frown.

"Besides," Renata said, the moisture from Sara's tongue cooling softly on her warm neck as she spoke, "the first lesson in how to top someone is delighting in making them wait."

Sara kissed Renata again, a soft groan filling her mouth. Renata's words stayed with her all the way home and into her bed, where she placed a hand between her legs and came almost instantly. Though somewhat disappointed that Renata wasn't sharing her bed tonight, she had to admit that Renata had a point. There was a beauty to it, a fervor, in being made to wait.

A few simple text messages, along with a photo of Renata, introducing the pegging idea to Mark was all it took to convince him.

When the night of the pegging arrived, however, the girls were nervous. They tried to quell their nerves with red wine and carbs, but they were too distracted by what was to come to eat or drink much.

Mark, eager to show what a good submissive he was, arrived 15 minutes early. He wore a white-button-down shirt and chinos, and Renata found herself judging him a little. Who shows up to a threesome dressed business casual? But then, she had to admit that it was far preferable than someone *not* trying.

She studied his all-American-white-boy features. His hips were angular and narrow and tapered up into a V, showcasing his wide, muscled shoulders. His eyes were sleepy and blue. When he held out his hand, Renata noted that his fingers were the most feminine thing about him—they were long and delicate and looked as if they needed to be upon a musical instrument— perhaps they soon would be, as Renata knew intimately the potential of Sara's body to sing.

He smiled easily and the three of them engaged in animated, nervous small talk in the living room. As Mark sat, hands folded in his lap, Sara felt a surprising surge coursing through her. She wanted very much to see how those hands looked in shackles, and hoped Renata had some cuffs in her goody drawer to mitigate this desire, as she herself had none.

After some discussion of boundaries, logistics, and consent, Sara suggested they retreat to the bedroom. Hand in hand in hand, the three walked down the hall, with Renata in the lead. She paused in the threshold of the doorway and kissed Sara softly on the lips, who in turn kissed Mark softly on the lips behind her. A trail of fire leading down and down and down among them.

"I've never had a threesome before," Mark said, his eyes taking on a doe-like appearance, his hands sweating.

"It'll be new for all of us then," Sara assuaged him, leading him by the hand until he stood before the two women who sat down on the edge of Renata's California king–size bed.

"Are you ready?" Renata asked, her fingers gliding along Sara's knee, stopping at the hem of her dress, mid-thigh, as she looked at the male form in front of her.

"Yes," he said, sheepish, eyes downcast.

The scene had begun.

"Good. First, a few rules. You will not speak unless spoken to," Renata said to Mark, her eyes hardening under thick lashes, her full, red mouth no longer betraying any ounce of sweetness. "And when you do, you will address us properly as "Miss,"

"Ma'am," or "Sir," if you're feeling gender-bendy. Do you understand?"

Mark, flustered, lifted his eyes back and forth between the firm line of Sara's jaw and Renata's heart-shaped face. Their eyes bored into him and he found his cock beginning to throb and twitch already. "Yes," he said.

"Yes what?"

"Yes, Ma'am."

"Good," Renata sighed. "Now take off your clothes and kneel before us with your hands clasped behind your neck. Keep your eyes on the ground."

Mark obeyed, and as he removed his pants swiftly and gracelessly, the women shared a sly glance. Sara smiled a little maniacally. Was this really happening?

Once he had disrobed and kneeled, the women set about examining him. Sara bent over him, running her fingers idly through his dark brown hair and gripping his thick neck in her hand, massaging the tightness there. Renata smoothed her hands over his chest, which was hard and lightly hairy. The contrast pleased her. She pinched each nipple, first with tender finesse, and then harder, tugging them between her thumb and forefinger and watching them harden and pinken. She could feel Mark's heart racing in his chest and this also delighted her. She hadn't even started yet.

At the touch of four hands upon him, Mark shivered almost imperceptibly, but made no sound. He kept his eyes trained to the ground, as if the light of the two women who stood in his shadow might blind him. He noticed their lower legs and feet, the electric blue nail polish that covered Sara's toes, the lithe indents in Renata's shapely calves that gave them a gazelle-like quality. He had never stopped to notice such things before, having been trained to focus on more obvious erogenous zones, and yet he couldn't help but marvel now at their details and forms.

Sara's hands moved down, across Mark's broad back, over the wings of his scapulas and the notches of spine that led to a dimple just above his round, muscled ass. She found that she wanted to trace this line of him with her tongue, and then realized that she *could.*

"I want to feel you with my tongue. Would you like that?" she said, knowing, of course, what the answer would be.

"Yes, Ma'am," he said eagerly.

Sara did so slowly, exploring the ridges and valleys of his back with her mouth, already feeling ever so slightly drunk on the power of doing as she pleased. Permission granted. Desire fulfilled. She was enjoying this newfound toppiness.

Renata kneeled to the side of him, pinching the flesh of his thighs, holding his hip bones in her hands, feeling the weight of him. He was sturdy, she noted, which meant he could probably take a good, hard pounding. It was a good thing there were two of them, since they could take turns accomplishing this feat, if one became fatigued.

Mark's breath turned uneven, and his cock rose as if an imaginary string had been attached, pulling it taut. His neck flushed at this unignorable sign that he could no longer hide his desire.

When the women had examined him to their satisfaction, Sara beckoned him to rise to his feet. He did so with a small amount of agony, as his feet and calves were full of needles. He teetered uneasily as the blood rushed back into them.

"Bend over the bed," Sara said.

"Yes, Ma'am," he said, as his forearms landed on the duvet.

"And spread your legs," Renata said. When he failed to do this quickly, she administered a series of hard, stinging slaps to his thighs. He winced, and spread his legs farther and faster. The women admired the round curve of his ass, which was hard yet supple, and held a dimple in each cheek. Sara admired the soft down of his thighs and clasped his cock loosely in her palm before giving it a tug. Mark groaned, his cries muffled by the covers near his mouth.

Renata's eyes became tiny points of fire when she heard Mark's cries, and she commanded him to spread his cheeks open for them with his hands so they could see him better. As he did so, his perineum and asshole thus exposed, Renata traced the ridge of this tender flesh with the pad of her finger. She placed a dollop of lube at the cleft and watched the line of it run down his cheeks, looking exactly like the precursor to desire that it was. She continued to rub the ridges near his entrance, teasing him idly, watching the skin pucker in response, as if blowing a kiss.

Mark's hips rose, offering himself more fully, more completely to the women, and Sara saw the veins in his forearms bulging with the strain of holding himself open. She smiled wickedly at Renata and kissed her, gently kneading her breast as Renata stroked Mark's secret spots.

"Feel how delicate he is, Sara," Renata said, placing her hand on top of hers. Sara was surprised how cool and commanding her hands felt massaging Mark's flesh, which was warm and slippery and yielding utterly to her slightest touches. She placed the tip of a lubed finger into his asshole and felt the orifice tighten around it, clasping her ecstatically. Feeling bolder now, she inserted her index finger up to the first knuckle. It clenched around her again, like a vice that could not escape the pleasure she intended to wring from it.

Mark groaned again, his breath galloping before him, neck straining from the position, and reddening.

"About an inch and a half in you'll feel a second inner sphincter," Renata told Sara, "and beyond that, the prostate. Press down with your finger toward the front wall, toward his belly button, and you'll feel it more intensely." Sara did so, increasing the pressure of her finger, which elicited another round of gasps from Mark, whose legs shook from anticipation and the strain of holding his cheeks open with his hands.

"How lovely," Sara said, the heat of her rising and pulsing as her finger dipped in and out of him. "His body is so responsive." Sara marveled briefly at how swift this transformation in her had occurred. A week ago she hadn't been able to even entertain the idea of topping a man and now here she was, fucking one with her right hand, while her left squeezed his balls hard, tugging them downward.

As she exuded this calm control over Mark, she felt her insides liquifying, turning into pure, molten energy. Her sex throbbed and no one had even touched her there. Yet.

From the dresser next to the bed, Renata grabbed a harness and small dildo, which was mauve and smooth and curved slightly upward. "He can probably take a much bigger dick than this," Renata said, "but this will do for a start." She removed the short black skirt and black corset she had been wearing. The black, lacy push-up bra followed, hitting the floor with a soft thud.

Now naked, Renata held out the harness for Sara to step into, and, reluctantly, she removed her finger from Mark's ass to disrobe herself. As she shed her sundress and stepped into the harness, Sara noticed the pleasant sensation the friction caused as it rubbed against her clit and pubic hair. With her right hand, she held onto the mauve dick, imagining it as an extension of herself. She stroked it lightly and this flooded her once more, her thighs and core burning brighter and hotter.

"Look at you," Renata marveled, twisting Sara's hips so she could see herself in the mirror by the closet, forgetting Mark's presence entirely. Sara too was shocked at herself, the black leather of the harness strode across her lower back and under each cheek, framing her petite ass like a portrait. Another slight turn and she could see the dildo and the curve of her breast. The juxtaposition both startled and entranced her. She squeezed the dildo, feeling a surge of power.

"Place the tip of the dick at the opening," Renata said, drizzling copious amounts of lube along the shaft, as well as Mark's taint and asshole, which pulsed and shuddered from the attention. As the dildo knocked softly at Mark's ass, his hips bucked backward, enveloping the head of the dick entirely.

"Someone is eager," Renata laughed, and reached forward to pinch his left nipple hard between her fingers. Mark tried to be still, but found himself squirming ever so slightly away from Renata's grasp. For this, she slapped his ass cheek swiftly and mercilessly, delighting in the reddened flesh that greeted her blows.

Sara found she was too excited to wait and thrust the full length of the dick into Mark's anus, ecstatic at the sight of it disappearing before her. She carefully inched it back out until everything but the head of it was visible, then thrust again, filling him completely, hearing the satisfying slap of her thighs meeting Mark's ass cheeks, along with his contented, muffled cries.

"Place your hands behind your back, Mark," Renata said.

"Yes, Ma'am," he said, grateful at not having to hold his cheeks open anymore, even though such a vulnerable position left him breathless and aroused. This one was easier on his neck. He turned his cheek, taking some of the strain off. He couldn't see much of what was happening, just the faint outline of Renata standing next to Sara. But he could *feel* her eyes on him, taking him, appreciating him. Her pleasure seemed to create a surge in his own body.

Sara thrust again, faster this time and with more exuberance. The feeling was so rich that Mark arched his back further, tilting his ass in the air higher to receive Sara's dick, offering himself like a cup upon which she alone could drink.

The sight of Sara's hips tilting forward and back and the slow slap of her and Mark's bodies together sent a wave of frantic heat through Renata. "Fuck," she said. "That is the hottest thing I've ever seen. Does it feel as good as it looks, Mark?"

Mark struggled to respond, his cock rigid and red and pulsing with an almost violence. "Yes, Ma'am," he whispered, craning his neck to the side, trying to get a glance of himself in the mirror near the bed, to get a better view of this delicious submission.

"Speak up," Renata said, sending another series of blows raining down upon his reddened cheeks. He squirmed, trying to avoid the blows, but knowing full well he couldn't escape them.

"Yes, Ma'am," he said again, louder, legs shaking.

Rearing toward Mark once more, Sara thrust into him, holding his hip in her hand and reaching forward to grab his neck with the other. Towering at six feet tall in heels, Sara had never been so grateful for her height before. Usually it intimidated men, but not Mark. Or perhaps he enjoyed being intimidated. Her eyes became wild, darting, as she arched her hips and dug her nails into the flesh and bone of his hip, to penetrate him deeper and harder and more completely. A sonorous ache formed between her legs and spread out like a ripple in a pond. As she moved in and out of him, her own pleasure moved with it. She felt the dildo's base nudge pleasantly against her clit and ground her pubic bone against it. Her head fell back; she could not stop smiling.

A sheen of sweat formed on Sara's brow as she continued to thrust. She felt immense, like Hydra, the three-headed sea god, or some other hundred-limbed, hundred-headed deity. Her lower back throbbed and her arms strained to hold onto Mark's hips and plummet deeper into his tight opening, which stretched easily to receive her.

Renata, noticing that Sara was overexerting herself, made her way behind Sara to offer her a subtle correction. She pressed her large, downy breasts into Sara's back and placed her hands on Sara's hips, which moved furiously and erratically, as if they could not contain the immensity of their own movements. Renata tilted Sara's pelvis forward slightly, as if it were a bowl she was intent on spilling. Sara slowed her movements until she was practically at rest. Renata's fingers grazed Sara's hip bones, guiding them the tiniest bit up and down. As she did so, Sara felt the soft swivel of Renata's breasts against her back, and closed her eyes, to better feel every subtle motion.

With Renata's gentle guidance, Sara continued to rock her hips back and forth, slower now, with more deliberate movements, sliding in and out of Mark, building speed once more and rhythm without overexerting herself. She burned to feel more of Renata's caresses than just the tips of her hands. Leaning back into Renata, she bit Sara playfully on the neck. She practiced tilting her hips, listening to the slow slap of her thighs meeting Mark's ass again. As she increased her rhythm and intensity, Mark's groans became more pronounced, more feral. He longed to bring his hand back to his cock but didn't dare move them without permission.

Sensing the tension that was pulsing to a furious beat between the three of them, Renata reached around and placed her left hand on Mark's cock, and her right on Sara's breast, massaging both between her fingers, squeezing them like the ripe fruits they were. She kissed Sara's shoulder blades while she continued to work them both, the exquisite ache of their supple flesh writhing on her hands was almost too much sensation to bear.

She knew her fingers alone would not satisfy their aches, but oh, how she enjoyed bringing them up to the edge of their deepest wants, their backs arching, their bodies sinking and rising and breaking like waves on the shores of her fingers. She relished it, the torment, the teasing. When it finally seemed as if they could stand it no longer, Renata placed her hands back on the points of

Sara's hips, stopping her.

"My turn," she said.

Mark gave a small cry when Sara exited him, and she noticed that his skin was red as a hot poker. "Stand up, Mark, and lie on your back with your knees and feet up."

"Yes, Ma'am," he said, visibly relieved to change out of this excruciating position in exchange for a more relaxed one. He laid on his back and raised his legs, feet dangling in the air.

"Straddle his face," she said to Sara, who did so obligingly, after she stepped out of the harness, which thudded wetly to the floor. Her face pointed toward Mark's feet, her cunt roaring as it made contact with Mark's sweet and hungry mouth.

Renata inched forward on her knees, positioning herself in front of Mark's legs. She inserted a strapless strap-on, which was bigger than the mauve dick and firmer, with a slight curve to its considerable girth. Grasping Mark by the thighs while he lapped at Sara's cunt, Renata poured lube onto the dick and penetrated him slowly, inch by inch, feeling Mark stretch and give and yield to her completely, while Sara rocked her hips forward over Mark's flicking tongue.

The women looked up, watching each other, transfixed, both thrusting into Mark, taking their pleasure from his varied sources, eyes full of birdsong, flushed, indulgent, and full of offering.

"You may touch yourself, Mark," Renata said, continuing to pound the full length of her rod into him, not breaking eye contact with Sara, but mesmerized by this strange and sudden intimacy, their faces so close and yet so far apart, the currents of their mutual desire sparking in futility, seeking connection, to close the circuit.

Mark glided his hand along his shaft, moving in slow and steady strokes until it throbbed and seemed to almost jump into his hands. A wave of Sara's desire bathed his face, and he savored the salt-sweat he knew was dripping down his chin and cheek. His tongue brushed the swolen ridges of Sara's sex, the tender flesh that adorned her opening like a crown.

Sara reached across the space made by their eager, grunting bodies and took Renata's breasts in her hands, feeling their heft and fullness and satin textures. As she gently worked at Renata's nipples, Renata felt her heart vibrating in her ribs. Sara's hands at her breasts sent her into a roar. She elongated her spine, thrusting harder and faster into Mark, the slap of their skin reverberating around the room. A smile stretched wide across her face as she looked at Sara, thinking about how they might look to an outside observer and knowing and taking satisfaction in how hot the three of them must look joined together in this way, the Euclidean geometry of their bodies, the hips and cunts and cocks and lips circling each other, all of them brimming and spilling and reaching for an imminent yet elusive arrival.

Sara ground her hips against Mark's face as Mark reddened and moaned beneath her. The pace of Sara's moving hips quickened and Sara leaned toward Renata, their faces drifting closer and closer until their lips found each other, never breaking stride or eye contact. Renata's lips were warm and red and invitingly swollen. With each thrust into Mark, Renata seemed to pull Sara deeper into her circle of wants. The slow slide of Renata's tongue, the sharp of her teeth, which grazed softly on Sara's lower lip— all of it unhinged her. The pleasure felt enormous, too immense to be contained in their puny bodies, the rapture rolling through them the way a wildfire levels a forest as they came, one after another after another, mouths open, hips releasing a hornet's nest of shudders and cries.

The women collapsed against each other's foreheads, the sweat and heat gathering and cooling there as the waves and ripples wrung yet further gasps from their wet throats.

As the two women looked down at Mark's torso, they saw the proof of his own desire on his chest and stomach, the cloudy white droplets glistening in a scattered display on his skin, like a Jackson Pollock painting. Renata draped her hand across Mark's chest, gathering the proof of his desire on her fingers and placing them in Mark's mouth, who sucked them clean.

Renata kissed Sara once more, tasting the cool breeze on her spent lips, and wondering if she would ever stop marveling.

She hoped not.

THE BICYCLE

They couldn't have been more different from each other.

Sabine was artsy, with thick black liner circling her eyes and black Docs studded with silver toe spikes. She was slow to warm to people, despite being the editor of both the newspaper and yearbook, and beautiful, but wouldn't know it for several more years. As such, she hid her full breasts and impossibly small waist under black clothes two sizes too large for her, emblazoned with the names of obscure death metal bands.

Michelle was a cheerleader and all-state track star, and a hoard of friends and acquaintances seemed to float about her constantly, the way woodland creatures followed Disney princesses. Thick, dark hair caressed the graceful slope of her shoulders, her skin smelled like cinnamon bubblegum, and her face seemed perfectly arranged for everyone's pleasure.

The most interaction the two high school seniors had with each other was the briefest of glances in the hallway between third and fourth period. Sabine always looked for Michelle, however, and Michelle always found Sabine's gaze, even when she didn't seem to be searching for it. Since their high school careers were ending in a few weeks and the two might never see each other again, Sabine began adding a dollop of a smile to the look she gave Michelle as she passed, and, lo and behold, Michelle smiled back. The flash of Michelle's dimple alone, only on the right side, Sabine noticed, could send Sabine into spasms of giddiness. Emboldened by the smile, Sabine followed the graceful arc of Michelle's neck down to the subtle swell of her cleavage, and wondered what it would be like to trace that line with her tongue.

Shy glances and passing grins aside, Sabine had no idea how to talk to Michelle. The most the two had spoken was for a Biology project in 10th grade—dissecting a cow eyeball—which was not a topic Sabine wanted to revisit and certainly not one that would lead them on the course of everlasting love. She pictured herself trying: *Remember 10th grade Bio? You mooooved me.*

No. Sabine picked at the chipped black nail polish on her fingers, deciding to leave the gross science experiments alone and focus on the future.

But what could they possibly have in common? How would she break the ice? Asking about her summer plans felt trite and obvious. She could ask about college—Michelle got a sports scholarship to a fancy-sounding school on the East Coast—but Sabine didn't know the first thing about track. *I want to jump you like a hurdle*, she thought, and then chastised herself. So not smooth.

Luckily for Sabine, however, an answer presented itself in the way of an early graduation present from her dad. It was a lowrider bicycle, glittering gold all the way from spokes to brakes, which her dad outfitted with a portable sound system and a velour banana saddle. Sabine was showing it off to her small, but adoring cadre of misfits after school, when Michelle and her woodland creatures strode past, lured by so much bling.

"Can I try it?" said the one who looked not unlike a squirrel—excitable, tiny eared, possibly on some kind of uppers.

Sabine looked to Michelle for reassurance, trusting her for reasons she couldn't articulate, and Michelle nodded slowly, signaling that the squirrel was all right, that she wouldn't break Sabine's new toy. One by one, the creatures took turns on the golden bicycle, until at last there was no one left but Michelle who had yet to take it for a ride. Sabine's friends had long gone home, and Michelle, perhaps needing a moment to herself (or a moment with Sabine?), told her crew she'd catch up with them later and sent them on their way.

"Do you mind?" Michelle asked. From this close distance, Sabine could see the constellation of freckles on Michelle's upper arm and smell the sweet, oily scent of her sunscreen—coconut. She felt she might faint from the scent alone.

"Of course not," Sabine managed to say in a squeak. In her head, she thought, She's just a person. She's just a person. A person like you. This helped to calm Sabine's jittery heart some.

Michelle straddled the long, velvety seat, which turned slightly up at the tip, and felt immediately the advantages to such a design. A bright spot of pleasure nestled itself between her legs and only increased as she set foot on the peddle and pushed. The friction of the seat and her denim-clad thighs sent a gentle wave of heat from sacrum to scapula, and a smile spread from lips to lips. Having never masturbated, as she had shared a bedroom with her sister her entire life and hence, never had any real privacy, Michelle hadn't experienced this direct sensation on her clit before and soon found herself flushed in the neck and chest and slightly dizzy. As she passed Sabine in a slow circle, the sensation and the cute goth girl smiling at her was too much for Michelle.

She crashed right into a bush.

Sabine, alarmed, went to her, and offered her a hand. "Are you okay?" she asked.

Michelle cupped her sex with her palm, embarrassed and throbbing, though she could not tell whether it was from pleasure, pain, or a mixture of the two. "I'm not sure," she said.

"Come with me," said Sabine, and ushered Michelle into the nearest bathroom, which was in the school's gymnasium. Their footsteps echoed against the high ceiling, and Sabine noticed that Michelle did not let go of her hand as they walked, even though she easily could have .

Sabine led them to an empty bathroom stall and locked the door. She sat on the toilet as Michelle stood with her back against the door. A piney, chemical smell tinged the air.

"Let's see it," Sabine said, with a boldness that surprised both of them.

"It?" Michelle asked.

"Your injury."

"Oh. Right."

Sabine reached up and unbuttoned the top button of Michelle's black cutoffs, looking up at her perfectly arranged face to see if this gesture was okay. Michelle didn't move Sabine's hand away, but she didn't look at her either. Sabine popped another button. And another. Michelle's heart thundered in her chest. She would never let the boys who were constantly trying to seduce her get this far on a first encounter, yet here was this mysterious girl, with blue mascara and an amazing rack she tried (and failed) to hide from the world, removing Michelle's pants in the first ten minutes. Michelle was confused, and, she admitted to herself, a little impressed.

The last button popped open and Sabine tugged the shorts down over Michelle's hips. Michelle was not that surprised to find her hips moving seemingly of their own accord, helping Sabine along, and with a final swish, they dropped to her ankles. The black cotton thong came down easily after them.

Michelle felt the shock of cold metal against her bare ass and stared straight ahead at the anarchist graffiti on the stall wall, along with a couple's initials, AP + TE = <3.

"It looks a little swollen," Sabine said, both legitimately concerned and dying a little at the proximity of her mouth to Michelle's cunt. "I hope you didn't damage any nerve endings."

"Is that bad?" Michelle asked, the undertow of her desire and vulnerability now mixed with fear. Sabine let her hand rest on the soft brown triangle of hair above Michelle's clit, desperate to explore it with her thumb.

"One time, in second grade, I got kicked in the crotch by Brad Perkins—" Sabine started.

"Ugh, I hate that kid. He used to try to flip up every skirt I wore to school. I stopped wearing skirts until ninth grade!"

"He did? That's awful!" Sabine's heart froze when she noticed Michelle's hand covering her own, pressing, guiding it closer to her cunt. Sabine attempted to finish her thought. "After he kicked me, I couldn't feel anything down there for an entire week."

"Oh my god," Michelle said, fingers drawing circles on Sabine's hand. "Could that happen to me?"

"I don't know," Sabine said. "Can you feel this?" She placed her thumb at the opening of Michelle's sex and massaged, softly, a slow line up to her clit, feeling the heat and slick of Michelle coat her thumb, wishing she could lick it clean.

Michelle, barely able to contain her pleasure at this touch, and who also could not bear for Sabine to stop, lied outright. "No," she said. "I don't feel anything."

"Hm," Sabine said, the salt of Michelle's cunt reached her nostrils, sprouting a new madness in her that she struggled mightily to subdue. "How about this?"

She kept her thumb on Michelle's clit, and with her other hand, made a V shape and pressed down and around the outside of her lips, feeling the folds swell and spring to her touch. Michelle's head tipped back against the stall door, the clang of it startling her, but still she said, breath catching in her throat, "No," she said, "nothing."

"How about this?" Sabine said, kneeling before Michelle, knees trembling as they met the cold, hard tiles. The position reminded Sabine of church, all those weekends her family made her attend mass against her will—all of it felt suddenly worthwhile, practice for this very moment of penitence and worship. She took Michelle in her mouth like the Eucharist, poised to melt every last ounce of Michelle's resolve.

Michelle's hand went to Sabine's hair, resting it gently, tentatively, forgetting altogether the game of "no" she was pretending to play. A soft moan fell from her lips, and Sabine, eager to prolong this stirring, stopped moving. She wanted—suddenly, fiendishly—to rouse and deprive Michelle of pleasure until she dropped the ruse, until her entire body vibrated with longing for Sabine's mercy.

Hair strewn across her face and eyes wild, Michelle looked down at Sabine, a look that begged, Don't stop, and so Sabine didn't. But instead of keeping her face pressed to the fire, Sabine slowly worked her way up Michelle's torso, kissing the sharp of her hip bones, the soft down of her belly hair, up and up, pushing the shirt, then the bra up and out of the way, kissing the soft fruit of her breasts, the pinch of her nipples, the sternum and collar bones, until she was standing upright, staring into Michelle's face, her face the pit-perfect center of a peach. Sabine felt momentarily struck dumb by the wild unreality of the moment and forgot her plan.

"How about this?" Michelle finished Sabine's sentence for her, but Sabine didn't have time to respond or move even an inch forward before Michelle's hands clasped her face and pulled her in violently for a kiss.

Feral with impatience and need, Michelle fell upon Sabine's mouth, sucking the traces of her own heat, touching gently their tongues, the bow of Sabine's rind-red lips, soft as snowmelt and plush as a stuffed toy. Michelle removed Sabine's too-large shirt and sports bra in one deft movement, surprising herself, and reached her fingers into the waistline of Sabine's pants, working the button and zipper without the aid of sight, as she pressed her teeth first to Sabine's neck, then to her ear, and back to her lips once more. Michelle felt suddenly like everything—even their own skin—was a barrier between them that must, at all costs, be done away with.

Michelle continued to struggle with the zipper when she remembered that there were certain benefits to large, ill-fitting pants, and tugged the whole affair down, underwear and all, swift as a knife. Sabine gasped at her sudden nakedness, the chill of the air and Michelle's lips like magnets pulling the iron from her blood, pulling the tides in her veins, and she could no longer stand the separation between their bodies. She pushed Michelle back against the stall door, hearing the satisfying metallic knock of it, and pressed her every place she possibly could, shins and knees and thighs and cunts and hips and ribs and breasts and mouths, all of them pulsing, swelling, dancing in the flames of their movements together.

But then, a whoosh and a thud. The bathroom door opened, and the patter of several footsteps stopped Michelle and Sabine cold. They were no longer alone, and froze, locked together as they were, hoping the girls would not see Michelle and Sabine's legs or the large pile of clothes under the stall door.

"Did you see the way he looked at me?" said one of the voices.

"Yes, girl, he so thirsty," said another.

"Bitch, you just jealous."

"Puh-lease, everyone knows Brad'd fuck a beehive he so thirsty."

A chorus of giggles echoed through the space, as Sabine, unable to stop the slow, exquisite ache that came from Michelle's cunt pressed against her own, began to tip her pelvis back and forth.

The heat of Michelle began to ripple and meld with her own. It began to feel surreal to Sabine, as if the more she touched Michelle, the more her own pleasure soared, until it was all she wanted, more touch and more life and more more.

The tilt of Sabine's hips, agonizingly slow, a fraction of an inch at a time, caused Michelle's hips to start rocking against her will, and she couldn't hold back a groan. Sabine clasped her hand over Michelle's mouth, waiting, breathless, to learn if they'd been discovered.

But they had not. The giggles and footsteps of the girls faded and the door slammed shut once more, leaving Michelle and Sabine to continue their tortuous escapades.

Michelle, seizing the nearness of Sabine's fingers, took four of them into her mouth, her tongue appropriating the salts and oils from them, as she grasped Sabine's ass with both hands, pulling her closer still, pulling her into the bright-red center of her wants, teaching her the rapture of gravity. The pressure building, nowhere to go except through. Their desire turned to steam and the steam rose and condensed and crystallized back into their bodies in a rhythmic rush of continuity that threatened to send them both toppling to the floor.

Michelle's head fell back and the length of her pressed against the stall door. Sabine worked her hips faster, harder, and as she did, she felt Michelle's thighs tense and flex and yield, their cunts moving together seamlessly, containing every collapse, limbs and hair and sweat and heat tangled, and merging, coming together and apart and together again, like a flock of starlings at dusk.

Michelle became Sabine, and Sabine Michelle, their moans ricocheting off the walls and tiles, becoming ten, then a hundred, then a thousand moans. Time contracted and elongated at once, until Michelle felt even the hairs on her arms pulsing with desire, and cupped the firm curve of Sabine's perfectly heart-shaped ass once more. Michelle's fingers reached and reached, spreading Sabine open, pressing and traveling until they found Sabine's opening. Michelle pushed gently, wetly inside. At this touch, something in Sabine snapped. She bucked wildly, so much so that Michelle lost her reach, and had to hold Sabine in place with her arm before feeling around once more for the spot that had set Sabine off.

Once back inside, Michelle pressed her fingers in farther, an immense and reckless satisfaction beaming on her face at the buck and curl of Sabine's body. Sabine dug her nails into Michelle's hips, but did not cease her own hips' motion. When Sabine pushed her hips upward, Michelle felt the bright, pleasant ache of their clits moving together. When Sabine pulled back, she felt Michelle's fingers pressing into her slick folds. Each back brought the other forward, and vice versa, both of them leaning precariously close to the edge, the pulsations and heat bearing down on them, each gasping and grasping, throats ragged with abandon, and both refusing to cease, to slow, to let go of the other's pleasure. Until.

Until the pulsing reached its tremorous, feverish peak and they came this way, limbs coiled, hair a snarl, one after the other, like too many objects dropped in their hands at once. They could not catch anything, not even their own breath, which finally, eventually slowed. Their sighs snagged in the air like dissonant music that dipped and dropped exquisitely together, a coin fitting somehow perfectly into its slot. Michelle collapsed against Sabine's collar bone, and she inhaled the skin there, beaded with honeyed sweat, a happiness nestling quietly inside her that she had not known was possible in all of her eighteen years.

But after the heat and intensity of their togetherness had cooled, Michelle felt a sudden and irrepressible urge to flee. Was it embarrassment? Fear? Some inner disapproval she wasn't yet aware of? She didn't know. She only knew she must vanish. And so she did, with scant so much as a peck goodbye, leaving Sabine to wonder and dress quickly and awkwardly in the stall by herself.

The next day at school, Sabine searched for Michelle everywhere, but Michelle was not to be found. Not even in the hallway between third and fourth period. Despondent, Sabine packed her things and made her way to the bike lockers to retrieve her gold companion and head dejectedly home.

It was there that she found Michelle, sitting astride the bicycle's upturned seat, looking for all the world like a queen on her rightful throne.

"Hey," Michelle said.

"Hey." Sabine felt timid, uncertain, and couldn't read Michelle's intentions.

"I went riding," Michelle said shyly, looking down at Sabine's navel. "I think I hurt myself again. I was hoping you might take a look?"

CHOOSE THE RIGHT

A Cautionary Tale

A friend and I are at an Italian restaurant in the Mission, sharing a bowl of handmade pasta and sparkling rose. She takes a ring off her finger and holds out her hand.

"What's this?" I say. This friend is always showering me with gifts. She's basically the best girlfriend I've never had.

"It's for you."

The ring is a silver signet with the letters CTR engraved in black. She sees me eyeing the letters quizzically, not sure how to respond.

"Do you know about 'choose the right'?"

I do not, so she proceeds to tell me that "choose the right" is the Mormon version of "What would Jesus do?" An abbreviated reminder to act in ways that are in accordance with one's beliefs and values.

My friend is not Mormon—in fact, she's Jewish—but she has always been strangely drawn to Mormonism. Parts of it, at least, like CTR, and the idea of a "true" name.

A Mormon's "true" name is given to them the first time they participate in an endowment ceremony. This name will be what they are called in the afterlife. A wife must tell her husband her true name, and no one else, as this is how he will summon her during the resurrection.

It's a romantic notion—that only one person can *know* you in this specific way, your soul belonging to theirs completely, during this life and all eternity.

As odd as it is that my Jewish friend has given me (an atheist) a Mormon purity ring, I'm delighted and charmed and slip it on my middle finger, the only place it will fit on my spindly, long fingers.

I suspect the real reason she is giving me this ring is because I am about to see my ex-girlfriend for the first time since we broke up, and she doesn't want me to fall back into the familiar, toxic pattern of our on-again, off-again tumult.

"Choose the right, Anna," she tells me, clutching my hand, a ringlet of curls bouncing on her nose in the chilly San Francisco evening.

"I'll be fine!" I tell her.

But I am not fine. I am anything but fine. I am, in fact, feral with longing, so desperate to see my ex and touch her and connect with her that my heart starts skipping beats. I clutch at my chest, trying to will the muscle to calm, but it doesn't work.

Leaving the restaurant, I trace the outline of the letters on my new ring and sigh. I need all the help I can get.

Because my ex and I have a pattern of immediately falling into bed together the first instance it is physically possible to do so —and we are trying to avoid this—our meetup requires some strategizing.

Several ideas are tossed out, then swiftly rejected. "What if you tied me up?" I text, thighs vibrating already at the thought of being restrained, the taut burn of rope against my bare skin.

"No," she texts back. "That would not do at all. What about a chaste, public place, like a playground."

"You mean like that playground we fucked in?" I say.

I remember that day perfectly. We climbed atop a yellow slide with the plastic green railing. No one else was around so she tugged my pants down and placed her tongue at the apex of my thighs. Her long hair blanketed my thighs, and it was raining but I could barely feel it. The rain became her; it was on us and in us and happening upon us the way her mouth was happening upon me as I looked up at the white fluff ringed with electric blue and discovered I was beautiful.

That chaste playground? That would not do either.

"We can't meet anywhere we've fucked—so, not our houses, no parks, no beaches, no dressing rooms, no hotels, no Cheesecake Factories, not my truck, no airports, no airplanes!" I said.

"I wasn't going to suggest we get on an airplane!" she replied.

"Well, knowing you, that's not out of the realm of possibility."

Approximately eight hundred texts later, we decide, or rather, *she* decides we will get a couples massage—something in public, relaxing, involving touch, but from other people. I am initially against this idea—because we will be naked—but she seems convinced and I don't have a better plan, so I agree to try it.

During the hour-long drive to her house, where I am to meet her but not set a foot inside, I feel as unhinged as I did the first time we met. My heart knocks against my ribs like a fly on a windowpane. I can't soothe it. Instead I scream along to Dashboard Confessional—and for some reason, a recording of Jewel singing the national anthem—in hopes that I will wear it out through exhaustion.

She greets me at the door dressed entirely in white—white sandals, tight white jeans that seem to grasp her curves like hands, and a white, flowy, drapey top that, when she extends her arms, gives her the illusion of wings.

At the door she devours me with her eyes, scanning my body so completely that I have to look away. I'm dressed in my usual attire, black tank top, maroon jeans, and black leather boots. My neck flushes pink and I pull her into my arms because I can't bear for her to see me as thoroughly as she's seeing me right now. Not yet. Maybe not ever.

In hugging her, I've already broken a rule. We are not supposed to touch. Because touching leads to kissing and kissing leads to more kissing and more touching and yet here we are, standing in her doorway, my hands wrapped around her slender waist, my hands skating along the white fabric, feeling the softness, the warmth of her, not believing it, some part of me, not believing it's real, that she's here, that I am holding her. We've been broken up for a month. The longest we've gone without touching in the year we've known each other.

We stay here for several minutes in this embrace, moving incrementally, like tidally locked planets, and I inhale her scent, my face lost to a blanket of her hair, the sweet cloud of her perfume. With the tips of my lips, I graze the skin where her neck meets shoulder, and feel her body tense and collapse at the same time. It's possible a moan escapes her. From the very start, our bodies have been attuned to each other's vibrations; there's no movement she makes that I don't also feel in my body.

Right now, in my arms, she radiates desire. She moans or I moan —I'm not sure at this distance—and my lips wander up the periphery of her, from neck to jaw to cheek, until our lips face each other, poised and attentive. I pause again. My hands are shaking.

We aren't supposed to kiss, which makes it that much likelier we will, because that is desire's whole premise. To want what is just beyond your grasp. To want what is forbidden to you.

I hover over her lips, brushing across them with my own so lightly that the sensation could be a moth's wing. The wait is excruciating. I wait because I want her to respond. To make some sign that she wants this as much as I do.

Her eyes close. We are almost the same height, so her touch is like a mirror—her hip bones, belly, ribs, breasts, all of them exquisitely touching my softest and sharpest terrains. My most urgent wants. I keep my eyes open. I want to watch us. I want to see everything I do to her and everything she does to me. With her eyes shut she looks pained, perhaps from pleasure or from the toll it takes to resist me. I feel like I could cry—and I will, later, but not yet.

My heart thunders against her chest when finally she kisses me, her lips cloud-full and soft as ice cream melting. The kiss is slow, frenzied but restrained, desperate wanderers drinking from each other's cup, two rushing rivers colliding in a vast, eternal sea. My tongue finds hers, and I savor it as if it were my last meal. I am dismantling now, my mouth eager to kiss her everywhere, to fill my tongue with the salt and sweat of her, and just as I am about to, her phone buzzes.

Our car is here. As we leave her house, she tells me that she called a Lyft as soon as she heard me ring the doorbell, so that we would have only a few minutes alone. Clever. Cruel. Perfect. We get in the Lyft. I have no idea what we talk about on the way to the massage, so nervous am I at the prospect of being fully naked in the same room with her, and still flush from the countries of our lips colliding. My skin feels like a hot-wired car. If she touches me again I will ignite.

◆ ◆ ◆

In the changing room, I disrobe quickly and unceremoniously. The lights are dim and the room smells like eucalyptus and lavender. I face her in my nakedness and she reaches out and gently clasps my breasts with her nails, pinching the tiniest amount when the tips reach my nipples. I love when she does this; even her lightest touch feels like possession.

She pulls back, scolds herself for touching me, and tells me my breasts have gotten bigger.

"That's impossible," I say. "I've lost weight. I haven't been eating."

The masseuse knocks and we lie down on separate beds. I am already turned on and the woman who touches me is young and attractive, and her hands on me only exacerbate my condition. I try to look over at my ex but her head is facing straight down. I want to know what she's thinking. I want to reach out across the short distance and take her hand in mine.

But I don't. I attempt to relax, to breathe deeply and let the oil and warmth of another's hands soak into my skin. The masseuse's hands aren't the hands I want, but they will do. For now.

After the massage, she takes me to lunch and, over a veggie scramble that I half-eat, tells me that she can't be a partner to me. Everything inside of me deflates, slowly, like the air of a tire hissing to death. After she says it, I want to leave the earth, to swim to a cave at the bottom of the ocean. But when I look up, I am disappointly still here, in this diner, and there is still one more activity on our No Fucking Day agenda—and it is the least erotic thing we could think up: an intake call with a therapist.

(Yes, we went to therapy post-breakup. Yes, it *is* the gayest thing you've ever heard.)

We take the call at her house, (dangerous) sitting side by side on her L-shaped couch, thighs touching, elbows touching (extremely dangerous). Talking to the therapist buoys my mood, but not enough. It's just an intake call, after all, going over rules and dates and insurance information.

After the call is over, it hits me that our relationship is over. The call, the entire day, a red herring. We're not traveling down this dusty road together. It's just me, alone, building altars to a woman who no longer exists.

I cry silently for all the bridges my ex and I will never cross together, and sink down into the couch. She lays down next to me and kisses my tears and it does not take long before she is kissing my cheek and neck and then her mouth is upon me and her hands claim me again and again and we are melting and pulling and humbling ourselves before lesser gods.

In our frenzy, we can't be bothered to remove our clothes entirely—pants remain half on, only one arm is released from a shirt, bras are pushed upward to reach and reveal dark, erect nipples. The soft sounds of us slapping together echo through the living room, our cries melding as we tear softly at each other's jagged edges. Random pieces of clothing start to come off—my bra, her shirt—but the rest stay on. I am frantic to touch her, to feel the proof of her desire for me, palpable, sharp as a blade, that I cannot wait until her pants are off. I pop the button of her jeans, tug the teeth of the zipper down, and cup her sex in my hand, over her thong, ecstatic to find that the fabric is drenched already.

I leave my hand there for a moment, unmoving, feeling the exquisite heat of her rising to my palm. I focus on kissing her, dragging my teeth up and down her neck until every nerve ending brightens and sings my name. Her hips rise to meet my hand, and I slip beneath the thin fabric, my fingers soon warm and slippery in her folds. I lay my middle finger at her opening and she invites me inside. As I move my finger slowly in and out, I press the base of my palm against her clit and make slow circles. I steadily build this rhythm into a melody into a hymn into a symphony, and soon she is writhing wildly, clutching my wrist in her hand, her mouth falling open, her mouth appearing as a grimace to anyone else, but I know, I know this face, I know she's close, and in just a few more slides of my hand, she will come toppling over this cliff face with me.

I thrust my finger in again wildly, as deep as it will go, joyful disbelief once more crowding my thoughts, and it is then that I feel it, the silver signet ring, slipping off my finger, the very finger, the only finger that is inside of her, poised to make her come. But I can't stop. I don't stop. I slide into her again, and feel the ring slip further still, past one knuckle now and moving steadily down. She is trembling beneath me. Her breath comes out in quick, staggered bursts. Her hips a wild current seeking completion. *Oh god*, I think, *please do not let this ring fall off, please stay there for a few more seconds, until she comes. Just a few more seconds.*

But the ring does not wait. It slides entirely off my finger and grazes the opening of her cunt, where I catch it and pull my hand out of her jeans. I place the ring, dripping and hot, on her coffee table, where it clatters and bounces. She looks at the ring on the coffee table and I look, too. It glistens in the bright afternoon light, slick with her desire and mine.

The sounds of us fill the room once more, but this time it's our riotous laughter. We cannot stop laughing. We have been twat-blocked by a Mormon purity ring. It's perfect. It's devastating. Choose the right, indeed. Right on cue.

"I feel so scolded," she says. And I blush all through my chest. I notice my bra on the floor. She wraps her arms around me and we lay together, my head buried in her neck, her lips against my collar bone. We do not go further. We choose, this time, to honor the message of the ring, to honor our higher selves and intentions, and hope that someday soon, we will get it right.

THE DOCTOR

Riva sat on the crinkly white paper, her legs dangling off the side of the examination table, feet not touching the floor, despite her considerably long legs. She pointed her toes down as she swung her legs, attempting to reach the linoleum, but failed, and in doing so felt a little like a child in a tall chair.

She hated these visits, the way her doctor condescended to her, mansplaining the ailments she had lived with her entire life, of which he could never cure, but loved to blather endlessly about.

Riva tried not to think about it, instead reading once more the elaborate hand-washing sign, which involved no fewer than eight steps and about that many illustrations. As she was puzzling over how an act so simple could require this many instructions, she heard a knock and felt a slight gust from the door as it opened.

Riva swiveled her head around and was startled to see this was not her usual doctor, but a much younger, and—Riva could not fail to notice—a much more attractive man. He held his hand out to her and flashed two perfect rows of flawless white teeth. Riva clasped his hand, the skin of his palm warm and softer than she expected. When he didn't immediately let go, Riva gave him a subtle once-over, and by the time her eyes found their way back to his broad jaw and charming sideburns, she swore she saw his eyes performing their own sly glances at her. She wore black jeans and a green tank top—nothing wow-inducing by any means but certainly one that showed off her curves. The cut of the top allowed the faintest glimpse of her breasts to show, which were full and round and seemed to rise further to attention when the doctor's eyes fell on them.

"You must be Riva," he said, in a British accent that sounded dewy, his syllables coated in a cool, morning mist. "I'm filling in for Dr. Johnson while he's at a conference."

"And you are...?"

"Charmed, naturally." He held his hand out once more, which Riva was all too eager to take.

"I'm similarly charmed," she smiled, clasping his long fingers in hers. "But I meant your name."

"Oh! Of course. Forgive me," his neck flushed through the opening in his white overcoat. "It's David. ... Lawrence. ... uh, Dr. Lawrence."

"Dr. Lawrence. Nice to meet you." He let go of Riva's hand and, flustered, stepped abruptly back, but as he did so his khaki-clad thigh brushed her knee and even through the fabric of her pants she felt the skin around the area awaken and brighten. She leaned back, surprised at this reaction, this betrayal of her body, this quiet yielding to a stranger. She rested her hands behind her on the white paper, which crackled unpleasantly.

The position allowed Dr. Lawrence to register once again her breasts, whose nipples had formed small round peaks that he could clearly see through her black top. He registered his own desire, which he had never before experienced with a patient in his years of medical practice. He shoved it down and recovered. "What seems to be the problem?"

The problem, Riva did not say, *is that your hands are not on my body, tip-toeing up my thighs and hips, sliding up to my tits and claiming them.*

Confused by the suddenness and alarmingness of this fantasy, this intrusion of her mind and lack of hands on her body, Riva did not answer him for several beats. It was only when his eyebrows arched in confusion that she remembered she had been spoken to.

She decided to do something wholly unlike her. "Well, it's a little weird," she said, looking down at her breasts, which perched as eagerly as two mounds of sugar awaiting tea.

"You can tell me, Riva. Everything that happens in this room is confidential, strictly between us." As he said this his fingers grazed her shoulder for a fraction of a second, and then departed. Riva shivered. This man was tuning her like an instrument, tightening every string in her body until it sang.

"I have this pain," she started.

"What kind of pain?"

"A throbbing kind. It starts at the underside of my breasts and spreads outward, almost like a fire."

"I see," he said. "And when was your last clinical breast exam?"

"Years ago," she lied.

"And did the doctor find anything unusual?"

"No," she said, eyebrows forming peaks of mock-concern. "Should I be worried? It's not cancer, is it?"

"Do you have a history of breast or ovarian cancer in your family?"

"Not that I know of."

"It's unlikely then, but I'll have to take a look. Would you mind removing your top and bra please?"

Riva stood and faced away from the doctor so he could not see the absolute satisfaction in her smile as she crossed her arms in front of her and slowly pulled the tank top over her head. Dr. Lawrence took in the lovely, sloping arc of her spine and the well-formed Latissimus dorsi muscles that stretched as she lifted her arms above her head.

With one hand, she reached for the bra strap and feigned to struggle with its clasp. She tried again with both hands, but it would not come undone. She cast an innocent eye in the direction of the doctor, and said, "Would you mind?"

He would not.

He stepped closer to her, and glancing over her shoulder, could see her breasts rising and falling at the pace of her breath, which he also noticed was shallow. He did not have to take out his stethoscope to know her heart was beating hard, as was his own. With skillful care, he placed his fingers gingerly on the band, and felt her push slightly back into him, the ample curve of her ass brushing against his crotch for the briefest of seconds. If he hadn't been so aware of his own desire, he might not have noticed it at all, that's how swift the movement came about.

The clasp popped open in his hands and Riva's skin shuddered both from the doctor's caress and the sudden cold of her now naked upper body. She set the bra and top on a nearby chair and sat back down on the table.

"Lie back please, and raise your left arm over your head."

Riva did as she was told, feeling once more the stiff paper greet her soft skin. Dr. Lawrence went to the sink and washed his hands, pulled two surgical gloves from a box. Riva smelled the slight chalkiness of the gloves as he snapped them on and something else she couldn't quite identify, possibly sage.

He stood over her now, her beauty on full display before him, her lips pulled taut in a half-smile that seemed pleased with itself. He steadied his breath, attempting to retain his professionalism, and to ignore once more the desire that caused his pants to tighten and stretch around it.

He placed one hand on her sternum, and with the other, using the three pads of his middle fingers, he pressed lightly against her breast in slow circles, feeling the skin warm and color at his touch. He kept his eyes to the back wall as he increased the pressure, not breaking contact with her breast, even when his palm brushed the nipple and it hardened. With a deftness known mainly to pickpockets or magicians, the doctor continued the up-and-down motion of the exam with the pads of his fingers while also grazing his palm over the nipple, feeling it rock sweetly and agonizingly against his hand, and harden further.

Riva bit her lip each time the doctor's palm found its way to her nipple, certain now that he had caught on, that they were playing the same game and that they must both keep it up, for the sake of her propriety and his profession. She was, however, also finding that the part of her brain prone to thinking was becoming ever blurrier with each subtle sweep of his hand on her delicate flesh.

The doctor continued to explore Riva's breast with his fingers in a most professional manner while his palm went everywhere his desire wanted to go. He kept his gaze steady, not daring to look at her face, but gauging her reaction by touch, the soft sigh of her breath, the slight lift of her back as he brushed against her, firmer now, as if she were offering herself to him, these ripe fruits, firm and full and harvested just for him. Emboldened by Riva's hips arching forward at his latest caress, the doctor extended his thumb outward and gave the flesh a cursory squeeze. The exquisite heft and yield of her breast fully in his clasp affected him violently, the swelling in his pants now visible to all who wished to see it.

Still his voice remained calm, unwavering. His composure a mask Riva would not yet lift. "Nothing unusual here," he reported. "But you said there was pain."

"Yes."

"Where?"

With a slight trembling, Riva placed her hand over his, guided the tips under the curve, its perfect C shape. "It starts here," she said.

"Only the left breast?"

"No, both," she said, taking his other hand from her sternum and placing it on the other breast, manipulating his hands into a position she enjoyed, with the outer edges of his pinkies pressing against her ribs, and his palms pushing her breasts up toward her chin. In this position, with his hands gripping her and her hands guiding, Riva felt faintly possessed. She didn't know how much longer she could keep her voice steady at this rate. But she endeavored to try, even as she could feel her desire dampening her pants. "It moves up and out," she said, tracing circles with his thumbs, "like the nerves are inflamed."

"Does anything help to alleviate the pain?" His hands hovered, poised and waiting for a signal, wanting desperately to crush the supple flesh and knead it in his fingers.

"Pressure," she said, looking him straight in the eyes now, daring him to go further, to break his considerable composure and end their agony.

"What kind of pressure?" he said, clinical, almost fatherly. If she wanted him this badly, then she would have to earn it, he thought.

"Like this." She pushed his thumb and forefinger closer together, so that it held her nipples once more.

"Like this?" he asked, and pinched the spot she had led him to, rolling the soft flesh between his fingers. Riva inhaled sharply, her breath caught in the surprise and pleasure of this small movement.

This was signal enough for the doctor, whose wire was hence tripped, and he fondled her breasts openly and with considerable vigor, hands pressing and possessing her. With firmer but still gentle strokes, he tugged at the nipples until they formed stiff peaks, and then placed his mouth there, sucking on the firmness he inspired.

Riva's moans turned wilder, singing further and further into abandon as the doctor kneaded one breast with his hand and the other with his mouth. Like a marionette doll, she felt her clit swell and rise each time he placed his mouth on her nipple, as if the two places were connected by string. The weight of him upon her caused her insides to simultaneously leap and sink further into the cushion of the examination table, whose paper continued to make an awful racket, but which Riva no longer paid attention to. His hands and mouth on her were like lightning, striking and illuminating her in ways she had never known were possible before. She seemed to feel him everywhere at once, and as his movements quickened and intensified, her cunt pulsed and her hips and ass bucked furiously against the table.

As Riva's quiet gasps gave way to madness, the doctor clasped his hand over her mouth and leaned into her, his breath hot against her neck. "Come," he whispered through his teeth. "Come now. I want to feel you scream into my hand." And with that, her orgasm sped out and through her like electricity. The doctor's hand proved to be a reliable barrier, muffling almost all of the sound that shook from Riva's lips, and he held her as the tremors slowed and subsided, catching her eyes and smiling as the pulsations fled her body.

When her heart had sufficiently calmed itself, she managed to sit up, her hair a lion's mane, her pants soaked through to the white paper beneath her.

The doctor smoothed her hair and then his own white overcoat as he allowed a little distance between what had just happened. He handed her clothes back to her, and Riva put them on in a daze.

"Well," he said, voice once again dewy with composure. "Your body has a perfectly healthy response system." She smiled at him, eyes slightly downturned, remembering the role of the innocent she had been playing. "But I'd still like to give you a full examination, to make sure we aren't missing anything." He reached into his pocket and fished out his card, which he held out to her.

She took the card, still woozy from this unexpected turn of events, and from the lingering traces his fingers made on her skin. Underneath these feelings was something more raw, vulnerable, a smattering of guilt at having behaved so publicly, so *shamelessly*. Though she had put her clothing back on, she still felt naked.

She eyed the card suspiciously. "Are you for real?"

The doctor smiled. "I understand your doubts," he said and placed his hand upon Riva's knee once more, which warmed just as it had the first time. "But here at Caspian Health, it's not just lip service. The patient really does come first."

He winked at her and together the sound of their laughter filled the small, white room.

She was still chuckling softly to herself when the sound of her own name startled her awake.

"Riva Vasquez? Dr. Johnson will see you now."

Riva wiped the wet that had seeped from her mouth, her cheek still flushed with arousal, surprise, and now embarrassment.

Wiping the sleep from her eyes, she rose, achy from the slim, sea-green chair, and sighed. "I'm coming."

DESERTERS

*The Roar That Swallows Silence, a
story by Paloma and Nadezhda*

T he horse would go no further. After weeks of traversing
the General Frost, past backwoods with snow drifts tall
as men and through secluded paths screaming with icy
brambles, it knelt—the air pushing past its wet nostrils in one
final, hot gust—and perished.

Arsène allowed herself to shed two tears—she could not spare
the moisture—before slitting open the beast's belly. She warmed
herself until the heat of its insides turned to hard, icy labyrinths.
With her cutlass, she carved out what meat she could bear to
carry, and set off on foot.

She'd lost track of how long she'd been traveling, the summer
coat that covered her soldier's uniform had not warmed her
since she marched across the Russian border on Napoleon's
orders. Torn at the shoulder, the gray cuffs were stiff and crusted
with old blood. Her own, yes, but also blood of the men she'd
killed. And now of the horse she'd stolen when she finally fled
the Grand Armée, sick for home and warmth and *ensaimada*, a
spiral yeast bun dusted with sugar, which Arsène hadn't tasted
in three long years.

Arsène tightened her coat closer around her now, warming some at the memory of her mother's *pa'amb oli* bread, dipped in steaming rice soup thick enough to chew. Warming at the thought of a dry, crackling hearth fire on her face.

As she walked, the frozen earth slapped her feet as if they were cobblestones. Her boots, which were separated almost entirely from their soles, flopped as she trudged ever forward, a need inside of her to live piercing her like the blade that hung from her tattered belt.

She knew she would not make it much longer. Even with the leather gloves she'd taken from a still-warm body on the battlefield, Arsène could feel her hands turning blue, could feel each little bone in the hand seizing and embalming. Her eyes, which were the only parts of her uncovered, had lost their wet in the relentless violence of the Russian winter.

The sun was sinking, a gray orb flaring in the gray sky. She would have to find shelter soon, she knew, though all she could see was gray. But then, on the periphery of her tired eyes, Arsène spotted a black shape amid the barren landscape. Could there be a house still standing after the Czar's scorched-earth campaign? Arsène ambled toward the shape, knowing it was her only hope.

As she got closer to it, her vision grew kaleidoscopic and her knees, which had been cracking and straining to support her tall frame all these weeks, gave way suddenly. Less than 30 paces from the house, Arsène hit the ground unceremoniously. The thud of her body meeting the knife of the earth roused whoever was inhabiting the house. A shadow loomed inside, cast from behind by a strange orange glow. Arsène crawled toward the glow, noticing the wood of the house had indeed been charred, but the roof was intact, flaring white with snowdrift. Head swimmy as soup, Arsène heard the door whine open, and knew that, depending on who answered, her French uniform alone might sentence her to death. But she knew also that death was all but certain in this cold. What choice did she have? A figure crouched before her, and Arsène struggled mightily to make it out before she lost consciousness, but was not certain her mind wasn't playing tricks on her. The light in her went dark, but not before Arsène saw the eyes of a wolf boring into her, the green of them gleaming like jewels in the snow.

When Arsène awoke, she was on the floor, naked, sweating under furs that had been draped over her bare skin. The blast of a fire hit her neck like a fervor. Lips chapped, hair matted to her forehead, she tried to sit up and found that her legs were shackled, the teeth of the traps digging into her skin, and winced at the raw red welts forming on her pale ankles.

"Don't struggle," said a voice. "The more you move against the leg irons, the worse they'll bite. And your ankles are far too pretty for such a fate."

The wolf.

Arsène ceased her movement. Her shoulder ached from where it had hit the ground, but she noticed that her wounds had been dressed. She lifted her eyes in the direction of her captor, who sat bolt upright in a plain wooden chair as if it were a throne, her hands resting delicately on the rickety arm rests. A thick, dark fur blanketed her captor's shoulders, though her eyes were winter-naked and shining like the sea. *Those eyes*, Arsène thought, remembering their image before she had passed out. *Those eyes could devour my entirety in one, savage sweep.*

"Who are you?" Arsène asked, mouth groggy from disuse, its rasp almost unrecognizable to herself.

The wolf narrowed her eyes, a hint of a smile betraying her lips as she watched Arsène struggle. "I'm the one asking the questions."

Arsène shifted her position on the floor, attempting to leverage a better view without disturbing the leg irons, and as she did so, the furs blanketing her torso fell from her shoulders, revealing the perfect pink of a nipple. Arsène quickly made to cover herself, but it was of little use.

As the furs fell, Volchitza sat up straighter in her chair. How she longed to crush the frail perfumes of that nipple between her teeth.

But she did not do this.

Instead she said, "Tell me. How does a girl dressed in boy's clothing manage to find herself collapsed at the door of a Russian peasant's house hundreds of miles from the nearest village?"

Arsène tried to hide the red that bloomed in her cheeks. She wasn't used to being *seen*, not this naked and not as a girl. It had been years, in fact, since her sex had been so exposed to a stranger. To combat her feelings of vulnerability and fear, Arsène went on the offensive. "I could ask you some version of the same. How does an aristocrat find herself in the house of a Russian peasant, rescuing a French soldier from death, only to bound her in irons?"

Volchitza could not hide her smile now, her jaw twitched wickedly. "Perhaps I merely enjoy seeing you in irons." Arsène cast her eyes to the floor to avoid the beguiling woman's gaze, heat rushing from her ribs down to her center. "What makes you think I'm an aristocrat?"

"*Vous parlez parfaitement le français,*" Arsène said, satisfaction blooming in her chest. She was right, she knew. If years of living as a man had taught Arsène anything, it was how to spot another deceiver.

Volchitza crossed her legs. Arsène continued: "Also, your posture betrays you. No peasant sits that tall. Years of toil beats the length out of him."

The wolf went silent, fire cracking at her fur-covered shins.

Clearly this was no ordinary soldier, Volchitza thought. But she had known that already. Knew it when she had been unconscious and Volchitza had stripped the statuesque creature of her uniform and discovered her startling femaleness. Knew it when she'd breathed the sweat and sour of Arsène's clothes and bent to toss the tatters in the hearth. But as she was about to do so, she had caught hold of a different scent. It stopped her. Overpowered her. And in a movement that both alarmed and startled her, she buried her face in the breeches of the stranger and inhaled her animal musk. Volchitza felt the room tilt on its axis then, and clutched at the stone hearth to steady herself. *Impossible,* she thought. *She smells like Anya.*

And here she was, this strange, sour fruit of a creature, this element loosed upon the wilds, telling Volchitza that her disguise was no disguise at all. "Very perceptive," was all she said. "And who, dear boy, are you running from?"

"That depends on who's asking." Arsène's skin felt damp, her legs shook in their prisons. "If I tell you, might you consider undoing these?"

"I will consider it," Volchitza said. "If your story suits me well enough."

Arsène struggled once more to face her captor fully, and as she did, she saw the wolf's eyes catch on the bare flesh of Arsène's neck, on the muscle that knots its way down the shoulder blades. As Volchitza's eyes traced Arsène's lines, Arsène felt her own blood rise. *Who is this woman with the startlingly serene face and the eyes hellbent on unmasking me?* She wondered, knowing full well that she would let herself be unmasked, that she welcomed it, longed for it, had longed for it for longer than she cared to admit. Arsène felt suddenly shy. She knew what happened when girls followed wolves into the woods, and yet, Arsène also found herself strangely at ease. There was something familiar about Volchitza, some madness she recognized, possibly because her own blood was drenched with it. Arsène felt that once she started talking, the chambers of her heart would never shut again.

But if a story was the key to Arsène's freedom, then the wolf would have one.

◆ ◆ ◆

She began.

I was born in a small coastal village in the Serra de Tramuntana, where the mountains meet the sea. My lot had always taken to the water—as fishers and traders, primarily. My father and brother would have prepared me to join them in this pursuit, had my mother not expressly forbidden it, saying no man wants a fisher for a wife.

She couldn't keep me from the sea, however, and each chance I could I was in the water, exploring its hidden caves and inlets, learning its moods and tempers, and teaching myself to hold my breath for longer and longer turns. This would turn out to be very useful, as you'll soon see.

Arsène touched her fingers to her lips then, a simple gesture, but one that gave Volchitza a startling rise. Her eyebrow arched and she crossed her legs in the chair. She noticed Arsène mouth, the soft O of it, lips as plump and inviting as an overstuffed ottoman. Moisture gathered in the cusp of Volchitza's thighs at the thought of this stranger's mouth buried there, not stopping, no need to come up for air, no. Very useful indeed.

"Do go on," she managed to say.

When I turned 16, I was bewitched by a girl whose thick, dark hair swept across her face in wild currents, her eyes green and alive as the mediterranean. She was harvesting olives on the hill when I saw her, the wind billowing her skirts like a sail. She appeared to be walking toward the sea. I followed her to the edge of a cliff whose drop would have startled most others. But not her. She shed her clothes, placed her olive basket in the grass, and plunged into the cool, clear waters below. What could I do? I dove in after her, my splash ten feet from her startling us both.

She swam toward me then, moving with as much ease and grace as one born with fins. Having not been trained properly in the ways of seduction, I had only childish games at my disposal, and so used them. I took a cup of sea in my palm and splashed her. She laughed, dove under my legs, and tugged me down with her as she passed. Each time I moved to touch her, she swam easily out of reach. Until, that is, she found herself at the cliff's smooth face, nowhere to go. I brought my body close to hers, our breasts pressed against each other as our legs kicked in the water below to stay afloat. When she kissed me, I felt all of her warmth pass through and into me. And then she moved away again.

She swam toward a small strip of sand, moored on both sides by red rocks, and naked of everything save for the sun, which dazzled the grains like stars. She beckoned me to join her, her bright-burst lips parted in a half-grin, half-laugh as she stretched out on the sand, her long, brown legs glistening.

I pressed my mouth to hers once more and felt every cell in my being stretch toward hers. Each place our bodies touched was flint turning to spark turning to bonfire turning to wildfire that threatened to extinguish us both. But we did not perish. And we did not stop. Her fingers traced my lips, and I took them in my mouth. They tasted of the sea and I sucked and sucked the salt from them, before moving down, paying heed to the sun-gold flesh of her breasts, tracing its darker peaks with my tongue and teeth, feeling her nipples harden in my mouth. I traveled the length of her beautiful body this way, gathering each taste and texture from it with my tongue, before settling myself between her thighs.

She offered her sex to me like an Ophrys Balearica, which only bloomed once a year, but for me opened each moment my lips sought her, and I drank of her, her fruit, both sun-drunk and too aware of the miracle of it, this rare and earthful unveiling. Her pleasure dismantled me. I came with my tongue inside her, my sex becoming a song she didn't even have to touch to crescendo. Moments later she reached her own peak, her hips bucking wild and her nails dug into my scalp, gripping and releasing with an almost violent shudder. Soon after, we both fell asleep on the sand.

I awoke hours later. The stars had replaced the sun's fiery gaze, and the girl was gone. Determined to find her, to prove I did not dream her, I set out along the northern shore. It was at that moment that I saw the fires.

Due to the frequent raids by Barbary pirates, the island had set up a series of watchtowers to warn citizens of attacks. Two such towers were visible on either side of the cliffs that flanked me, and the fires in each were lit. This meant the ships were coming straight to me. I dove under the water, scanning by memory for a cave I could hide in until the raid past, but before I could find a toehold in the cove, a galley carrying at least 50 fighting men appeared, their cutlasses gleaming like gravestones in the moonlight.

I was captured and put in irons, prepped to be sold on the Ottoman slave trade. But I knew the Barbary corsairs were headed north along the Balearic sea, and I was determined to make my escape before the waters became utterly unfamiliar to me. The chains that held me were man-sized, and with my small wrists I found I could slip out of them, but knew I must wait until the ships glimpsed the southern shores of France. Once I was certain the shore was within swimming distance, I wriggled free of my chains and dropped like a stone overboard, holding my breath and myself far under the water for 12 minutes, as I had practiced.

Gasping like a fish breathing its first shock of sky, I managed to reach the shore. I fled inward, away from the sea. I knew the only way I'd make it back home alive and unscathed was as a boy, so I became one. I named myself Arsène, cut off my long hair, and stole the clothes of a farm boy I passed who was dozing naked in a field. My plan to cross the country by foot was not much of a plan at all, but it was the only one I had. Without money or anything to beg or barter for, except my wits and my life, I set about walking.

I was startled at the surprising amount of generosity people bestowed upon me as a boy. The goatherds and fishermen slapped my back and spared more food than they could to a stranger and taught me some necessary French phrases (mostly filthy ones) before sending me on my way.

I had almost made it to the Spanish border when the trouble came. The family who was housing me had a son about my age, and when La Grande Armée rolled through, they conscripted me in his stead, passing me off as him to spare their family. At the time I cursed their entire bloodline, but I can't say that I would have done differently if I had been in their shoes.

And that is how I became a soldier. For three years I toiled and trudged, waiting, planning my escape, marching, marching endlessly, and watching men far braver than I attempt to flee, only to be found and shown the rope.

Here Volchitza interjected. "How on earth did you manage to live undetected as a boy in the Grand Armée for three years?"

"You'd be dismayed at all the things men do not notice," she replied.

"I assure you I would not," Volchitza smiled. "But what a fantastic tale. Do you expect me to believe it?"

"You don't have to believe it," Arsène said, her eyes dancing in the light of the fire. "I'm only telling the truth."

Volchitza rose from her chair, which gave Arsène the first full-length view of her. She took a long, cool drink of her captor, noting the lithe form and impossible waist, the dark hair spilling like champagne over her face, falling against the swell of her breasts, whose roundness was concealed not at all by the linen shirt that covered her.

She knelt on the rug that held Arsène, and their eyes locked like rams' horns on each other. Starting at the knee, Volchitza ran the tips of her fingers down Arsène's legs, over the soft flesh of her calves and the hard bone of her ankles. The touch was so light Arsène could barely feel it, and still she shivered. She shivered again when she felt Volchitza's hair caress her shin when she fit the key into the lock at her ankle. She hesitated, looked up once more at Arsène's feral eyes hovering.

"You don't trust me," Arsène said, her heart racing, though whether it was from Volchitza's caress or her hesitation, she could not say.

Volchitza's brow arched in amusement. "Stories don't earn trust, darling. Only actions do." And with that, her long, slender fingers turned the key. The lock popped open, and Arsène was freed. She soothed her sore flesh with shaking hands, willing the feeling back into her frozen feet.

"Thank you," she said, circling her ankles, rising to her knees to test out the motion and strength of her limbs, which were weak, but holding. She found herself kneeling in front of Volchitza, who had not moved from her position, her face close enough to Arsène that she could see Volchitza's breath flaring her nostrils. She was breathing hard, so much so that Arsène swore she could almost hear it thundering. Emboldened by this, her freedom, and the trust Volchitza's action imbued in her, she decided to respond with a similar, bold action. "Where I come from, we say thank you with a kiss on each cheek."

As she said this, she leaned forward, and placed her lips on Volchitza's right cheek, tasting its salt, its dazzling soft, before pulling slowly back to kiss the left. Seeing as Volchitza did not move to accommodate this gesture, Arsène swiveled and elongated her neck to reach the other cheek, which didn't quite make it, instead landing on the corner of Volchitza's lips, which had curled into a smile.

The burning wood of the fire popped behind them, sending a small stream of embers toward the kneeling women, neither of whom moved. Arsène's mind whirled like the sirocco, the brute winds that blew in from Africa, fraying the nerves and scattering dust into every crevice.

As the seconds ticked past, Arsène feared she had overstepped her bounds. But she couldn't know that Volchitza had not been stirred by so brief an embrace since Anya. The closeness of their faces unsteadied her, but she could not move away. Arsène's whisper of a kiss had pulled all the heat to the surface of her skin. She was stirred and she did not know how to feel about it. Just as Arsène was about to fall back on her heels, Volchitza lifted Arsène's chin with the knuckle of her index finger. If she was going to plunge into this ocean of uncertainty, she was determined to take her time. She wanted to admire the fullness of her mouth once more, to savor it like a meal—the upper lip high-tensile as a bow string, lower sharp as a lashing.

"Where I come from," she said, "we say it on the lips." Volchitza's heart pounded as she tilted her head to the side and crushed her lips against Arsène's. The ferocity of this gesture unmoored Arsène, who let out a drowsy moan, her throat still unsteady, her voice full of sap and heat and need. A longing for touch that had not been satisfied since that day years ago on the beach. She gripped Volchitza with her hands, one clutching at the back of her neck and the other at her jaw and earlobe.

Behind them, a log cracked, louder this time, the force of it startling the women apart. "The fire is dying," Volchitza sighed. "It will not last much longer."

"No," Arsène agreed. "But it may be a blessing. The smoke could be seen by passersby and give us up."

"We must find some other way to warm ourselves." Volchitza stroked Arsène's cheek.

Arsène's breath quickened. "I'm certain we'll think of something. But the night is yet long and since tomorrow brings with it only uncertainty, will you tell me something—anything—about you?"

"What do you want to know?"

"The same question you asked of me. Who are you running from?"

Paloma stared at the blinking cursor, at the untamed blankness of the screen in front of her, her eyes bleary and red from overuse, and sighed. She rubbed the back of her neck with her hand, which was stiff from writing for hours, from the fever of unbroken concentration and the warmth that had flooded her from remembering.

On her body was the robe Nadezhda had given her, its cool black, satin caressed her skin the way clouds moved across a desert sky. On the corner of her desk sat a framed photo of them, which Paloma had turned face down the day Nadezhda left. Paloma couldn't bear to get rid of the photo, an accidental selfie of them taken on a train ride through the Pacific Northwest. Their bodies a blur of motion, their bodies melding into one another. The photo managed to make the women appear as they both felt at the time—inseparable, as close as two humans could be without existing inside of one another.

They had conceived of the story of Arsène and Volchitza together on that train ride, read the characters like braille into their fingertips as the train rumbled and roared, as they wound around each other in the tiny cabin bed, naked and spent and delirious with happiness. The wolf and the soldier. The Napoleonic wars. *Tell me,* Nadezhda had said, her face between Paloma's thighs, nipping at the soft skin. *Tell me about Arsène.* And Paloma did, or tried to at least, while Nadezhda pressed her tongue against Paloma's warm folds. *Don't stop,* Nadezhda told her, when Paloma's words went woozy, her pulse a soft hammer beating in Nadezhda's perfect mouth. *Don't stop.*

Paloma glanced once more at the downturned photo on her desk. She didn't need to see the picture to experience its poignancy. Even facing down, she could feel Nadezhda's emerald, sky-lit eyes following her around the room, could still hear the quiet scorn in her voice from their last fight, the way Nadezhda had said her name like the hiss of a tire deflating.

And here she was a year later, faced with finishing the story, Volchitza's story, and drawing a sharp blank. *How can I possibly finish our story without you?* Paloma asked the silent room. And as she did so, a wild longing took hold. She printed what she had written of the story thus far, pushed the chair back from her desk, and stood up. On top of the printed pages, she placed a post-it, on which she wrote, simply: "Finish it—P."

She stuffed the pages into an envelope and dropped it in the mail. Paloma knew it was an extremely long shot. They hadn't spoken in months. She didn't know how Nadezhda was doing, or where she was, or if she had forgotten about Paloma entirely. All she knew was that she had to try.

Paloma felt frantic, all the intensity and longing of their relationship flooding her. Their own love story might have been over, but perhaps it could live on in another's, she thought. Perhaps they could grow this fictional love the way they had grown their own, with sweat and sighs, teeth and sinew. The only limit to their love was what their imaginations could dream up. Paloma sat back down at her desk, inhaled deeply, and prepared to wait.

Weeks passed. Paloma had all but given up when she spied an envelope fat and full as a rain cloud pressed between the credit card offers and glossy grocery store flyers. With shaking hands, she went to her desk and sat down once more. She pressed the pages to her chest and inhaled the pulpy scent of the paper. Nadezhda always scented her letters—one more way in which she haunted Paloma's every sense—and this letter was no exception. Breathing in the sweet, woody florals and bright citruses of Nadezhda's perfume, Paloma thought she might faint, and was glad she was at least sitting down.

When her heart slowed to a near-human pace, she dipped a finger into the envelope's fold, and gently pried it open.

The pages were hand-written in Nadezhda's sloping cursive, and torn out of what appeared to be a journal. The violence of the jagged edges caused Paloma's heart to quicken. She was suddenly afraid of what her former lover might have written, afraid of what she might do to Arsène and Volchitza's love. But it was too late now. The story was no longer in her hands alone.

She read:

Volchitza lay down on the floor, head in her hand, and beckoned Arsène to join her. Arsène lay on her back and Volchitza stroked the hair near Arsène's temple. She removed one of the furs from her shoulders and draped it around their bodies. Finally, she spoke. "For the longest time, I thought I was running from my husband," she said, tracing a finger along the curve of Arsène's hip bone. "It was only after his blood was on my hands that I knew. I was running from myself."

Volchitza spoke quickly, as though she were confessing, eyes downcast, eyes looking everywhere but at Arsène. She scanned the plain room as if her eyes were trying to recall every detail of her life up until this fateful moment.

She began.

I could tell you a hundred stories about me—about my upbringing, my family and its particular unhappinesses. I could tell you tales of grand balls and opulent feasts and the most ordinary cruelties we inflict upon those we love most. But the only thing you truly need to know is this: My life has been too full of men. Their wishes, their whims, their black moods and blacker wants.

Ever since I was a child I've had the same dream. In the dream I am a bird in a beautiful, gilded cage. Strangers visit me in this form. Some starve me. Some put me on display. Some beckon me to sing and rattle my cage if I do not. But one dear soul always opens the door of my cage and releases me. The person who set me free in the dream varied as the years passed, but what remained the same throughout was her eyes. I would recognize those eyes anywhere.

It took 25 years, but finally she came to me, in the form of a housekeeper my husband Andrei sent for, to replace the last one he had ruined. At first I didn't recognize Anya as the girl from my dream, as her eyes were always lowered when she went about her duties. But one day, as she was pinning sheets to the line, I heard her singing. She could not see me from my perch, cloaked by the sheets as she was, so I stayed and listened to her for a while, enchanted by the deep, syrupy swell of her voice. I moved closer, beckoned by her shadow on the other side of the fabric, its rhythmic sway, her song enchanting, slowing my senses, drawing me near. When we were inches from each other, she pulled down the sheet and looked me full in the face for the first time.

We both sprung back slightly, as if scalded—she, out of surprise, and I, familiarity. But soon the shock left her and a wave of recognition replaced it. She took my face in her hands, examined it as if it were her own face in the mirror, and drew me to her. I gazed into her cinnamon eyes, rings flecked with gold, and when she closed them, I placed my lips against her eyelids, as if in blessing.

"It's you," I whispered into her neck. "It's you."

At first we could only meet late at night, and only for the briefest encounters. Andrei often stayed up into the early hours, entertaining guests and drinking himself into oblivion. Once the sounds of his snores threshing in the night found my ears, I crept out of bed and went to her.

She knelt over my body during these stolen hours, as the dawn crept up through the small window of the cellar, where we placed our body offerings. Her long fingers slid into me like fire as I lay beneath her, the cold earth against my back. Her heat undressed me slow as sunrise, as her fingers moved everywhere they wanted to, filling and emptying and filling me. And as the sun made its way to our entangled bodies, she held her fingers up, her fingers full of my desire for her, glistening in the light. She brought them to my lips and I took them greedily. Her chest heaved as I sucked her dripping fingers, breath furious as I extracted each drop of my longing for her from her tips.

The dawn was our master, our cue that we must once again part. I kissed her eyelids each time I had to leave her, and one day I cast a last fervent glance at my beloved. Perhaps a part of me knew it would be the last time. The last image I would have of the way the light worshipped her. I memorized her form, the way her sweat beaded like honey, mouth ragged with pleasure, the way her body twisted to fit my every moan and sigh.

When I finally turned to creep back up the cellar steps, she grabbed my wrist. In that small touch, I could feel our hearts beating in unison. Even now, I can feel the pulse of her within me so sturdy I could walk it like a plank.

Her eyes bore into mine as she said, "You are bound to me, sinew to scar, soul to cell, wave to collapse. Do not forget."

I pressed her lips to mine, as if this altar we made each night with our bodies alone could change the course of the world, our fate, as if it could make our every prayer come true.

But, as with all beautiful things, the more you try to hold on to them, the sooner they slip from your grasp. Andrei found us out and sent Anya away. I tried desperately to find out where he planned to send her, and hoped on my life she would not be sent to the katorga camps, but when my husband heard me eavesdropping, he flew into a rage and locked me in the cellar. The place that had brought me the sweetest freedom I had ever tasted had become my prison.

When he let me out five days later, I began plotting my escape from him. He would never let me go of my own accord, as this would unalterably tarnish his precious reputation, particularly in the political circles in which I was well-known. And he could not simply send me away, as he did Anya, though I'm sure he would have if he could have gotten away with it. I could have fled with a horse under cloak of night, but, he would have sent out a search party and, once caught, I would be brought back only to be punished further, and more severely.

My respite came in a most unlikely form, for soon after, the orders reached us that Napoleon was coming for Moscow and that the city was to be evacuated and burned. In the ensuing melee to flee the city, I knew this was my only chance to act. My plan was thwarted when a servant spied me shoving clothing into a parcel and went straight for my husband. In seconds he was upon me, dragging me by the hair to the cellar where he planned to lock me in it once more and set the house aflame before fleeing himself, a convenient alibi. As we reached the landing to the cellar, I clutched at a candlestick that had fallen in the scrum, and swung at him with all my might. He tumbled down the stairwell, face a garish pulp, into the darkness below.

I didn't know if he was dead or merely unconscious but had no time to make certain. I locked the cellar door, grabbed what meager stores I could carry, and set out into the night. As I rode, an ominous orange glow filled the sky behind me. It was extraordinary to see the flames —to know that everything you once held dear could perish in an instant.

The city would burn, I knew, but I would not. Not that night, at least.

Here Arsène chimed in, "But how did you know where to go?"

I didn't. I had no map, no clues, little food, and even less hope. I did the only thing I could think of, which was to go to sleep. When I did, Anya came to me in a dream. This time she was the bird, a hooded crow, and she instructed me to follow her. When I woke, I gazed out into the perilous grey sky and what do you think I saw, some 30 feet from where I slept? The black wings and ash-grey chest of a hoodie. Beckoning me. Having nowhere else to turn, I followed it.

For days, this guide kept me away from marauding troops, from starvation and frostbite. And now it has led me here, to this very house, and to you.

Arsène stared in abject bewilderment at Volchitza's tale, her face a black canvas washed in skepticism.

"Ah," Volchitza said. "She doesn't believe me. Go to the window, *golubchik*. You will see a crow perched on a low branch of the nearest tree."

Arsène rose from the floor and made her way slowly to the window, gooseflesh rising on her arms and legs. She looked outside and saw that what Volchitza said was true. The crow swiveled its head, glancing between the window and the great beyond, as if keeping watch. "Unbelievable," she whispered.

"You don't have to believe me," Volchitza jested. "I'm only telling the truth."

Arsène shivered from her place by the window and hurried back to the warmth of the furs and Volchitza's lithe frame. The fire was waning, its embers casting a pale glow on Volchitza's contours. "What do we do now?" Arsène asked, pressing her cold feet against Volchitza's shins.

"We toast," Volchitza said, her eyes smileless, but her lips radiant as the midday sun. Arsène searched Volchitza's face for signs of possible madness, but found none. The wolf gestured with her eyes to a leather satchel sitting next to the wooden chair she had recently claimed for a throne. "Bring it to me," she said.

Arsène obeyed.

"With the city in flames and my haste to escape, I did not pay close attention to what supplies I was grabbing from the pantry before I fled. Look inside and you'll see I chose poorly for survival, but marvelously for a celebration."

Reaching into the satchel, Arsène pulled out a bottle of champagne, a wine-colored handkerchief that was wrapped around a small jar of caviar, two portions of pickled beets, and half a loaf of blackened, crusty bread. Arsène eyed each object, brow knotted, a slow grin creeping up her face.

Volchitza opened the caviar, which was as black as her own dark wants. "If we were at the palace, I would serve this Ossetra to you on blinis with créme fraiche." Her fingers clawed into the bread, in a gesture somehow both delicate and savage. "But this will have to do," she sighed.

"Who *are* you?" Arsène marveled, taking the bread she offered, using her finger to spread the caviar on top.

"Your enemy, technically." She popped the champagne cork, sending a stream of foam arching into the still, cold air.

Arsène saluted her. "La Grande Armée! Valeur et discipline!" Volchitza handed her the bottle, and she drank from it, long and deep.

"The Imperial Guard never retreats, darling." Volchitza pressed her lips to the bottle, tilted her head back, and sipped. When she had satisfied her need of food and drink, her face relaxed into a sleepy moon. It was too much, all of it, the champagne, the stories, Arsène's wild eyes and bloodful cheeks. Volchitza felt drugged. She felt as if she had never tasted champagne before, and never would again. It could exist only now, only here, with Arsène. All else would turn to ash in her mouth she was certain.

As she thought the words, the last embers of the fire sputtered and turned to gray.

Volchitza closed her eyes, heart beating wildly, but also at peace, as if she had no cares in the world, as if she were not possibly being hunted this very moment by her husband and his power-ful friends, by military men and scavengers, as if she were not homeless, and her love had not been taken from her to a place she knew not where, as if they might not die tonight in this abandoned peasant house without a fire to warm them.

As if sensing Volchitza's thoughts, Arsène said, "We could break apart the chairs, the furniture, to use as kindling..."

Volchitza's eyes sparked, a kind of demoniac flush fanning her brown eyes. "Or, we could harness this power..." She glided her hand down Arsène's arm, skating softly over her chest, belly, and hip, until she reached her thighs, and traced the opening there with her fingers. "The heat of our bodies."

Arsène's mouth fell open in a sigh as Volchitza gently pried her legs apart, the animal in her rearing up, ready to fight, to survive. When Volchitza's hand found its way into her warmth, Arsène had the sudden, desperate urge to claw at Volchitza's skin, to tear her way inside, to be that close.

She tilted her head up, her lips reaching for the neck. The pulse. Sank her teeth in. Volchitza's head fell back as she let out a deep, animal groan. From this distance, Arsène could smell the sweet rouge of Volchitza's skin, the verve and pomp of her. She kissed the line up to her jaw and nibbled softly there and there, and at her ear.

As she did so, Arsène felt her own sex pulsing, a grasping, hungry mouth, desperate to speak. Arsène threw the furs off her shoulder, without heed for the cold. She only knew it was a barrier between her and Volchitza and so it must be done away with.

Kneeling, Arsène set about undoing Volchitza's boots, slowly, methodically, as if it were her life's task. Though the fire had gone out, Arsène swore she could see Volchitza's eyes blazing like the ruins of her city, her eyes the most beautiful destruction she'd ever witnessed. She decided at that moment that she would follow Volchitza anywhere, even into an open grave.

Once the boots had been removed, she moved up Volchitza's legs, clasping first her shins, knees, and thighs, before reaching the buttons of her trousers, feeling each snap open in her fingers, and revealing an ounce more of Volchitza's supple skin, the dark hair that guarded the entrance to Eden. When she reached the last button, Arsène noticed the thin boning of a corset under Volchitza's linen shirt. Hands quickening as Arsène placed both on her impossible waist, Volchitza clasped her by the shoulder then and pushed her sternly to the ground. Arsène's shoulder hit the floor and Volchitza was soon on top of her, straddling her hips and pinning her arms above her head.

"Am I to be shackled again?" Arsène's voice strained, though from surprise or excitement, she could not tell.

"Would you like that?"

But before Arsène could even dream up a response, Volchitza's mouth was upon her once more, tongue flicking and curling over her nipple, the soft hill of her breast. Volchita's white linen neck cloths teased the skin at Arsène's belly as she worked her way down, her grip releasing Arsène's hands, her nails raking hot, pink streaks down her arms. The sharp of Volchitza's touch was searing, and Arsène welcomed it. Arsène wanted it so much, to be hurt, to be marked. She wanted this proof of her aliveness, of the unreality of their chance encounter. She longed for Volchitza to possess her body, to alter it, the way she knew her life would be forever altered on this night. She wanted to offer up her body to Volchitza, to be its sacrifice, a witness to their every unchecked longing.

Still hovering over Arsène's hips, Volchitza wriggled out of her trousers, and kicked them to the side. She pushed Arsène's legs open wide like a well-loved book and traced its long, wet seam with her tongue, then watched as Arsène's eyes shut and her head fell back in ecstasy. As her tongue edged inside Arsène's cunt, Volchitza's hand moved over and around it, and cupped the taut, hard muscles of her ass, which flexed and bucked at the unbluntness of Volchitza's nails claiming her there. As she worked her hands along Arsène's ass, her thighs, and lips, the blood followed and warmed her, obeying Volchitza's heat and movements as if her body no longer had a will of its own. Arsène's jaw tightened, her cunt an ocean of burning wants. She knew she was at the precipice already, that she would go tumbling over the edge in a few more curls of Volchitza's deft tongue.

And it was then that Volchitza stopped all of her movements. "Not yet," she said, when Arsène raised her hips, whimpering. "I want you like this, poised and drunk and vibrating between my lips. Over and over and over. Do not come until I tell you to."

Arsène was so aroused she could not speak. Her words tumbled out in a cloud of sound, eyes closed, head nodding, she hoped, in the direction of yes and yes and yes.

Placing a hand on Arsène's sternum, Volchitza crouched over her, straddling her hips, a starved lust bearing down on them, her cunt hovering just out of Arsène's reach. Arsène waited breathlessly, watching it pulse, her hands on Volchitza's thighs poised to strike on command, her hands two poems begging the white space.

After what felt like an impossible lapse in time, Volchitza

lowered her hips onto Arsène's, the tip of her clit waltzing over Arsène's slippery, opened folds. This slight pressure of their clits meeting caused Arsène's thighs and ass to tense involuntarily and her head to fall back against the floor. Slowly, slowly Volchitza began to move her hips in small circles, the slick, warm silk of them mingling and heating and charging the air around them. Arsène thought she might pass out from the pleasure of this tiny movement alone before she realized she had, in fact, stopped breathing in the drugged rush of Volchitza's cunt on hers. Arsène unclenched her jaw, letting her lungs empty.

Volchitza continued the slow drag of her hips as she reached out and ran her fingernails down the front of Arsène's body, the tips clasping her breasts and digging ever so briefly into her nipples, caging them. Arsène moaned, the entirety of her skin set shivering at this touch. When she did, Volchitza's breath sharpened and her eyes shut tight. "I could come just from hearing you moan," she said.

"Please," Arsène whispered.

"Not yet."

Over and over Volchitza brought them to the brink of the cliff face, and just as they were about to go careening over its edge, she stopped, leaving Arsène breathless and feverish, until she seemed to grow an entire new body, toes and backs arched and flexed, everything heightened and static, every cell vibrating and sparking with desire. Volchitza's movements quickened. The pressure building and boiling and aching as they melted into one another, their cunts pressed together like two hot irons. Who, Arsène wondered, was branding whom?

"Tell me what you feel," Volchitza said.

"I cannot," Arsène cried. "I cannot. I would need a hundred tongues. A hundred hands to touch you, a hundred hearts to lay before your feet."

Arsène's body dilated—every part of her opened and opening to let Volchitza in, everything, even her gaze, her voice, her pulse found its way inside, into her blood, her cells, until they were one flesh, one soul, one gravity. This was the only closeness, Arsène knew. The only sex. The only hunger. Everything that came before this was but preparation.

A moan fell from Volchitza's lips. Her voice keeping Arsène near. Her moans so bright Arsène almost couldn't bear their radiance. Not then. Not ever.

As her cunt continued its slow, nearly unbearable slide over Arsène's, Volchitza's mouth pressed against her clavicle, her neck and sternum. She relished the pain, the teeth pulling the blood to the surface of her skin once more. Each mark Volchitza left on Arsène's body singing *I am yours I am yours no matter what happens tomorrow I am yours.*

Finally, near dawn, they collapsed, spent, warm, satiated, all moisture drained from them but that which had pooled in the molten center of their sexes.

A crow cawed. Was it Volchitza's guide beckoning?

They lay entwined in each other's arms, limbs and hair and hips knotted, their bodies speaking a language no one else could possibly understand.

"It's time," Volchitza whispered.

Arsène breathed into her neck, eyes shut tight against the warmth of her lover's skin. "I beg of you, do not go."

"We must, *golubchik*. You to your island, and I to my Anya."

Arsène clutched in her fist an edge of the fur blanketing them. She wanted to cry, but wasn't sure she could make her eyes obey her anguish. "I cannot bear the thought of leaving you," she said.

"But you aren't leaving me. You've given me the most precious gift. I will take you with me, your scents and sighs, your reflection, your obstinate nose and frozen feet, your wild hair and wilder imaginings." Volchitza paused, swept a hand across Arsène's cheek, where the tears had begun to blanket it.

Arsène wrapped her arm around Volchitza's waist, holding her tight, letting the wet tears warm her cheeks. "You are poetry, color, brilliance. I don't know how I could possibly bear my life away from you. You make every earthly aim feel false."

"We were born of the same passions, my darling girl. The same madnesses." Volchitza reached for the wine-colored handkerchief that had held the caviar, and tied it tenderly around Arsène's wrist. "Take this. Then I will always be with you. A part of you. No one can tear that from us. Not the ravages of time, not war, not the countless lives you'll live without me once we part."

Arsène clasped a hand on top of the handkerchief, her face a wall of grief, her mind whirling like a cyclone. "I wish I could do better," Volchitza said. "I would offer you my blood, lay my bones at your feet, but this will have to suffice. Until we meet again."

Tears crowded Volchitza's eyes and with them came a deep, wrenching sob, which felt like several lifetimes of anguish unfurling. She kissed Arsène's eyelashes, her eyelids. She kissed the tips of her hair, which smelled of smoke and the Caspian sea. She kissed her jaw and chin and the bones of each of her ten fingers. It was not enough. It would never be enough. And yet, it had to be.

The crow cawed once more, louder this time, and Volchitza gathered her belongings, leaving a linen shirt and trousers for Arsène, to replace the soiled uniform she had burned. Standing before her soldier, she kissed her one last time, pressed her mouth hard against Arsène's chapped lips, one hand on her neck and the other clasping her waist, pulling her hips once more into the circle of her hunger.

At the door, Arsène willed Volchitza to turn around and come back into her arms, to admit this whole exit had been an elaborate joke, a ruse. But she didn't turn around, didn't so much as glance back at Arsène, for fear that if she did, she would never have the courage to leave.

The crow flew to Volchitza and perched on her shoulder. Arsène watched the wolf become a smaller and smaller figure on the horizon. When the figure became a dot and then indistinguishable from the white, woolen landscape, Arsène allowed herself to turn away from the window. She dressed and gathered her few meager possessions, hung the cutlass at her waist, secured the handkerchief tighter about her wrist.

She did not cry, for she knew she would live again and again, breaching the knot and swim of Volchitza's love, as cool and clear as the roar that swallows silence.

Paloma set the pages down, hands trembling, the smooth wood of the desk feeling like the most inadequate caress imaginable, but it was all she had. She placed her palms down flat in the hopes that it would prevent her from collapsing in a heap of sobs. It didn't last long though, her head felt so heavy, so oppressed by gravity, that she pressed it against the desk, letting the torrent of grief wash over and through her at having read Nadezhda's words. The tears felt good, baptismal, and she did not hold back. Wail upon wail rushed out, her cries unrecognizable to her, her cries coming from some shadow place inside of her that she rarely had access to.

When the waves receded, Paloma's eyes fell upon the envelope that the pages had come in. Peeking out of a corner was the edge of something, its color blushing against the white paper. Paloma reached inside and pulled out a wine-colored handkerchief, neatly folded. She pressed the fabric against her nose and mouth and inhaled the sweet scent of honeysuckle paired with something bright and effervescent, almost like champagne.

The scent of Nadezhda sent a new wave of pain through her and she rode it out, breathing hard against the fabric until it subsided and she was calm once more. Then she unfolded the square and tied it tight on her wrist, the knot of it digging slightly into her pulse point, reminding her of her aliveness, reminding her that she had this day, this life ahead of her and behind her and spilling out in every direction she could fathom.

Hand unsteady and face puffy, she smoothed her hair behind her ear and stood, deciding that she might as well live it.

THE DANCE

An Erotic Interlude

1 :41 a.m. and I am still thinking of my hands on your hips, the heat of us rising like a phoenix in someone else's myth.

I am still thinking of the salt on your neck that I did not baptize with my tongue.

The way you said my name and I couldn't tell if it was an invocation or a warning. The way you fed me pie from your hand, the crumbs of it edging past my lips, the glimpse of your fingers leaving my mouth. They tasted sweet and creamy from the dessert. The way the crowded living room swelled with our lungs to the music, and the swing band swung and everything else fell away.

The way another person would call this feeling *regret*, but I am enjoying too much collapsing in this heap of almosts.

Something unmoors me when we dance. Something about how my desire for you goes every which way, a tugging toward and a reaching back at once. The brief, dire poem of our hands meeting, hips meeting. The bodily postcard of you. The sweat glistening on your collar bones. The way you gave me a sleepy look and mussed my drenched hair across my face. A toppy move for such a bottom.

The way I pressed your hips to mine through the cotton and pleather and sweat and skin. There are always so many obstacles between us. When we dance my hips want to grind you to dust. They are searching for your center, the clear, molten core of you that bones can never reach.

The way we have not kissed and probably never will. You have a partner and I'm trying to have integrity for once. There's something to that, as well. The exquisite torture of the almost-having. The purity of anticipation. You and I will never disappoint each other. Because we won't get the chance to.

But I would love nothing more than if you saved me a dance.

THE BICYCLE, PART TWO

50 Shades of Gay

The summer after they graduated high school, Michelle and Sabine were inseparable. They were both new to sleeping with women—and, as such, they were eager to try every sexual act they could conceive of (and a few they could not) before Michelle left for college on the East Coast that fall.

And because, at the time, one could not throw a rainbow dildo out of a window without it landing on a *Fifty Shades of Grey* reference, the girls decided it might be time to try their hands at some light bondage. Where to start, though?

Sabine tried to read the book, but stopped about 30 pages in. She did not understand why protagonist Anastasia started every sentence with "Holy crap!" Or why, when Christian Grey took Anastasia's virginity, she responded the way a comic book villain who had just stubbed his toe might. That is to say, "Argh!"

Who is turned on by this? Sabine wondered, looking suspiciously at her mother, who was baking vegan muffins and probably dreaming of a man who had the gumption to make her say *argh*.

Sabine texted Michelle some snippets of the most egregious *Fifty*

Shades dialogue offenses and Michelle responded with a litany of barf emojis.

"Maybe the movie is better?" Michelle texted.

"We better break into your dad's Jameson again just to be sure."

Two nights later, Michelle's dad dropped her off at Sabine's house, with the pilfered liquor in tow. Sabine's parents were divorced and her mom had an extremely hands-off attitude about sleepovers, even with boys. This startled Michelle, whose parents were strict and WASPy and had no idea that Sabine was more than "just a friend."

Michelle would cross that bridge with them eventually, but not tonight. Tonight, the girls would get tipsy and tie each other up with scarves. Or something. Michelle wasn't exactly sure what bondage was. She did notice, however, that her skin flushed white hot the time Sabine had slapped her ass—in a public park, no less!—and was hoping she could work up the courage to ask her outright for more.

She blushed at the thought of the warmth that spread through her lower body when Sabine's palm met her flesh. She tugged a little at her cut-off shorts, the center seam of which chafed pleasantly against her sex.

Sabine greeted Michelle at the door and hooked her finger into Michelle's belt loop to bring her closer, then kissed her full and bright on the lips. Michelle never tired of kissing Sabine. Every kiss felt like the first, and her heart ping-ponged around each time Sabine's lips so much as brushed her own.

She opened her eyes to look at her lover. Her *lover*! It was all so new to Michelle, who, despite a few lackluster jacuzzi hand jobs and movie theater makeouts, didn't have much in the way of sexual experiences. Sabine had a few more, having been briefly involved in the local rave scene, and who, as such, learned to spin fire, which earned her a handful of admirers eager to get their hands on Sabine's other heat sources.

They both had been virgins before they started fucking each other, and disagreed as to when they had officially "sealed the deal." Michelle thought it had been the first time, in the bathroom in the school's gymnasium, when Sabine had fucked her briefly with her mouth, then her hand, then with their cunts pressed together to the point of collapse. But Sabine, who was prone to romantic inclinations, preferred to say it happened a week later, when they were laying on a real bed and not surrounded by the chemical smell of bathroom cleaning agents.

Once back in Sabine's room, Michelle pressed her against the door, gripping Sabine's face in her hands, and kissed her deeper —her breasts, hips, and thighs coinciding with Sabine's. Sabine trembled, her head lightly hitting the door with the force of Michelle's body knocking against hers, and the thud of it caused Michelle to pause briefly in her ardor.

"You okay?"

"Guess we're bondage-ing already," Sabine smiled.

"Not even close," Michelle said, grabbing hold of Sabine's wrists and placing them both above her head. She pressed her face close to her lover's and felt the pleasant heaving of Sabine's breath in her own nostrils.

"Kiss me," Sabine said, eyes half-closed, back arched and hips desperate to connect once more with Michelle's. Michelle was enjoying this position of power, however. With one hand still on Sabine's wrists, she moved her other down and cupped Sabine's left breast, feeling its suppleness yield at once to her touch. She switched to the right one next, clasping the nipple through her shirt and bra, and watching it harden through the fabric. It was only then that Michelle kissed her once more, the weight of her lips aching to explore Sabine's soft mouth.

Michelle realized quite suddenly that she did not know if she'd be able to make it through an entire movie without tearing at Sabine's clothing. Sabine, her breath and heart racing at Michelle's display of toppiness, also began to wonder how long she'd last.

They both wanted to pace themselves—they had the entire night, after all—but the intensity of their desire for each other made this a challenge. They decided to make a few rules.

1. They could touch each other and kiss each other as much as they wanted, but no one could come until the movie was over.
2. To help ensure this would happen, they could not remove any clothing, except shoes.
3. If one of them did accidentally come, the other got to decide an appropriate punishment and enforce it.

"I'm turned on already just writing these rules," Michelle said, her neck blushing red as her hands stroked Sabine's flushed cheek.

"I cannot wait to punish you then," Sabine smiled, unsteady, as she was also vibrating with anticipation.

Sabine set the laptop on the end of her bed and pressed play. The girls settled into the mattress, reclining on top of the covers, holding hands as the opening credits rolled. The heat of their thighs pressed together was already distracted Michelle, who trailed her hand up the edge of Sabine's forearm, watching the soft blonde hairs rise and shiver. Sabine leaned into Michelle's neck, inhaling the coconut scent of her body wash, and pressing her lips to the lobe of her ear. Michelle moaned, turning her face away from the screen to kiss Sabine fully. She then ran her teeth along the soft edge of Sabine's lower lip.

It was not long before Michelle had climbed on top of Sabine, her hands playfully tugging, teasing, and edging along Sabine's beautiful curves. Sabine half-resisted, not wanting to lose the "challenge," but soon her hands were twisting in the sheets and her hips rose to greet the wild friction of Michelle's undulations. Michelle's pulse galloped with momentum as she sat astride Sabine, gently biting at Sabine's neck and her nipples through the clothing. She found that she liked to see Sabine try to resist her and fail utterly, but with this excitement, Michelle felt herself pushing toward orgasm.

Sabine shuddered underneath her, and Michelle, channeling some inner resolve from a place she didn't entirely know where, slowed her movements, and lay still on top of Sabine. She breathed deeply for a moment, regaining her composure, then slid to the side and forced herself to watch the screen.

It appeared that Christian was about to "rip through" Anastasia's virginity. Michelle felt a little repulsed and a little excited—not by what was happening on screen, but by the thought of what was to come. Or not come, as it were. Michelle was struck by two competing desires—the desire to "win" the challenge, and the one to "lose" and be punished. She wanted both! She was too excited though, and didn't want to come this quickly.

Sabine had other plans, it seemed. She parted Michelle's legs and reached easily into the bottom of her cut-offs, feeling the silky dampness that lay so readily at the surface of her sex.

Michelle gasped and placed her hand on top of Sabine's. "Cheating!" she said.

"What rule have I broken? I haven't removed any clothing," Sabine smirked. "You happen to be wearing very revealing attire."

Michelle conceded the point, but did not release Sabine's hand. With her other, Michelle grasped Sabine's face and forced it toward the screen, where they watched as Christian bound Anastasia's hands with her own shirt.

Oh, that's a good move, Sabine noted inwardly, filing it away for future use. As they watched, their breath slowed to normal and they settled in once more as placid viewers. Michelle struggled to keep up with the plot, distracted as she was by Sabine's body, so accessible, so near, so *there*. Sabine was similarly distracted by Michelle, and also the itch of discomfort that came with watching Christian bully Anastasia into submission.

"Anal fisting? Really, Christian? What idiot would sign that kind of contract on, like, the second date!" she said to Michelle.

"Dude's got mommy issues," Michelle laughed, absent mindedly stroking Sabine's abdomen, which was warm and smooth against Michelle's cold hands. The light touch was enough to bring the warmth to Michelle's own skin, which glowed and hummed and ached with aliveness.

She made small circles on Sabine's skin, widening them slowly, until her fingers dipped into the waistband of Sabine's baggy jeans, then back out and up towards her breasts, where she stopped to massage them, to admire their heft and firmness. Michelle continued in this fashion, making lazy, teasing circles on Sabine's breasts, abdomen, and the edge of her pubic mound, not glancing away from the screen, until Sabine's desire was too visible to be ignored.

This time it was Sabine who climbed on top of Michelle, kissing her face and neck and collarbones and working her way down. Sabine gripped Michelle's bare thighs and pushed them outward, causing Michelle to shudder loudly. When Sabine's teeth greeted Michelle's soft inner thighs, Michelle's back arched involuntarily, but Sabine kept an arm on her hips to hold her down, and steady her. Sabine bit into the denim that covered Michelle's sex, pressing her chin and jaw against the opening, just below Michelle's clit, and Michelle rocked on the bed again, gripping her lover's hair in her hands.

With her hand, Sabine pushed the denim and the cotton underwear underneath it to the side, and traced one slow line with her tongue up Michelle's damp folds, rejoicing in the abandon that tumbled out of Michelle's mouth upon contact.

Michelle held onto Sabine's hair tighter now, and the muscles of her thighs clenched and ached with each thrust of Sabine's long tongue. Michelle glanced briefly up to see Christian and Anastasia fighting about something, but had no idea what. *Who cares, who cares?* she thought, her head falling back against the pillow, her nerves blushing vibrant and taut as Sabine kissed and sucked on the small amounts of flesh she could reach through the openings of the fabric.

Sabine, wild with the pleasure of seeing her lover so unhinged, pressed her own cunt against the mattress and swiveled her hips around. Her whole lower body felt hot, but mildly so. She knew she probably couldn't come from the friction alone, but if Michelle's gasps and moans kept up, it might be enough to send Sabine over the edge.

Michelle, drenched and writhing, struggled to stay still enough through this exquisite torment for Sabine's tongue to find her and trace the edges of her abandon. Each time it seemed Sabine was striking the right rhythm against Michelle's clit, the denim stymied her.

Growing somewhat frustrated by these various obstacles, Sabine got an idea.

"Turn over," she said. Michelle obeyed, a pillow placed strategically under her torso, lifting her ass into the air. From this position, Sabine could more easily push the denim out of the way. She glided a finger along and into Michelle's sex, slick and slippery with heat and writhing and madness, as she continued to explore her with her tongue. She nibbled at Michelle's thighs, the soft creases and downy hair. She licked at Michelle's lips and felt them swell and redden as her finger gently probed in and out and in.

Michelle's back arched again, giving Sabine a fuller and more enticing view of her entire backside, whose display made Sabine's excitement grow tenfold. Her own cunt pulsed as she ground her hips into the bed, trying to hold the momentum with Michelle's quickening gasps and sighs. She knew if she could hold out a minute longer, she would win the challenge and Michelle would be hers to command for the night.

Sabine knew exactly what the punishment would be. She'd been thinking of it for weeks but was too afraid to ask, worried that Michelle might be squeamish or not into it. The thought of her desire alone was almost enough to make Sabine lose her edge, and she concentrated all her efforts as Michelle bucked and clenched underneath her, losing all composure in a rush of release that felt, even to Sabine, like an avalanche felling every rock, tree, and piece of debris in its path.

After, Sabine slid her finger out of Michelle's cunt, resting her hand on the curve of Michelle's beautiful ass. Michelle's breath slowed and steadied. They both laid still for several moments, eyes closed, mouths red and spent, until Michelle said, her voice muffled by a pillow. "That was amazing."

"You're amazing," Sabine replied. She craned her neck back toward her laptop and noted that they had not made it even halfway through the movie. She stopped it anyway, and rested her head against Michelle's warm thigh.

"Come here," Michelle beckoned, and Sabine inched her way up and into Michelle's arms. She kissed her eyelids, her nose, the corners of her mouth. Michelle couldn't stop smiling.

After a few moments of tenderness, Sabine couldn't help but gloat a little. "You lost!"

Michelle blushed and slapped Sabine playfully on the shoulder. "You would've lost too, if you'd been in my position!" She laughed.

"Are you ready for your punishment or do you need a moment?"

Michelle kissed her, letting her teeth gently tug on Sabine's lower lip. "With you, I always seem to be ready." She blushed again, and buried her face in Sabine's neck.

"Take your clothes off," Sabine said. "Lay back down on your stomach and face the laptop."

Sabine removed her own clothing as well, and told Michelle to scroll to the Wikipedia page for *Fifty Shades*.

"Since we missed the movie, I want you to read the plot summary," Sabine said. "Don't stop reading it no matter what I do to you."

A wave of heat rode itself through Michelle's body when Sabine said this, and she shivered in anticipation as she felt Sabine straddle her ass, the heat of her cunt pressed against the dimple above Michelle's tailbone.

"Begin," Sabine said, thankful Michelle could not see her smiling like an idiot. She had never been so commanding before and couldn't tell if it was working. As Michelle began reading the summary, Sabine pressed her naked breasts against Michelle's back, and slowly slid them down and down, past the dip in her lower back, and the perfect rounds of her ass.

When she had snaked her body down far enough that her face was eye-level once more with Michelle's firm cheeks, she reached up with her left hand and gave it a playful smack, relishing the satisfying sound of it.

Michelle gasped and briefly forgot her task of reading. Sabine slapped her other cheek in response, harder this time, watching a small red mark form where her hand had been. Michelle continued to read, repeating sentences and missing words and hoping Sabine didn't notice how turned on she was each time Sabine's palm made contact with her ass.

Sabine could feel the heat and moisture of Michelle's sex rising toward her face each time she administered a blow. She kept the slaps mild, with just enough force to bring the color to Michelle's cheeks and make her arch a little off the bed.

With her left hand, Sabine gripped the flesh of Michelle's ass fully, watching the center line open, revealing Michelle's sex to her once more and the tight bud above it. Sabine kissed her way down the cleft, letting her nose and tongue edge their way along the rift, taking her time, making sure Michelle was okay with this.

She noticed that Michelle had stopped reading again and drew her right hand up once more. Sabine dealt her another blow, smiling at how easily distracted Michelle was. Michelle picked up her reading again, not that Sabine was paying attention in the slightest to the words themselves. She was enjoying this scene too much, the warmth, the animal scent of Michelle so close to her nose, and placed her face once more to the fire.

Michelle's asshole clenched and released when Sabine flattened her tongue against it, and she let out another long, slow moan. With both hands, Sabine gripped the flesh of Michelle's ass, opening her more, giving herself a wide berth to explore and lick and savor everything she found in this new, uncharted territory. Michelle's thighs clasped against Sabine's head as she did so, and Sabine relished the sensation of being trapped in the strong vise of Michelle's muscled legs while her tongue pushed gently into the opening.

Michelle writhed again, her moans growing louder and freer. She felt entirely vulnerable, feral, helpless in a way she wasn't sure she had the right to enjoy this much, and also utterly, utterly incapable of reading another word about *Fifty Shades*.

Thankfully, it seemed Sabine was sufficiently distracted herself as not to mind this, and continued to trace her tongue along Michelle's perineum, lapping at the tender flesh there, kissing her cheeks, massaging them, possessing Michelle. She shifted her whole lower body on the bed, moving to the force of her hands kneading and her mouth sliding as she lapped and rocked and nudged. Michelle's flesh felt like velvet on her tongue, and her face grew entirely damp. She felt drunk, sure that her own pleasure was similarly soaking the bed. To test it, Sabine pressed her hips once more into the mattress and felt a surge of heat slip throughout her pelvis.

Sabine slapped Michelle's left cheek once more, harder still, hearing it reverberate throughout the room, and keeping her tongue pressed to the opening of her asshole, which seemed to want to envelop her entirely, all of her wet and hot and open and opening.

With a fervor that felt beyond her immediate control, Sabine's hips began to move as if a riot was forming inside of her. The momentum could not be quelled. Its fire raged, the torches lit, the mob in chaotic formation. The hair near Sabine's face was matted and damp but *who cares who cares?* She thought.

She undulated, her heart a wild bird in a cage as her hips pulsed in tandem with her tongue against Michelle, the ring of her contracting and expanding, until Sabine could no longer bear it, and her body was thrown into a long spasm and she collapsed just as Michelle was coming for the second time.

They lay there panting for several beats. Sabine tried to kiss the back of Michelle's thigh once more but found she couldn't lift her head. She gave up, content to heave and sigh and die a little at the unbelievable pleasure of all that had just occurred.

"Oh my god," Michelle kept repeating, her face mashed into the snarled comforter. "Oh my god, oh my god." She reached back to stroke Sabine's head and hair with the tips of her fingers, while Sabine smiled sleepily, her face a bouquet of Michelle's thick, pungent aromas, her neck pleasantly sore. "Oh my god."

BLIND HEAT

I t's my second date with James.

The first involved a romantic, though chaste, walk in the rain through Mountain View Cemetery in Oakland. He smelled of cigarettes and black coffee and Old Spice. Something Boy Scout about him, maybe how he held the door open for me, or the easy way he smiled, though his eyes betrayed a distinctly handsy look. At least, that's what I was hoping. I wanted to see what was under his sheen of politeness and chivalry. I wanted also to see what was under his faded Levi's.

We sat on a bench of a mausoleum in a line of mausoleums known as Millionaire's Row, as the rain fell in a quiet spray on our faces. I hadn't been touched in months and was starting to feel unhinged, that I might spring upon the next person who looked at me half a second too long. I was very much hoping it would be James who looked. We bonded over our recentish breakups, along with a shared dislike of Murakami books. ("Really? Another talking cat?") We laughed easily. He told me he used to be a glass artist, that the place a glassblower forms their work is called a "Glory Hole," and how the 1,000-degree glass has to stay in constant motion or it'll lose its shape.

"You must perform well under pressure then," I said, knocking against his arm, and gave him a wink.

He grinned shyly, but I could tell he was warming to me. Our arms brushed together as we strolled the labyrinthine lawn of the cemetery, gravestones like smiles gleaming. The tension pulsed between us.

"Thanks for going out with me," he said.

"Did you just thank me?" I laughed.

At the end of the night, he walked me to my car. I put my umbrella down, leaned closer. His embrace caught me by surprise. One arm swooping in around my waist to draw me into a hug, pulling me against his broad chest, and even that small motion was enough to set my particles jostling. But he didn't stop there. Instead, he picked me up off the ground, my legs locked around his waist, and held me there.

"You're so light," he said. "How much do you weigh?"

"125," I said.

"You weigh the same as my dog."

"I … don't know how to feel about that," I laughed.

He set me down. We said our awkward, first-date goodbyes. No kiss. But that was okay. I was high, literally, off of his sudden, swooping embrace alone. I thought of it for days after. It felt like a scene out of *Dirty Dancing*. I decided I could be patient. At least for a little bit longer.

We text and flirt throughout the week. He sends me a YouTube video of a psychic who specializes in BitCoin prophesying. I send him back a video of a material scientist who makes knives out of things like Jell-O, milk, and cardboard. Eventually, the conversation deepens. I tell him about the death of my father, how I didn't know how to go on for months, and James tells me how he used to be Jamie, how he could no longer go on living a lie, and how his mother, though sweet and tacitly accepting, still accidentally refers to him sometimes as *she*.

Feeling emboldened by the budding intimacy and trust between us, I take a chance, tell him about a sex party I'm thinking of going to, partly provocation and partly to gauge his interest in such things. If he's squeamish about sex, we might not be a good fit after all. Best to learn such things now rather than later.

"Let's go," he texts back, without hesitation. I pump my fist silently in the air, mouth the word *yes*. The Boy Scout has an exhibitionist side. This is good to know.

For our second date, I suggest we go to an indie movie theater, the kind that has a toppings bar for popcorn and antique leather couches instead of seats—I don't want the barrier of an arm rest between our bodies. I don't want any barrier between our bodies. "Where should we meet?" he texts. "Or should I blindly feel my way to you in the dark theater?"

Oh. Once he says that, I can't stop thinking about him blindfolded. His hands on me in the dark. The slight callous of his thumb tracing the curve from breast to sternum, his fingers starting bonfires on my ribs, the heat of my desire rising to his palm.

"Actually...that gives me an idea," I tell him. "How invested are you in watching a movie?"

I text him a cursory outline of my fantasy. He seems intrigued, but a little hesitant. I assure him by telling him I'll keep watch the whole time he's blindfolded, and if anything seems out of sorts, we can put the brakes on and change routes. "We can stop anytime," I reassure him.

"Okay," he says, "I'm down."

This is going to be fun.

The day arrives. I choose the worst movie I can think of—some blow-things-up action flick—so fewer people are likely to be there. It's also a Wednesday, mid-afternoon. Like our first date at the cemetery, this place is predictably dead. In the theater, I find us a spot in the very back row, and we sit on a white leather loveseat, so worn and saggy in the middle that it folds us up in it instantly, the sides of our bodies pressed together in a not-exactly-agreed-upon embrace. Not that I mind. He bites off a hunk of red licorice he got at concessions and chews slowly. Smiles at me. I can't read how he's feeling, but cross my legs in my short black skirt, angling my knees toward his.

"You look nice," he says, eyes running the length of my body like a gauntlet.

"Thank you." There's that handsy look I was waiting for.

The lights in the theater go dark. I hear a few scattered coughs and the groans of bodies shifting on old furniture—there are maybe four other people watching with us, the closest is an older, balding man in a grandpa sweater eight rows ahead of us—but no one is close to where we're sitting.

We wait an agonizing 20 minutes, watching the movie tensely, arms to our sides. I dare not even look at James. Not yet. I'm too unhinged still. I fear if I touch any more of him than his outer arm, I may pounce. The waiting is strategic, too. I want to make sure no latecomers burst upon us in the theater unexpectedly, and also for the noise and action of the film to start, to muffle our own action.

During the first car chase scene, I take a deep breath. In my mind, everything is perfectly executed, but it's always when you're least prepared that life throws you a curveball. Or in this case, a blue ball.

I squeeze his arm, which I notice is so muscled I doubt I could get both hands around it. I cannot wait to learn the canvas of his body. Perhaps he'll let me.

"Ready?" I breathe low and soft in his ear.

He nods, smiling, not quite meeting my gaze.

I pull a black hankie from my purse, and secure it over his eyes, my face so close to his I can hear his heart thundering in his chest. He's nervous. How sweet, I think, only somewhat oblivious to my own hands shaking. I place my lips against his ear, nipping slightly at the soft flesh of lobe. He breathes out hard and hot against my neck.

"Here's the rules," I say. "You can touch me anywhere you want —"

"Anywhere?" he asks, surprised.

"Anywhere," I say. "But you can't remove the blindfold. You have to rely on your other senses. You have 15 minutes."

I set a timer on my phone, making sure it's set to vibrate, so as not to alert the other moviegoers to our activities, or god forbid, the theater staff.

His hands pat the air, fingers finding the curve of my shoulder, orienting himself to the shape of my body. After this cursory inspection, he wastes no time, grabs me first under the knees and lifts, so that my thighs drape across his lap. The other hand goes to the back of my neck. His fingers are so soft that I'm taken momentarily off guard when he fists the hair there and pulls my face sharply toward his. With his other hand, he traces a line up from clavicle to throat, his fingers reading me like braille, and I can't stop a moan from escaping my lips.

I glance around the theater furtively. All eyes are glued to the screen. The balding man scratches at the back of his head. James dips a finger into my mouth, perhaps to stifle another moan, and I suck the salt eagerly from it. In spite of their softness, he tastes like someone who works with his hands. I picture myself then, a piece of molten glass, burning 1,000 degrees on the end of a pipe James is turning and shaping and making endlessly beautiful.

Both palms cup the sides of my face and neck now as his mouth finds mine in the dark. Our lips crushed together, something violent in it, something holy and ragged, this touching. The taste of his lips is sweet and bitter at once, the sharp of tobacco mingling with the licorice he ate earlier. I lose myself for a moment in the exquisite weather of his mouth, until the booming, hollow voices of the film startle their way into my consciousness. I glance up to see someone—a terrorist? A cop?—is dropping C-4 down an elevator shaft, blowing up an entire floor of a New York high rise.

The loud of the movie thankfully disguises my gasp this time, as James moves one hand down the side of my neck, tracing the hollow near my collarbones, still kissing me, his teeth lightly chewing on my lower lip, sending a warm flush from the base of my spine all the way up to the top of my head.

His warm hand finds an opening in my shirt, fingers unclasping a button, now two, and then he pauses, his warm hand revving at my ribs. "Oh God, don't stop," I whisper, and he cups, gently at first, my breast, then harder, feeling the nipple tense and yield to his touch.

"Do you like that?" he says.

"Yes, yes," I say, practically baring my teeth at him. And he pulls back then, a devil grin on his face. Runs his fingers lightly up and down my arms, turning my skin into a giant, staticky pulse. He's teasing me. Here I thought I was holding the cards and how quickly I'm reminded that I'm the one at his mercy.

He finds his way back to my chest, traces slow circles around my nipples, massaging me through the thin fabric of the bra, before pushing it up out of the way and cupping both breasts firmly in his hands.

It feels so good I want to cry out but the movie has gone quiet —bound and tied-up hostages whisper to themselves from their

123

places on the floor, helpless, as I feel helpless in James' hands, his mouth dazzling me like a drug—so instead I bite my lip to stifle a moan. I can tell I'm wet already and he hasn't even touched me below the waist. I let my legs fall open just slightly, the hem of my black skirt bunching up and up toward the apex of my thighs. Does he notice? Can he feel the heat of me reaching for him?

He senses me shift positions and—surprising me again—grabs me by the hips and ass and pulls me deftly onto his lap, my back against his chest, thighs touching, torsos touching. His breath quickens and his lips graze my ear as he takes one hand and pushes the hair out of my face, traces my neck with his teeth. I can't stop the sound from escaping my throat, and he places his hand tenderly over my mouth and holds it there. The balding man eight rows away turns his head sharply to the left, causing my heart to push wildly at my throat, but then, thank the gods, another explosion—anti-tank missiles blow up an armored SWAT car—and his eyes flit back to the screen. The other hand winds its way down, past my belly, the sharp of my hip bones, pushing the fabric of the skirt up as his fingers graze my thighs, yes, tips hinting at my clit, god yes, and I want the agony of this waiting to both last forever and not a single second more. The muscles in my legs tense and release and my hips buck involuntarily as his hand hovers over me, my cunt a river now, a river of wants bending and snapping in the dark theater that is in no way big enough to hold these desires.

After what seems like hours of this light, agonizing touch, he pushes my underwear to the side, traces the sides of my lips. Up and down and back. I'm so turned on I can feel my heart beating in my cunt.

I want you inside me, I think, but don't say because his hand is still covering my mouth. But he intuits this request, miraculously, dips one finger, then two inside, as his lips find my neck and ear once more. His thrusts are slow and deep, and each time, as he winds his way back out, his fingers find my clit, the pressure pooling and building in my center, before he enters me again.

My body is full of writhing now, synapses coiled like a snake, and it is a good thing his hand is clasped over my mouth because I can't contain this pleasure, the slick warm silk of me burning to a crescendo with each steady movement of his deft hand. Again and again and again and don't stop now please don't stop and the wave of me crests and breaks against him and everything tenses and limps and tenses as I come, collapse fully back into him, cunt shuddering against his fingers.

Chest heaving deep sighs as I rest on his lap, sweaty and spent, my hand clasping his muscled arm, the one thing keeping me from sliding to the floor in a heap. He kisses once more the skin at the base of my neck at the moment that my phone timer goes off. The vibration startles us both. He removes the blindfold, looks at me with a ferocity so tender I almost can't stand it, and puts the blindfold over my eyes.

Breathes into my ear: "Your turn."

THE HOLY GRAIL

Nyla and Anastasia decided they wanted to have sex with a man.

But, as they were the kind of women whom men bent over backwards to open doors for, who received free drinks from men, free oil changes, the occasional free electronic device, and, of course, a daily dose of free harassment, Nyla and Anastasia knew they couldn't simply post an ad online, because they'd get bombarded with messages.

So, they devised a different strategy over tea one Sunday morning. A creamy light filtered into their bedroom. Nyla lazily read *The Economist* in a black satin robe, while Anastasia waltzed in with a tray holding two cups of earl gray and a chocolate croissant.

Nyla's eyes drifted above the magazine to admire her lover when she came in. Long brown hair tied in a loose braid framed her heart-shaped face. Dressed in athleisure wear, Anastasia exuded a lithe extravagance. She was marble smooth and quick as a cat. Her utterly feminine body and boyish face tended to disarm people. The combination made women flirtatious and men feel simultaneously threatened and aroused.

"Thank you, darling," Nyla said, as Anastasia set the tray down in front of her. When Anastasia attempted to rise, Nyla grabbed her wrist, stopping her. Anastasia looked up at her lover, the V of skin highlighted by her loosely belted robe showing the suggestive swell of Nyla's breasts.

Even in repose, Anastasia thought, *Nyla is pure suspense.*

Gold-brown skin, skylit eyes, proportions that not even corsets dared to compete with—all of these leading down to an apex that seemed poised to strike at the slightest provocation.

In short, Nyla's body was a feast that refused to be consumed.

Anastasia leaned in and offered her mouth to her lover, who took it as if it were fruit from the Tree of Life. As they kissed, Nyla kept hold of Anastasia's wrist, guiding her where she wanted her to go until Anastasia was laying on top of her, their hips aligned, their feet entangled. Nyla's robe fell open, and she clasped her legs around Anastasia, digging her heels softly into Anastasia's high, round ass.

Nyla's cunt pressed against Anastasia's. She moved her hips in small, slow circles. Anastasia loved that she could feel Nyla's desire by the anointment Nyla was making on her yoga pants as she continued to swing her hips.

"Stop," Nyla said suddenly. Anastasia ceased her movements, even her lips, which fell into a pout. "As much as I can't resist you, we can't start fucking again. Not until we've figured out how to find our third, at least."

"Yes, Ma'am," Anastasia said, trailing her lips over Nyla's skin, and nipping at the soft fold of her earlobe. Nyla moaned, lost herself briefly, then recomposed. She gripped Anastasia's face in her hand, so that her full lips bunched together like a heap of sighs on her face.

Nyla released her, patted the bed. "Come. Lay next to me." Anastasia obeyed.

"Have you given it more thought?" Nyla asked.

"Yes, though I'm not sure you'll like my idea."

"Tell me."

"You know how a male-female-female threesome is often lauded as the Holy Grail of sex acts? The thing men are supposed to aspire towards?"

"Mmhmm."

"If that's true, and we are the 'prize,' then why not make the men who seek it go on a similar quest as those seeking the actual Holy Grail?"

"A quest? I'm intrigued."

"A quest, yes. A series of challenges, each harder than the last."

Nyla's eyes widened in excitement, her thick, wavy hair tumbled over her shoulders. "I love it. And what will the challenges entail?"

Anastasia sat up straighter, her eyes a fiery, emerald trail. As Nyla's submissive, Anastasia so rarely got to design or implement her own pleasure schemes. Not that she didn't relish giving up her power to Nyla, but she also couldn't help but enjoy this slight role-reversal.

"The challenges," she said, "will involve making these men experience what it's like to be women."

"Scrutinized?"

"Yes."

"Condescended to?"

"Yes!"

"Objectified? Harassed? Emotionally labored?"

"And they had better do it all with a smile."

Nyla kissed her firmly on the mouth. "That's brilliant. You're brilliant. I just might let you come today." She placed a long, tapered finger at the apex of Anastasia's crossed thighs, and nudged them apart. Her hand dipped into Anastasia's yoga pants and hovered there, at the entrance. The suggestion of Nyla's fingers inside of her alone was enough to make Anastasia wet.

"But first," Nyla said. "Tell me everything you have planned in that wicked brain of yours."

Nyla's hand still hovered. She allowed a single finger to curve inward, tracing the wetness in one long, slow arc. Anastasia was practically panting. "I may need you to … do … not that … if I'm to use this wicked brain of mine at all."

Nyla smiled, increased the pressure and speed of her gently probing finger. "Not a chance."

Several hours and several orgasms later (three for Nyla, one for Anastasia), the women had a plan in place and were ready to set it in motion. They placed an ad on Craigslist that outlined their desires as well as the challenges would be involved. The challenges were described in vague but intriguing terms, along with several photos of the two women together in various states of undress.

As expected, they received hundreds of responses, a perhaps unsurprising amount of which were angry, misogynist screeds. *How dare you make me work for sex? Who do you think you are? You should be ashamed of yourselves.* Some called the women cunts and whores, or, as one man spelled it, "hores." The angrier and more entitled the emails were, the stronger Nyla and Anastasia's conviction and commitment to the idea of the quest became.

Out of the slush came a few dozen viable contenders, and Anastasia sent these men the first challenge, which was this:

A package will arrive in the mail for you in two days. Inside will be a weighted bra, the size and shape of a DD rack, Nyla's cup size. You will wear this rack for 24 hours and go about your day as usual. You must spend at least four of those hours in a public place. You cannot take the bra off at any point, no matter how tired you are or how much it hurts. If you do, you will have failed the challenge. At 1900, you will go to the Rosewood Sand Hill bar, where you will buy every woman a drink who asks you to. They will explain things to you, and you will not contradict what they say or argue in any way. We will be watching your efforts. May the best man win.

xo,
Nyla and Anastasia

❖ ❖ ❖

Jeremi's eyes widened when he received the message. He was boyishly handsome, with thick eyebrows that were constantly knotted together in anger, confusion, or both. Though in his early thirties, he wore an expression of misplaced condescension, as if he had never grown out of being a misunderstood teenager.

Being the kind of heterosexual man who was not very comfortable with his masculinity, Jeremi had never worn any garment that could conceivably be read as female, not even for a cheeky Halloween costume or prank, and he had certainly never experienced the kind of public humiliation that was being requested of him by these two hot strangers. He pursed his lips into a sulk. These bitches reminded him of his ex, Rhea, who had blocked him on every platform. When he realized he could still reach her on Venmo, he sent her $1 so he could tell her off one last time. Who did she think she was treating him like that? And who did these random-ass girls think *they* were?

Jeremi had to admit, however, that he did enjoy a certain amount of suffering in his day-to-day life. He sought punishing exercise that had caused him to throw up on more than one occasion; he dated impossibly high-maintenance women whom he could never satisfy, and when given the option, he always chose the least comfortable chair. To prove ... something. But the thought of walking into his office—where he sold headphones specifically designed for video game users—dressed as a Mrs. Doubtfire situation repulsed him so much that his finger hovered over the delete button.

Who are these crazy bitches? He wondered.

But something stopped him. He looked once more at the women, at the pictures they'd sent. One was taken outdoors, in a place Jeremi didn't recognize. They lay in a shallow river bed, steam rising around their prone, inert bodies. Jeremi couldn't help but notice that the women were beautifully matched. Even in static, they radiated sensuality, a fresh-bloodedness, each cell poised in offering, in opening—for him. The steam from the river gave their allure an almost mythical quality. They looked like goddesses of fire. He wondered if the women had ever been fucked by a man before, and the thought of being the first to do so excited him greatly. Plus, a threesome with two hot-ass lesbians would sure show Rhea what she had lost out on!

Jeremi felt his blood rising. He focused on the darker-skinned woman, Nyla, and imagined taking her DD breasts into his mouth, while the lighter-skinned woman's lips circled his cock. He had an erection now, and released it from his pants, tugging it absent-mindedly with his thumb and two fingers, thinking of four hands upon him, two mouths engulfing him. As he stroked himself, he closed his eyes, trying to hold the women in his mind, to view his hand as their hands. If he could keep his mind focused on Nyla and Anastasia, he thought he might be able to endure the challenge.

Besides, he told himself, it was only for a single day. He could endure anything for a day. He once spent six consecutive hours on a Peloton machine! *I ain't no pussy*, he told himself.

Then he sent off a clipped reply—"yo i'm in"—no time for punctuation or grammar, before hopping in the shower to finish the fantasy he had started.

As promised, the package arrived two days later. Jeremi unwrapped it unceremoniously and flung his temporary breasts on the bed. He'd always loved women with big breasts and felt a secret thrill at getting to fondle them all day, even if it was *himself* he was technically fondling.

He reached down and gave the right one a squeeze. It yielded to his hand exquisitely. He strapped the breasts onto his body and secured them in place. In the mirror he checked himself out.

"Not bad, hombre," he said to his reflection, running his hands along the beige fabric and flicking his imaginary nipples.

As he opened his closet to see what might fit over these mammaries, he felt a twinge between his deltoids. These puppies were heavier than he thought, but no problemo. He stood up straighter, and pulled a large, navy button-down shirt from a hanger. As he buttoned the shirt over his newfound augmentations, he found he could not close the shirt. A gap greeted him, ludely, no matter how much he tugged the shirt down or smoothed it over. He tried a different shirt, same problem. All looked ludicrous, all made him appear to be what he suddenly saw he was: a man with enormous breasts. Defeated, he pulled a large sweater that his mother had given him years ago when he was still "fluffy" (as she put it) from the back of his closet, knowing still that it wouldn't conceal his endowment, and hurried out the door. He was running late for work as it was.

No less than three cars honked at Jeremi as he walked the seven or so blocks to the train station. When the fourth one laid on its horn, he erupted, yelling, "Fuck you!" to the black BMW that passed. When the car pumped its brakes a hundred yards from him and a door opened, Jeremi panicked and ducked into a nearby alley, panting, hands shaking. He clutched at his chest, winded from the adrenaline and his new top-heavy center of gravity. After a few minutes, he popped his head back out, relieved to see that the car had vanished.

He took a deep breath before resuming his clipped walk to the train, but he hadn't made it more than a block before he felt the presence of another car behind him. Jeremi didn't turn around this time, not wanting to aggravate the situation further, and thinking that he was being unduly paranoid. He balled his hands into fists and walked faster. The car continued to stalk him, slowly creeping up behind him, until Jeremi had no choice but to turn around. He did so just in time to see a bald, white man in an SUV masturbating furiously in the driver seat. A cloud of disgust formed its perfect weather on Jeremi's face, which evidently turned the man on even more, for when he registered Jeremi's disgust, he came, laughing wildly, a stream of his perversity splashing out of the window and onto the dashboard.

Horrified, Jeremi once again started running. An onslaught of questions plagued him: What the fuck was wrong with people? Was this guy a plant hired by Anastasia and Nyla to taunt him? Or was this a microcosm of a reality he'd simply never understood? A very small and unpleasant sample of what it meant to walk through the world with tits? As he ran, he checked his sweater to make sure no cum had landed on him, and his horror was renewed when he found a tiny drop.

Jeremi cried out as if scalded, and held the sweater away from his body. "Fuck you, you fucking pervert," he muttered to himself as he reached the entrance to the train station and made his way down the steps. As he did so, two teenagers grabbed his breasts when Jeremi walked past, making a grotesque honking noise as they did, and laughed.

Jeremi's eyes narrowed into a hard, thin line. He half-chased the teens, shaking his fist and shouting obscenities at them as they bolted. "Fuckers," he muttered again, suddenly exhausted—and he had only been wearing tits for ten minutes! If he could just make it to his office, he told himself, he'd be somewhat safe. Protectively, he walked with his arms across his chest, holding himself tight as a snuggie, and boarded his train.

He'd already concocted a story for the inevitable questions that would arise when he walked into work, which was that he had lost a bet and this was his penance. Mostly this seemed to put an end to further questions, but it did not stop his colleagues from grabbing his breasts and pawing at them, and why did they keep making that wretched honking sound? Did they think that was cute?

Jeremi paused after the eighth or ninth unscripted fondling, and wondered if he himself had ever done this to a woman. He was ashamed to remember that he had, once, in college. A woman was passed out on a couch at a party and he walked by and groped her briefly. Just once! But still, he'd done it. He wasn't proud of it, and a small part of him wondered if these fondlings were his comeuppance, payback for the millions of small, unchecked grievances he had caused women to suffer.

On his way to the bathroom, Joel in accounting reached out and squeezed Jeremi's breast. Jeremi slapped his hand away. "Dude, what's your problem?" Joel said. And when Jeremi only glowered at him, he added, "You're acting like a chick," and walked off.

On and on it went. Jeremi found, to his dismay, that if he tried to stop the groping, he was instead met with ire, indignation, and name-calling. As if it was his fault! As if he had brought this upon himself! To add further insult to injury, his back throbbed from the heavy breasts, the hours spent hunched over his computer, and from all the swatting. No amount of bolt-upright posture or gentle massage seemed to alleviate the pain. In his cubicle, he shifted like a caged tiger, keeping an eye over his shoulder in case another would-be groper should try to sneak up on him.

In his fatigue and discomfort, Jeremi realized that he hadn't fondled his breasts once since that morning, and did so now, out of stubbornness. It brought him no joy. He closed his eyes and tried again, picturing the breasts as Nyla's, how firm they would feel in his hands, how supple, and how, once bared, Jeremi would pop the nipples in his mouth as if they were candy. This brought him a momentary sense of relief before the ache in his back set in once more, and his fantasy caress went from tender to perfunctory, as he cupped them underneath and pushed the breasts up high, towards his chin, to take some of the pressure off of his back.

Jeremi suddenly couldn't wait to complete the rest of the challenge, as it involved drinking at a bar, even if he knew it meant further humiliation in front of the Bay Area's most cosmopolitan women. He knew all about the Redwood Sand Hill's reputation as a gathering place for elite, beautiful women, and the men who desperately wanted to bed them.

To avoid further honking and men masturbating at him in cars, Jeremi decided to take a Lyft to the bar. As he stepped into the car, the driver ogled his breasts openly. He placed his backpack on his lap, in hopes of disguising them, but it was too late.

"What are you?" the driver said.

"Excuse me?"

"Like, are you one of them shemales or something?"

"Dude, look, I lost a bet okay? Just drive."

"Oh, phew. Cuz you sure is a ugly-ass woman."

"Well, *you* sure is a ugly-ass man, motherfucker. Don't talk to me."

"Why you all up in arms, ladyman? Do you hate your dick or something? Does it work?"

"Stop the fucking car."

"What?"

"I said stop the car!"

Jeremi flung the door open before the car had come to a full stop, almost falling to the pavement, but catching himself. He slammed the door shut. Rage and helplessness burned through him. As the car sped off, he paced up and down the sidewalk, feeling tears erupt like spit in his eyes. Punching a nearby recycling bin, and knocking it over, gave him a distinct kind of pleasure. He then kicked it, watching the milk containers and bottles scatter on the sidewalk.

Seething, he reached into his sweater to remove the source of his misery. But as his hand hovered on the clasp, Jeremi paused. If he took off the bra now, the entire day would have been in vain. Every humiliation, every insult, every honk and bodily injustice. After all he'd endured in the last 10 hours, Jeremi couldn't stand the thought of this day coming to nothing. He gritted his teeth, slapped himself once on the cheek, and called another Lyft.

This driver was a woman, who, aside from exchanging casual pleasantries, said nothing for the remainder of the trip. If she noticed his breasts, she did not remark upon them. Jeremi sighed in relief.

When the car pulled up to the Rosewood Sand Hill, Jeremi realized how underdressed he was. Suits and cocktail dresses abounded, while he tugged sheepishly at his oversize sweater, with the cum stain he realized he hadn't dealt with, and headed immediately to the bathroom to do so.

Standing in front of the restroom sign with the stick figure man, he paused. What harassment lay beyond these doors? Jeremi held his breath and entered. Thankfully, no one was inside. He scrubbed at the small white stain on his sweater until it dissipated, which took a surprisingly long time, then pressed himself under the hand dryer.

While he did so, he remembered a lover who wouldn't have sex with him for weeks. She had wild hair like a lion and cinnamon skin. "You can't fuck me," she would tell him coyly, "But you can come on my tits." And he did, night after night, as she teased and taunted him, with her hands, her mouth, to the point of oblivion, but never letting him take her. Possess her. This almost-having, Jeremi realized years later, was so much better than the having would have been. He still thought of this woman, and how, even though he had painted the smooth skin of her body's canvas all those nights, it was *she* who was, in fact, marking him, the core of him, all along. He smiled at the memory, and made his way to the rooftop deck, where a throng of beautifully coiffed bodies awaited him.

The first woman who approached him and asked him for a drink was so meticulously dressed and sculpted that Jeremi felt unmoored, as if merely looking at her was like unwrapping a Christmas present two weeks early. The drink she ordered was called the "Mrs. Doubtfire," and it was delivered with a wink. *This must be a friend of Nyla and Anastasia*, he thought.

He ordered one for himself, and the two engaged in polite chitchat.

"Do you follow college basketball?" the woman asked.

"Yes!" he said, elated to talk about one of his favorite topics.

"Who are you voting for?" the woman asked.

"Voting?" he asked.

"Yes—voting." She looked at him sourly.

"Do you mean—" and here he stopped himself. The directive was to not correct or argue with what the women said. He finally understood. No mansplaining. He allowed his sentence to hover in the air, unfinished.

"Yeah?" she said again, smile bright as a bomb. "Who are you voting for to win the basket bowl?"

"Duke," he said through his teeth, wincing at this egregious misfiring of words about a sport he worshipped almost as much as sex.

"Oh, I love Duke. Go Blue Demons!"

Jeremi winced again. *It's Devils*, he did not say. *Blue Devils.* A twitch began to develop in his jaw. He tapped his face to calm it. "Yes, go Demons," he sputtered.

On and on it went. The women who approached him seemed to have a preternatural ability to discern which topics of conversation would most irk him. It was as if they had meticulously combed his life, his social media profiles, his public passions and private pains, and created the precise scripts of misinformation that would drive him insane.

"Do you know about the ketogenic diet?"

"Let me tell you how blockchain works."

"Jeremi? No, you're saying it wrong. It's pronounced Jer-em-*aye*."

"...So then Peter Parker touches a spider and becomes radioactive, thus giving him an allergy to spiders and also the ability to fly. It's next level. You should read the comics."

"Did you know San Francisco has its own football team? ... Really? Tell me then, Mr. Smarty Pants. ... That was a lucky guess."

By the end of the hour, a vein had appeared in the middle of Jeremi's forehead the size of a ballpoint pen. He was concerned it might rupture if he had to endure these mansplainers for much longer. Thankfully, the booze had unwound him some, and one gorgeous woman had even given him a generous hit of her vape, but not first without explaining to him what vaping was and how it could help what she called his "obvious mood disorder."

As the smoke eased into his lungs, Jeremi thanked her, and as the sun dipped below the evergreen hills of the peninsula, he made a silent vow to try to catch himself the next time he unintentionally condescended to a woman he was talking to. He thought it was unintentional, at least. He was pretty sure.

A wood fire popped pleasantly in his ears as he bid his adieu to his tormentors, and made his way back to his apartment.

The first challenge had exceeded Nyla and Ana's wildest expectations. To ensure the men were not cheating, and also to discern what was happening to them, Nyla had installed small, nearly undetectable voice recorders into the bras. All day the women had been tuning into the misadventures of the contenders as they went about their quests. Half had failed to follow the directive to go out in public, so they were out. The ones who did, Ana noticed, were not being spared an ounce of pain. Nyla had briefly considered hiring friends to deliver well-timed doses of danger, insults, and injustices to the men, but gave it up as too labor-intensive. But it turned out they needn't have worried. Strange men were doing it on their own. And with particular aplomb and cruelty.

The world was a horrifying enough place as it was. Witnessing these unscripted assaults, even only auditorily, gave Ana pause.

She had wanted to teach these men what it was like to be a woman, but maybe this was going too far. What if someone got seriously injured? Or outright attacked? Ana found herself especially sympathizing with Contender #12, whose name she looked up on the spreadsheet and discovered was Jeremi. He seemed to be having a real brute of a day with his fellow men. A few interactions sounded violent even.

"Brute brute heart of a brute like you," Ana hummed to herself, quoting Emily Dickinson as she wondered if the quest would lead to actual bloodshed. She wondered as she folded Nyla's lingerie, caressing the purple satin, the delicate lace of the trim, as if she were caressing Nyla herself.

Then, as if in response to Ana's clothing caresses, Nyla herself appeared, placing her hand on the back of Anastasia's neck, squeezing lightly, kneading the taut muscles.

"You're tense," Nyla said.

"I've been listening to the men."

"Has it been awful? I tuned out around lunch time."

"It has. More so than I expected."

"Poor darling," Nyla cooed, patting the bed. "Come here. Let me loosen some of these knots."

Nyla leaned back against the headboard and Ana in turn leaned against Nyla's body, feeling her scapula rest against Nyla's breasts. Nyla ran her nails through the hair at Ana's temples, lingering on its silky sheen, before trailing her fingers down to the tips.

With her thumbs, Nyla began to press into Ana's neck, holding the pressure at the center of a knot. Anastasia smiled sleepily and let her arms drop to her sides. Nyla's perfume found her nostrils and Anastasia inhaled its woody lavenders as the tissues in her neck yielded to Nyla's firm grasp. As Nyla dug deeper into a tender spot, a noise loosed itself from Ana's throat, which startled her a little. She had sounded like an animal that was about to go off somewhere to die.

Self-conscious, Anastasia swallowed the remainder of the moan.

"Do you remember when I made you kneel in uncooked rice?" Nyla asked, kissing her soundlessly.

"That was so Catholic of you."

"You made a noise like that when you got up." Anastasia couldn't see Nyla's face, but she knew she was smiling wistfully. Nyla continued, "You suffer beautifully."

"Only for you," Ana replied.

"Mmm, I love when you tell me things like that, even if they're not true."

"They *are* true," Ana said, hurt that her lover would doubt the sincerity of her submission. "I've never suffered for anyone the way I do you."

Nyla's hands inched their way forward, over the rounds of Anastasia's sloping shoulders, glimpsing the points of her collar bones, and continued until they had reached the hem of Ana's tank top, the rise of her breasts. Dipping her fingers under Ana's shirt, Nyla found the two soft centers of her nipples, and pressed them. They hardened at the subtle pinch as if on command, as if Nyla had trained Ana's body to respond, like a seal, like Pavlov's dogs, like hypnosis. Nyla relished Ana's body, its animal responses, the way her body never lied, the sharp scent of her, the biology that refused to be ignored.

She held Ana's nipples between her thumb and forefingers, pulling them gently, kneading, massaging, as Ana squirmed against her. Anastasia loved to be possessed by Nyla in this way, to be this held, to be this unafraid of her own hunger, to be wild like a poem, a work of art, to grip the slippery edge of unreality with every twist of Nyla's lithe fingertips.

Nyla pressed the nipples harder, her hands circling the firm flesh, the tender points, and Ana cried out, her head shaking back and forth, her skin a fire that could burn down the world.

"Don't come," Nyla said, sensing the fire in her, letting the heat of Ana strike her own like flint.

"Okay," Ana managed to whisper, clasping her thighs tight together until something popped. There were times, Anastasia knew, that her desire for Nyla felt like a force that could break her, even her lightest caresses, *especially* her lightest caresses, which drove her to exquisite madness.

She felt herself dissolving, the current of Nyla's hands shooting straight to her sacrum. Her hips lurched, she twisted on the bed, wild, possessed, but held still. She was a good submissive. She would not come.

Nyla continued to fondle her breasts, to mold and shape Anastasia's body as she desired. "Don't come," she said again, her voice dreamy, ethereal. Ana wondered if this warning was for herself or for Nyla, whose own body seemed to swim underneath hers, as if they were two currents sending heat to the far poles of the earth.

Ana felt Nyla's hips moving under her and knew that Nyla was in fact on the verge of coming, on the verge of taking her own pleasure as she readily withheld Anastasia from taking hers. Nyla's mouth opened softly against Ana's scalp as Ana pressed her ass back into the cradle of Nyla's pelvis, her undulating hips, hoping the pressure would pop the cork. But as she did so, Nyla's resolve returned somewhat, the intense pleasure she took from waiting, from drawing out her pleasure. Nyla ceased rocking her hips, and dug her nails into Ana's soft areolas, causing her to yip, and little pink crescent moons to appear on her flushed skin.

After a few moments, their breath slowed, their desires once more in check, Nyla returned her hands to Ana's shoulders and neck, resting them there.

"Are logistics for the second challenge in place?" Nyla asked.

Anastasia hesitated. "I'll watch, but I don't want to be involved in the judging."

"Are you sure?"

"Yes."

"As you wish. I'll handle them."

"And Ratu?"

"No one handles Ratu, but she'll be there. And so will Micah and Dahlia."

"Micah, too?"

"Of course. He's the most ruthless queen this side of the Mississippi."

"What a spectacle this is shaping up to be."

"I know," Nyla said, nipping at Anastasia's neck, the itch of power revving her once more. "I can't wait to see how the men will do."

◆ ◆ ◆

Subject: Challenge #2

You will come to the address listed below at 1400 this Sunday. A masked man will greet you outside the entrance and blindfold you. He will escort you into a loft where you will complete the next challenge, which will be this: You will be judged on your physical appearance by a select, discerning panel of women and one drag queen. You may be asked to alter your appearance, if it displeases the panel, and to comply without question or complaint. Should you speak or complain, you will be eliminated from the Quest. Service subs will be on hand to complete grooming and other altercations.

Other challengers will be in the room with you, but you will all be blindfolded, and as such, your anonymity will be protected. May the best man win.

Xo,
Nyla and Anastasia

Jeremi received this message with enthusiasm. His body was his livelihood, his temple. As much as he prized other aspects of his identity—his entrepreneurial spirit, his determination and grit—Jeremi knew that, at the end of the day, his body was the best thing he had going for himself, and thus treated it accordingly.

He groomed meticulously, ruthlessly adhered to stringent diet and exercise modules, and even once, at the request of a lover, waxed his balls. It didn't hurt nearly as much as he thought it would, and her response and touch to Jeremi's freshly shorn boys more than made up for the 20 minutes of pain. How lovingly she caressed him with her hands and tongue, applying expensive oils to the pink, tender skin afterward, then wrapping her mouth around the shaft, taking all of him in, as she cupped and pressed and smoothed his balls. The memory aroused Jeremi so much he pondered waxing them again this moment, but decided to let Nyla and Anastasia determine his fate. He dropped to the floor to do 20 pushups, feeling the pleasant spring and ache of his pectoral muscles and delts as he did so. *Yes*, he thought, he would ace this challenge.

Ratu's SOMA loft was spacious and airy, with exposed brick walls and 20-foot ceilings. Her bedroom was made for extravagant sexual liaisons, and held four beds, two love seats, a chaise lounge, as well as a corner draped with pillows and blankets, in case she decided she wanted to fuck on the floor. She called it her fuck palace, and palatial it was. Ratu demanded variety, was prone to whimsy and flights of fancy, and as such, her fuck palace was a cornucopia of textural sensations—softnessess and hardnesses, metals, brass, wood, silks, satins, rubbers, and beyond. Whatever her textural imagination dreamed up, Ratu lived to see her fantasies come to fruition, and particularly how each sensation shaped and distorted her pleasure.

Next to the fuck palace was a proper dungeon, outfitted with a St. Andrew's cross, suspension beams, a medical station, two spanking benches, and, just for fun, a wooden pillory Ratu acquired when a porn site had its liquidation sale. She almost took the human hamster wheel, but couldn't sacrifice the floor space for something she knew she wouldn't use. Ratu admired the pillory, tracing her hands along the wood. She didn't think she'd be putting anyone in the stocks today, but well, you just never knew. She snapped her fingers and a service sub appeared at her side and kneeled.

"Dust this," she said, stroking his hair and chin a little before sending him off to his task.

In addition to stepping on the scrotums of Silicon Valley CEOs —the higher up the corporate ladder, the more extreme the pain they wanted—Ratu also made a decent livelihood as a kind of sex coach. She trained submissives on how to be better ones. It was, she smiled gleefully, the best business and personal decision she'd ever made.

Snapping her fingers once more brought a different sub to Ratu's feet. This one was tasked with oiling Ratu's curly black hair and powdering her ample bosom. The girls would arrive any minute now, and Ratu wanted to ensure that the place was ship-shape. Or at least, whip-shape. The men who would also arrive would be blindfolded, she knew, but no top should ever abandon her sense of decorum and hospitality.

A platter of crustless sandwiches sat delicately on a low table near the parlour, next to an assortment of teas, coffees, petit fours, and beignets for Micah, who was from Louisiana and whom she knew had a weakness for the French donuts.

Yes, today her friends would get "full service," Ratu laughed to herself, thinking of her halcyon days at Mr. Tom's Peeping Parlour, when full service meant something else entirely. She smoothed a teal throw pillow, picking a speck of fluff from it, and ran her stiletto nails along the back of the black leather couch, admiring the buttery give of its cool surface. This is where they would be conducting their inquisition. Ratu was quite used to public humiliations, of course, but never when the men didn't explicitly ask for it. She was curious how the afternoon would go.

As she nibbled on a cucumber sandwich, the doorbell rang and a collared girl with a shaved head and enormous THEY/THEM earrings escorted Nyla, Anastasia, Micah, and Dahlia inside, where shouts of glee and hugs were exchanged. Micah, in particular, was beside himself with excitement, making jumpy little leaps and air-kissing Ratu a queeny number of times.

"You are giving me such hashtag realness right now I can't even stand it," Micah said. Ratu struck a pose in response and Micah snapped an imaginary picture with his hands.

"How long has it been anyway? Since 'Piss Off'?" Ratu asked.

"Did we miss your latest piece, Micah?" Anastasia chimed in.

"It was brilliant, Ana," Ratu said. "When 45 revoked many of the trans bathroom guidelines that Obama had put into place, Micah staged a shit-in in several of the capitol buildings across the US to reclaim public bathrooms as safe spaces for anyone, of any gender."

"America! We're number two," Nyla said, sipping an earl gray that had been placed in her hand by a sub without her even having to ask.

"I even interviewed him for the podcast," Dahlia chimed in, wrapping Ratu in a belated hug.

"The TERFs must've gone absolutely batty over that," Ana said.

Dahlia smiled. "Oh they always do. Let them wail in their subreddits and leave the rest of us to our real work."

"Speaking of," Micah said, sniffing the air conspiratorially, "I smell the impending tears of several heterosexual men. ... And beignets. Are there beignets!?"

"Just for you, darling," Ratu said, beckoning a sub to feed the hot fried dough crusted with powdered sugar directly into Micah's glitter-red lips.

After all her guests had been greeted and were settling in, Ratu turned to Nyla. "So how medieval are we going on these guys?"

Nyla, now sipping a blood orange mimosa and casually treading her finger along the hem of Anastasia's yoga pants, considered her reply. After a beat, she said, "If most of these men *don't* leave here sobbing, then we haven't done our job."

Micah clinked her glass, followed by Dahlia and Ratu. Anastasia, who held no glass, fist-bumped the trio with a beignet, shaking powdered sugar on the leather cushion. "Oops," she said.

"Don't worry," Ratu replied. She snapped her fingers and a sub kneeled before her, lapping up the white specks of sugar from the sofa with a long pink tongue. Two other subs hovered nearby, and Ana caught on that the subs were not merely there to feed, fan, and clear the dishes away, that they were also there to *service* the queens, should they require such service.

For all in the room except Ana, humiliating men publicly was a point of erotic activism that bordered on religious. As such,

Ratu was wise to think they might need a little … relief for their efforts. Anastasia eyed the sub kneeling before Nyla suspiciously. *Don't even think about it,* her eyes broadcast, and gripped Nyla's hand in hers. She was shocked at this sudden surge of jealousy, knowing that Nyla wouldn't dare let another submissive touch her in Ana's presence, but she also knew the erotic potential of the scene about to unfold, especially in a room full of such elegant sadists.

"Come here," Ana told the sub, and lifted her feet off the ground. The sub, who was beautifully rubenesque and wearing little more than an apron and garters, understood Ana's gesture and made herself into an ottoman. Ana rested her feet upon the sub's back. The sub smiled blissfully. Nyla, watching all of this, raised her eyebrows at Ana.

"What?" she said, shrugging as nonchalantly as she could. She couldn't stop the corner of her lip from rising, however. Nyla leaned over and kissed her wetly on the neck.

Micah, for his part, called over a cute white boy with jet black hair and deep dimples, asking him to rub his feet. The sub returned with lavender oils and started working them slowly into Micah's high arches. He sighed dreamily. "Y'all need to have threesomes every damn week."

The girls laughed, while Dahlia busied herself playing with the nipples of the sub with the shaved head, all while she commanded her to pour a mimosa directly into Dahlia's full wet mouth. "Don't spill it," Dahlia warned, tweaking and tugging the hard little buds until the girl was practically humming. But she did not spill it. Dahlia sipped the sweet, bubbly nectar and relaxed back into the couch.

The doorbell rang again. The men had arrived.

"Shall we?" Ratu looked at her compatriots, who were getting a little too sleepy and complacent with the pampering.

"We shall," Nyla said.

The men were led single file into the hallway across from the parlour. Each had been stripped of their clothing and possessions, save for a black satin blindfold covering their eyes.

"Bring in #1," Ratu's voice rang out in the echoey loft.

Without the use of his sight, Jeremi had no idea what "number" he was, or how many men were within spitting distance of his own naked body. He could smell the Homme Intense on them, hear their breathing, the creak of their feet shuffling on the hardwood floor. Unaware of his own body in space, Jeremi stuck an elbow out and hit something hard but fleshy. Was it ribs? Another arm?

"Watch it, man!" Came the grumpy whisper in reply.

Jeremi extended the other elbow and was greeted with flesh, along with a mild static electricity shock. *How?* Jeremi recoiled. Had he touched something metal on the man next to him? A piercing? Some kind of electric sex toy?

He tried not to think about it, focusing instead on the firing squad he was about to walk in front of. In the distance, Jeremi smelled baked goods and his stomach rumbled. He probably shouldn't have skipped breakfast, but he wanted to get in one last workout before coming here. Besides, he'd found that he was too nervous to eat anyway, except a protein shake with collagen powder and MCT oil.

The sound of uproarious laughter filled the room beyond and Jeremi strained to hear the words flying towards the unnamed, naked man.

"Honestly, not loving the Khal Drogo vibe," Jeremi heard a voice say to the man. "That hair has got to go." Silence ensued next, the light tinkling of champagne glasses, followed by the velcro-ripping sound of a man who had, presumably, just had a large strip of his (chest?) hair removed. More cries and groans followed as the leitmotif repeated itself, a pouring and a ripping and a stripping and a groaning.

"Better," said another voice, after the symphony of unvarnished agony appeared to have subsided. "But now he looks too young. Like a bald baby bird. Put a little hair back."

Laughter followed this request as something was smacked back onto the man's body.

"Let us see your teeth," said another voice, this one sounded male, Jeremi thought, though a faggy kind of male.

Next he heard gagging and whimpering noises as the man was subjected to what Jeremi could only surmise to be an unpleasant oral examination. "Wider," said the voice. "That's it. Now bend over and cough for me. ... Ooh, honey, that hairy *culo* will not do." He snapped his fingers. "More wax!"

As the verbal and physical onslaught progressed, the voices grew quieter, making it more difficult for Jeremi to hear. The rest came in waves and fragments, a perverse kind of poetry.

"Why aren't you smiling? ... Could definitely stand to lose ten pounds ... look at those precious little cankles ... sad little mushroom ... do you call that an erection? ... Your face is just, it's so derivative ... who cuts your hair? Smile, darling, smile ..."

Until finally the clearest sound coming from the room was that of a grown man weeping. It grew louder as the man was brought back into the hallway. Jeremy felt the breeze of his body as he was ushered past the line and the rustle of a plastic bag that probably held the man's clothes. A door opened, heat from the afternoon filtered in briefly upon Jeremi's face, then vanished.

Three other men were tried and prosecuted before his ears. Two similarly left in tears, though the third started shouting ethnic slurs and obscenities after one of the women criticized his nipples as "too spherical." His stamping and yelling was silenced by the sharp, electric lick of what might have been a taser, the current of which Jeremi swore he could feel from where he stood. The man's body hit the floor with a thud, like a sack of potatoes. He made one last attempt to spew his anger, and another shock silenced him for the time being.

"Get him out of here," a voice commanded, and Jeremi felt the soft patter of bare feet ghosting by, along with the slow shuffle of the man's limp weight as he was dragged by. Hearing this, Jeremi's heart began ping-ponging around his chest. His hands tremored, clammy to the touch. He realized suddenly that he was shivering in the airy hallway without a stitch of clothing to warm him. And also, a premonition. He was next.

Panicked, he sucked in the .5% body fat in his flat stomach and did not dare let go. His breath left his lungs in spastic stutters as he did a full body scan, attempting to pinpoint his flaws and mock them himself, as if this could take some of the sting out of it, to practice his resolve. But as he thought back to the voices' particular cruelty, he couldn't make any rhyme nor reason out of it.

Their criticisms of the men's appearance and behavior seemed arbitrary, draconian, and inconsistent. One was criticized for following their rules too well, and another was punished for breaking them. As Jeremi went over the list of things he did not like about his body—his toenails were yellowish, his forearms puny, his nose a little wide, and his dick a little slender—he realized that the game, if that's what this was, was intentionally unwinnable.

Jeremi shivered again, and stuck his hands in his armpits, to warm them.

"Next," a voice commanded. No more time to ponder. A hand clutched his elbow. Jeremi exhaled and slapped the winning-est smile his angular face could muster as he was led to slaughter.

◆ ◆ ◆

Dahlia wolf-whistled as Jeremi was led into the parlour and placed before them. "We've got a live one."

The sub who had poured a mimosa past Dahlia's lips now had her head firmly buried in Dahlia's ruffled skirts, and was gently, meticulously lapping at the delicate flesh between her thighs. When she hit a particularly tender spot, Dahlia held her head in place and let out a slow, near soundless groan. "Look at this smug little potato pancake," she said when Jeremi was placed in front of her.

"Little is right," Ratu chimed in. "What are you, 5'6"?"

"You must be this tall to ride this train, honey," Micah laughed and smacked his haunches. The rest joined in. All but Anastasia, of course, who had watched the proceedings unfold in silence, as she had requested. She'd tried, in vain, to get into the spirit of things, but found it brought her little joy. *Perhaps I'm just not a sadist*, she thought disappointedly.

She studied Jeremi, the chiseled-ness of his form, the hard meat of him. He had a body like a Rodin sculpture, she thought, admiring his smooth lines and the veins that popped on his forearms. Anastasia's eyes widened as a service sub brought Jeremi's dick to attention.

Sure, she thought, he *was* on the short side and his nose was a little wide and his dick lacked a certain girth, but on the whole, his body was a marvel, and Ana would rather fixate on the exquisiteness of the human body than to critique its imperfections. She admired the lean slope of his calf muscles, the sharp little hip bones, and the errant incisor that stuck out just so. Ana had always admired the unconventional bits of people, and as she found herself doing this with Jeremi, she felt a heat rise between her thighs. It surprised her. She blinked, flushed with a pink on her neck she knew was visible to others. Nyla, feeling Ana's weight shift on the couch, looked over at her, and a flash of thunderous jealousy poured through her. Her lover was looking at this man with hunger, a hunger reserved for Nyla.

This would not do. Without taking her eyes off of Anastasia, Nyla pressed the tiny remote she had in her purse, which activated the vibrator nestled against Anastasia's clit. Ana gave a start, her hips lurching forward at the sudden, inescapable pleasure. She had forgotten about the panties Nyla had requested she wear that day, had forgotten her lover's tendency to subject her body to all manners of sensations when she was least expecting it. Such as now. She folded her hands in her lap, trying to calm herself.

"Everything okay, darling?" Ratu said, glancing over at Ana in between insults of Jeremi's "whimpering calves" and "sniveling nipples."

"Mmh," Ana half-nodded through clenched teeth as Nyla pressed the remote again, increasing the speed of the vibration as the panel crucified Jeremi's cock. Their voices became softer, then became a blur as warmth spread through Ana's hips and ass and along her lower spine. The vibrator beat its insistent rhythm against her clit, slipping against the moisture at the apex of her thighs. She stared once again at Jeremi's cock, imagined it inside of her. *There was something so ordinary about it,* she thought, *and yet...*

Nyla increased the intensity of the vibration once more, and Ana struggled to sit still. She clenched her legs together, which only made the ache in her cunt more persistent, so she released them. As the vibe surged, she pictured Jeremi's cock surging into her, inch by inch, sensation reaching entirely through her, past her womb, her belly, her toes, each thrust opening something in her, bringing the shadows of her dark selves more and more into the sunlight.

Ana started to perspire. She could feel the sweat gathering at the dimple just above her ass. Throughout, Nyla carried on as if nothing at all was happening, as if she were not in fact bending Ana to her every whim, teasing her, torturing her. Nyla registered the absolute pleasure of fucking Ana so privately and so publicly.

Nyla looked up as Micah said, "...and not an ounce of fat on him! Boy, eat a carb. It won't kill you. Sheesh, I can see the veins in your stomach!"

Ana rocked a little in her seat, feeling the outline of an orgasm arching its way through her. Her muscles went hard, rigid, her breath galloped like a racehorse, and an exquisite fire burned its way through the forest of her body. Just as she was about to walk up and over that ledge, however, Nyla clicked the remote. The vibrations ceased, and Ana was left with a furious disappointment. She glanced at her lover with a hurt, angry look on her face—a look she knew she would pay for later, but which she also could not control. Nyla paid her no mind at all, however, just continued on with the roast of this unknown man, a man who stood stock still through every assault, almost meditatively, as if he was a living statue or the Buddha, come back to teach them some mystical, paradoxical lesson about nonresistance.

Nyla admired the man's resolve, but because of it, and because of the bratty look Ana had just bestowed upon her, which she would definitely pay for later, Nyla wanted to break him all the more. She unleashed a litany of barbs aimed at his manhood, his masculinity, and even his mother. While the latter did send a furrow of discord through Jeremi's placid exterior, he refused to go down.

Nyla looked at Micah, whose sub licked and sucked and bobbed pretty as a bow on his dick, which Micah barely seemed to register, so in thrall he was lashing out at Jeremi, that both he and Nyla said at the same time, "Get the wax."

They let him keep his eyebrows, but the rest of Jeremi was up for grabs. Legs, scrotum, arms, armpits, and even his toes were stripped of their knuckle tufts. Throughout this slow baring of his flesh, the swift agonies of the strips pulled, the burning and cooling, Jeremi's blindfold began to slip, to loosen, and he could see a sliver of light, of the room he was in. He saw before him a couch, with people sitting on it, and tried to assign voices to the legs in his limited vision. One pair was silent, and he found himself fixating on her. Her legs were clad in yoga pants, gray, tight as a second skin. Her legs were crossed, impossibly long, gazelle-like even, which led to bare feet, one of which dangled on top of the other, as if dispelling its own nervous, restless energy.

Another strip of wax was applied, this time to his happy trail, and Jeremi focused all his energy on the legs so as not to cry out. He focused on the legs as if they were a patron saint, a savior, a guiding light, as if they alone would get him through this humiliation. He knew it was crazy to think so, but he could swear that the legs were reaching for him, offering him compassion, a cool, soothing washcloth applied to the fire of his skin. He memorized their forms, the slimness of the ankles, the sharp jut of knee, the taut, muscular thighs. A hand ripped the strip from his torso and Jeremi winced. How much more of him was left to remove? He wondered.

He fixated on the legs once more, imagined them wrapped around his neck, his tongue buried in the soft folds of her, tasting the salt-sea and sweat therein. This image pulled the blood back from his skin into the center of his body, and Jeremi knew he was getting hard again. The pleasure of his fantasy contrasting with the pain of the wax made for confusing bedfellows in his body. His skin felt both flushed and freezing, naked and covered, and the paradoxical-ness of these conflicting sensations excited him even more.

"Fuck, you guys. He's into it," Micah said.

"The straighter they are, the more masochistic," Ratu replied. "Should I break out the TENS machine?"

"No," Nyla said, defeat palpable in her sighs. "We've wasted enough time on this one already. Send him along. He passes."

Ratu snapped her fingers and the waxing stopped, leaving Jeremi lopsided on one arm and wildly perceptive to the faintest of breezes. He'd have to finish the job himself at home if he didn't want to look like Two-Face. Or Two-Arm, he supposed.

As a hand gripped his elbow and he was led away from the room and the couch and the legs, he said goodbye inwardly to the beautiful pair that had gotten him through this ordeal. He smiled, a real smile this time, not the plastic smile of endurance and stubbornness he'd worn on for the judges, to deprive them at least that small amount of satisfaction.

He'd made it though. He hadn't cried. He passed!

The light of the alley hit him intensely as he was spat out into the waning afternoon. The blindfold was removed, his clothing handed to him, and a metal door shut with a monstrous clang behind him. It took Jeremi a moment to remember where he was, and even who he was. He stretched his limbs and examined his new, mismatched arms. Pink as a shrimp. Despite this, Jeremi was finding that, with each challenge, with each bit of suffering he endured for Nyla and Anastasia, the more suffering he *could* endure. It was as if his body, his desires, his attentions were labyrinths that they somehow had the map to.

He also realized, with some surprise, that he liked it. These women took care of everything. They thought of every detail. Their execution was on par with Fortune 500 CEOs. As such, Jeremi didn't have to do a thing other than show up and subject himself to their whims. He found great freedom in this, and even, paradoxically, a kind of power. He was exhausted by the thousands of decisions—both mundane and monumental—he had to make each day. There was, he thought, a purity, a serenity, to not making them. To be told exactly what to do, when to show up, what to wear or not wear. It gave him a sense of direction, a purposefulness, a goal to strive for. These commands, these horrible tasks, were not so unlike his punishing CrossFit workouts, his Ironman triathlons, his flipping over tractor tires in the mud. If he welcomed *that* pain, why not this? Especially if he would get laid at the end of all this. In other instances, he got nothing, except a whey protein shake and an Instagram #humblebrag, if anything.

As he walked, back to his life with its uncertainties and problems, he felt a delicious exhaustion. Even the air swirling around the shit-strewn streets of SOMA gave him pleasure, and he found himself missing the torture room already, the lovely legs, the low-grade pain of having to wait for the next challenge to arrive. He wondered if this was how charismatic leaders formed their cults, and realized, horrifically, that he was just the kind of person who would have drunk the Kool-Aid.

Subject: Challenge #3

Congratulations! You've made it to the third round of the Quest for the Holy Grail. The challengers are dwindling and we will select our victor very soon. But first, for this challenge, you will go to a club in the Castro called Stormy Leather on Thursday night at 2300. You will order a drink of your choosing and proceed to the dance floor. There, you will let anyone who wants to touch you do so, even if the touch is unwanted, even if it violates your boundaries and personal space and bodily integrity. After a man touches you, you are to thank them.

We will be at the club, though we will not reveal ourselves. But rest assured, we will be watching you. At 0100, you are free to leave. May the best man win.

Yours,
Nyla and Anastasia

Mister Fister wasn't an ordinary gay club, but a leather bar, with two raised stages which held men in leather jockstraps and aviators slowly gyrating their pelvises and rubbing their contents on the faces of men wandering by the platforms. Dressed in dark, baggy jeans and a button-down shirt half-undone, Jeremi tugged at the thin gold chain around his neck and felt suddenly nervous, and out of place.

The bass from the music sent vibrations up through his trainers as he scanned the room for Nyla and Anastasia. The bar held a smattering of women, though it was hard to tell which were real and which were drag queens in the low lighting. On the second floor of the bar was a railing made of a chain-link fence, and Jeremi spied a group of women dressed in neon latex with gloves to match. The black lights made them glow ethereally, like shadows with no bodies attached. He decided that was probably them and headed to the bar to get his obligatory drink before the torture started. He wore an extra pair of underwear—briefs under boxers—in an effort to give his member a small amount of protection against the roving hands that would soon make his acquaintance on the dance floor.

At the bar, he ordered a double, and as he did so, Jeremi felt a hand cup his ass, giving his cheek the slightest squeeze as they walked past. He turned around to give whoever it was a dirty look, but couldn't tell who it was—the place was packed and the crowd only getting tighter. Jeremi let it go, figuring he probably didn't want to know who it was anyway.

An older woman stood next to him waving a $20 in her hand spastically. "Hello! I've been here 15 minutes already. Who do you have to flash to get a goddamn drink around here?"

The bartender ignored her, continuing to serve only men. "Let me try," Jeremi said. "What do you want?"

"A gimlet please, vodka."

Jeremi lifted his shirt over his head and made his pecs dance, one at a time, popping them like a morse code message at the bartender, who made a beeline for Jeremi and his snake-charming nipples. He ordered the woman's drink and she thanked him, placing a dollar bill into his waistband playfully. When she left the bar, Jeremi marveled at this ordinary kindness. He couldn't remember the last time he'd done something sweet for a woman he didn't want to have sex with. Must be something in the water, he mused.

After downing the whiskey and ordering another double, he cracked his knuckles and exhaled low and loud. It occurred to him that he wasn't the only man here responding to the challenge, and wondered what other poor schmucks were here with him in this strange arena. The idea of outlasting these other men pleased him greatly. The thought of triumphing, being the last man standing was almost enough to give him a semi. He glanced at his watch, 10:58 p.m., and pushed his way onto the dance floor, through the waves of bare-chested bodies, the sea of harnesses and chaps, the wigs and glitter and gold booty shorts.

Once again he glanced up at the chain-link fence above, at the women in latex. One wore a bright pink wig, which glowed luminescent in the black light. He winked at her, hoping she belonged to the pair of legs that had bewitched him from the Inquisition, and then shut his eyes, allowing the pulse of the music to find its way into his bones, and move them.

It did not take long for the crowd to begin taking its liberties with his body. He felt first a hairy arm clutch him from behind, and pull him back against a broad chest. The arm held Jeremi in place, as they swayed lightly, the man's breath coming out in hot, wet puffs against Jeremi's neck. He kept his eyes closed as he felt teeth graze his neck and then a tongue bathe the top knot of his spine.

Jeremi shuddered at this wet embrace, but the arm held him in place. The man's saliva cooled on his neck as his other hand slowly worked its way around, forming a loose claw at Jeremi's hip. Jeremi focused with all his might on the image of Nyla and Anastasia in the hot river, the steam rising around their bodies. He imagined moving the thin bikini bottom out of the way, exposing the delicate flesh there, what it would feel like to push into them from behind, one at a time, back and forth between them, their bodies prone and gasping as the water splashed around him.

His imaginings worked a little too well, however, for now he was fully hard. The man holding him by the chest swiveled Jeremi around so they were facing each other, and thrust his tongue deep into Jeremi's mouth. As he did so, Jeremi felt the man's cock push against him as well, against his abs, and tensed against it. This caused the man to press against him harder. His beard chafed Jeremi's lips as he devoured Jeremi's mouth.

Before Jeremi had time to be embarrassed about being hard, two more hands were on him from behind, kneading his ass. Unlike the man assaulting his face, these hands were gentler, handling his ass as if it were a sculpture, tracing its contours, its firmness, weighing the roundness and heft. Jeremi found that he rather enjoyed this embrace, and wished it was distracting him from the bearded man's alarming and grotesque tongue. Now his captor was holding Jeremi by the back of the neck and darting in and out of his mouth with great force. He felt himself on the verge of gagging, and turned his head away and down, where the man continued to gnaw at his neck.

And still the gentle hands behind him traced and shaped his ass. The hands reached into his baggy jeans now, reached easily under the boxers and the briefs and rested hotly on his bare skin, where they continued their caresses. Slowly the fingers fanned out, spread Jeremi's cheeks, opened them like a fan or an umbrella. Jeremi had never felt more vulnerable. He clenched the muscles in his ass, to protect this most delicate part of him, to let even the loving hands know he had his limits.

The bearded man gripped Jeremi's chin in his hand, forcing Jeremi to finally look at the man's face. He wore aviators, so his eyes were mirrors, and his large, bear-like paw mashed Jeremi's cheeks together, the way his terrible uncle would when Jeremi was a child.

"What do you say?" he barked.

Jeremi hardened, the vein in the middle of his forehead thick and pulsing. He shook his head no.

The man gripped Jeremi by the throat with enough force to cut off his air supply. Any more and Jeremi would be lifted off the ground entirely. "What do you say?" he said again.

The man released Jeremi's throat enough for him to form words, his calloused fingers scratching at the base of Jeremi's neck. "Thank you," he choked, his pride quickly dwindling in the face of this much bigger man's strength.

The beard licked Jeremi's face one last time and vanished in the crowd. *Thank god*, Jeremi thought to himself, wiping his face with the sleeve of his shirt. Meanwhile, the gentle hands guided him around so that Jeremi was facing this new stranger. Jeremi closed his eyes suddenly—he couldn't bear to be seen. Not like this, not now.

Without the frontal assault distracting him, Jeremi softened, let his head rest on the man's shoulder as they undulated to the music, his hands continuing to knead and unwind him, these deft hands loosening the knots in his glutes, stroking and opening, stroking and opening him, until the man's finger rested at the opening of his anus, and gently knocked.

A wave of pleasure and revulsion greeted Jeremi and once more the muscles of his ass clenched and stiffened. Though this time, the finger was between them, and clenching around it seemed to push it further inside him, just the tip of it, and the added pressure of this finger between his cheeks, lightly probing, caused his sphincter to contract and release. Hot blood went coursing through Jeremi's body until it rushed, mercifully, to his cock.

The bodies swelled around him on the dance floor, and Jeremi let the sensations wash over him. He didn't fight it, not his hard-on or the shame that rose around it, not the sweat pooling in his lower back or the wild longing that lodged at the back of his throat as the finger dipped in and out of him. He was getting fucked—like a girl!—and he didn't exactly want it to stop.

As soon as he thought it, though, the hand broke away and the body went with it. He didn't ask Jeremi to thank him, as the other man had, but nonetheless he whispered it to the sea of bodies, whispered it so quietly that there's no way the man could have heard him, but still he said it, and in his own mute and alarmed way, he meant it.

Men continued to swarm him. They cupped his balls and pulled on his nipples, rubbed their sweaty bodies along his and tongued the salt from his neck. A few more fingers penetrated his ass, but none with the same precision or care as the first. Indeed, these fingers seemed intent on hurting him, humiliating him. Another grabbed Jeremi's dick and laughed right in his face when it wilted. But Jeremi just smiled; he knew his purgatory was almost up, and found himself strangely buffered by his own fortitude, his ability to withstand such blatant violation. It made him feel more alive, more manly somehow, more *more*. He even stayed five extra minutes on the dance floor, as if to say to the women watching, "What else you got?"

At 1:05, he pushed his way back out of the throng, smoothed his clothing, buttoned his shirt, and headed out into the cool, black night, chin held high. In his own bed later, while watching porn, he reached his left hand back behind him and gently stroked the delicate ridge of his perineum that had awakened so much pleasure in him earlier. With his other hand on his dick, he moved his fingers around the opening of his anus, feeling it wink in response. It was a little sore, he noticed, so he tread lightly, timing the movements with the rhythms of his hand working the front, until he felt his blood rising, every nerve ending standing at attention like a well-trained foot soldier. He came seconds later, sighing in relief.

"I don't think Gus has ever had as much fun as he did tonight," Nyla said, dousing herself with talc powder so she could remove the skin-tight latex gloves from her arms.

"Oh, I know. And did you see Jonathan tea-bag the tall one in the Keds from the stage?" Anastasia replied.

"Damn, no. I can't believe I missed that," Nyla said. "We'll have to get a complete report from the boys at the next boozy brunch. Did Derek pick a place yet?"

She turned around, gestured for Anastasia to help her loosen the stays of her corset. Anastasia kneeled and set about freeing her lover from its teeth. "You know he picks the same place every time."

"I Wanna Hold Your Ham!" They both said in unison, laughing.

As their laughter subsided and the room fell silent, Nyla turned around, corset half-undone, her cunt staring straight at Anastasia's pouty mouth.

"Did it turn you on?" Nyla asked, sliding her fingers through Anastasia's hair. Anastasia closed her eyes contentedly.

"What?"

"Tonight."

"Yes."

Nyla's hand made a fist at the back of Anastasia's head and pulled it toward her hips. The tip of Anastasia's nose nestled against her clit. Nyla was wet already. The sight of Anastasia on her knees was often enough to bring this response out of her, but still she was surprised. She slowly pressed Anastasia's face against her fire, coating her mouth and cheeks and chin with wet. Anastasia parted her lips and let her tongue soak up whatever remnants of Nyla's desire her cheeks and chin did not catch. "Tell me what turned you on."

Anastasia lifted her eyes, pulled her tongue back enough to speak. "I liked watching them, knowing I had orchestrated it, knowing that every touch and caress and kiss those men received was from me, an extension of me even. I felt like I had a hundred hands, a hundred mouths. I felt like I was fucking them all."

Nyla moaned, pressed Anastasia's face against her sex once again. "You do have a hundred hands, darling. I feel you everywhere. Your tongue is on my clit but it's also at my ear, it's whispering my name, it's marking my thighs."

Anastasia increased the pressure of her tongue, moved her head slowly from side to side, as if shaking her head no, to protest, and also to tease the tender flesh there with her lips. Nyla's head sank back and she leaned against the vanity. Her sharp nails moved down, gripping the softness of Anastasia's shoulder and leaving little bonfires in their wake.

As Nyla's legs clenched and her breath grew shallow, she knew she would soon come if Anastasia kept this up. As she would never give her lover such easy satisfaction, Nyla once again bent Anastasia's head back, away from her sex, and looked admiringly at her red, languorous mouth, her cheeks flushed and glistening in the light. The sight alone was almost enough to tip Nyla over the edge, so she quickly turned around, and beckoned her lover to finish removing the corset. Anastasia did so, but couldn't help but take one last nibble as she worked the stays, her mouth guiding over Nyla's curves, the perfect swell of her heart-shaped ass, her teeth leaving the faintest mark on her left cheek.

"You're gonna pay for that later," Nyla said.

"Yes, Ma'am."

After the girls had undressed and fucked and redressed and fucked again, they lay back against the soft grey sheets, Anastasia's head resting on Nyla's clavicle.

"What shall we do next?" Anastasia said, her voice a contented purr.

"Is my little pupusa still not satisfied?" A blush spread from Anastasia's coccyx to her scapula as Nyla raked her fingers casually across her arm.

"I mean with the quest... but please don't stop doing that."

"Ah, the grail! Yes. What shall we make them endure next? Have someone blow them with a ghost pepper in their mouth? Send them a barrage of dick pics that never stop coming? Ooh, or. Or! We force them to hand over their phones and then spread photos and videos of their man goodies all over the porn sites."

Anastasia stiffened. Nyla craned her head back to look into her eyes. "Too much?"

"It's a bit much, yes."

"Are you okay? Having hesitations again?"

"It's just that—I mean, where does it end? I don't want to *become* the terrible monsters we're trying to destroy. To become gleeful, aroused even, by the cruelty we inflict—"

Nyla's eyes widened, flashing with mischief.

"—doesn't it make us, well, just like misogynists we claim to abhor Or worse?"

Nyla sat up straighter, considering. "Are you proposing we end the quest then? We still have half a dozen men in the running."

"Jesus," Ana said. "Still? How is that possible? We're putting them through so much!"

Nyla traced the long, arcing slope of Ana's hip bone as it curved into her sex. Ana shuddered. "*This* is how, darling. You are the feast of Herod, Wagner's entire Ring cycle, all 1.8 million words of the *Mahābhārata*. You are salvation. Temptation. These men would sooner castrate themselves than give up the chance of a night with you."

"The things you say to me."

"I speak only the truth."

"Still. I don't know how much longer I can keep this going."

"Then we shall stop. Pick a boy. I'm fine with whoever pleases you. Do you know their names?"

"No," Anastasia was embarrassed to admit. "But there was one. At Ratu's. I remember we waxed him and he, well, he seemed to rather enjoy it. There was a softness about him. Despite the obsessive Peloton body."

"Yes, and the terrible tattoo."

"What was it?"

"Tinkerbell, I believe, with a fairy wand up her—."

"Good gods." Ana exclaimed. "But still. A warmth emanated from him. He had no menace, despite all the cruelty we hurled at him. He seemed to me like a boy who'd simply lost his way.

Nyla consulted the spreadsheet on her phone to find his identifying information. "That one is named Jeremi with an i."

"With an i?"

"Yes."

Anastasia winced, scrunching her face up in displeasure.

"You can back out at any time, you know," Nyla said, beckoning Ana to lay back down upon her shoulder. "We don't have to go through with it."

"No, I—I want to, I do."

"Jeremi then?"

"Jeremi it is," Ana said. Nyla resumed her soft stroking of Ana's arms, shoulders, and the soft swell of her torso. As they both fell sleepy, drifting on the edge of consciousness, Ana said, almost inaudibly. "And no ghost peppers. That is a torture only for me to enjoy."

Nyla smiled, her eyes still closed. "As you wish."

The day of the threesome arrived. Nyla and Anastasia had sent a note to Jeremi's apartment with instructions as to how he should prepare for the evening. He would bathe and groom himself, the note said, and remove all hair from his nether region. Attached to the note was an elegant straight razor and perfumed shave cream. After, he would dress plainly, aside from the black, satin blindfold that he was to put on, and wait outside his apartment for the limousine, which would pick him up at 2000 exactly.

Jeremi was so nervous and excited that he blindfolded himself and stood outside of his apartment 35 minutes early. He paced one step in every direction, the small radius in which he was sure he would not run into or trip on anything, engaging in an agonizing and restless square dance that, had he been not a white man, would have no doubt caused some aggrieved Karen to call several police departments on him.

Alas, he was, and they did not.

Jeremi's ears craned toward the whoosh of every passing car, and deflated when it did not stop. Eventually he heard a crunch of wheels upon the gravel driveway, as well as the sound of a door closing, and another opening.

"This way please," a voice said, at some distance. Taking one tiny step forward after another, Jeremi, hands outstretched, hobbled toward the sound, which had all but vanished, and hoped his anxious steps would not soon be met with a face full of gravel.

Groping his way along, his hands met fabric, which appeared to belong to the stolid arm of the limo driver. He followed it up to the man's shoulder, and then across his torso, and then to the hood of the car, until he found the entryway he was searching for. The limo driver was not helping Jeremi at all in this endeavor, and though blindfolded, he was sure the grin on the limo driver's face was as long as the limo itself.

Let him laugh all he wants, Jeremi thought. *I'ma get me some toniiiiight.*

With that, the glee broke upon his face and he settled in as comfortably as he could without the use of one of his senses. He was on his way.

"You're nervous," Nyla said to Ana.

"I am not," Ana replied, wiping down a nightstand with a washcloth.

"You always clean when you're nervous, darling. But this is the penthouse suite. I assure you it's sterling."

Before Ana could falsely protest that she was, in fact, panic-cleaning, there was a knock at the door.

"Showtime," Nyla said. "Are we really doing this?"

"Kiss me first."

Without hesitation, Nyla encircled her lover's lips with her own, with enough intensity to bring a swift patch of red to Ana's cheeks, and then released her.

Nyla opened the door, where Jeremi stood, along with the bell-boy Nyla paid to escort him to their room. She slipped another wad of bills in the bell boy's hand as he led Jeremi's to a straight-backed, armless wooden chair that stood at the foot of the bed.

A soft sigh of rose water emanated from Jeremi as he passed, which pleased Ana, as it meant he had followed the directions she had sent to the letter. A true submissive! Perhaps when they were done with him, they'd send him to Ratu for proper training. She could make much use of such a willing subservient.

The grin still wide across Jeremi's face, he sat in the chair, and *almost* didn't notice the fur-lined shackles that were being placed on his wrists and ankles until the last strap was tightened on the last cuff. "Wait a minute," he said, "Can we—"

But before he could finish, Nyla placed a single finger against Jeremi's lips. "Shhhh," she said. "Just relax."

The syrupy hush of Nyla's voice quieted Jeremi immediately, especially as it was followed by the brush of her soft breasts against his face. He ceased straining against the cuffs.

While Nyla readied the room and the instruments, Anastasia removed Jeremi's white tank top and took him in more fully. His arms were muscled and tanned. His fingers long, dainty almost, slightly yellowed at the tips, with clean, almost immaculate nails cut to the quick. She scanned down further and was delighted to find that, through the black athletic pants, she could see his excitement growing already. When his chest rose and fell as he breathed, Ana wondered what it might be like to press herself against it.

"I'm pleased you chose these pants, Jason."

"It's Jeremi?" he said, suddenly unsure of his own name.

"Right, whatever," Nyla continued. "I had planned to cut them off, but I see yours come with … side snaps."

He could barely suppress his joy at having pleased Nyla with his purchase. "Yeah, yeah. Got these 20% off at the Dick's Sporting Goods near the mall."

Nyla rolled her eyes in Ana's direction, but maintained her icy, emotionless tone.

To Ana she said, "Remove them." Ana kneeled before Jeremi, placing one hand at each cuffed ankle and slowly began to unsnap the white buttons, sliding her fingers along the skin and hair of Jeremi's calves. Ana could tell he was nervous; his tension was palpable, but as she gently caressed his lower legs, then his knees and very pale thighs, removing his pants while she did so, he seemed to relax. As she unfastened the last snaps from his hips, Ana realized he wore no underwear. This pleased her, and she brushed her bare nipples against his thighs, which caused him to stiffen again, this time from pleasure.

"I want to see you," Jeremi said, his voice somewhere between a whine and a pleading.

"In time," Nyla replied. "But first..."

A soft pair of lips greeted his—he presumed they belonged to Ana—and his breath quickened. Instinctively he tried to use his hands to clasp her hips or breasts, before realizing they were bound behind his back. The cuffs chafed against his wrists, but yielded not more than an inch.

As his tongue and lips performed their dance, Ana found herself immured in conflicting emotions. She hadn't kissed a boy since high school and it was so unmemorable then that she had almost forgotten it entirely. Then she thought how different Jeremi's lips and mouth were from Nyla's—the coarse stubble, the hardness, the intense pressure of his movements—it fascinated and dismayed her. She wasn't sure *how* she felt, which baffled her further. As a test, she let her hands wander down his chest, feeling the taut muscles of his pecs before gripping each pink nipple between her thumb and forefinger and squeezing. As she did so, she felt Jeremi harden further beneath her, his cock pressing warmly against her stomach, as she knelt between his knees.

It was at this moment, when Jeremi thought he might come with just a few more accidental brushes of Anna's stomach against his cock, that he received a different shock—a literal one. Both he and Ana jumped at the jolt that passed through their shared embrace.

"This is a cattle prod," Nyla said casually, as if she was pointing out that the sky was blue. Nyla pressed the metal tongs against Jeremi's thigh and he winced in anticipation, even though the prod was off now, and all he felt was a slight sharpness from their pointy ends.

"You're lucky," Nyla went on. "I've stripped you naked for a reason. With clothes, the spark gap would be wider, and, as such, the greater the shock." She trailed the prod along his lower torso, and then down the length of his shaft, which twitched at her caress. Nyla enjoyed seeing the tension in Jeremi, the short, staccato rise and fall of his chest at the fear that Nyla could press the trigger at any time—and might.

But no shock came. Not then, at least. So he tried to relax once more, and to normalize his breathing. The trials that Nyla and Ana had put him through had prepared him for the exquisite confusion of pleasure and pain experienced together in equal measures. He also had realized his propensity for pain—his delight even!—in giving the reins up to someone else, especially if those someones were beautiful women. Indeed, he felt, dare he say, pleased? Excited? Though he squinted at the fear of electric volts placed anywhere near his man goodies, he sat up straighter in his chair, feeling a little like a patriot at a baseball game when the national anthem is sung.

"Are you ready for your final test, Jeremi?" Ana asked, letting the tips of her manicured nails trail through his hair and along his face.

"I was born ready," he said, winking, and then realizing that she wouldn't see it because of the blindfold.

"Then pay attention," Nyla said. "Anastasia and I will be testing you on key issues that affect women and gender nonconforming people. If you answer the questions correctly, Ana will please your body in any way she sees fit to do so. If you answer incorrectly, you will be shocked. Do you understand the rules?"

"Yes," he said. Jeremi's chest tightened once more. He didn't know anything about women's issues, except what he read in that Nancy Friday book *The Secret Garden*. That was women's studies, right? His heart pounded. He could feel the sweat on his palms slick and faintly sticky. For the first time, he wished Nyla would just whip him until he passed out. He wished he was before the horrid scrutiny of the queens again. Anything would be better than this.

"My first question is, what is patriarchy?"

He exhaled slowly. Okay, he could do this. "Uh, it's, like, male domination."

"I will accept that as an answer," Nyla said. At this, Ana's lips formed a soft O at the tip of Jeremi's cock, and began sucking gently. He groaned, thighs tightening at this unexpected embrace. Nyla continued, "I also would have accepted: a gendered social and political structure in which the most powerful men impose their will on others, including legal systems, family systems, schools, religions, the media, the medical establishment, and the workplace."

But Jeremi didn't hear the rest of Nyla's sentence, too entranced was he to pay attention to anything other than the soft lips and curling tongue melting him into the chair.

"Next question." Ana leaned back on her knees, releasing Jeremi from her mouth. "When did women receive the right to vote?"

"They didn't always have it?"

The pain struck his cock the way lighting would fell a tree. He pulled so hard against his shackles, he thought he might break them. But the chains held. The wetness from Ana's lips concentrated the shock all in the head of his cock, the most sensitive area. His head lolled forward. The current shot through him and then fell silent. His heart pounded.

"Incorrect. Women were granted the right to vote thanks to the 19th amendment, which occurred a few months before 1920."

"Damn, I didn't know that," Jeremi breathed, trying to recover.

A genuineness in his voice made even the hardened, icy Nyla pause.

She added, "Even after the 19th amendment passed, some women were still excluded from voting, based on race, age, education level, and whether they were married or not."

"That's bullshit."

"It is," Ana chimed in.

"Next question: Name a black woman who has had an impact on you—"

Jeremi pressed his lips together swiftly in anticipation, before Nyla added, "—someone other than Beyonce."

He sank back in his chair, his whole body at half mast, except for his cock, which stood erect as ever. He had always struggled with this in the past, and yet with Nyla and Ana at the helm, his dick was suddenly as predictable as the expiration date on a milk carton.

"Okay, I got this," he said, licking his chapped lips. "Nina Simone. Home girl's got mad skills. JAY-Z built a whole track around "Four Women." She's also been sampled by Kanye, Wayne, Timbaland, and lots more."

Nyla and Ana looked at each other in dismay. Then Ana leaned forward again, smiling, and placed her hands and arms on Jeremi's thighs as she took him into her mouth once more, this time widening her mouth and throat to take the full length of him inside. He shuddered softly. The blindfold made him feel everything so intensely. He almost didn't want to take it off now. But he wanted to *see* her, wanted to see himself disappear inside her. When Ana's tongue grazed the thick veins on his shaft, he swore he could feel each groove. The pleasure bore down into the base of his spine and in a momentary embarrassment, felt that he might come any second.

But this thought wore away as soon as Nyla asked another question and Ana sat back on her knees dutifully.

The next four questions in a row Jeremi answered wrong. He couldn't list an issue impacting indigenous women; he didn't realize the extensiveness of the income inequality gap; he did not know the difference between sex work and sex trafficking; and he could not name a single LGBTQ elected official—not one! Not even after living in San Francisco for the last eight years. The fact of this particular ignorance would have shocked him if he hadn't also been quite literally shocked by Nyla's menacing, unceasing electrified blows.

He felt the pain of each wrong answer in a different, demonic way. Some shocks were stingy and short, others fat and traveled the full length of him. Still others made him feel as if his manhood had been run over by a semi. And others yet felt as if his most delicate flesh was being seared by a waffle iron.

His head rolled back, his muscles limp with agony. He did not know how much more of this he could take. Though blindfolded, the room had ceased to be. His body disappeared, the pleasure of Ana's lips on him a faded, distant glimpse of a memory. Now all he tasted was iron. Even the fillings in his teeth ached.

"Last question, Jeremi, as we do not want you to collapse before you'll be of any sexual use to us. It's a simple question: True or false, one out of three women worldwide will experience sexual violence in their lifetime."

Jeremi knitted his brows. He pondered: One out of three was *a lot* of women. That was too high, right? How could it possibly be that high? Yet, none of Nyla's questions had been misleading or worded to trick him. Maybe this was evidence that the statement was true. He took a guess. "False?"

The electric tongue of the cattle prod rained upon him so quickly and so intensely that his body arched off the chair entirely.

"Incorrect," Nyla said. "This statistic comes from the World Health Organization."

He struggled to speak, his lips numb, his face muscles drunk with pain. He seemed incapable of parting to let anything other than a wail come through. "That number ... seemed ... too ... high."

Jeremi heard the cattle prod hit the floor and groaned in relief. "Let me ask you something, Jeremi," Nyla said.

He groaned again.

"When we asked you to wear the weighted bra, did you receive unwanted sexual attention?"

Jeremi admitted that he had, though he kept the particular and unsavory details about the man in the car to himself, unrealizing that Ana had heard everything.

"What you experienced was a very small glimpse of what it's like for women to exist in the world, sometimes every single day. Let me tell you something that happened to me just last week. I'll give you a benign example, so as not to upset you or Anastasia. I was driving to a taqueria just past sunset. When I pulled into the parking lot, a man noticed me and stood outside my window. I tried to wave him away, but he did not leave. Instead, he began to pound on the glass, beckoning me to open it. I refused, looking straight ahead, willing him to leave. After five agonizing minutes, he shook his fist into the glass, not breaking it, thankfully, and called me a cunt before storming off."

Anastasia reached for Nyla's hand, squeezing the tips of her fingers as she spoke.

"That's just one very small example of the gawking, the scrutiny, the fear, and humiliation. All of it, and for no reason, other than I'm a woman—different. What do you think of that, Jeremi?"

He had no answer, but shook his head softly, eyes searching the darkness that was this cruel lesson, looking for the light. Jeremi hated that that had happened to Nyla but he also knew he wasn't responsible for it. Was he? Was that the point she was making? The Jeremi before the quest would have resisted all of this—the blindfold, the uncertainty, the violation upon violation done to his body, his spirit. But something had happened to him during these weeks of trials, of pleasure and pain, delight and embarrassment. He grew to, well, not exactly *like* these feelings or experiences, but to become curious about them, about himself and ease in his day to day life he had taken for granted.

Whereas at first Jeremi was merely angry at these cunty bitches for putting his nuts through the ringer, he now felt strangely *special*, the chosen one, the one to receive their harsh lessons of femaleness, of retribution. He also felt in awe of how much work they had put into these quests—how many people and how much time and money and care and details went into crafting the days and nights and agony they had put him through.

How could he tell Nyla and Ana this? What could he say other than the cliche, the utterly simple and profound, the too-big and too-little words: "Thank you."

Nyla stood up, the clacking of her heels echoed brightly on the wood floors as he waited for her to say something—anything. But she did not. Instead, he felt the cuff of his left hand being loosened and released, and then his right one. He rubbed his sore wrists, which were raw and chafed from the straining.

It was Ana who whispered to him to rise from the chair—his feet were still bound in leather cuffs connected by a chain. He was led to a bed, the comforter soft against his ass and thighs as he felt his way onto it and sat. And it was also Ana who soothed the tender flesh that had been stung by the prod, rubbing scented oils into his thighs, nipples, and finally his cock, which began to harden once more under Ana's firm yet gentle fingers.

He heard a soft rustling of movement as Ana crawled onto the sprawling California King. Someone roughly, Nyla, he presumed, stood Jeremi up and placed his hands onto Ana's now-naked hips. His hands gripped her hip bones, the flesh soft and hard at once. Oh, how he had longed for this moment! Tentatively, he glided the palm of his hand inward and cupped the firm flesh of Ana's ass, which he would have spanked had he not feared swift and certain punishment from Nyla.

Still, he knew better than to move much more until directed. He satisfied himself by exploring Ana's contours in tiny moments, feeling the sharp of her pelvic bones, the soft down of her outer thighs, the notches of spine that sloped slightly down as Anastasia arched her back more fully, seeming to purr at his light touches.

"You're going to fuck her from behind," Nyla said with a detached, managerial air. "Hold out your right hand."

Jeremi's palm shot outward, practically shivering with delight. As he unwrapped the condom he had been given and put it on, he was glad that he couldn't see how much his hands were shaking.

Nyla finished reattaching his ankle cuffs to the top and bottom bed posts on one side of the bed, before adding, "And I'm going to fuck *you* from behind."

"Whoa, whoa," he said, his first protest of the night, and indeed, his first protest through the entire quest. "I ... I can't. I'm not ... gay."

"Since when does having sex with not one, but two women make a man gay, Jeremi?" Nyla said, without a trace of anger.

"Well, no, okay, but no—I can't..."

"Alright," Nyla said. "That's disappointing." She took a step back and Jeremi felt Ana's hips begin to wriggle out of his grasp. Nyla added: "Anastasia was very much looking forward to this. But, it's your choice. Let's go, love."

"Wait! No. No, no no." Jeremi's voice pitched against the words. It could not end now, like this. "I'm...into it. I'm just ... nervous. Can you be ... gentle?"

"Like the sweet man at the club the other night?" Ana whispered.

Jeremi's face reddened. "You saw that?"

"I orchestrated it, Jeremi. And from what my associate reported back, your response was—what did he say, love?

"I believe the word he used was *besotted*," Nyla said.

Jeremi had nearly forgotten the anonymous stranger who had explored that most vulnerable of places in him. He didn't want to think about what it might *mean* to enjoy such a thing, so he had filed the night away in his DO NOT DISTURB memory bank.

"Yes, like that. Loving, gentle," Jeremi whispered.

"So you did like it." Nyla traced the curve of Jeremi's taut, muscled backside with a single finger, then traced the ridge that separated his cheeks with a hushed deliberation.

"Yes."

"Then ask for it, and do so with some manners this time, for god's sake."

When Jeremi hesitated, Nyla placed the cattle prod's forked tongue into his left asscheek, and held it there, the electricity unceasing, the pain twisting and searing his flesh so much that he emitted a series of high-pitched screams.

"Please! Sir, ma'am, Nyla! Fuck me, please. I want it. I want it so bad!" He was breathless when the blows stopped, panting and bent like a parenthesis.

With a nudge of her high heel, Nyla tapped Jeremi's feet until he widened his stance enough to suit her. She then placed a dollop of lube on her hand and spread it along the length of his sheathed cock. Jeremi placed his hands back on Ana's hips as Nyla guided him inside her, the rush of which was so overwhelming that he barely noticed the pinch of pain when Nyla's cock entered him from behind.

Ana moaned, then Jeremi. He leaned forward, pressing himself into Ana's back and cupping her breasts, squeezing the nipples just slightly before Nyla thrust more fully and deeply into him, causing him to gasp.

Each time he thrust his cock into Ana, he felt the savageness of Nyla behind him. The slippery fire of Ana's cunt melted him, expanded and contracted every nerve in his body, and transformed into its own wild heat. The sensation of filling and being filled at once made him leap like a wild animal. He began thrusting harder and faster, which in turn made Nyla thrust harder and faster, too. Her hands on his hips, the slap of skin beat its animal pace as they rocked back and forth. Neither were artful in their movements, but eventually they found a rhythm.

Jeremi placed one hand on Ana's shoulder and the other on her ass. Sweat sheened on his face, but he did not wipe it away. He wanted every ounce of fluid drenching him. The more he felt possessed by Nyla, the more Jeremi felt he had to possess Ana in response, to retain some ounce of himself and not be merely an extension of Nyla's desire, Nyla's wants.

Ana tightened around him. The bed began to shake as they melded together, clutching and rippling and spilling out. Nyla answered every moan with a deeper thrust. Ana panted, making louder and louder gasps. Jeremi could feel her losing control under him and threaded his fingers through her hair, tugging it as her hips bucked and her body shook in uncontrollable spasms. The undulations were so intense that he slipped out of her. As the orgasm spread through her, Ana collapsed onto the bed and Jeremi collapsed on top of her, which caused Nyla's cock to slip out of Jeremi abruptly, making him wince.

Nyla smiled at the luster, admiring the dick that glistened with a satisfying sheen before her.

Ana got up off the bed and padded softly to the "powder room," as she called it. Jeremi lay where he was, his arms holding the space Anastasia had occupied on the bed. His ankles were still bound to the bed posts, so it was a bit awkward, his belly on the mattress, his neck straining to the side against the twisted sheets.

When he heard footsteps, he propped himself up on his elbows, ready and rearing for round two. He bet he could make Ana come at least two or three more times. Maybe she was even a squirter!

He felt his blindfold coming off, the light of the room nearly blinding him in its brilliance. Jeremi saw that it was Anastasia who had removed it, gently, delicately, as if her slightest touch might hurt him, despite the pounding he had just received from her girlfriend!

As the cloth fell around his neck, Jeremi was shocked to see that Ana was now fully clothed; and Nyla was, too. Ana kissed him first, soft and sweet on the lips, with just the tip of her tongue touching his as he struggled to reach her and understand what was happening. Nyla's kiss that followed was, perhaps unsur-prisingly, more forceful. She took his lower lip into her mouth, biting, but not hard enough to draw blood. His own blood surged at the touch. He reached for her with his right hand, but as he did she backed away. The leg cuffs yielded a few inches, but binding him to his place on the bed. His eyes begged, beckoning them closer. But they stayed just out of reach.

"Thank you, Jeremi, for this unique and formative experiment."

"Thank you? You mean, it's over? But it can't be over!" Jeremi began to struggle harder against the chains, feeling suddenly like a caged animal.

"And yet, It is," Nyla said. "The key to your handcuffs are in this room. I'm afraid we can't tell you exactly where they are, but we have no doubt about your resourcefulness, Jeremi. Or, if you can't find the keys yourself, you can always reach the nightstand and call the front desk, though it'll be interesting to think what explanation you'll come up with as to how you got yourself in this situation."

Jeremi's cries came out pleadingly, pityingly. "Please! Nyla, Anastasia, come on. I ... I didn't even come yet!"

It was the wrong thing to say, he knew it even as the words formed on his lips, and yet he could not stop himself. He had *earned* this. Who did these bitches think they were walking away *now*?

Nyla and Ana looked at each other wryly, and then back at the man laying prone before them on the 1,000 thread count sheets. "Oh, Jeremi. One more thing," Nyla said.

Thank god, he thought. *They aren't leaving*. This was just part of the game. He had played along so well. Surely the next challenge awaited him and he would triumph yet again.

The women began to walk toward the door. Ana looked over her shoulder one last time at his sorrowful brown eyes, wanting to memorialize them in this moment, before she said, "If you tell anyone what happened, no one will believe you."

Jeremi heard the door open, its bottom edge sliding along the carpet as it did so, and then the cold snap of its hinges as it closed and locked back in place. After that, he could hear nothing else, not their shoes down the hallway, nor the whir of the air conditioning, nor the labor of his own shortened breaths going in and out, in and out, in and out.

Hours had passed before Jeremi, ankles rubbed raw from pulling and twisting against his shackles, was ready to call the front desk for help. Even with his hands free, he couldn't find the damn key. He tore the room apart, as much as he could while ankle-cuffed to the bedposts, and for nothing. Now he had to piss badly and his mouth was bone-dry from not having had a drink of water in the last 12 hours. He thought about urinating right where he was, but the small part of him that still retained its dignity refused to let him.

His face contorted in a grim cry and a single tear fell down his cheek as he picked up the phone on the bedside table, ready to humiliate himself once more to whatever cleaning lady would be forced to come unshackle him. It was only after he lifted the receiver that he noticed the shiny silver key. *Damn*, he thought. It had been there all this time! And all he would have had to do was swallow his pride. Admit he needed help. And he hadn't. Instead he had kneeled here for hours, cursing himself and his captors.

As he turned the key in the lock, something broke in him, released itself of years of turmoil and anguish. He had wanted this, he realized, all of it, had wanted to be broken, to bend himself so utterly that his very resistance would buckle and he would feel alive once again, whole, the way he had felt before Rhea had tamped down his heart.

The tears streamed freely down his face now, and as they flowed he took his cock in his hands once more, stroking himself furiously and wildly. He kissed the key with his free hand, remembering Nyla's cock inside of him, the ring of flesh yielding easily and exquisitely to her power.

And as he came in hot spurts against the mattress and floor, he called out their names, whimpering as the last spasms shot through him, "Thank you, thank you…"

HROTICA, PART TWO

The Age of Cumpliance

A fter the sex Julia and Clare had had in her office, Clare's body wouldn't stop vibrating. She kept smoothing her skirt, getting up to pace, then sitting back down. Seeing her coffee from that morning, she took a long sip from it, relishing the cold, creamy sweetness. After taking another deep breath to calm her nervous system, she got to work. She read the Employee Operations Manual cover to cover, and cross-referenced it against local, state, and even federal laws to be as thorough and precise as possible. Lucky for her, Clare loved to nerd out on this precise kind of data. When the last bylaw was checked with the company's core values, she shut her laptop triumphantly, her smile as long as her slender legs, which were still fatigued from the desk sex earlier, and picked up her phone.

When Julia answered on the first ring, Clare swallowed her excitement and spoke instead in an even, calm tone. She wanted to be face to face when she told Julia, so for now, she feigned a neutral, casual voice. "Hey," Clare said breezily. "I have news. Can we meet at yours? … Perfect. Let me get a pen to write down the address … see you at 8." Before hanging up, she couldn't help but add, "Can't wait."

The second Julia hung up the phone, she began to madly tidy up her studio apartment, throwing shoes in the closet, kicking her Hitachi Magic Wand under the bed, and scrambling to clean the remnants of the tofu chorizo scramble off the skillet she'd left on the stove that morning. She didn't know why Clare was coming over exactly—in her excitement, she forgot to ask—but she didn't want to come off as a slob, especially since she hadn't had a woman in her apartment since her ex, Britt, moved out.

Britt had been a bit OCD about cleaning—she claimed she couldn't have sex if the house was dirty or disorderly, that it interfered with the "vibe"—so Julia had kept the place spotless. It was only after Britt left her for a gazelle-like creature who ran an all-women farming commune in Florida that Julia began to slacken, and then outright rebel against cleaning, to spite her ex. *Let the place turn into a pig sty, what do I care!* she choke-laughed, tossing a few cheesy poofs in the air like deranged confetti. *It's still better than fucking in an actual pig sty. Good luck with that, farmer Britt!*

As the months passed and Julia's depression turned to ordinary sadness and then eventually acceptance, she also returned to a satisfactory, non-sad-human level of tidying. But with Clare coming over, Julia suddenly felt panicky. Clare liked order, didn't she? Wasn't that kind of the whole HR shtick? Rules and such? And so, Julia *dashed*. She wiped and sprayed and scrubbed until her apartment resembled a state that would not elicit passive-aggressive comments from her WASPy mother.

Once finished, she had just enough time to run a brush through her hair, reapply mascara and lip gloss, and change out of her fuzzy Christmas pajamas and into jeans and a tight red shirt that showed just enough cleavage to be inappropriate for work. But they weren't at work now, were they? Julia could be as inappropriate as she wanted in her own home, and oh how she hoped Clare wanted to be similarly inappropriate with her.

Five minutes before Clare was due to arrive, Julia practiced seeming casual. She placed her arm on the wall, arcing her body away in a pose she saw regularly on Instagram, and nodded at no one. No, too obvious. She crossed her arms over her stomach and leaned against the door frame blankly. No, too cold! As she attempted a third pose, which involved hooking her thumbs into the belt loops of her jeans, the doorbell rang.

Clare didn't expect to be as nervous as she was when she walked up to Julia's apartment, but her hand shook as she pressed the small white button. When Julia answered immediately, Clare's hand still hung in the air, not having had the chance to return to her side.

"Hi," Julia said, her voice causing Clare's heart rate to quicken to a punk-rock tempo.

She noticed Julia's plunging neckline immediately, the two perfect half-moons rising and falling with her breath, and bit her lip. Had Julia been exercising? Her golden skin seemed to shimmer in the soft light.

"Hi," Clare said.

Julia stepped aside to usher Clare past the doorway, apologizing for "the mess."

"If this is messy then you are never allowed to see my house," Clare joked.

"Thank god," Julia said, audibly relieved. "Drink?" She rummaged through a cupboard. "I have white and white and peach Schnapps? Why?"

"White is perfect," Clare laughed. It felt intimate to be sharing so small a space with Julia and to get such a personal glimpse into her life. Erik had only invited her over a few times, and even then she never slept over, a fact which now struck her as so obvious she could have kicked herself.

As Julia poured them wine, Clare surveyed the studio apartment, taking in the boho-chic aesthetic, admiring the white lacy curtains, macrame plant hangers, the photos of Julia with people she didn't know, and the bookshelf that took up an entire wall. She picked up a librarian action figure, whose hair was in a severe bun. She wore cat-eye glasses, and her finger was poised in a perpetual *shush*.

Julia came back into the room holding two wine glasses as Clare put the action figure back in its place. "I was a library science major in college," Julia said.

"Were you?"

"Yep."

"I can totally see it," Clare said. Because there was nowhere else to sit, she sat down on the bed's bright red duvet cover and, noticing the brown plastic eyeglasses on the nightstand, picked them up and put them on Julia's face. "You would've been the hottest librarian."

Julia sat down next to her on the bed, pushed the glasses down on her nose, and gave Clare a stern wink. "I would have waived all your overdue book fees."

Clare felt a familiar warmth wash over her, heat and light radiating up and down her spine. She hadn't felt this way in, well, she didn't even know how long. Erik, had been, what, eight years ago? And she'd been wracked with guilt almost the entire time. At three months in, Clare discovered that Erik was married. He was not "traveling for work," as he had told her. He was traveling to his real life. The life he did not share with her. Clare was devastated, and spent the next year trying to break it off, only to be wooed back with lofty, empty promises, lavish gifts, and trips. Once she finally, mercifully, freed herself from his clutches, she swore that she would never break the rules again— that she would never be illicit, a secret, something to be hidden and tucked away out of sight.

"You said you had news?" Julia asked, hopeful, excitable, her small, mauve lips poised in anticipation.

"Yes!" Clare said. "I did some research into the company's divisions and hierarchies, and though I'm technically still senior to you, we don't operate in the same reporting structure!"

"That's fantastic!" Julia said, not understanding a word of it, but distracted nonetheless by Clare's eyes, which appeared green today, and the pencil holding her dark hair in place, begging to be freed. "What does that mean? In non-HR-speak please."

"It means," Clare said, taking Julia's wine glass and setting it on the nightstand, and then removing Julia's glasses and placing them next to it, "that we can do this." Clare took Julia's face in her hands and kissed her softly. Julia relished Clare's lips, which tasted like vanilla lip balm, and welcomed the cold pads of Clare's fingers touching her neck, melting her into a heap of sighs.

Their mouths met again, harder this time, faster, and Julia removed the pencil from Clare's hair, watching the strands shake loose and fall to her slender shoulders. Trailing her fingers down Clare's arms, Julia noticed the fine dark hairs that came to attention under her teasing caress.

She guided Clare's arms up and over her head, then removed her blouse, admiring the lacy, teal bra she wore by outlining the straps with her fingers. Julia then kissed the supple mounds that peaked out from the bra, running her tongue down each slope and valley, before unclasping the bra, and letting it drop to the floor.

As Julia gently pushed Clare down onto the bed, nudging Clare's knees open with her own, the foot that was still touching the floor kicked something hard and a loud buzzing ensued.

"Is that—?" Clare said.

"Fuck." Julia reached down to silence the Hitachi that she had accidentally switched on, and was about to shove it under the bed once more when Clare stopped her.

"Wait." She took the wand from Julia and placed it between her thighs, then beckoned Julia on top of her. Julia straddled her hips, feeling the gentle pressure of the vibrator between them. With one hand, Clare positioned the wand against their clits and turned it to the lowest setting, while the other hand massaged and pinched Julia's nipple through her tight shirt and sports bra. It hardened immediately and the ache of the vibration below sent her soaking right through her underwear and jeans.

She leaned forward to kiss Clare full and hard once more, her hair falling around them, and shaking her head in disbelief. She couldn't believe this was really happening. Just a few days ago, Clare had told her no, deemed it impossible, and now here Clare was in her bed, legs butterflied open, eyes blanketing Julia's face with tenderness and heat.

Julia kissed along Clare's neck and jaw, down and down, until she reached Clare's breast, the pink murmur of her areola, and circled it with her tongue. Clare increased the speed of the vibrator, which sent a thousand surrenders coursing through Julia's entire body. Julia gently ran her teeth along Clare's nipple and, hearing her moan in response, increased the pressure there. They moved their hips in unison, each matching the other's fervent rhythms until they were galloping wildly, legs straining, sweat pooling at the base of Julia's spine. She wanted suddenly to remove all the barriers between them—how had she not even undressed?—but her desire for Clare could not be stopped. She leaned back, placing her hands on Clare's thighs as they rocked together, the vibration between them pitching to a fever, until they both came, and Julia collapsed on top of Clare, riding the last few waves of orgasm as they shocked through her.

Several moments later, as Julia lay on Clare's chest, her mouth resting against Clare's collarbone, she whispered, "I'd love to take you on a date this Friday."

Clare squeezed Julia tighter. "Friday, like tomorrow?"

"Yes."

"I'd love to."

The next morning, Clare was still buzzing from the unexpected and beautiful night she'd shared with Julia when she walked into the office. She wore an all white pantsuit with a red power tie to celebrate the momentous occasion.

Her smile faded when she opened the door to her office and found Nikki sitting in her chair, a severe, almost cartoonish smirk on her face. Clare and Nikki had briefly been lovers. In fact, Clare had gotten Nikki a job at the company. Once Clare realized how incompatible they were, she broke things off, which is when Nikki's true "job" started—making Clare's work life hell.

"You should really clean your desk once in a while," Nikki said. "Or are you secretly auditioning for a spot on *Hoarders*?"

Clare swallowed hard and set her purse down on the desk. When Nikki didn't get up from Clare's chair, Clare glanced at her aspirational calendar, which read, *The best revenge? No revenge. Move on, babe.*

"Good morning, Nikki," she said. "To what do I owe this unexpected pleasure?"

"Yolanda called a last-minute meeting with HR, finance, and several of the C-suiters. I was told to summon you."

"And you chose not to use your cauldron this time? Classy." The best revenge was passive-aggressive comments, she decided. Nikki glared at Clare before rising and tossing one of Clare's pens on the desk.

"10 minutes. Conference room C. Don't be late."

"What's this about anyway?"

"Your guess is as good as mine, sunshine."

Julia barely had time to place the lid on her oat-milk latte before Paula had grabbed her by the elbow and steered her away from her desk toward a conference room.

"You're needed," Paula said, walking them briskly down the grey hall before Julia had time to protest or question her.

"Aw, I need you too, bae, but I also really need to pee, so gimme two minutes—"

"Not by me. You're needed in conference room C. I'm just the messenger."

"Oh! This isn't about Callie not texting you back?"

"No, but yes—later! I do need you to read this text message draft and tell me if it sounds too co-do. But first—" Paula opened the door to the conference room and ushered Julia inside, where she was greeted by a sea of C's—the COO, CFO, CHRO, and others she couldn't place, having worked there only a short time.

Panic gripped her. This was it. She was going to be fired. For the harassment claim? For the desk sex? They'd been so careful, she'd sworn they hadn't been caught, but had they missed something? She gripped her latte hard, trying to calm the storm swirling around her stomach.

A few seconds later, Clare walked in, and Julia felt as if she might throw up. They'd both be fired! And this was all her fault! Clare had been right. Why had she been so foolish? Why did she let her stampeding desire for Clare get in the way of her common sense? Julia looked at Clare for reassurance, but Clare merely glanced at her, then took a seat at the far end of the table.

When everyone was seated, the COO, a bald man in a grey suit and cornflower blue tie smiled cordially. "Thank you all for joining us, Rob and Bastien, in particular, thank you for coming in from the corporate office."

Corporate? Did that mean lawyers? Was she going to jail on top of losing her job? Julia blew on the too-hot latte, casting her eyes into its milky swirl, as if it could tell her the future.

The COO continued, "This is a very exciting day for us, and we hope for all of you."

Julia raised her head back up tentatively, fidgeting with the cardboard insulator on her coffee cup.

"We are excited to announce a new initiative at the company promoting visibility of female leadership in the field, and we want all of you involved."

Julia and Clare shared an uncertain glance at each other. "Now," the COO said, "Before you ask the obvious question, yes, this project does mean longer hours on top of your normal workload. We want you to present your plan for the new initiative to the board at the annual meeting in Los Angeles."

Here Nikki interjected, "But that's only one month away!"

"We know it's fast, and that's why we've assembled the team you see in this room. You're going to work together to pull off the impossible. And the position doesn't come without benefits. Nikki, if you accept, we're making you Senior VP of People."

"What?" Clare cried out. "That's my title."

Nikki cast a smug smile in Clare's direction and Julia had a sudden urge to toss her hot coffee across the table at Nikki.

"Ah yes, thank you for bringing that up, Clare," the CHRO was speaking now, an elderly bespectacled man with two wild tufts of white hair seeming to spring straight from his ears. "I'm retiring at the end of the month, and I'd like you to succeed me."

"You're making me Chief HR Officer?"

"If you'll have it," he said. "The department is yours. You've earned it."

"Oh my god, sir, I'm so honored. Of course I accept."

"Excellent." He reached across the table to shake Clare's hand as Nikki tried and failed to suppress a pout. "As for the rest of you, Yolanda, Julia, Ben, Terese, you'll each be receiving new titles as well, along with salary increases."

Excitement coursed through Julia—a promotion! And here she thought she was about to be fired. But as the spark wiggled its way around Julia's stomach, another fear stormed in.

"Does this alter the reporting structure?" Julia asked, a slight tremor in her voice.

"Yes," the COO said. "You'll all be reporting to Clare now, who I'm sure you'll agree, is the exact person you want to be under."

"Yes, I, well—" Julia stammered, as the weight of the news sunk in. Clare was her boss, effective today. She'd have to cancel the reservations she'd made for dinner tonight. There could be no date. No Clare. Not now. A pebble lodged itself in her throat, refusing to budge. But she refused to let herself cry, certainly not here, in front of all the higher ups, and definitely not in front of

Nikki, whom she didn't know but already disliked intensely.

"Now, I know you have a lot of questions," the COO said, "so I'm turning this over to Rob and Bastien, who'll be walking you through the roles and budget of the initiative."

Julia sat quietly through the rest of the meeting, wanting desperately to speak to Clare, but Clare wouldn't so much as look at her. Out of the corner of her eye, Julia could see that Clare's leg was shaking. Up and down, up and down the leg went, an ocean roiling and toiling beneath the surface of her skin while above, Clare's face showed nothing but placid, unflappable calm.

"Get out."

"I came to congratulate you," Nikki said, sitting once again in Clare's chair, after the meeting had ended. "And to scope out my new office. What do you think about a taupe rug right here?"

Clare grabbed Nikki a little too hard by the upper arm and escorted her to the door. Right before Clare shut it, she whispered in Nikki's ear. "Great idea. It's basic. Like you." And slammed the door. The best revenge was revenge, after all, it turned out.

Sitting back down at her desk, she lay her face in her hands, feeling her face about to crumble like a cake taken out of the oven too soon. Happiness and devastation eddied about inside of her like a revolting soup. She was Chief HR Officer. A C-suite position! The job she had been coveting ever since she started here two years ago, and which she thought was still years beyond her grasp, now set directly in her lap. And she couldn't even celebrate, couldn't kiss the one person she wanted to in the world, Julia.

She couldn't bring herself to look at Julia during the meeting, for fear that she would never be able to stop, that she would dissolve into a puddle of whipped cream and sadness right there on the office floor. And how on earth were they supposed to work together now with all the *possibility* that lay between them? She imagined the long, late hours side by side, Julia's sleeves rolled to her elbows, sharing furtive glances as the tips of their fingers met over a stack of Excel charts. Thinking about even the small meeting of their fingers across a table sent a wave of desire through Clare, who fanned herself with a spreadsheet like a corseted southern belle in need of smelling salts.

Maybe this could still work! she told herself, desperation dotting her cheeks with red. Maybe if they only—no, that wouldn't help. Or what about—no, she had just checked that yesterday. She rapped her fingers against the desk, thinking, *thinking*.

But it was hopeless. She'd heard what the COO had said. Julia would report directly to Clare. There was no loophole, no workaround. She could either choose her dream job—or the girl of her dreams. There was no in-between, no third choice, no obscure bylaw that would save them. Defeated, she reached for the bottle of Cognac hidden in her desk drawer and took a long swig. The fire it sent down her throat soothed, if only for a moment, the fire that Julia had ignited in Clare's heart.

A soft knock.

It was well after work hours and Clare was still in her office. Julia had waited as long as she could for Clare to emerge, but at this rate, she'd be waiting all night. And so, she knocked. A mouse knock. A whisper-mouse knock. When Clare didn't answer, Julia opened the door, walked in, and shut it quickly behind her.

"Hi," Julia said, sitting down across from Clare, whose head lay in her arms on her desk.

"Hi," Clare said, not lifting her head. Julia noticed the almost empty bottle of amber liquid by her head and took a swig straight from the bottle. The burn felt harsh and good. "You can't be in here."

"I know."

Clare raised her head off the desk, her red tie dangling like a beautiful noose. "You're killing me in that tie, you know," Julia said. "All day I've wanted to take it in my fist and use it to pull you into a kiss."

Clare smiled sadly. "I wore it for you."

Julia took another swig of Cognac and wiped her mouth. She felt a little like a sheriff in a western, except it was herself who was about to be carted off to jail. Emotional jail! The valves in her heart opened and shut like saloon doors.

"I'm happy for you, you know," Julia said.

"I'm happy for you, too. Associate VP of Operations. That's big. You should be proud."

Clare clasped her hands in front of her on the table and Julia longed more than anything to hold them. "I made a reservation at Salt tonight. For us. But I suppose now we shouldn't go. Right?"

"No," Clare said. "We shouldn't."

Julia didn't realize until she said it outloud that she was hoping Clare would argue with her, that Clare would fight the stupid rules that aimed to keep them apart, that Clare would fight for *her*.

"Don't look at me like that," Clare begged, tears welling in her eyes. "This is killing me, don't you know that? Don't you know that I can't stop thinking about you? That I'm half-drunk and moments away from offering my resignation if it means I have one more chance to kiss you?"

Julia clasped Clare's hands across the table, wiping at a tear that rolled down Clare's cheek. "You can't do that. I won't let you, okay? Don't even think it."

Clare kissed the tips of Julia's fingers as two tears rolled down her own cheeks. "What if," Julia offered, sadness unfurling in her throat, "we dated in secret? No one would have to know."

"No, I can't do that again—I won't." Julia paused at the word *again* but was too distraught to ask Clare about it. Clare wiped her eyes and straightened her shoulders, regaining herself. "It's going to be okay. I mean, it's going to be terrible, but we can do it. Because we have to. Now I want you to leave this office and take yourself to dinner. Charge it to the expense account."

Julia smiled. She had admired Clare's take-charge attitude before, but she loved it especially so now, in her time of distress. "Is that an official request?" Julia asked, smiling through her tears.

"It's an order."

A week went by without incident. Clare and Julia worked together with their new team, brainstorming and building a plan that they could bring to the board. Because time was not on their side—they had just three weeks left before they were due to present the initiative—this worked in Julia and Clare's favor, as they barely had a moment to blink or breathe, let alone fantasize about the relationship that could have been, or about anything else. The distraction was especially welcome to Clare, who often threw herself into her work whenever she found her emotional life too taxing. Had she not done this very thing when Erik chose his wife over her? And had she not worked her ass off then? And was she not now the new Chief HR Officer? She was! Her avoidance had paid off then, so why couldn't it work again? Thankfully, she found the demands of her new role especially

challenging. She wasn't used to being responsible for so many people, and welcomed the relief of having something to fixate on other than Julia.

Late on Friday evening, after the team had worked through two rounds of drafts and several helpings of takeout Thai food, Clare and Julia found themselves alone for the first time that week. Even the meandering, disruptive Nikki had gone home, but not first before complaining that Clare was setting an unhealthy work-life example for the team.

Sifting through the remnants of a plastic container of pad see ew, Clare plopped herself down on the modular grey couch, exhausted. Julia joined her, grabbing her pad Thai and sitting as far away from Clare on the couch as she could.

"I'm so tired," Julia said. "I don't think I've been this tired since I worked 80 hour days in the Peace Corps."

"You were in the Peace Corps?"

"In Romania, yep. Education."

"A librarian, an educator, and now this."

"I was also briefly a wedding planner."

"Stop."

"What?" Julia smirked. "I take direction well."

"How many lives have you lived?"

Julia stretched her sore neck, cracking it to the right and left. "Too many," she said. "I stayed on for two extra years after my volunteer stint with the Peace Corps was up, supporting the NGO that worked with the Roma and Turkish minority groups I was teaching. And then, they fired me."

"What? Why?"

"Because I wouldn't have sex with my boss," Julia said, almost nonchalantly. Clare felt indignant on Julia's behalf, and con-flicted by her own desire for Julia. Wasn't she Julia's boss now? Wasn't she no better than these men? "I would babysit his kids sometimes. We had a cordial relationship. No one was more shocked than me when he threw a hissy fit after I turned him down."

"I'm so sorry."

"It's okay. It was a long time ago," Julia said, staring ahead at some unfixed place on the back wall.

"Still. It's bullshit. And even more so that it happened to you here, too."

"And you put a stop to it," Julia said, smiling. "My knight in shining ... suspenders." Clare tried not to laugh too hard at the thought of being anyone's knight in shining anything.

Julia continued, "I know that I can come off as kind of a bimbo—"

"Not at all—"

"No, I do. I accept it. But I thought if I worked hard enough I could convince people to take me seriously, which is all I've ever wanted."

Clare closed the distance between them, taking one of Julia's hands. "I take you seriously."

Their eyes met and Clare felt herself move to Julia like a magnet once more. She leaned forward, drawn by some perverse other gravity, some alternate force that led her ever back to the soft O of Julia's mouth. As Julia leaned toward Clare in kind, their movements as slow as tectonic plates shifting, Clare awakened from her trance and stiffened, dropping Julia's hand and sitting bolt upright on the couch once more. Not knowing what to do with her hands, Clare absentmindedly began to trace the scar next to her lower lip.

"How'd you get that?" Julia asked.

"Pardon?"

"That scar. The one shaped like an unlucky backward 7."

"Oh, it's stupid really."

"Tell me. I have lots of stupid stories."

Clare thought about lying, about telling the usual story she told people whom she didn't want to know—that she had fought an IKEA lamp during assembly, and lost—but faced with the quiet fact of Julia, Clare realized she couldn't keep anything from her, and didn't want to. Clare wanted Julia to know her, for better or worse. "Ever hear the expression, 'Don't let the door hit you on the way out'?"

"Of course."

Clare went quiet for a moment, gathering up her nerves before telling Julia about the ill-fated day she discovered Erik was married. It was the one of the view times he'd invited her to his house. She remembered it was raining, the thunder so loud it seemed the floor was splitting each time the storm cracked its whip at the night sky.

The thunder was also the reason they hadn't heard her open the door. It was only as his wife called to him from the stairs that Erik heard and panicked, urging Clare out of the second-story window, amid her alarmed protests, where she then had to shimmy down a drain pipe in her socks in that pissing rain. When she had made it across the backyard without managing to be detected, the gate wouldn't open. She pulled and pulled, silently cursing, the rain barreling down upon her, and still the gate wouldn't budge. It was only after she placed one of her feet against the wall and used the full force of her body that the gate opened, sending its ruddy wood surface right at her face, and giving her a scar she would bear for the rest of her life.

Julia clenched her face. "The worst part is, I kept seeing him after that." Clare shook her head in disgust. "Can you believe it?"

"I can," Julia said, sweeping her hand up and laying it flat on Clare's chest. "The heart is an asshole."

Clare gripped Julia's hand on her heart. "This is why we can't. I don't want to do that to you. I don't want you to know what that feels like, to be someone's secret, to lie to people you care about. It's awful."

Tears welled in Julia's eyes. "Could it really be worse than this, having you inches away from me when I can't kiss you? To work alongside you almost every day, pretending that the mere sight of you doesn't unravel me? Is it really more awful than that?"

Clare kissed her then, pushing Julia down onto the couch and reaching, unthinkingly, for Julia's shirt, to pull it over her head. Julia moaned in response, taking Clare's lower lip in hers, but also placing her hands over Clare's, to stop Clare from removing her shirt.

"We can't. You just said—" Julia said.

"Forget what I just said. I want you. I need you—"

"You need to keep your shiny new job and I need to keep mine, so you will stay right where you are," she said, with a confidence that startled Clare, until she added, "If that's okay."

Clare stiffened, feeling scolded, even though she knew Julia was right. She smoothed her hair, attempting to compose herself in the torment of this all-consuming desire. The strap of Julia's red bra fell from her shoulder and Clare longed desperately to return it to its place.

Clare leaned toward her, to fix the bra strap, but Julia stopped her. "No, we can't touch each other."

"We can't?"

"No," Julia hesitated, "but..." she paused for a moment, the weight of every word she might say bearing down on Clare's chest. "I can touch me. And you can touch you. And that's not breaking any rules."

"Okay," Clare said, breathless, her skin aflame with the desire to touch Julia anywhere and everywhere. "Okay."

"I can feel you," Julia said, eyes boring into Clare's like two bonfires threatening to escape their pits.

"Where do you feel me?"

Julia dipped a hand into her bra on the side where the strap had fallen and massaged slow circles around her nipple. "Here," she said. "And here." With the other hand, she undid the button of her pants, then the zipper, and reached between her thighs. "Do you feel how wet I am? Do you feel me touching you?"

Clare pulled the suspenders off her shoulders and reached into her pants. She placed a single finger at the seam, shocked to feel it glistening with moisture already. She began touching herself slowly, a little hesitant, tracing the outer lips that were filled with blood and tender. Clare realized that she hadn't been this open, this vulnerable, with someone in such a long time. "Yes," she whispered, "yes, I feel you. I feel your hand on me, here. I feel my heat rising to meet your palm. Your long fingers tracing the edges of me—"

"Yes, please," Julia said, her back arching into the couch as her hips pressed forward, the hand inside her pants picking up speed, the movements intensifying. "Do you want more? Do you want me inside of you?"

"Yes!" Clare groaned.

"Do it."

Clare plunged her fingers deep inside of herself, her palm pressed firmly against her clit as she drove in, holding pressure there for a moment until she dipped in again. "Oh god."

Julia increased the speed of the circles she made on her clit, gripping and pulling at her nipple with her free hand. Julia threw her head back, a fury overtaking her when Clare said, "I want to taste you. Let me taste you," and Julia removed her hand from her pants, slipping two glistening fingers inside her own mouth, cheeks hollowing as she sucked every last trace of moisture from them.

Clare bit her lip so hard watching Julia's fingers exit her mouth that she thought she might break the skin, but instead she erupted below, the spasms of her orgasm sending her careening back toward the arm of the couch. As the last tremors hollowed and rocked her, she opened her eyes just in time to see Julia coming herself, her face mashed against the cushion, mouth open, hands a flurry of motion as her hips buckled and roared and quaked.

After the delirium had worked its way through her body, Clare half-lay on the couch, hair matted with sweat. She inhaled the dander and chemical clean of fake leather from the modular couch, as her breath slowed to normal. "You're really something," Clare said, looking up at Julia, but unable yet to make her limbs obey her.

Julia smiled, face still pressed against the couch cushion. "I told you I take direction well."

The heat in Los Angeles was sweltering, but Julia barely felt it inside the air-conditioned hotel that was hosting the conference. She and Clare were slated to present their initiative on visibility of female leadership to the board in 20 minutes.

Ever the early bird, Julia was already outside the room, pacing. She couldn't eat or drink anything, her stomach a tilt-o-whirl, so she instead fixed her attention on the hotel's curious carpet, whose geometric pattern and green-yellow-orange colors were clearly a holdover from groovier times.

Clare wasn't here yet, which comforted Julia. They hadn't had any more "slips," as Clare quaintly referred to them, since that night on the couch, but Julia had begun to feel strange when Clare was around. She recognized this bubbling and tipping and flurrying sensation as the beginnings of love, but Julia hadn't expected them to come so quickly or so aggressively.

Besides, she had no idea how Clare really felt about her. They spent so much time trying *not* to feel, it seemed, that things had muddied in Julia's mind. Perhaps Julia was making things bigger than they actually were. In the real estate of Julia's heart, Clare had gone and built an amusement park. She admitted to herself that she had a grandiose imagination. Perhaps Clare merely viewed Julia as an enticement, a new shiny, and that was all. Plus, so much was riding on this initiative, perhaps Clare hadn't even had time to consider Julia as anything other than a colleague. A colleague she had intense sexual chemistry with, yes, but a colleague nonetheless.

"Nice blazer, Julia, " Ben said, chucking her shoulder as he walked by. "Break a leg in there."

"Thank you."

She at least looked the part of a woman who was put together, taking a cue from Clare and tapping into her inner-dandy, a side she hadn't paid heed to since her college days as an amateur drag king. Her stage name had been Mister Fister, and nothing delighted him more than performing showtunes and jazzy covers of "Baby Got Back" to a small but enthusiastic crowd of women's studies minors, Students Against Sweatshops activists, and a scrum of intramural rugby players.

Today she wasn't quite so over the top in her attire, choosing grey tweed pants and a matching vest, her hair styled in a high, severe ponytail that she hoped made her appear older than she was. A red pocket square provided the only pop of color on her person. That is, until Clare walked up, sending a splash of crimson to each pale cheek.

"You look sharp," Clare said. "Ready to K some A?"

"Yes. I mean, I think—I hope," Julia demurred.

"You're nervous," Clare said, smiling. "Want to do it again?"

Julia's heart pounded and her vision blurred. "What?"

"Do you want to practice your part of the presentation again?"

"Oh," Julia stifled a smile. Of course Clare had not been suggesting *that*. "Yeah, actually, that'll help me calm down some, I think. Let's walk while we do it so I can burn off some of this nervous energy."

"Okay." They set off down the hall, making a wide circle around the hotel's perimeter. "First," Clare said, "I'll do my part of the presentation, and then I'll introduce you. You'll start on slide 14."

"Right," Julia said. She rehearsed once again the lines she'd practiced with Clare over and over again the last week as they slowly walked passed the coffee stand, row after row of monotonous conference rooms, and the sleepy, unopened restaurant. After they'd made four rotations, Julia's breath began to soften and her confidence rose. She had this presentation down, she was certain.

And just when she was about to suggest to Clare that they head back, Julia overheard someone say her name. She glanced to her left, about 15 feet away, where Nikki sat, her back to Julia, on a plump orange chair, talking to someone Julia didn't recognize.

Julia placed a hand on Clare's shoulder to slow her and steered them toward where Nikki sat. She didn't know why exactly, curiosity perhaps, or masochism, or a preternatural ability to discern when others were talking about her behind her back.

"I couldn't tell you," Nikki was saying. "Maybe they chose her because she looks good on a company brochure. Whatever, she's a ditz."

Julia's stomach sank. Was her fear really coming true again? Did people not respect her because of her looks *again*? Julia's fists clenched at their sides. She hated the idea that Nikki was talking about her, especially since she had been studiously avoiding Nikki at work—her negativity cast a sour stench upon everything she touched. Plus, the way Nikki treated Clare was only a shade above appalling. Maybe that was it, Julia thought. She had snubbed Nikki by ignoring her at work and this was Nikki's way of getting back at her. Before she had time to follow this trail of thought further, however, they were close enough that Nikki's companion saw them and gave Nikki a little kick under the table. "We should be getting back, yeah?" he said too loudly.

Nikki glanced behind her to see Julia and Clare a few feet away and stammered, "Ye-yeah we should. Let's go."

When they were out of earshot, Clare squeezed Julia's hand and let it go. "She's jealous. Don't let her get to you. That's exactly what she wants."

Julia's eyes found the carpet once again, losing herself in the maze of its bright colors and shapes as her mind burned. She wished suddenly that she had a cigarette. Not because she smoked, but because she wanted *something* in this moment that she could stomp on the ground.

Clare watched Julia's mouth twist. She couldn't tell if Julia was about to laugh or burst into tears. Not knowing what to do, Clare reached for her, but Julia's arm jutted out to stop her.

"If you hug me, I'll fall apart, and I can't fall apart," she said, her eyes shining wetly. "Not here. Not now."

"Okay," Clare said. She rubbed the back of her own neck, feeling helpless. She wanted more than anything to comfort Julia, to say something that might take the sting out of Nikki's ignorant words, and to reassure Julia that they were utterly false, but when she opened her mouth to try, nothing came out.

She felt useless and strange, struck dumb once again by Julia's brightness. How do you begin to comfort someone so radiant? Someone so smart and funny and tender and loving? Clare couldn't begin to tell Julia how much she meant to her, how even knowing Julia for a few short weeks had changed her. Faced with the surging and inappropriate need to confess these things, Clare stopped herself. "We should get back," she said. "It's time."

—

Clare's stomach was in knots when she walked up to the podium to present her piece of the initiative. Looking out at the sea of faces, some stern, some familiar, some shifted in their seats as the silence between them grew. At the end of the first row of beige chairs, Clare saw Julia sitting on her hands, legs crossed, her top knee bouncing restlessly. When Clare's eyes fell upon Julia, the bouncing paused, and even though it was obvious to Clare that Julia was distressed, she still gave Clare an unsubtle wink. Clare glanced at her index cards, and then set them aside on the podium. She knew what she wanted to say.

"Thank you, Gerry, for that lovely introduction, and thanks to all of you for attending," Clare started, her voice rising and falling before settling into her usual calm, melodious tone. "Before I get started, I'd like to thank all my colleagues who contributed to this presentation, and whose hard work, long hours, and dedication made all of this possible."

She paused, her hands shaking. She was glad the podium hid them from view. And she was even more surprised that her voice did not falter as she continued, "I'd like to give special thanks to one colleague in particular, Julia Dawes, who embodies the commitment, keen insight, and fierce determination that we are striving to model in this initiative on female leadership." Clare scanned the crowd as she spoke, but her eyes lingered on Julia's, a sureness in her voice tamping down every fear and doubt that loomed inside of her as she said, "I can't imagine having a more dedicated person on my team, or a better partner, than her. You'll hear from her next. But first, I'm going to talk a little bit about compliance."

Picking up the index cards in front of her, a lightness overtook Clare. She smoothed down her shirt and noticed that her hands had stopped shaking. She marveled at this, that something so simple—so cliche—could have this effect on her. She shook her head, a half smile tilting upward. The truth, it *did* set you free. What she didn't know was what the hell she planned to do about it, now that she knew she was falling for Julia, that she wanted to be her partner. She steeled herself as uncertainty wound its way through her.

"Next slide please."

The rest of the day blurred for Julia. As soon as Clare had said her name, had said those lovely, inspiring words about her in front of the board and all her colleagues, Julia felt as if she had gone into a low-grade black out. Still reeling from Nikki's words, but bolstered now by an audacity to prove Nikki wrong, and by a surging affection for Clare, time passed for Julia in fits and starts.

Here was another person shaking her hand, congratulating her on her presentation, and thrusting a business card in her direction. And here was Ben, telling Julia that she had killed it, and that they were all meeting in the hotel bar for drinks. And here was the board chair, regaling her with his own memories of his time in the Peace Corps. She must have mentioned her history to him, but she had no recollection of it. Still, he was smiling, and enthusiastic in the board's unanimous approval of the initiative. And here was Yolanda, telling Julia that she and Clare made a terrific team, and that they could look forward to working closely together over the next year to put the initiative in action.

She smiled through all of this, at the rotating cast of faces offering their hands, their praise, their stories, all the while searching for Clare in the crowd. Where had she gone? Julia had lost her in the aftermath of bodies and grins and handshakes, and each time she set about trying to look for her, another person swarmed in.

"Come on, Julia," someone tugged at her elbow. "First drink's on me!"

"I'll meet you there," she smiled, pulling away. "I just need to—" she jerked her thumb in the air behind her, and took off down the hall in search of Clare, leaving the rest of her sentence to dangle in the air unfinished.

She wasn't at the cafe, or the coffee cart, or by the hotel pool. She wasn't outside with the smokers or sitting in the lounge area. From a distance, Julia even peeked into the bar, where everyone had gathered, drinks sweating in their glasses, but Clare wasn't there either.

Riding the elevator up to her room, Julia wondered if perhaps Clare didn't want to be found. Maybe she regretted what she had said about Julia earlier. Or maybe it was spoken in haste in order to make Julia feel better and now she was embarrassed. But as

Julia unlocked the door to her room and stepped inside, she found Clare sitting on the edge of the bed, chin in hand.

When Julia walked in, Clare rose and stood before her. "The porter let me in," she spoke quickly, as if not used to such simple transgressions. "I told him I lost my key."

Julia smiled, and closed the distance between them. "There's a rule-breaker in you yet."

Clare blushed and looked down, away from Julia. Julia reached for her, placing her palm on the back of Clare's neck, drawing her closer, as she said, "Did you mean it? What you said?"

"Every word."

At this simple, monumental admission, Julia gently pushed Clare back onto the bed, straddling her hips and kissing her as she sat on Clare's lap. Clare closed her eyes and Julia noticed her eyelashes for the first time, which were long and black, with tips that lightened at the end. She kissed each eyelid, inhaling the salt of Clare's skin. Clare's hands gripped Julia's waist tighter as she performed this ritual, reverence mixing with desire and tenderness. The room's A/C whirred awake, which sent an army of goosebumps to Julia's skin. She trembled when Clare's hands ran the lengths of her arms, warming and igniting her, amazed that they could read each other so well without saying a word.

Mind spinning, Julia pushed Clare back onto the bed so she was laying on top of her, and slipped her tongue into Clare's mouth, relishing the taste that was at once foreign and familiar to her. How strange to feel so strong and weak in Clare's hands, the pleasure of it so intense it bordered on pain, each sensation kaleidoscopic, as if a hundred hands extended from her body and a hundred hands reached back toward her own.

Not wanting to repeat her mistake from their previous night together, Julia paused in her ardor, removing all of her clothes as swiftly as she could, and kicking the last tangle of pants onto the floor before climbing back on top of Clare.

Clare's head thrust back into the white bedspread when Julia placed her mouth upon the hollow of her throat. When Clare moaned, she pressed a little harder, teeth dragging a jagged line across the pure, unmarred canvas of Clare's skin. Julia had the sudden urge to mark Clare, to possess her, even if it would fade in a few days, but held back, as she didn't know if such a gesture would be well received.

Julia worked her way down, unbuttoning the crisp white shirt Clare wore and lavishing her breasts with attention and softness. Clare gripped the back of Julia's head, pressing her closer, and then surprised her by urging Julia's body upward, pulling her until Julia's thighs straddled Clare's face, her cunt poised directly above Clare's eager mouth.

The suddenness and intimacy of this position unhinged Julia. A surge of wetness coursed through her. Her cunt brushed against the tip of Clare's nose, but Clare did not greet it with her tongue. Instead, she slowly drew her tongue along the ridge between thigh and lip, nibbling softly at the flesh all around it. Clare's mouth was so firm and so soft that Julia felt every insecurity and doubt melting away, leaving a tremulous trail of desire and longing in its wake.

Clare's hands massaged Julia's thighs, which were tense from holding herself up, and relaxed when she leaned back a little, letting her ass rest on Clare's chest. Clare's hands continued to explore Julia's body, tentatively, and then more assuredly cupping Julia's cheeks with both hands as she pressed her tongue to the most sensitive part of Julia. Julia groaned as Clare's tongue teased and tasted her, and she moved her hips slowly back and forth in rhythm with Clare's movements. When Clare glided her hands upward, along Julia's back and then around to her breasts, Julia clenched her thighs around Clare's face, pleading for more.

Pinching and rolling Julia's nipples in her fingers, Clare's tongue began to move faster, and Julia didn't know how much more of this she could bear before losing herself entirely. She felt the sensations everywhere, each pinch of her nipples sending trails of fire from the base of her skull down through her toes. Her skin prickled with cold from the A/C, mingling from the sweat on her torso and lower back as she pitched herself harder against Clare's mouth. And then, it seemed, Clare also couldn't stand to wait much longer, as her right hand left Julia's nipple and reached between her own thighs, where they began to rub furiously. Now Clare's hips rocked with the same ferocity as Julia's and together they rode the wave of each other's pleasure, a fury and agony overtaking them, until Julia felt that she might shatter into a million pieces. Right before she felt her body disassembling, she called out Clare's name, her voice almost unrecognizable to herself, her voice a wild bird caught in the throat, her thighs singing, trilling to a song her mind had forgotten but which her body knew by heart.

After the strength in her limbs had returned, after Clare had clung to Julia like a salve for hours and hours in the large, unfamiliar hotel bed, their legs twisted in the sheets, Clare broke away from their embrace, stretching her body in a full, cat-like arc. She had no idea what time it was, the light from outside having long since extinguished. Kissing a sleeping Julia on the forehead, she dressed quickly, and, even though it was dark, she knew her clothes were hopelessly wrinkled, her hair disheveled, and her neck throbbed in the place where Julia had raked her teeth against it. Clare both wanted and did not want a bruise to appear there, but she wouldn't know for sure until she surveyed the damage under the unforgiving light of the hotel bathroom.

Thoughts short-circuited and whirled around in her mind as she lay there. She thought about how long it had been since she'd felt this connected to someone, how Julia had awakened a desire in her, and a trust, that Clare thought she had long since locked in a bottle and thrown into the sea. And how cruel it was that, in spite of how rare and wonderful it was, Julia was the one person she was not *allowed* to want.

Clare glanced over at her, watching her breath rise and fall under the sheets, and sighed contentedly. Clare could no longer pretend that what she and Julia were doing was an accident or a mistake. The rules and protocols that ordinarily brought her a sense of peace and order in a chaotic world failed completely when it came to Julia. This was personal. Deeply personal. Clare couldn't deny it much longer. Wouldn't deny it.

And yet, they had broken so many rules already. How could they possibly keep this up? Surely they would get caught. And if they did, what then? Would Clare be able to lie about her feelings for Julia when she felt so strongly? Could their reputations recover from a scandal like this? Would these lapses in judgment doom the careers they had worked so hard to build?

Fear and uncertainty began to wind up the base of Clare's spine as she considered the uncertainty of the future. Then, in spite of everything, there was Julia's scent, which lingered on Clare's breath, her face, lips, and fingers. She placed a hand up against her nose and mouth, breathing in the delicious salt and musk and jasmine of Julia, letting it fill her lungs. The smell of Julia was a balm that eased Clare's troubled, stricken mind. It coated her breath and skin, winding its way down through her nerves and synapses. For now, she let it be enough.

THANKS FOR READING!

Like this collection? Head to annapulley.com/transgressions to receive three bonus stories—one is the start of an erotic re-imagining of Beauty and the Beast, where Beauty is a pick-up artist, and Beast is a dominatrix. The other two stories are erotic fan fiction, starring Sherlock Holmes and characters from a certain very popular wizard series.

They are playful, humorous, fun, and involve nefarious pop culture references, man-on-man action, a witch orgy, and other good stuff.

Want more?

Website: annapulley.com
Newsletter: annapulley.substack.com
Instagram: @lezbianna
Twitter: @annapulley

ACKNOWLEDGEMENTS

A heartfelt and lusty thank you to Vika, who read, inspired, brainstormed, and edited many of these stories.

Thanks so much to my beta readers: Elizabeth, Toni, Danny, Jonathan, Michelle, and Barbara. Your feedback was immensely helpful.

Thanks to Kelly, as usual, for your sharp and incisive eye. Thanks also to Avery, Kelsey, Sam, Reaux, and Anni for your encouragement.

And to my father, the late John Pulley, who always supported me, no matter what.

Thanks to Jeanette Winterson, whose book *The Passion*, partially inspired the story "The Deserters."

And thanks to all of you who picked up this book. Without you, it wouldn't exist. Well, okay, it *would* exist, but it's like a tree-falling-in-the-forest situation and we're not here for philosophical thought experiments! Thank you for making this book a non-philosophical-thought-experiment.

ABOUT THE AUTHOR

Anastasia Fleur

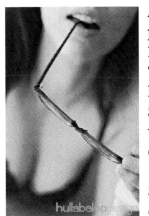

Anastasia Fleur is the not-very-secret pseudonym for Anna Pulley, author of The Lesbian Sex Haiku Book (with Cats!), which Tegan and Sara said was "an adorable and hilarious way to start the day," Cheryl Strayed called a "must-read," and Bound actress Jennifer Tilly said was "thoroughly charming."

She writes a weekly sex and dating advice column for The Tribune Content Agency and has been published in New York magazine, Mother Jones magazine, The Washington Post, San Francisco magazine (the issue she contributed to won a National Magazine Award), Vice, Salon, BuzzFeed, and many others. She was also named a Top LGBTQ Writer on Medium. Her writing was excerpted/quoted in Esther Perel's book, The State of Affairs. She's been a repeat guest on Dan Savage's podcast, Savage Love, on Daniel M. Lavery's "Dear Prudence" podcast, and most recently on the 99% Invisible podcast.

Printed in Great Britain
by Amazon